An Archive of the Catastrophe

SUNY SERIES IN CONTEMPORARY JEWISH LITERATURE AND CULTURE
EZRA CAPPELL, EDITOR

Dan Shiffman, *College Bound:*
The Pursuit of Education in Jewish American Literature, 1896–1944

Eric J. Sundquist, editor, *Writing in Witness:*
A Holocaust Reader

Noam Pines, *The Infrahuman: Animality in Modern Jewish Literature*

Oded Nir, *Signatures of Struggle: The Figuration of Collectivity in Israeli Fiction*

Zohar Weiman-Kelman, *Queer Expectations:*
A Genealogy of Jewish Women's Poetry

Richard J. Fein, translator, *The Full Pomegranate:*
Poems of Avrom Sutzkever

Victoria Aarons and Holli Levitsky, editors,
New Directions in Jewish American and Holocaust Literatures: Reading and Teaching

Ruthie Abeliovich, *Possessed Voices:*
Aural Remains from Modernist Hebrew Theater

Jennifer Cazenave, *An Archive of the Catastrophe:*
The Unused Footage of Claude Lanzmann's Shoah

An Archive of the Catastrophe
The Unused Footage of Claude Lanzmann's *Shoah*

JENNIFER CAZENAVE

SUNY
PRESS

Cover: Francine Kaufmann, Yitzhak "Antek" Zuckerman, and Claude Lanzmann during the making of *Shoah*. (Created by Claude Lanzmann during the filming of *Shoah*. Used by permission of the United States Holocaust Memorial Museum and Yad Vashem, the Holocaust Martyrs and Heroes' Remembrance Authority, Jerusalem.)

Published by State University of New York Press, Albany

© 2019 State University of New York

All rights reserved

No part of this book may be used or reproduced in any manner whatsoever without written permission. No part of this book may be stored in a retrieval system or transmitted in any form or by any means including electronic, electrostatic, magnetic tape, mechanical, photocopying, recording, or otherwise without the prior permission in writing of the publisher.

For information, contact State University of New York Press, Albany, NY
www.sunypress.edu

Library of Congress Cataloging-in-Publication Data

Names: Cazenave, Jennifer, author.
Title: An archive of the catastrophe : the unused footage of Claude Lanzmann's *Shoah* / Jennifer Cazenave.
Description: Albany : State University of New York Press, [2019] | Series: SUNY series in contemporary Jewish literature and culture | Includes bibliographical references and index.
Identifiers: LCCN 2018033291 | ISBN 9781438474779 (hardcover : alk. paper) | ISBN 9781438474762 (pbk. : alk. paper) | ISBN 9781438474786 (ebook)
Subjects: LCSH: *Shoah* (Motion picture) | Holocaust, Jewish (1939–1945), in motion pictures.
Classification: LCC PN1997.S4755 C39 2019 | DDC 791.43/72–dc23
LC record available at https://lccn.loc.gov/2018033291

10   9   8   7   6   5   4   3   2   1

For my grandfathers—
Roland Cazenave and Albert Suissa

CONTENTS

List of Illustrations, ix

Acknowledgments, xv

Chronology, xix

Introduction: The Making of the *Shoah* Archive, xxiii

1 The Formation of a Paradigm, 1

2 Recasting 1961: *Shoah* and the Eichmann Trial, 55

3 Off-Frame: Trauma and the Feminine, 113

4 The Question of Rescue and Refugees, 175

Conclusion: The Deep Time of Testimony, 227

Notes, 231

Bibliography, 273

Index, 287

ILLUSTRATIONS

I.1 The cardboard boxes containing the *Shoah* outtakes in Joinville-le-Pont — xxvi

I.2 Tin canisters and reels of the interview with the Holocaust historian Raul Hilberg — xxviii

1.1 Yael Perlov editing *Shoah* at the LTC film laboratory in Saint-Cloud — 2

1.2 Claude Lanzmann, Richard Glazar, and a largely off-screen Corinna Coulmas holding the clapboard — 13

1.3–4 Claude Lanzmann, Leib Garfunkel, and Irena Steinfeldt; a close-up of the survivor — 22

1.5 An annotated page from the Leib Garfunkel transcript — 24

1.6 Claude Lanzmann evidencing his "bookish [...] knowledge" during the interview with Benjamin Murmelstein — 27

1.7 Claude Lanzmann and Benjamin Murmelstein on the last day of the interview — 28

1.8 The clapboard of the Franz Suchomel interview showing the "artist-technician couple" Lanzmann and Lubtchansky — 32

1.9 Corinna Coulmas, with the handbag containing the Paluche, and Claude Lanzmann outside of Eduard Kryshak's residence — 43

1.10–11 Abraham Bomba (close-up) by the boardwalk in Tel Aviv — 46

2.1 Henryk Ross and Stefania Ross, from the film *Memories of the Eichmann Trial*, directed by David Perlov — 57

2.2 Rivka Yoselewska, from the film *Memories of the Eichmann Trial*, directed by David Perlov — 59

2.3 Ada Lichtman at the witness stand during the Eichmann trial — 66

2.4–5 Ada Lichtman mending dolls during her filmed interview with Claude Lanzmann — 68

2.6–7 Ada and Itzhak (close-up) Lichtman — 71

2.8–9 Claude Lanzmann holding Abraham Bomba's hand the day before the reenactment in the barbershop — 75

2.10 Mordechai Podchlebnik with Claude Lanzmann, whose left hand is clenched to a fist — 77

2.11–12 Gideon Hausner during the testimony of Mordechai Podchlebnik, here sitting at the witness stand — 78

2.13–14 Close-ups of Yehuda Lerner and Claude Lanzmann in 1979 — 85

2.15 Abba Kovner at Kibbutz Ein HaHoresh in the opening moments of the interview — 89

2.16 The children of survivors raise their hands during a film course at Yad Vashem — 95

2.17 The military students in front of the Monument to the Ghetto Heroes at Yad Vashem — 96

2.18 Francine Kaufmann, Itzhak "Antek" Zuckerman, and Claude Lanzmann at the Ghetto Fighters' Museum — 100

2.19 The resistance hero Hersh Smolar displaying his medals — 109

2.20 Tadeusz Pankiewicz with Claude Lanzmann — 110

2.21 The reenactment in the pharmacy — 111

3.1 Jacob and Malka Goldberg, as Malka points at the number tattooed on her left arm — 114

3.2 Claude Lanzmann enters the frame, insisting that Malka Goldberg and the two men perform "Undzer shtetl brent!" again — 115

3.3–4 Seeing the making of *Shoah*: the filmmaker, the survivor, and the crew; the cinematographer William "Bob" Lubtchansky — 118

3.5–6 Claude Lanzmann listening to the testimonies of Benjamin Murmelstein in the spring of 1976 and of Paula Biren in the winter of 1978–1979 — 120

3.7	Claude Lanzmann interviewing Paula Biren in a hotel room	121
3.8	The two-page list of themes included in the transcript of Paula Biren's interview	122
3.9	Claude Lanzmann (right) speaking with three Jewish policemen of the Riga ghetto	129
3.10–11	Lore Oppenheimer and Hermann Ziering (close-up) with his back to the camera	131
3.12–13	Gertrude Schneider (center), Charlotte Hirschhorn (right), and Rita Wasserman (close-up) singing "Azoy muss sein" in the outtakes; in the finished film, Wasserman remains off-frame	136
3.14	A page from the French summary of the Gertrude Schneider interview with "Les chansons [the songs]" highlighted and an arrow pointing to "MALE BIALE [*sic*] DOMEK" at the bottom	139
3.15	A tracking shot of Theresienstadt in 1979	140
3.16	Claude Lanzmann telling Andre Steiner about the making of *Shoah* and his investigation of the transport of children from Białystok to Theresienstadt	143
3.17	Ruth Elias during the silent opening moments of her testimony	145
3.18	Ruth Elias's notes adjacent to Claude Lanzmann's on the table	151
3.19	The filmmaker takes notes while the survivor narrates her account of the years of persecution	155
3.20	A transcribed page from the Inge Deutschkron interview, whose annotations are accompanied by the letter *C* and the number 7	156
3.21–22	Martha Michelsohn, Claude Lanzmann, and the photograph of Erhard Michelsohn (close-up) at her home in Lage	159
3.23	Inge Deutschkron narrating the years of persecution at Café Kranzler with West Berlin visible behind her	162
3.24–25	The facade of Café Kranzler, and a close-up of Claude Lanzmann and Inge Deutschkron sitting by the window	163
3.26	Inge Deutschkron, "the last Jew of Berlin," on a train departing from the Grunewald railway station	164

3.27	Claude Lanzmann, Dr. Ernst Marton (photograph), and Hanna Marton at her home in Jerusalem	166
3.28	Hansi Brand during her filmed interview	169
4.1–2	The cans containing the Nahum Goldmann negatives; interview color-coded film cans, including the footage with the historian Raul Hilberg (in blue), the survivor Inge Deutschkron (in green), and the SS officer Franz Suchomel (in red and also labeled "La Solution")	182
4.3	An anonymous technician holding the clapboard appears briefly on-screen during the interview with Nahum Goldmann	183
4.4	A close-up of the "prophet of gloom" Nahum Goldmann	185
4.5	A second camera films Claude Lanzmann and Jan Karski sitting across from each other during the interview	189
4.6–7	A close-up of Szmul Zygielbojm's portrait in the outtakes captured at the home of his brother Faivel	194
4.8	The 1968 Hebrew edition of the diary kept by Adam Czerniaków in the Warsaw ghetto	195
4.9	Jan Karski incarnating Szmul Zygielbojm reacting to the request for a hunger strike	198
4.10	Claude Lanzmann driving to the Bay Point resort community	201
4.11	Ambassador Reams and his wife Dotty "living the good life on a golf course in Panama City"	202
4.12–13	The filmmaker fishing and golfing in Panama City with Ambassador Reams	204
4.14–15	Claude Lanzmann and Richard Rubenstein in the Floridian wetlands and the evocative image of an alligator	207
4.16–17	A walk in the woods: the former WRB director John Pehle raking leaves and picking up branches	210
4.18	The extreme close-up as homage in the excluded interview with John Pehle	211

4.19   Peter Bergson (left) and Samuel Merlin (right) discussing the   214
       newspaper advertisements they sponsored in 1943

4.20   In search of Rabbi Weissmandl: Mr. Becher and Claude Lanzmann   217
       walking in November 1978 near the Nitra Yeshiva

4.21–22   The ICRC headquarters in Geneva, where Jean Pictet is inter-   222
          viewed in the spring of 1979

ACKNOWLEDGMENTS

Akin to the story of *Shoah* it recounts, this book has traveled significantly over the course of its making. From Chicago to Washington, DC, to Paris to Tampa to Los Angeles, and, finally, to Boston, many friends, family members, mentors, colleagues, and archivists have supported this project and inspired me along the way. To them, I owe much gratitude.

The research, writing, and production of this book was made possible by generous financial support from several institutions: at Boston University, the Center for the Humanities (BUCH) and the Elie Wiesel Center for Jewish Studies (EWCJS) provided subvention awards; the American Council of Learned Societies (ACLS) funded a crucial fellowship during the 2017–2018 academic year; the Humanities Institute at the University of South Florida awarded me a 2017 Summer Grant; the Jack, Joseph and Morton Mandel Center for Advanced Holocaust Studies at the United States Holocaust Memorial Museum (USHMM) provided a Charles H. Revson Foundation Fellowship that funded research in their film and video archive. At an early phase of the project, I also benefited from a fellowship from the SPFFA (Society of French and Francophone Teachers of America, Bourse Jeanne Marandon) and several doctoral grants from Northwestern University, including a Crown Family Fellowship for Jewish Studies and a Mellon Grant from the Alice Kaplan Institute for the Humanities.

This book would not exist in its printed form without the dedication of several individuals at State University of New York Press. I thank in particular Rafael Chaiken for his enthusiastic reception of the project, Diane Ganeles for her editorial support, and the two anonymous reviewers for the time and attention they gave to the manuscript.

An Archive of the Catastrophe began as a dissertation undertaken jointly between Northwestern University and Université Paris Diderot (Paris 7). I thank my former advisors Eric Marty and Samuel Weber for their encouragement and intellectual rigor, and for calling my attention, time and again, to the off-screen. I am grateful to Hannah Feldman for her unwavering interest in this project; she has been an essential source of inspiration and support from beginning to end. Peter Hayes, Sylvie Lindeperg, and Marcus Moseley have also contributed intellectually to this book. Robert Kelly has had a profound influence on my trajectory and I thank him warmly for his continued presence since my undergraduate days at Bard College.

Throughout my research, I benefited from the assistance and expertise of specialists, archivists, and librarians at the USHMM, the Bibliothèque nationale de France (BnF), and the Institut national de l'audiovisuel (INA). In fact, I could never have written this book without the remarkable preservation work on the *Shoah* outtakes undertaken by Raye Farr, Leslie Swift, and Lindsay Zarwell at the USHMM. They have been a source of support and encouragement over the years, and I thank them wholeheartedly for their generosity. The USHMM constituted, as well, a first forum in which to share my research. For their scholarship and humor, I would like to thank former fellows Donald Bloxham, Emil Kerenji, Devin Pendas, Mark Roseman, and Martin Shuster. Ron Coleman and Vincent Slatt provided incredible research assistance at the museum's library.

Several individuals have enriched this book in myriad ways: Karine Granier-Deferre has been an important interlocutor and supporter for more than a decade; Nelly de Freitas, a confidante and source of encouragement; Ophélie Hetzel, an intellectual ally since our very first conversation on *Shoah* years ago at the BnF; and Claire Nazikian, a wonderful friend and cinephile. In Paris and beyond, my gratitude also goes to Jean-Christophe Blum, Thomas Clerc, Clara Kuperberg, Julia Kuperberg, Laura Mamelok, Frédéric Voillemot, and Lily Woodruff. I wish to thank, as well, the late Claude Lanzmann for his generosity and Corinna Coulmas for sharing with me her memories of the making of *Shoah*. Finally, I am deeply indebted to Isabelle Arnould-Chardon for her unfailing engagement and encouragement.

At the University of South Florida, I wish to thank Margit Grieb, Anne Latowski, Christine Probes, Heike Scharm, and Stephan Schindler. In Tampa, Scott Ferguson, Julia Irwin, Steve Prince, and Amy Rust also provided camaraderie, intellectual exchanges, and ongoing conversations; Angel Forester offered encouragement and support. In Los Angeles, Jennifer Croft and Kymm Swank were inspiring friends. At Boston University, I am grateful to Odile Cazenave, Nancy Harrowitz, Christopher Maurer, and my colleagues in the Department of Romance Studies.

Over the course of my travels and of writing this book, I have been fortunate to always have the support of my family. I am deeply grateful to my mother Vanessa Briand-Suissa. A constant source of inspiration and strength, she patiently listened as I read to her over the telephone sentences that became paragraphs, paragraphs that became chapters, and chapters that became this book. My brother Larry Cazenave has been my best friend for as long as I can remember, and I thank him for his presence, intelligence, and humor. I also wish to acknowledge the kindness of my sister-in-law Lorri Hicks-Cazenave.

This book is dedicated to my grandfathers, from whom I inherited stories of the Second World War. The memory of the many women in my family also permeates these pages. This book is for them, too.

CHRONOLOGY

1973

- *Israel, Why* premieres at the New York Film Festival.
- Following this first documentary, CLAUDE LANZMANN is commissioned by the State of Israel to make a film about the Holocaust.
- He hires CORINNA COULMAS and IRENA STEINFELDT to assist him in conducting archival research and preliminary interviews.

1975

- In January, the Zionist leader NAHUM GOLDMANN is the first protagonist filmed for *Shoah*.
- In early March, Lanzmann attends a Holocaust conference in New York City. He meets scholars and witnesses whom he later films: the historians YEHUDA BAUER, HENRY FEINGOLD, RAUL HILBERG, and RICHARD RUBENSTEIN; the Vilna partisan ABBA KOVNER; and the Auschwitz survivor PAULA BIREN.
- That year, he visits Theresienstadt for the first time.

1976

- In March, the Kovno ghetto survivor LEIB GARFUNKEL is recorded in Israel; BENJAMIN MURMELSTEIN is filmed in Rome for nearly twelve hours.
- A month later, assisted by the French cinematographer WILLIAM LUBTCHANSKY, Lanzmann secretly films the perpetrator FRANZ SUCHOMEL with a small camera called the Paluche.

1977

- In an introductory letter to ROSWELL MCCLELLAND, a former War Refugee Board representative, Lanzmann describes the film he is making as a vast investigation of the Holocaust that will encompass topics such as Allied politics of rescue and the fate of Hungarian Jewry.

1978

- March: Lanzmann travels to Poland for the first time.
- September: he films the famous return of SIMON SREBNIK to Chełmno and the Jewish survivors of Corfu singing in a synagogue.
- October–November: GERTRUDE SCHNEIDER and several other survivors of the Riga ghetto are interviewed for *Shoah* in New York. The Auschwitz escapee RUDOLF VRBA is also recorded. In both Washington, DC, and New York, Lanzmann films several "bystanders" of the West: the Polish courier JAN KARSKI, the former director of the War Refugee Board JOHN PEHLE, ROSWELL MCCLELLAND, and the activists PETER BERGSON and SAMUEL MERLIN.
- That winter, he films ROBERT BORDEN REAMS, the former refugee specialist of the State Department, in Panama City; there, he also records PAULA BIREN. Near Tallahassee, he interviews the scholar RICHARD RUBENSTEIN on the question of Jewish refugees and the Évian Conference. In Atlanta, he films the survivor ANDRE STEINER, who worked alongside RABBI MICHAEL DOV WEISSMANDL and GISI FLEISCHMANN to rescue the Jews of Europe.

1979

- January: RAUL HILBERG is interviewed for *Shoah* at his home in Burlington, Vermont. Several weeks later, the historian HENRY FEINGOLD is filmed in New York City.
- Between March and April, the filmmaker and his crew capture location footage in Theresienstadt. They then travel to Poland and film several eyewitnesses, including TADEUSZ PANKIEWICZ, the celebrated Polish pharmacist of the Krakow ghetto.
- Weeks later, in Switzerland, Lanzmann interviews former ICRC delegate MAURICE ROSSEL, the vice president of the ICRC JEAN PICTET, and the Treblinka survivor RICHARD GLAZAR.
- In West Germany, he films survivors INGE DEUTSCHKRON and FILIP MULLER, as well as "ordinary" Germans, among them workers at the factory owned by the family of JOSEF MENGELE, the SS physician at Auschwitz. Accompanied by CORINNA COULMAS, Lanzmann also clandestinely records perpetrators, including EDUARD KRYSHAK, PERY BROAD, and HEINZ SCHUBERT.
- At the end of the summer, Lanzmann and his crew travel to Israel to shoot the final interviews. He hires the Hebrew interpreter FRANCINE KAUFMANN and films a number of *Shoah* protagonists: the heroes of the

Warsaw ghetto YITZHAK "ANTEK" ZUCKERMAN and SIMHA "KAZIK" ROTEM, the *Sonderkommando* members of Vilna MOTKE ZAIDEL and ITZAK DUGIN, the Auschwitz survivor RUTH ELIAS, and the "barber of Treblinka" ABRAHAM BOMBA. Among the survivors interviewed whose testimonies remained on the cutting room floor are ABBA KOVNER, several women (HANSI BRAND, MALKA GOLDBERG, ADA LICHTMAN, and HANNA MARTON), the Minsk ghetto resistance leader HERSH SMOLAR, and the Sobibór eyewitness YEHUDA LERNER.
- In September, ZIVA POSTEC begins editing the film. Over the next five and a half years, she works alongside Lanzmann and several other collaborators, including the sound editor SABINE MAMOU, to compose a nine-and-a-half-hour Holocaust film from nearly 230 hours of material.

1985

- April: *Shoah* premieres at the Théâtre de l'Empire in Paris.
- June: the body of JOSEF MENGELE, who died in 1979, is exhumed in Brazil. Lanzmann retrieves from the remaining 220 hours of outtakes the unused interviews at the Mengele factory and edits a sequence seemingly intended for French television. This sequence is never shown.

1986

- June: *Shoah* premieres at the Jerusalem Cinematheque.

1996

- The United States Holocaust Memorial Museum (USHMM) purchases the *Shoah* outtakes.

1997

- Lanzmann makes *A Visitor from the Living* with the unedited MAURICE ROSSEL interview.

2001

- Lanzmann makes *Sobibór, October 14, 1943, 4 p.m.* with the unused testimony of YEHUDA LERNER.

2010

- Made from the remaining JAN KARSKI outtakes, *The Karski Report* airs on French television.

2013

- *The Last of the Unjust*, which incorporates the BENJAMIN MURMELSTEIN outtakes, is released.

2017

- Lanzmann's final film, *The Four Sisters,* premieres at the New York Film Festival. It centers on the interviews with RUTH ELIAS, PAULA BIREN, ADA LICHTMAN, and HANNA MARTON.

Introduction

THE MAKING OF THE *SHOAH* ARCHIVE

> P.S.: [...] I calculated that a can of film (the metal can+half an hour of sound and picture) weights [*sic*] 2 kilos and a half. I multiplied that, including the negative, the ¼ inch [audio] and the resumés and transcriptions and arrived to 2.600 kilos. (2 TONS+600 KILOS). Filminger would ship by plane to Washington the whole thing, including their work to the customs for 15.000 Francs.
> —Letter from Sabine Mamou to Raye Farr, Film and Video Archive Administrative Files, United States Holocaust Memorial Museum

ON JANUARY 21, 1997, the *Shoah* archive reached the warehouse of the United States Holocaust Memorial Museum (USHMM). Sabine Mamou had prepared the transfer from Paris to Washington, DC, of more than two tons of original materials accumulated during the making of Claude Lanzmann's cinematographic opus between 1973 and 1985. The sound editor of *Shoah*, Mamou later edited Lanzmann's *A Visitor from the Living* (1997) and *Sobibór, October 14, 1943, 4 p.m.* (2001), the first two documentaries made from the film's outtakes. The 155 cardboard boxes shipped by Filminger contained tin canisters with sixteen-millimeter silent color negatives and negative trims, quarter-inch audio tape reels, and interview transcripts and summaries.

Following the release of *Shoah*, this monumental filmic and paper archive remained scattered between the filmmaker's apartment in Paris and the LTC film laboratory in the suburb of Saint-Cloud. In 1994, Lanzmann discussed with the Holocaust historian and *Shoah* protagonist Raul Hilberg the possibility of selling the 220 hours of outtakes (originally estimated at 350 hours) to the USHMM, which had opened its doors only a year before. Hilberg had played a decisive role in the creation of the museum and, in particular, of its Permanent Exhibition, which Raye Farr directed between 1990 and 1993. On March 18, 1994, he recounted his conversation with Lanzmann in a letter addressed to Michael Berenbaum, the director of the museum's Research Institute that housed the Film and Video Department. "I would be happy to be an intermediary in any feasible deal that would make the museum the capable custodian of his film, outtakes, transcripts, and records," Hilberg wrote, before adding that Lanzmann wished for *Shoah* to be screened several times a year in the museum.[1] That fall, only a few days before Yom Kippur, Lanzmann visited the USHMM for the first time and met with Berenbaum and Farr, now director of the Film and Video Department, to discuss a possible acquisition. Lanzmann had prepared an eight-page document titled "Material of 'Shoah'" detailing—and succinctly appraising through adjectives like "unique" and "extraordinary"—the contents of a filmic archive comprised of 185 hours of testimonies and 35 hours of location footage captured in Germany, Greece, Israel, Poland, Switzerland, and the United States. Only days before Lanzmann's visit to the USHMM, and in the wake of the success of *Schindler's List* (1993), Steven Spielberg had announced the creation of the Survivors of the Shoah Visual History Foundation (today the USC Shoah Foundation). Motivated by the imminent passing of one of the last generations of survivors, he pledged to collect at least 50,000 filmed testimonies around the world over the next three years, effectively generating the largest oral history repository.[2]

Two decades earlier, a similar sense of urgency had permeated the making of *Shoah*, resulting in the creation of a unique archive of Holocaust testimonies. In a 1977 letter addressed to Roswell McClelland, the former War Refugee Board (WRB) representative in Switzerland, Lanzmann explains that the protagonists of his film "are the surviving witnesses" before deploring the fact that "in a few years from now it will be too late."[3] While working on *Shoah* for more than a decade, he accumulated the vast majority of nearly 200 hours of testimonies during the years 1978 and 1979. In a subsequent letter to McClelland, Lanzmann's research assistant Irena Steinfeldt captures this rushed shooting schedule when she describes the filmmaker as "travelling all over the continent, working around the clock, without being able to pause for a moment."[4] This accelerated collection of testimonies over the course of two years attests to what Thomas Trezise terms a certain "anxiety of historical transmission" that itself accounts for the creation of equally colossal video archives such as the Survivors of the Shoah Visual History Foundation.[5] At the same time, this "archival impulse" bears witness to Lanzmann's own sense, revealed in his 1977 letter to McClelland, of a certain failure of cinema to represent the catastrophe—a failure from which emerged the production of a monumental film and, ultimately, an equally monumental archive intended to "restore this major event of contemporary history in all its magnitude."[6]

On October 28, 1994, in the wake of Lanzmann's visit, the USHMM announced the establishment of the Steven Spielberg Film and Video Archive. According to Berenbaum, this archive would serve—not unlike the mission of the Survivors of the Shoah Visual History Foundation—as the "foremost repository for Holocaust-related moving images in the United States." In turn, it would enable the USHMM to obtain and preserve "what otherwise might deteriorate—important material that would be lost to future generations."[7] There is of course some irony in the fact that the philanthropy of the director of *Schindler's List*, a Holocaust fiction that Lanzmann had dismissed only months earlier as a distortion of history, rendered possible the acquisition of the *Shoah* outtakes by the USHMM.[8] Yet the mission of the newly founded archive perfectly encapsulated, in 1994, the status of the reels left on the cutting room floor of the LTC film laboratory and the urgency underlying their acquisition, restoration, and transfer to video format. Accordingly, Berenbaum and Farr spent the year 1995 making a case for the purchase of this unprecedented collection, all the while estimating preservation costs and potential technical challenges.

Neither archival footage nor oral history, the excluded material of Lanzmann's acclaimed work constituted a vast and distinct filmic record on the Holocaust. If the excluded footage was acquired, the role of the USHMM would greatly exceed that of a "custodian." As envisioned by Berenbaum and Farr, the museum would effectively rescue, at a time when the last witnesses were disappearing, an immense repository of testimonies and ensure their transmission to future generations through public access. They also emphasized the constitutive openness of the *Shoah* collection, arguing that the excluded footage could be edited anew and deployed in museum exhibitions, films, and television broadcasts.[9] In a letter to Berenbaum dated August 17, 1995, Hilberg further endorsed the purchase of the unused interviews of *Shoah*. Likening Lanzmann's opus to "a giant experiment in film making [*sic*]," he argued that existing scholarship on *Shoah*, no matter how insightful, could not be decisive without "the missing passages in the 340 [*sic*] omitted hours."[10]

A crucial turning point in the acquisition process occurred in February 1996, when Berenbaum and Farr attended a screening of these "missing passages" organized by Lanzmann and Mamou in the Parisian suburb of Joinville-le-Pont. Over the course of nine days, they viewed portions of twenty-two interviews, out of the seventy recorded between 1973 and 1985. Among them were witnesses left out from the finished film and some of the most memorable protagonists of *Shoah*, notably the Chełmno survivor Simon Srebnik and the member of the Auschwitz *Sonderkommando* Filip Müller. The screening included testimonies most highly regarded in "Material of 'Shoah.'" In February 1996, Lanzmann selected the future protagonists of all but one—*The Karski Report* (2010)—of the documentaries he later made from *Shoah* outtakes: the "extraordinary" accounts of both Red Cross delegate Maurice Rossel (*A Visitor from the Living*) and survivor of the Sobibór uprising Yehuda Lerner (*Sobibór, October 14, 1943, 4 p.m.*); the "unique" narrative of Theresienstadt offered by Benjamin Murmelstein (*The Last of the Unjust*, 2013); the "heartbreaking" and "magnificent" stories of women survivors Paula Biren, Ruth Elias, Ada Lichtman, and Hanna Marton (*The Four Sisters*, 2017).[11] He also chose, among

FIGURE I.1. The cardboard boxes containing the *Shoah* outtakes in Joinville-le-Pont (Created by Claude Lanzmann during the filming of *Shoah*. Used by permission of the United States Holocaust Memorial Museum and Yad Vashem, the Holocaust Martyrs and Heroes' Remembrance Authority, Jerusalem).

several others, John Pehle ("Unique") and Andre Steiner ("First class"), two protagonists in his investigation into wartime politics of rescue; the Kovno ghetto survivor Leib Garfunkel, who passed away shortly after the interview ("Heartbreaking"); and several perpetrators, including Karl Kretschmer, clandestinely recorded with a hidden camera, whom Lanzmann would recall years later in his memoir *The Patagonian Hare* (2009).

The selected testimonies partially shown in Joinville-le-Pont further underscored the uniqueness of the *Shoah* outtakes previously intimated by Berenbaum and Farr. "We concur that these interviews are among the highest quality personal testimonies on the subject that we have seen in our respective long careers in this field," they boldly affirm in their report of the screening. Deeming Lanzmann's interview methods "far more resonant" than those deployed by contemporaneous oral history projects of the Holocaust, whether that of the USHMM or the Fortunoff Video Archive for Holocaust Testimonies at Yale University, they also stress the relative temporal proximity to the event of these testimonies captured two decades earlier and the heterogeneous nature of the collection as a whole. "It is not possible to place a specific dollar value on these films. On some levels they are priceless," Berenbaum and Farr remark before listing potential documentaries that could be made using the *Shoah* outtakes. Anticipating *The Four Sisters*, *The Last of the Unjust*, and *Sobibór, October 14, 1943, 4 p.m.*, they specify "women in the Holocaust," "Theresienstadt," and "the uprising in Sobibor [*sic*]" as topics for these future films.[12]

Several months after the screening in Joinville-le-Pont, the Steven Spielberg Film and Video Archive made its first major acquisition: the Claude Lanzmann *Shoah* Collection. The arrival of the outtakes at the museum's off-site storage facility in January 1997 marked the commencement of an unprecedented preservation project more than twenty years in the making and estimated at two million dollars. The nearly twelve-hour-long Murmelstein interview—the longest in the archive—alone cost over $51,000 to restore and transfer to video.

What is today a digital archive comprised of interviews, location footage, and transcripts, jointly owned with Yad Vashem, began as "an enormous puzzle."[13] The first step of this puzzle entailed the minute reassembly of hundreds and hundreds of rolls and pieces of sixteen-millimeter original negatives, which bore not interviewee names but a manufactured edge code number. Then, these negatives had to be synchronized with the corresponding hundreds and hundreds of rolls and pieces of sixteen-millimeter magnetic soundtrack. The initial organization of Lanzmann's filmic and paper archive was rendered all the more inscrutable by the absence of a master log during the making of *Shoah*, which would have contained interviewee names, interview locations and dates, and edge code information.[14] Once re-created, interviews and location footage could be restored by an off-site film laboratory, transferred to video, cataloged, and, beginning in 2007, digitized and uploaded onto the USHMM website.

In 1998, the testimonies of Paula Biren, Ruth Elias, Leib Garfunkel, Karl Kretschmer, Filip Müller, and Gertrude Schneider were the first to be selected for preservation. With the exception of the testimony of Schneider, who appears briefly in the finished film alongside her unnamed mother, these interviews were partially shown during the screening in Joinville-le-Pont. In "Material of 'Shoah,'" Lanzmann deemed them among the most significant. All but two (Kretschmer and Müller) were in English, a language that, as an American institution, the USHMM prioritized. Finally, half of these inaugural interviews were conducted with women survivors. Largely missing from *Shoah*, they too were prioritized by the staff of the Steven Spielberg Film and Video Archive during the early years of preservation.[15]

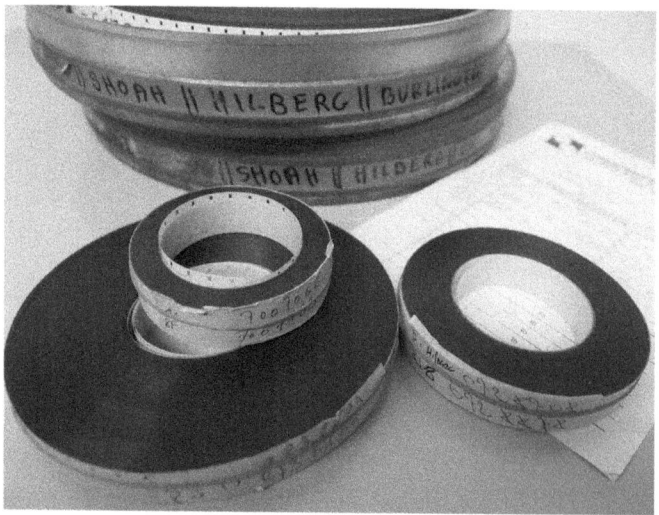

FIGURE I.2. Tin canisters and reels of the interview with the Holocaust historian Raul Hilberg (Created by Claude Lanzmann during the filming of *Shoah*. Used by permission of the United States Holocaust Memorial Museum and Yad Vashem, the Holocaust Martyrs and Heroes' Remembrance Authority, Jerusalem).

UNPACKING THE ARCHIVE

In his letter of endorsement, Hilberg never identifies the contents of the unused material—an archive of the catastrophe that the USHMM would only progressively, a handful of interviews at a time, reassemble and render accessible to the public. In 1995, the historian reiterates the now-familiar consecration of *Shoah* as an unparalleled filmic record of the Holocaust and of Lanzmann as a docu-auteur with a signature style.[16] "The interviews were produced by one man," the historian affirms. "They sprang from his conception and vision. Never did he use more than one camera. Never did he rehearse or repeat a series of questions and answers. Neither did he interpolate footage of 1933–1945. [...] For two or three years, Lanzmann cut and reduced these 350 [*sic*] hours to 9½ hours."[17]

These words encapsulate not the excluded footage but a certain conceptualization of the finished film as a sui generis composition, devoid of archival images and indissociable from a certain discourse about the limits of Holocaust representation. This discourse is itself derived from Lanzmann's writings; he was a director-critic in the style of the French New Wave, who in 1979, the final year of the shooting phase, published an essay condemning Marvin Chomsky's award-winning American miniseries *Holocaust* and its fictionalization of the event—an artistic stance he likened to an ethical transgression and to which the film he was making would offer a counter-representation (in 1994, Lanzmann rebuked Spielberg in identical terms for his fictional reconstruction of the Holocaust in *Schindler's List*).[18] The significance of this authorial voice that, already in 1979 exceeds, all the while consecrating, *Shoah* finds an echo in Hilberg's framing of the film as the work of the true auteur: "one man" endowed with an original "conception and vision" and a talent for eliciting testimonial performances sans rehearsal or repetitions. Since the release of *Shoah* in 1985, such uncritical panegyrics have repeatedly informed debates on the limits of representation and traumatic memory.

The outtakes salvaged by the USHMM, however, present a major challenge to this narrative of *Shoah* in rendering visible the significant contributions made by Lanzmann's crew, as well as the process and inevitable selection over the course of which a work comes into existence. Rather than the "one-man" tradition of documentary cinema put forward by the historian, an important number of collaborators accompanied Lanzmann throughout the making of *Shoah*, among them some of the greatest talents of French cinema: William Lubtchansky, the celebrated cinematographer of the New Wave and of auteurs such as Jean-Luc Godard and Jacques Rivette; Dominique Chapuis, whose career as cinematographer began in 1975 alongside Lubtchansky on the early video works of Godard; Caroline Champetier, Lubtchansky's assistant for *Shoah* and today the acclaimed cinematographer of Leos Carax, Xavier Beauvois, and Margarethe von Trotta, among many others; the sound engineer Bernard Aubouy, an expert of direct sound known for his contributions to the cinema of Jean Eustache and Diane Kurys; Mamou herself, deemed by the time of her death in 2003 "one of the most respected editors of French cinema," particularly of New Wave pioneers Agnès Varda and Jacques Demy;[19] the editor Ziva Postec who, at the LTC film laboratory between September 1979 and April 1985, physically cut and spliced film frames, ultimately transforming the 230 hours of footage into a nine-and-a-half-hour work.[20]

In 1983, Postec was filmed cutting *Shoah* reels by her director-neighbor Claude Thiébaut for his documentary short *Bernardins Bernardines*. The gesture she performs in front of the camera is far from insignificant: it calls our attention to all that Lanzmann had to exclude in order for the finished film to emerge as an unprecedented work of Holocaust representation, originating from his authorial "conception and vision." *Shoah*, in fact, is constructed around a series of omissions: the omission of the title "Holocaust" visible on the clapboard throughout the shooting phase, abandoned in the wake of the popular success of the eponymous miniseries; the omission of Lanzmann's investigation of politics of rescue, itself never evoked in the 1994 critique of *Schindler's List*, in which he condemns Spielberg's decision to focus on several hundred individuals saved rather than the six million murdered; the omission of the legacy of the foundational 1961 Eichmann trial, both in the selection of eyewitnesses and Lanzmann's significant engagement with the accusations leveled against the Jewish leadership by Hannah Arendt; the omission of archival images present in several interviews, beginning with the one filmed for *Shoah* in March 1976 with Leib Garfunkel; the omission of repetitions in unused takes; the omission of rehearsals in the form of preliminary interviews during which Lanzmann gathered extensive notes about each eyewitness that he subsequently used during their filmed testimonies; the omission of these notes visible in the outtakes; the omission of reverse shots of the filmmaker and the omission of a second camera used to record them; the omission of Lanzmann, whose largely off-frame authorial presence persists in the testimonial performances he elicits and produces, such as the tears of Filip Müller and of the "barber of Treblinka" Abraham Bomba; the omission of intersecting scenes of survival and remembrance—above all in the largely unedited testimonies of women survivors—that resist the momentary reliving of the past, or resurgence of deep memory, exemplified and universalized by *Shoah*.

Lawrence Langer introduced—and privileged—the category of deep memory in his groundbreaking study of the Fortunoff Video Archive, which he published several years after the release of Lanzmann's film. In recent scholarship on the mediation of video interviews, notably those archived at Yale, this form of remembrance persists as a dominant index of measure in determining the authenticity and depth of traumatic experience.[21]

Shoah, writes Michael Renov, is a "massive (indeed, obsessive) project [...] a work of mourning [...] doomed to failure for Lanzmann, as for many of his witnesses. There will never be words enough to fill the void left by the six million."[22] Akin to the finished film and its obsessions—the Final Solution, the painstaking excavation of deep memory, the tracking shots in killing centers or "non-sites of memory" (to borrow Lanzmann's terminology) devoid of traces of the past—the *Shoah* archive is equally massive and obsessive.[23] Extending beyond the years of extermination, it encompasses detailed accounts of the years of persecution in Nazi Germany; extending beyond the East, it investigates politics of rescue in the West; extending beyond the narratives of the male members of the *Sonderkommando*, tasked with disposing of the corpses, it retrieves over twenty hours of footage with women survivors. Further capturing the docu-auteur's unceasing attempts at engendering reenactment, particularly through song, the excluded footage of *Shoah* also bears witness to his untiring search for perpetrators, carefully staged in front of the camera, and to his efforts to snatch their testimonies at all costs.

RECOVERING THE *SHOAH* OUTTAKES

An Archive of the Catastrophe recuperates this colossal repository attesting to an "anxiety of historical transmission" and to a work of mourning always incomplete and never ending. The term "catastrophe," the English translation of the Hebrew word *sho'ah* (a word popularized by Lanzmann's film in France, where the Holocaust is called "la Shoah"), designates the destruction of the European Jews; it also conveys an annihilation of unprecedented magnitude, to which the hundreds and hundreds of reels of filmed testimonies obsessively amassed bear witness.

This book approaches the study of the Claude Lanzmann *Shoah* Collection at the USHMM by focusing attention to these words—no matter how insufficient—recorded and relegated to the margins; to the reception and, at times, nonreception of alternative accounts of the catastrophe, as well as to the momentary suspension of authorial intent; to the shaping of testimony by witnesses unseen and unheard; to processes of remembrance yet to be integrated into theoretical discourses on testimony and trauma. Accordingly, it challenges the continued rhetorical deployment of deep memory as a referent to not only the limits but also the ethics of representing the Holocaust and, more broadly, genocide. Positing the outtakes as critical and significant texts in unearthing new meanings and mobilizations of both the finished film and audiovisual testimony, this book argues that the omitted interviews underscore not the resurgence of but a resistance to this process of excavating the past. In keeping with the tradition of genetic criticism exemplified by the scholarship of film historian Sylvie Lindeperg, *An Archive of the Catastrophe* reconstructs the making of *Shoah* through a study of the excluded material while framing broader questions about Holocaust historiography, traumatic memory, and filmic legacies.[24]

"One common misunderstanding of Lanzmann's purpose in making *Shoah*," Stuart Liebman aptly observes, "is that he wanted to provide a comprehensive history of the Holocaust in all its dimensions."[25] Despite its size, the archive of testimonies and location footage rescued by the USHMM also does not encompass the catastrophe in its entirety. Although spanning the years of both persecution and extermination, the outtakes first and foremost reflect the major historiographical trends and debates—and their own omissions—concurrent with the making of *Shoah*. If Lanzmann investigated Arendt's controversial condemnation of Jewish leaders in 1961 and the equally tendentious topic of wartime Allied inaction, he explored only minimally the experiences and survival strategies of women in ghettos and camps, and he barely integrated them in the finished film. In the seventies, women were still largely missing from the history of the Holocaust. Questions of gender would only begin to be voiced around the time of the release of the film, notably through the work of the feminist historian Joan Ringelheim who, already in 1979, had started interviewing women survivors.[26] The Claude Lanzmann *Shoah* Collection, then, is at once "conservative and revolutionary" (to borrow Amit Pinchevski's characterization of the Fortunoff Video Archive).[27] Notwithstanding the testimonies of the ten Jewish women filmed for *Shoah*, the unused material primarily focuses on the perspectives of male eyewitnesses. Similarly, while largely restricted to the contemporaneous scholarship that informs Lanzmann's investigation of the Holocaust in the seventies, the outtakes include rare interviews of Jewish leaders, as well as Nazis, the latter secretly filmed using emerging video technologies in revolutionary ways.

Rather than proceed chronologically, the four chapters of *An Archive of the Catastrophe* focus on contentious and uncharted historiographical legacies that, in turn, reveal the "conservative and revolutionary" contours of Lanzmann's vast inquiry. Varied archival sources inform this book's narrative: the *Shoah* outtakes, the interview transcripts and summaries whose annotations made in the editing room further evidence the selection process between 1979 and 1985, the correspondence between the filmmaker and several protagonists of his investigation, the footage of the Eichmann trial, and oral testimonies of survivors previously interviewed for *Shoah*. The book also incorporates Lanzmann's writings and, in particular, his account of the film's making in *The Patagonian Hare*, an account itself constructed around a series of omissions and here recast through the lens of the material preserved by the USHMM.

Chapter 1, "The Formation of a Paradigm," grounds the book's undermining of the finished film as a sui generis cinematic work and of Lanzmann as a singular auteur through a critical narrative of the four principal phases in the genesis of *Shoah*. This chapter takes particular focus on the historiographical influences informing the selection and performances of witnesses, the decisive contributions of the film crew members, and the evolution—and contradictions—of Lanzmann's directorial method. I begin with the preliminary research phase between 1973 and 1974, during which Lanzmann and his research assistants Corinna Coulmas and Irena Steinfeldt defined the scope of their investigation of the Holocaust and conducted hundreds of preliminary interviews. A major source were existing testimonies from trials, including the first Treblinka trial held in Dusseldorf in 1964, where two future protagonists of *Shoah* took the witness stand: the SS officer Franz Suchomel and the survivor Richard Glazar. Prior to being filmed by Lanzmann, the two men were extensively interviewed by Gitta Sereny for her journalistic biography, *Into That Darkness* (1974), of the death camp commandant Franz Stangl. In analyzing these overlapping testimonies, recovered in the excluded portions of their accounts for *Shoah*, I argue that Sereny effectively rehearsed Suchomel and Glazar for their subsequent testimonial performances retained in the finished film. The first recorded interviews with the Jewish leaders Garfunkel and Murmelstein in 1976 further reveal the significance of postwar trials for the making of Lanzmann's opus. More than an inaugural probing into the Arendt controversy, however, these two unused testimonies also signify the imminent passing of survivors. At the same time, they capture an ethics of representation still largely in the making, whether in the aforementioned presence of archival images or the centrality of not deep but common memory.

This chapter further subverts the auteur myth through an in-depth analysis of the interviews secretly filmed with perpetrators—beginning in 1976—by means of a Paluche, a miniature video camera equipped with an ultra-high-frequency transmitter that relayed images to a monitor in a minivan. The Paluche was the timely invention of Jean-Pierre Beauviala, who created his equipment in close collaboration with New Wave filmmakers and technicians, including Lubtchansky. In my analysis of this clandestine footage, I reveal the cinematographer's crucial role in providing Lanzmann with the technological means to record perpetrators, first and foremost, in converting the crew's minivan into a mobile video studio. Finally, I turn to the editing phase. In *The Patagonian Hare*, Lanzmann likens his selection process to the Leibnizian notion of the incompossible, which denotes the existence of an infinite number of mutually exclusive possible worlds from which God chooses the most just and harmonious one. Refuting the finality of choice in the use of the incompossible as a metaphor for the inevitable selection in the editing room, I theorize what it means for the finished film and the digitized outtakes to coexist.

In his account of the film's making, Lanzmann dismisses the significance of the Eichmann trial, which nevertheless foregrounded the public emergence of the witness and whose date—1961—constitutes a critical marker for the articulation of transnational memory politics.[28] Chapter 2, "Recasting 1961: *Shoah* and the Eichmann Trial," offers an account of this obscured cinematic and historiographical filiation that unearths multifarious frameworks of remembrance. Likewise, this chapter repositions theoretical paradigms of testimony and trauma sustained by the finished film, notably including what Trezise terms "a silencing reenactment" exemplified in Bomba's oft-cited performance staged in a barbershop.[30] While further demonstrating the significance of the controversy sparked by Arendt's report of the trial, including in an unedited interview with the historian Yehuda Bauer, this chapter maps the ways in which Lanzmann's investigation and selection of witnesses for *Shoah* intersect with debates surrounding the emergence of Holocaust memory in Israel. Numerous outtakes address the contentious dichotomy between the supposed passivity of victims led "like sheep to their slaughter" and armed uprisings in ghettos and camps. Lanzmann not only filmed the two mythical figures of the Jewish resistance, Yitzhak "Antek" Zuckerman and Abba Kovner, but in fact, many of the male protagonists in the finished film either participated in revolts or escaped from extermination camps.

As this chapter demonstrates, these heroic narratives prevail in the excluded portions of their interviews and reveal, on the part of Lanzmann, a former member of the French Resistance, an admiration for and identification with these men, many of whom were his contemporaries. By contrast, the story of the Sobibór revolt is silenced in the unedited testimony of Ada Lichtman, one of the most memorable witnesses of the Eichmann trial. An exceptional mise-en-scène premised on reenactment mediates her performance for *Shoah*: she recounts her experience as a seamstress in the extermination camp while mending dolls scattered over a coffee table. Beyond this staged performance, Lanzmann attempts to provoke the resurgence of deep memory by prompting her to sing several times. Lichtman, however, continuously reframes her testimonial performance through facial expressions of incredulity and by ultimately interrupting her own singing to comment on the lyrics. If her performance epitomizes the auteur's failure to mold her process of remembrance, such an analysis forces a sustained comparison in this chapter to the "silencing reenactment" of Bomba and other male protagonists. It also provides an opportunity to engage with the ethics of editing *Shoah* and the concept of the incompossible. In omitting the striking verbal resistance of a woman survivor, Lanzmann, I argue, produced a universalizing—and overwhelmingly masculine—representation of traumatic memory in the present.

The recovery of Lichtman's testimonial performance calls attention to the absence of feminine perspectives in *Shoah*, an absence eloquently probed in a 1993 essay by Marianne Hirsch and Leo Spitzer. "What would it have meant [...]," they asked in their conclusion, "to confront masculine and feminine modes of survival and remembrance?"[30] This compelling question serves as the premise for the book's third chapter, "Off-Frame: Trauma and the Feminine," which recounts the exceptional stories of the remaining nine women survivors interviewed for *Shoah*. This chapter aims to respond to Hirsch and Spitzer not only by putting these narratives and performances in dialogue with the finished film. It also situates them within Lanzmann's broad investigation of the Holocaust, including the themes of Jewish leadership, Theresienstadt, and rescue politics. Central to my analysis is the reception of these gendered testimonies, which further illuminates the ethics of editing *Shoah*. Here I also stress the defining leitmotif of the tragedy of choice in these tales of survival that strikingly approximates the notion of the incompossible.

I begin with Paula Biren, first of the five women to briefly appear in *Shoah*. Her testimony provides a rare portrait of the Łódź ghetto, as well as of its controversial leader Chaim Rumkowski and the Jewish police force. Biren herself worked in the women's squad. Rather than probe the moral choices that confronted Biren, however, Lanzmann unsuccessfully attempts to elicit from her an account that bears witness to the experiences of the men in the police. I then turn to his examination of the unique case of the Riga ghetto: in

December 1941, thirty thousand Latvian Jews were murdered to make room for the arrival of sixteen thousand Jews from the German Reich. In *Shoah*, Lanzmann never reveals that Schneider and her mother, who sing a Yiddish melody, are survivors of this ghetto. In the outtakes, the docu-auteur imposes his demands of Holocaust representation visible in the finished film through "a silencing reenactment" centered on songs from the Riga ghetto. The story of this unique ghetto is also recovered in the excluded joint testimony of Lore Oppenheimer and Hermann Ziering, the sole footage to juxtapose feminine and masculine perspectives.

In this chapter, I examine as well the unthinkable trauma underlying the story of Ruth Elias: pregnant when she arrived from Theresienstadt to Auschwitz, she ended her newborn's life with an injection of morphine. This narrative, I argue, epitomizes the absence of gender differences in the finished film, while tragically exemplifying the incompossible. I then turn to the years of persecution in Nazi Germany and the story of Inge Deutschkron. While she provides the longest testimony of any of the women survivors, the exclusion of a gendered narrative defines its reception: on camera, she never recounts how she and her mother survived the war in hiding. This chapter concludes by returning to the question of Jewish leadership in the material captured with Hansi Brand and Hanna Marton, neither of whom appear in *Shoah*. Their testimonies center on a unique episode that once more invokes the incompossible: the 1944 negotiations between Eichmann and Jewish leaders in Budapest resulting in the rescue of 1,684 Jews, while four hundred thousand others were deported from Hungary to Auschwitz.

The book's fourth and final chapter, "The Question of Rescue and Refugees," details the unused investigation—unique in the *Shoah* archive for having been entirely left on the cutting room floor—of wartime efforts to save European Jewry. The year 1944 itself constitutes a pivotal moment in this chapter of the Holocaust. Invoking a shot reverse shot, it moves from East to West: from the Jews of Hungary, the largest Jewish community still alive, to the War Refugee Board, established by President Franklin D. Roosevelt in January of that year; from the en masse deportation and annihilation of Hungarian Jewry between May and July, to the WRB's attempt to rescue them. A tragic multidirectionality, I contend, also informs the year 1943 in the unused footage of *Shoah* and offers a unique counterpoint to the story of the Warsaw ghetto uprising, with which the finished film ends. On April 19, 1943, the day the revolt began, American and British delegates gathered in Bermuda to discuss possible measures to rescue the Jews of Europe. This conference, held thousands of miles away from Warsaw, produced dismal results. More than the question of rescue, then, these outtakes reveal an extensive engagement with the controversial topic of Allied and, in particular, American inaction.

In this chapter, I frame my analysis of this excluded material in conversation with the so-called "Karski affair" sparked by the 2009 French publication of Yannick Haenel's novel *The Messenger*. In his fictional portrait of the *Shoah* protagonist and Polish courier Jan Karski, who informed the Western governments of the annihilation, Haenel decries Allied indifference, despite their knowledge, to the plight of the Jews—a *parti pris* Lanzmann bitterly condemned in an article before making *The Karski Report*. As this chapter demonstrates, several of the "bystanders" in the West interviewed for *Shoah*, among them Karski, level on camera similar accusations as those subsequently voiced by Haenel. This excluded footage, I reveal, concomitantly recovers an attempt to recast, and effectively diminish, the controversy through the lens of a crisis of representation, encapsulated in a single question repeatedly posed by Lanzmann: how to imagine Treblinka from Washington, DC, or New York. Accordingly, those among the "bystanders" whom I term "messengers of the catastrophe" occupy a central position in this chapter. Beyond Karski, they include the story of Szmul "Artur" Zygielbojm, who, in the final days of the Warsaw ghetto revolt, committed suicide in London to protest the silence of the Allied governments he had tried to warn.

In 1994, Lanzmann returned to the question of rescue when he published his critique of *Schindler's List*. Never invoking his unused investigation for *Shoah*, he does intimate the ways in which these outtakes with "bystanders" in the West established the roots of a representational dilemma. As though projecting onto Spielberg the very predicament that awaited him at the LTC film laboratory between 1979 and 1985, he writes: "I told myself he was going to be faced with a dilemma. He could not tell Schindler's story without also saying what the Holocaust was."[31] In the end, it was Lanzmann himself who could not tell the story of both the destruction of the European Jews *and* of the efforts to save them. Nor could he include the condemnations against Jewish leaders or the gendered narratives of women survivors. Unvoiced, then, in his critique of *Schindler's List* is the making of *Shoah* and the five and a half years Lanzmann spent composing with incompossibles in the editing room.[32] This book aims to tell that story.

CHAPTER I

The Formation of a Paradigm

IN 1973—the year Claude Lanzmann began working on *Shoah*—the Israeli filmmaker David Perlov undertook *Diary*, a six-hour personal documentary recorded and edited over the course of a decade. This monumental cinematic journal opens with a shot of Perlov's apartment window in Tel Aviv and his voice-over foregrounding a method and ethics of representation still in the making. "May 1973," he begins. "I buy a camera. I want to start filming by myself and for myself. Professional cinema does no longer attract me. To look for something else, I want to approach the everyday, above all in anonymity. It takes time to learn how to do it."

Between 1973 and 1983, Perlov progressively crafted a chronicle of his quotidian that included his wife Mira and their twin daughters Naomi and Yael. This quotidian is punctuated in *Diary* with several returns not only to Perlov's native Brazil but also to France, to which he had immigrated in 1952 before permanently settling in Israel several years later. In Paris, Perlov studied painting and then turned to cinema; he assisted the director of the Cinémathèque française, Henri Langlois, and collaborated with the Dutch documentary filmmaker Joris Ivens. There, he also met the French writer André Schwarz-Bart, who shared with him parts of the manuscript that became *The Last of the Just*, his 1959 award-winning novel spanning from the Middle Ages to the Holocaust and centered on the persecution of several generations of a single Jewish family.

Perlov later credited Schwarz-Bart for suggesting in 1973 that he make a cinematic journal.[1] He also filmed him a decade later during a trip to Paris recorded in the penultimate chapter of *Diary*. Speaking in front of the camera with Perlov's daughter Yael, the author of *The Last of the Just* never recounts the traumatic history of his own family. He recalls instead a comical visit to the dentist as a child in the company of his father shortly after the outbreak of the Second World War. Perlov, however, concludes this segment of *Diary* titled "A meeting with Andre Shwartz-Bart [*sic*]" with a shot of the Gare de l'Est train station in Paris and his own voice-over recounting a very different

1

memory the French novelist had described off-camera that same afternoon: the endless nights spent in a train station at the end of the war waiting in vain for his parents, who had been deported in 1941, to return from the camps.

In this chapter of *Diary* dated 1983, the memory of the Holocaust and the limits that inform its representation once more resurface when Perlov films Lanzmann working on *Shoah* alongside his editor Ziva Postec—herself assisted by the diarist's daughter Yael—at the LTC film laboratory in the Parisian suburb of Saint-Cloud. Inside the editing room, the voice of Franz Suchomel, the SS officer at the Treblinka extermination camp who appears in *Shoah*, resonates in the background. Perlov's camera first lingers on Yael at the editing table, innumerable film cans and interview transcripts shelved behind her. His voice-over remarks: "Like myself, Yael admires this man who has devoted already years to this project with untiring persistence, with no comprise. His approach is dry, unemotional, like that of a legal prosecutor who needs no rhetoric, no artistic emphasis; he needs only documents." Calling to mind his personal credo formulated in the opening of *Diary* ("filming by myself and for myself") as well as his own devotion over the course of its making between 1973 and 1983, Perlov emphasizes in this segment dedicated to *Shoah* the method and ethics of Lanzmann's counter-representation of the catastrophe. Similarly, much like Raul Hilberg's conceptualization of *Shoah* in 1995 as a work "produced by

FIGURE 1.1. Yael Perlov editing *Shoah* at the LTC film laboratory in Saint-Cloud (*Diary*, 1983).

one man" and emanating from the director's "vision and conception," Perlov posits Lanzmann—despite the presence of Ziva Postec—as a singular auteur and sole creator of a unique cinematic document on the Holocaust.² On camera, Lanzmann reinforces this *parti pris* by aligning his unfinished opus with the representational dictum he would reiterate countless times after the release of *Shoah* in 1985. "There is an absolute coincidence, an absolute identity in this film between ethics and aesthetics," he affirms in *Diary*. On a white board behind him the names of the film's male protagonists are visible: the SS officer Suchomel; the survivors Abraham Bomba, Filip Müller, and Rudolf Vrba.

This segment of *Diary* shot at the LTC film laboratory in 1983 presents *Shoah* in its nearly completed form, both as a film and a discourse on the limits of representation. Although Perlov's camera lingers on the rows of film cans and interview transcripts shelved in the editing room, the hundreds of hours of footage that Lanzmann accumulated are never evoked. In 1983, *Diary* unwillingly obscures Lanzmann's archive of the catastrophe, an archive constituted over the course of a twelve-year transnational journey. Much like Perlov's own search for a form and method ("it takes time to learn how to do it," he declares at the beginning of *Diary*), this excluded footage transferred to the USHMM in 1997 uncovers the progressive emergence of a historiographical, representational, and theoretical paradigm that began inside the library and archives of Yad Vashem as a vast investigation into the Holocaust.

"A FILM THAT *IS* THE SHOAH": PRELIMINARY RESEARCH AND INTERVIEWS (1973–1974)

In the closing moments of Lanzmann's first documentary *Israel, Why*, a three-hour portrait of the Jewish state that premiered at the New York Film Festival in 1973, the camera slowly traverses the "Room of Names" at the Yad Vashem library. In this dim space filled with *yizkor* books commemorating the Jewish communities destroyed in the Holocaust, the camera pivots before revealing the filmmaker standing next to an unnamed archivist who reads a list of victims bearing the surname Lanzmann. As the archivist falls silent and places the memorial book back on the shelf, Lanzmann turns to his cinematographer William Lubtchansky and exclaims, "Cut!" *Israel, Why* ends precisely where *Shoah* would begin in 1973: with the memory of the catastrophe and with Yad Vashem, where the filmmaker first researched the destruction of the European Jews.

Despite this thematic continuity, the idea of undertaking a film on the Holocaust in 1973 did not originate with Lanzmann. According to the filmmaker's memoir, *The Patagonian Hare*, it was his friend Aloup Hareven who, following a private screening of *Israel, Why*, summoned him to his office at the Israeli Ministry of Foreign Affairs and commissioned him to make a cinematographic document on the catastrophe. "There is no film about the Shoah," Hareven purportedly told Lanzmann, "no film that takes in what happened in all its magnitude, no film that shows it from our point of view, the viewpoint of the Jews. It's not a matter of making a film *about* the Shoah, but a film that *is* the Shoah."[3] Seemingly shocked by this proposal, Lanzmann recalls how he "left that meeting stunned and shaking" before returning to Paris, where "something powerful, even violent, inside [him] urged [him] to accept."[4] Yet he never comments on Hareven's peculiar formulation: namely, to make "a film that *is* the Shoah." Indeed, what would it mean to embark on a cinematic endeavor defined as the catastrophe or the destruction itself? Does such a proposal imply the film *be* (to borrow the definition of the Final Solution put forth by Hilberg in *Shoah*) "something unprecedented, [...] something new," whether in its form or scale? Or did Hareven intend, as Sue Vice suggests, Lanzmann to create a film that would "constitute a piece of reality and not be simply a reflection of it"?[5]

A letter of introduction written by Lanzmann in February 1977 and addressed to Roswell McClelland, the former War Refugee Board (WRB) representative in Switzerland whom the filmmaker here asks to be "one of the film's personalities," reveals that *Shoah* was initially conceived not as a discourse on Holocaust representation but as an unprecedented all-encompassing investigation of the catastrophe—a film that, in its sheer monumentality, would *be* the Shoah. Evoking, in line with Hareven's opaque wording, "a work which will [...] *be* History," Lanzmann describes "a full-length documentary [...] conceived and constructed like an investigation of the Holocaust carried out today."[6] As suggested by the word "documentary," a genre Lanzmann would repudiate in a 1985 interview with *Cahiers du cinéma* because of the film's staged scenes, this presentation of *Shoah* lacks the ethical-aesthetic dimension invoked by the filmmaker six years later in front of Perlov's camera.[7]

Penned at a time when Lanzmann had shot only a mere handful of the seventy interviews he ultimately amassed, this letter describes a work concerned, four years into its making, with investigating and representing the catastrophe in its totality. The filmmaker thus explains: "Instead of limiting myself, as has been done up until now, to a specific chapter or episode of the Holocaust, I on the contrary intend to treat it in its entirety, in all its gigantic dimensions." In 1977, Lanzmann defines the unprecedented nature of his documentary in terms of its envisioned historiographical breadth, which was to include "the attitudes of the governments and international organizations" and "the question of the rescue of Hungarian Jews," two themes omitted, in the end, from *Shoah*.[8] During the editing process several years later, the filmmaker-turned-archivist of the catastrophe reframed this all-encompassing investigation into a detailed exposition of the destruction process—an exposition that evidenced "diverse investigatory processes" (an essential trait of the docu-auteur for Linda Williams), ranging from interviews with Holocaust historians to secret recordings with perpetrators.[9] Focused on the killing centers in occupied Poland and privileging the perspective of male witnesses, Lanzmann's nine-and-a-half-hour document notably omitted archival images, juxtaposing instead eyewitness testimony and non-sites of memory. What became a film heralded, following its release in 1985, as the definitive cinematographic work on the Holocaust nevertheless subsists, always incomplete, in the shadow of 220 hours of outtakes.

"The cinematographic image," writes the French critic and director Pascal Bonitzer, "is haunted by what is not there."[10] *Shoah* is a film haunted by the destruction of the European Jews, by the absence of archival footage of the extermination, and by the erasure of traces in the present day. Guided by the voices of witnesses and their faces, by the sound and images of moving trains, by the silence in former extermination sites, and by staged scenes of reenactment, the viewer of Lanzmann's monumental work is called on to visualize what remains unseen. Accordingly, as Libby Saxton observes, *Shoah* constitutes "a paradigm for exploration of the challenges the Holocaust poses to representation."[11] The defining representational innovation of *Shoah* (what Lanzmann terms in *Diary* the "coincidence" or "absolute identity" of ethics and aesthetics) lies, precisely, in a subtle interplay of the image and its absence. Conceptually, the film deploys what Noël Burch terms "the two kinds of space" in cinema: on-screen and off-screen space—inside and outside the frame.[12]

Yet *Shoah* is equally haunted by the choices and cuts made at the LTC film laboratory, by the excluded footage left out in the editing room, by an archive of the catastrophe displaced beyond the frame of the finished film. More than three decades since the release of Lanzmann's opus, the existence of these outtakes calls forth a paradigm shift away from the representational ethics that continue to inform its reception and toward the ethics of editing a monumental repository of testimonies into a film over nine hours long. This paradigm shift, in turn, stages an encounter between "the two [other] kinds of space" that also define Lanzmann's twelve-year-long cinematographic endeavor: the finished film and the excluded footage. Such an encounter with the off-screen invites ethics of another sort, ethics that necessitate, as Eyal Peretz suggests in his investigation of what lies outside the cinematic frame, "remaining open to excess" and "giv[ing] a place to what has no place."[13] Specifically, the unused footage of *Shoah* calls on us to reintegrate into the narrative of the Holocaust heterogeneous voices and histories captured by the camera but ultimately left on the cutting room floor.

In the summer of 1973, when he began working on *Shoah*, Lanzmann set out on a twofold investigation: to define and delimit the major chapters of the Holocaust and to find the film's protagonists. He began his research at the library and archives of Yad Vashem, where he had been given a small office. There, he was asked to report on his progress to an academic committee headed by the Holocaust scholar and Prague native Yehuda Bauer. In his memoir, the filmmaker credits Bauer for having told him about Müller and Vrba, two survivors of Auschwitz whose names appear in *Diary*.[14] He also filmed the historian for *Shoah* in 1979 at his home at Shoval Kibbutz in the Negev desert. In this unused two-hour interview, Lanzmann and Bauer discuss at length "the question of the rescue of Hungarian Jews" mentioned in the 1977 letter to McClelland.

Upon embarking on his investigation of the Holocaust and searching for witnesses, Lanzmann hired Irena Steinfeldt, an Israeli student fluent in Hebrew, German, English, and French, to assist him. A few months later, she was joined by Corinna Coulmas, a native German speaker who had completed a PhD at the Sorbonne on the Jewish community of Florence. In the closing credits of *Shoah*, Steinfeldt and Coulmas appear as "assistants to the director." Working from the very beginning on the film, they in fact became two of Lanzmann's closest collaborators over the course of its making. Between 1973 and 1985, they conducted archival research and preliminary meetings with witnesses, prepared and participated in the shooting of the interviews (often appearing at the filmmaker's side in the outtakes), and finally—in the case of Coulmas—transcribed the recorded testimonies and made frequent trips to the LTC film laboratory to view the assembled material.

When they undertook the investigation in 1973–1974, Lanzmann and his assistants began by reading extensively on the Holocaust, watching available films, looking for archival documents, and locating eyewitnesses. Dividing their time between Paris and Jerusalem, they individually researched different topics. As Coulmas recalls, "The three of us worked together during the research phase, but each one had a specific task: Irena, for example, was in charge of the State Department and individuals living in America. [...] I was, amongst other things, in charge of the Vatican. The three of us shared the same office, we were always talking, digging different aspects of the problem, slowly elaborating a conception for the next phase."[15] While Lanzmann would record several interviews in 1978 on the rescue efforts attempted by the WRB, he abandoned the topic of the Vatican for budgetary reasons. The research Coulmas undertook in Italy, however, gave way to a noteworthy encounter. There, she conducted a preliminary interview for *Shoah* with the prominent Auschwitz survivor and writer Primo Levi at his home in Turin. Although by far the most famous witness approached by Lanzmann and his assistants, he was one of hundreds of individuals considered and interviewed in preparation for the film, many of whom, like Levi, had already told their story before. Indeed, Steinfeldt recalls, "When looking for people to interview, one of the sources were existing testimonies from trials or people who had written books or were mentioned in books."[16]

Lanzmann and his two assistants took extensive notes during these initial meetings with eyewitnesses, at times even making audio recordings. Such is the case of Shlomo Gol, who was recorded on audiocassette in the spring of 1977 in Jacksonville, Florida. During the Holocaust, he had been selected to burn the bodies of victims murdered in the Ponar forest before escaping alongside Itzak Dugin and Motke Zaidel, both of whom appear in the finished film. In the unused portion of their joint testimony filmed in Israel at the end of the summer of 1979, his name is first invoked by Dugin who recalls that Gol, like himself, had discovered the bodies of his entire family when they opened the mass graves. Instead of commenting on this particular memory, the docu-auteur mentions much later in the interview having spoken with Gol. (Although he never filmed Gol, Lanzmann returned to Florida in the winter of 1978–1979 to record the Auschwitz survivor Paula Biren, the former State Department refugee specialist Robert Borden Reams, and the Holocaust theologian Richard Rubenstein.) If, as Steinfeldt notes regarding the preliminary search for witnesses, "in many cases one person told us about another," Lanzmann surely heard of Gol when he conducted a preliminary interview with Zaidel and Dugin or vice versa.[17]

Recounting this initial research phase in *The Patagonian Hare*, Lanzmann singles out two influential readings on the death camp at Treblinka—an extermination site central to the representation of the destruction process in *Shoah*—in which he first encountered the testimonies of the SS officer Suchomel and the survivor Richard Glazar, both of whom appear in the film. The first was the transcript of the inaugural Treblinka trial held in Düsseldorf in 1964, where the two men testified, and the second Gitta Sereny's account of the extermination camp, *Into That Darkness* (1974). Sereny based her book on lengthy interviews conducted with the former camp commandant Franz Stangl as well as with Suchomel and Glazar. Deeming her approach in *Into That Darkness* "purely psychological" for attempting to grapple with the question of evil, Lanzmann sharply contrasts in his memoir her undertaking and his own, which was instead marked by "the refusal to understand."[18] Yet, much like the description of the film found in his correspondence with McClelland, *Into That Darkness* endeavors a comprehensive account of the catastrophe (devoid, however, of any bibliographical reference to Hilberg's 1961 study that proved crucial for Lanzmann's historical investigation).

Indeed, to borrow Lanzmann's wording from the 1977 letter, Sereny's book encompasses "the attitudes of the governments and international organizations" (including the State Department and the Vatican), along with the three killing centers Bełżec, Sobibór, and Treblinka of Operation Reinhardt, the code name for the Nazi plan to exterminate the two million Jews in German-occupied Poland, discussed in *Shoah* by the prosecutor of the Treblinka trial, Alfred Spiess. In addition to her interviews with Suchomel and Glazar, Sereny includes not only the voices of bystanders (such as Franciszek Zabecki, the traffic controller of the town of Treblinka and member of the Polish underground), but also the stories of several witnesses found in both Lanzmann's finished film and the excluded material: the Polish courier Jan Karski, "now a professor at Georgetown University in Washington, D.C." (Lanzmann filmed him at his home in the fall of the 1978);[19] the SS officer at Bełżec, Josef Oberhauser, who "was said to be working in a Munich wine cellar" (in *Shoah*, Lanzmann attempts to interview him in a beer hall in the summer of 1979);[20] Adam Czerniaków, the president of the Jewish council in the Warsaw ghetto who committed suicide in 1942 upon realizing that he could not stop the deportation of children (in the film, Hilberg reads excerpts from Czerniaków's diary, including his final entry);[21] Szmul Zygielbojm, the leader of the Jewish Bund who, in the face of the silence and inaction of the world, committed suicide in 1943 (his story is narrated not only by Karski in the unused portion of his interview with Lanzmann but also by Faivel Zygielbojm, who reads in front of the camera several of his late brother's letters).[22]

Among the dozen interviews with survivors, perpetrators, and bystanders referenced in *Into That Darkness* is the testimony of Sobibór survivor Stanislaw Szmajzner, whose story bears a striking similitude to that of Simon Srebnik, the first protagonist to appear in Lanzmann's film. "He was a boy of fifteen when he broke out of Sobibor [sic] in October 1943; so he was only forty-three when we met," Sereny writes upon introducing Szmajzner.²³ In the opening crawl text of *Shoah*, Lanzmann tells the story of Srebnik, "a boy of thirteen when he was sent to Chełmno" who returned with him to the extermination camp in the late seventies; "he was then forty-seven years old." Sereny never went to Sobibór in the company of Szmajzner, but she recounts in her book a visit to Treblinka with the survivor Berek Rojzman. She lingers here over the camp's memorial, of which she includes a photograph: "thousands of granite slabs, the different sizes representing the number of people killed from different cities and towns in Europe," the very stones Lanzmann would film "like a madman" and include in *Shoah*.²⁴

Juxtaposing "site and speech" (one of Lanzmann's early titles for the film) and a historical investigation, Sereny's book on Treblinka echoes the conception of *Shoah* described by Lanzmann in 1977.²⁵ More importantly, it anticipates certain aspects of the finished film's mise-en-scène and two of its most memorable witnesses. *Into That Darkness* permeates in particular the polyphonic representation of the extermination through the juxtaposition of the voices of perpetrators, victims, and bystanders (to borrow Hilberg's post-*Shoah* tripartite distinction and eponymous study of the Holocaust).²⁶ It also seemingly informs the editing of Suchomel's and Glazar's testimonies in *Shoah*. In the finished film, both men recount anecdotes included by Sereny, such as the women who, according to the perpetrator, supposedly defecated while waiting to enter the gas chamber at Treblinka (when speaking to Lanzmann, Suchomel specifies that he "didn't see them do it"). Another anecdote is Glazar's first recollection in the film, where he mentions an opera singer from Warsaw who was chanting as they watched the flames the night they began to burn bodies. Similarly, if Suchomel's first appearance in *Shoah* opens with Lanzmann inquiring about his heart, Sereny introduces him in her book by specifying that, after having interviewed him at his home, they then "communicated by letter because he suffers from a heart condition and said it was too taxing for him to *talk* about it."²⁷

Also anticipating Suchomel's testimonial performance in *Shoah*, where the perpetrator avidly describes the destruction process in front of Lanzmann's secret camera, Sereny comments in her book on his willingness to bear witness. "But the last word, as often, was Suchomel's, for whom recalling the details of Treblinka has become something of a passion," she aptly remarks.²⁸ The importance of Sereny's book is further evidenced in the outtakes of Suchomel's filmed testimony. Here, Lanzmann directly refers to *Into That Darkness*. "I read that you arrived on August 20th," he states within the first five minutes of the interview; "there is an interesting thing in the Sereny book...," he says much later, looking through his notes.[29] Similar to the seven-and-a-half-hour-long interview Lanzmann subsequently filmed with Glazar in the spring of 1979, his lengthy testimony scattered throughout *Into That Darkness* constitutes the most extensive survivor account included by Sereny. It also largely exceeds the scope of Treblinka. In both the book and the unused portion of his filmed interview, Glazar describes his upbringing in Prague, his deportation in 1942 to the camp-ghetto of Theresienstadt, where he stayed for a month, and then to Treblinka. He recounts, as well, his escape from the death camp following the uprising in August 1943 and the two years he spent living in Germany as a foreign worker under a false identity. There, he saw at the cinema Josef von Báky's comedy, *Münchhausen*, on the adventures of the famous fictional German baron. "It was ridiculous, just ridiculous after Treblinka," he is quoted as saying by Sereny of this 1943 film commissioned by the Nazi propaganda minister Joseph Goebbels.[30]

Toward the end of both his testimony cited in *Into That Darkness* and the *Shoah* outtakes, Glazar shows Sereny and Lanzmann, respectively, several objects he escaped with from Treblinka, including an old shaving kit and a piece of soap. "Probably that's the only object which remains to this day from the 800,000 people [murdered in the extermination camp]," he tells Lanzmann.[31] Quite rare in the outtakes and more prevalent in accounts filmed by audiovisual archives, these objects constitute a fitting epilogue to Glazar's incredible tale of survival. As Jeffrey Shandler writes in his analysis of such visual elements found in the testimonies collected by the USC Shoah Foundation, "Beyond these objects' value as evidence of the Holocaust, they testify, if largely tacitly, to the survivor's postwar endurance."[32] In the case of Glazar, these objects also intimate a certain closeness between interviewer and interviewee that transpires in both the Sereny book and the unused portion of his testimony recorded for *Shoah*.

This closeness approximates Lanzmann's account in *The Patagonian Hare* of his initial 1975 encounter with the other Treblinka survivor included in the finished film, Abraham Bomba (in the Glazar outtakes, Lanzmann refers twice to Bomba's escape from the death camp several months before the 1943 revolt). Describing the weekend with Bomba in a cabin in the Catskills several years before he filmed him in Israel for *Shoah*, he notes how "in his rough, imperfect English, Bomba [...] spoke to me as I believe he had never spoken to anyone; as though he were doing so for the first time."[33] In the filmmaker's memoir, Bomba emerges as a paradigm for the unprecedented relationship—suggested by the present tense "I believe"—that Lanzmann forged with each one of his (male) protagonists over the course of making the film. After all, it was this relationship and proximity that enabled the docu-auteur to undertake the labor of testimony and elicit what one might call the exemplary testimonial performances later included in *Shoah*.

In his comparative study of audiovisual archives, Noah Shenker puts forth the category of the "exemplary witness" as a framework for discussing internal criteria that determine the selection of filmed testimonies for circulation. More specifically, institutions incorporate in their exhibitions and pedagogical programs filmed testimonies deemed to be "exemplary in terms of projecting or embodying the particular preferences of their respective archive or memorial sites."[34] Transposed to *Shoah*, the category of the exemplary witness designates survivors, perpetrators, and bystanders whose testimonial performances in the finished film epitomize Lanzmann's demands of Holocaust representation and exhibit the "personal imprint of the auteur."[35] First, a certain proximity to the catastrophe, defined by the filmmaker as the perspective of men who witnessed the destruction process most closely: the Polish courier Karski, who secretly visited the Warsaw ghetto in 1942; the clandestinely captured testimonies of perpetrators such as Suchomel; the members of the *Sonderkommando*, among them Müller, who removed corpses from the gas chambers; Bomba and Glazar, the escapees of Treblinka, a site which solely functioned as a killing center.[36] Second, the production of detailed and inevitably lengthy accounts of the catastrophe attesting to Lanzmann's own obsessions as investigator, notably the transports to the East, the arrival in the camps, and the victims' final moments. Third, testimonial ruptures where common memory, which "offers detached portraits, from the vantage point of today," suddenly gives way to deep memory or an emotionally charged reliving of past events.[37] Indeed, in the finished film, an exemplary witness *"communicates"* the details of the machinery of destruction as well as *"expresses* affect (tears) and the inability to communicate (his choked words)."[38] Finally, carefully crafted mise-en-scène, including the staged reenactment in the barbershop with Bomba or the staged return to Chełmno with Srebnik, which evinces Lanzmann's conception of testimony "as a form of acting."[39]

In *Shoah*, the filmmaker elicits and requires from witnesses "exemplary" testimonies exhibiting memorable performative gestures such as Bomba cutting hair in front of the camera, Srebnik singing on the River Ner, or Müller crying upon remembering his Czech compatriots inside the gas chamber. Such performances do not simply reflect Lanzmann's "particular preferences." They also crystallize what Linda Williams identifies as "the persona of the documentarian": the role played by the postmodern docu-auteur in "calling the shots," intervening in the labor of testimony and truth, and "constructing and staging" narratives of the catastrophe—and, I would add, disseminating and imposing in the form of interviews, articles, and a memoir his privileged approach of ethics and aesthetics.[40] In turn, the exemplarity of these testimonial performances premised on mise-en-scène exceeds well beyond *Shoah* to become a reference point for theorizing Holocaust representation. "I think we need more, not fewer, Holocaust documentaries that incorporate reenactment, staging, and other fictive strategies through which the Holocaust may be remembered and disremembered," affirms Janet Walker in her important study of trauma cinema.[41] Similarly, *Shoah* has informed decades of dominant discourses around Holocaust testimony, from Lawrence Langer's privileging of deep memory in his landmark study of the Fortunoff Video Archive to Cathy Caruth's Lanzmannian likening of reenactment to "*the truth of an event,* and *the truth of its incomprehensibility*" in her influential writings on trauma.[42]

In his reinterpretation of dominant theoretical frameworks that have shaped the reception of Holocaust survivor testimony, Thomas Trezise examines the ways in which Caruth's theory of traumatic memory "exhibits its affinity" with *Shoah*, particularly in situating the possibility of transmission in what he terms "a silencing reenactment."[43] This silencing reenactment rendered exemplary by *Shoah* lies in the appropriation of testimony by the docu-auteur who "calls the shots" and imposes his demands of Holocaust representation onto his witnesses. At the same time, however, it points to all that Lanzmann had to exclude, or silence, in order for the film's male protagonists to emerge as exemplary: all the *choices* and *cuts* made during the stages of filming and editing *Shoah* and which the outtakes render visible and audible. The footage left out recovers not only rehearsals and multiple takes of staged scenes but also counter-performances that are marked by a resistance to such demands of Holocaust representation and to such a censoring of agency. The exclusion of the women survivors filmed for *Shoah* is a case in point: despite more than twenty hours of footage, their combined on-screen time amounts to a mere ten minutes. This sheer brevity contrasts with the lengthy accounts of the film's male protagonists. More importantly, it precludes in the finished film exemplary performances encompassing either a detailed account of the destruction process, the resurgence of deep memory, or an interviewer-interviewee proximity.

In the outtakes of the Glazar interview, the closeness underlying the labor of testimony and the production of an exemplary testimonial performance transpires through Lanzmann's use of the informal second-person German pronoun *du* and the partial filming of the interview in the survivor's living room. This familiarity evidencing the mark of the docu-auteur finds a precedent in the lengthy interview Sereny conducted with Glazar, the only protagonist referred to exclusively by first name in *Into That Darkness*, at his home in Bern where she "went to stay with him and his family in the late autumn of 1972."⁴⁴ Similarly, "the many many hours Richard and [Sereny] talked," an interview followed by a correspondence over the course of which Glazar added to his testimony, appear in retrospect as a rehearsal for the nearly eight-hour-long interview Lanzmann filmed with the Treblinka survivor, who is seen a total of eight times in *Shoah*.⁴⁵

Beyond the repetition of several episodes included by Sereny in her book, Glazar's ability and willingness to recollect the past in front of the camera is crystallized in an important segment left in the editing room: sitting in a café by the Aar River, Lanzmann successfully prompts Glazar to sing the Treblinka hymn prisoners were forced to chant in the death camp—the very hymn sung in *Shoah* by Suchomel. "Do you remember," Lanzmann first inquires in these outtakes, "Suchomel told me about [...] the choir [...] did you sing?" After Glazar evokes the Treblinka hymn, the familiar voice of the docu-auteur asks: "Do you remember it? Can you sing it?" When the survivor suggests he recite the words rather than sing them, Lanzmann adds, speaking over him, "Please—*you must try*."⁴⁶ At that very moment, Glazar proceeds to sing the hymn once, his face framed in a close-up. Retrieved from the archive, this excluded fragment constitutes a unique countershot to Suchomel's

FIGURE 1.2. Claude Lanzmann, Richard Glazar, and a largely off-screen Corinna Coulmas holding the clapboard (Created by Claude Lanzmann during the filming of *Shoah*. Used by permission of the United States Holocaust Memorial Museum and Yad Vashem, the Holocaust Martyrs and Heroes' Remembrance Authority, Jerusalem).

performance in *Shoah*, which the SS officer concludes by affirming: "That's unique. No Jew knows that today." In order to retain the sheer horror in the words pronounced by Suchomel in the finished film, Lanzmann had to exclude Glazar's performance of the same song.

In the final paragraph devoted to Glazar in *Into That Darkness*, Sereny intuits the singularity of both his survival and testimony. "But there is a great deal more to the story of Richard Glazar's escape," she notes, "and I feel it should be left to him to tell it in print one day" (the survivor published his memoir, *Trap with a Green Fence*, in German in 1992).[47] Sereny then evokes Glazar's 1968 "Open Letter" to Jean-François Steiner, which, archived at Yad Vashem, remains unpublished to this day. Steiner authored the bestselling yet controversial nonfiction novel *Treblinka: The Revolt of an Extermination Camp*, a book Glazar considered a misrepresentation of both the 1943 revolt and the Jewish victims. First published in France in 1966, this fictionalized account of the revolt draws on interviews Steiner conducted in Israel with nine Treblinka survivors. It was prefaced, as the complete text of *Shoah* would be in 1985, by Simone de Beauvoir.

Invoking the famous phrase coined by the partisan and poet Abba Kovner in the Vilna ghetto in 1942 in a call for resistance, de Beauvoir's preface opens with a question: "'Why did the Jews allow themselves to be led to the slaughterhouse like sheep?' the young *sabras* of Israel asked each other indignantly at the time of the Eichmann trial."[48] This query summarizes the central thesis of Steiner's book: namely, what he perceives to be the complicity and passivity of the Jews during the Holocaust. For the French author, whose father perished in the Auschwitz subcamp of Gleiwitz, the Treblinka revolt constitutes a rare counternarrative to the insinuation of Jewish collaboration. This contentious topic had already been broached by Hilberg in *The Destruction of the European Jews* and infamously reiterated by Hannah Arendt in her report of the Eichmann trial—two books translated into French only after *Treblinka* in 1985 and 1966, respectively.

The publication of Steiner's book sparked a profound controversy in postwar France. In his reconstruction of the so-called "Treblinka affair" in which he cites several passages of Glazar's "Open Letter," Samuel Moyn meticulously argues for the significance of Steiner's book in "the emergence and development of post-Holocaust consciousness in France and beyond."[49] He emphasizes the crucial distinction made by *Treblinka* (visible in its original French subtitle, *La révolte d'un camp d'extermination* [The revolt of an extermination camp], but omitted in the English translation) between concentration camps and killing centers, such as Treblinka. Moyn also notes that "Steiner raised, for perhaps the first time before a large audience, the *Sonderkommando* at Treblinka and the other Nazi death camps"—albeit as emblematic figures of Jewish complicity who, in the end, decided to revolt.[50] Years later, Lanzmann chose these men, who had been in charge of disposing the victims' bodies inside the extermination camps, as the protagonists of his Holocaust opus.

In the final moments of his interview filmed for *Shoah*, Glazar indirectly references Steiner's book. "In the discussions after the war about Treblinka," he begins in take 49, "the question continually arose: 'Yes, why didn't you defend yourselves, why didn't you put up more resistance? Why were you such cowards?'" He is suddenly interrupted by Lanzmann, who exclaims in German, "*Nein, nein, nein, nein, nein* [no, no, no, no, no]," before asking Lubtchansky to cut (Glazar returns very briefly to this question at the end of the following take, asserting that Jews were "incapable of acts of violence").[51] Comparable to the fact that any proper discussion of the 1966 book that profoundly marked postwar intellectual life in France is absent in these outtakes, neither Steiner nor the "Treblinka affair" are ever referenced in the filmmaker's memoir, *The Patagonian Hare*.

Yet, as Moyn remarks, "Steiner's book provoked some of the first statements on the genocide by new actors in the generation who would decisively shape what it would mean later in their country and indeed around the world—for example, Claude Lanzmann."[52] Moyn refers specifically to Lanzmann's participation, alongside the French Jewish intellectual Richard Marienstras, in an interview with de Beauvoir for *Le Nouvel Observateur* in the midst of the "Treblinka affair." Much like the cover of the April 27, 1966, issue that reads, "The Jews of Treblinka: Simone de Beauvoir Responds," Moyn focuses on de Beauvoir's defense of Steiner's book. During this interview, however, Lanzmann formulates several criticisms that anticipate the representation of the extermination in *Shoah*. These underscore the significance of the "Treblinka affair" and, in particular, his subsequent decision to select—in order to redeem—the members of the *Sonderkommando* as the protagonists of his Holocaust opus.

First asserting that "it is truly inacceptable to write [that the Jews 'went like sheep to the slaughter']," Lanzmann remarks in 1966: "Never has the idea come to me to consider the men of the *Sonderkommando* as collaborators or traitors. I consider them to be martyrs just like any other martyr and many of them I actually consider heroes."[53] Two decades later, *Shoah* rehabilitated these men and reframed their representation from "collaborators" to "heroes" (in line with Lanzmann, French critics and scholars described his Jewish protagonists as "heroes," following the release of the film in 1985).[54] To recast them as "heroes," the docu-auteur had to exclude from the finished film not only the interview he recorded with Abba Kovner but also tales of revolt and escape found in the testimonies of many Jewish survivors, including Glazar. Lanzmann's second refutation of Steiner's theses and in particular the claim of Jewish passivity came in 2001 when he released *Sobibór, October 14, 1943, 4 p.m.*, a documentary centered on the account of Yehuda Lerner, one of the leaders of the revolt in the death camp.

Toward the end of the 1966 interview with de Beauvoir and Marienstras, Lanzmann cites Schwarz-Bart's *The Last of the Just*, a novel whose success also sparked controversy in postwar France partly based on accusations of plagiarism and historical inaccuracies (incidentally, Francine Kaufmann, who served as Lanzmann's Hebrew interpreter for *Shoah*, devoted her doctoral dissertation to the novel and its reception).[55] Deeming Steiner's answers to claims of passivity and collaboration to be "a bit quick," Lanzmann contrasts his approach to that of Schwarz-Bart who, "to describe, to explain Nazism, began with the Middle Ages and summoned the entire tradition of pogroms and Jewish Martyrdom."[56] Reminiscent of a *longue durée* history of anti-Semitism Hilberg describes in *Shoah*, the mention of Schwarz-Bart's novel also anticipates Perlov's juxtaposition of his encounters with the writer and the filmmaker in 1983: two men of the same generation (a generation, as Lanzmann notes in the interview with de Beauvoir and Marienstras, before Steiner's) whose respective opuses profoundly shaped at different times and in different ways the memory of the extermination in France.

The reference to Schwarz-Bart further illustrates the impact the 1966 Holocaust controversy would have on *Shoah*. When the actual shooting phase began in March 1976, Lanzmann and his cinematographer Lubtchansky first filmed Leib Garfunkel and Benjamin Murmelstein. Both men had served as members of a Jewish council or *Judenrat*, the administrative entity established by the Germans in ghettos, whose compliance Arendt compared to collaboration in her report of the Eichmann trial. She asserted, "if the Jewish people had really been unorganized and leaderless, there would have been chaos and plenty of misery but the total number of victims would hardly have been between four and a half and six million people."[57] Neither man appears in *Shoah*. Lanzmann would wait until 2013 to draw on the Murmelstein outtakes to make *The Last of the Unjust*, a transparent allusion to Schwarz-Bart and a belated response to claims of complicity.

"A RACE AGAINST DEATH": THE FIRST FILMED INTERVIEWS (1975–1976)

When McClelland received Lanzmann's letter in 1977, he wrote to the historian Lucy Dawidowicz, author of the bestselling monograph *The War Against the Jews: 1933–1945*. Published in 1975, the book marked a turning point for Holocaust memory in America, crystallized three years later by Marvin Chomsky's miniseries.[58] McClelland and Dawidowicz had begun a five-year-long irregular correspondence in December 1974. In this collection of letters, which the former WRB representative carefully archived, he notably describes how Yehuda Bauer interviewed him in 1969 on the cooperation between the Board and the American Jewish Joint Distribution Committee in New York.

In 1977, McClelland wrote to Dawidowicz to inquire about Lanzmann and his Holocaust documentary. In her response, she reveals that she met with the French director in New York during the spring of 1975 to discuss the film he was making. "Lanzmann," she writes, "made a good impression—our conversation lasted nearly three hours, I think. My book had just come out and I gave him a copy. He seems to know the people to see and talk to." Dawidowicz mentions historians Henry Feingold and Raul Hilberg, both of whom were subsequently interviewed for *Shoah* in early 1979. Hilberg, she adds, "wrote an extraordinarily well documented book which, until mine appeared, was the best source available on the subject."[59] The three-hour meeting remembered by Dawidowicz evidences the initial interviews conducted by the filmmaker and his assistants during the research phase. The reframing of *The Destruction of the European Jews* through the lens of *The War Against the Jews* intimates, for its part, a certain friction between Hilberg and her that possibly influenced Lanzmann's decision to not record her for *Shoah*. This friction also transpires in Hilberg's memoir, *The Politics of Memory* (1996), in which he bitterly dismisses the historiographical importance of *The War Against the Jews* and discredits its portrayal of the Jewish councils as "powerless entities."[60]

In *The Patagonian Hare*, Lanzmann never mentions his meeting with Dawidowicz, let alone *The War Against the Jews*, an account of the Holocaust that nonetheless informed his project. Rather, the year 1975 appears only in passing when he recalls a Holocaust conference he attended in New York at the beginning of March. It was there, and thus in the same trip during which he met with Dawidowicz, that he was introduced to Hilberg and Feingold.[61] Titled "The Holocaust—A Generation After," this international symposium organized by Bauer gathered nearly sixty scholars, several of whom would, in due course, play a part in the making of *Shoah*. Beyond future protagonists Hilberg, Feingold, and Rubenstein, Lanzmann met Isaiah Trunk, the author of *Judenrat: The Jewish Councils in Eastern Europe under Nazi Occupation* (1972). Trunk later provided names of people to interview about the ghettos. Also present was the Vilna survivor Abba Kovner, who on this occasion refuted claims of passivity his 1942 phrase "like sheep to the slaughter" had incited in the postwar period.[62] Bauer, along with the Israeli philosopher Nathan Rotenstreich, subsequently published a dozen of the proceedings in the 1981 volume titled *The Holocaust as Historical Experience*. While the original conference grappled broadly with the legacy of the catastrophe, the published essays examine, to quote from the book's introduction, "what has become perhaps the most controversial question in the whole field: the issue of the Jewish leadership in Nazi-dominated Europe."[63]

Of the book's ten articles, seven consider the varied responses of Jewish leaders across Europe as well as postwar claims of collaboration. They engage in particular with Arendt's controversial generalizations and Trunk's wide-ranging study. The edited volume concludes with an abridged transcription of a round-table discussion titled "The *Judenrat* and the Jewish Response," during which Hilberg aptly summarized the dilemma faced by the leaders of the ghettos. "Jewish councils everywhere," he explained, "came face to face with the basic paradox inherent in their role as preservers of Jewish life in a framework of German destruction. They could not serve the Jews indefinitely while simultaneously obeying the Germans" (this paradox echoes Dawidowicz's own formulation in *The War Against the Jews* of the "dichotomization" of the *Judenrat* who "tried to reconcile their irreconcilable tasks").[64] In the version of his 1975 conference paper included in *The Holocaust as Historical Experience*, Hilberg reflects on the generalizations produced by Trunk's study, which does not examine Jewish councils individually but rather draws on each ghetto to illustrate the general situation of the *Judenrat* during the war. Hilberg counters this collective portrait through the example of the Warsaw ghetto and its council president Adam Czerniaków. Incidentally, in Steiner's *Treblinka*, Czerniaków's suicide is deployed by the French author to illustrate the absence of any revolt on the part of Jewish councils.[65]

Much like his conference paper in the Bauer and Rotenstreich volume, Hilberg provides the sole representation of the Jewish council in *Shoah* by reading and commenting on excerpts of Czerniaków's diary, a document originally written in Polish that Hilberg, Stanislaw Staron, and Josef Kermisz coedited for the 1979 English translation. In the finished film, Hilberg's account of Czerniaków's growing despair in the ghetto erases the moral ambiguities that surrounded the *Judenrat* after the war and persisted well into the making of *Shoah*, as evidenced by the New York conference and the subsequent publication of the proceedings. The representation of Czerniaków as an absent protagonist to whom the historian lends his voice also differs by sheer physical presence alone from the interviews Lanzmann filmed with Garfunkel and Murmelstein.

In his 1977 letter to McClelland, Lanzmann explains that the film's protagonists will be "the surviving witnesses." Concomitantly invoking their imminent passing, he notes that, as an investigation into the catastrophe, the film he is making will chronicle "its nature of urgency and a race against death."[66] This sense of urgency permeates the first interview shot for *Shoah* in Israel in March 1976 with Garfunkel, three years after he had been interviewed by the rabbi Joseph Rudavsky for a book on the Jewish ghettos of Eastern Europe.[67] At the time of his filmed testimony, Garfunkel was nearly eighty years old; he passed away shortly thereafter. During the war, he served as vice chairman of the Kovno *Judenrat* in central Lithuania. Like Czerniaków, he secretly kept a diary in Yiddish and recorded meticulous accounts of several important events in the history of the ghetto: its establishment in 1941, the so-called "Great Action" on October 28 of that year during which the Germans murdered 9,200 Jews, the transports to the death camps beginning in 1943. Garfunkel was deported to Kaufering, a subcamp of Dachau whose inmates were used as forced labor in fighter aircraft production. He survived and emigrated to Israel in 1948.

A decade later, Garfunkel drew on his wartime diary to write a historical monograph in Hebrew titled *The Destruction of Kovno's Jewry*, which was published in 1959.[68] Rather than his testimony, this book becomes the centerpiece of the two-and-a-half-hour-long interview Lanzmann conducted in English with him a year after attending the New York conference. Coupled with the issue of the *Judenrat*, the centrality of this paper memory approximates the representation in *Shoah* of Czerniaków who—as Hilberg and Staron speculate in their introduction to the English translation—also possibly kept a diary "with a view to writing a book later on."[69]

"I would like Irene [sic] to read a part of your book," begins Lanzmann. Sitting in Garfunkel's living room, he is assisted by Irena Steinfeldt over the course of the interview.[70] Unlike Kaufmann, Lanzmann's Hebrew interpreter who remains off-screen in both the outtakes and the finished film, Steinfeldt translates in front of the camera several lengthy passages from *The Destruction of Kovno's Jewry* aloud into English. Garfunkel, with the book balanced on his knees and his appearance rather frail, interrupts from time to time, either by briefly commenting or simply turning toward the filmmaker, nodding his head silently in order to highlight the importance of certain facts as they are being cited. Lanzmann does not have a copy of *The Destruction of Kovno's Jewry*. Instead, he listens to both the interpreter and the survivor, periodically writing down notes. This gesture captured by the camera appears less performative than indicative of a certain lack of historiographical knowledge described by Lanzmann upon recounting the making of *Shoah* in his memoir. "I later learned that one needs a vast body of knowledge before questioning [someone]. At the time I really didn't know enough," he observes regarding the preliminary research phase during which he met with hundreds of survivors. Along with his papers scattered on the coffee table in Garfunkel's living room, the note-taking seen in these outtakes illustrates "the position of an attentive listener" Lanzmann first adopted during the making of *Shoah*.[71] Of this position, there would remain no trace by either the end of the shooting phase or in the finished film. In fact, to ensure they would "know enough," the filmmaker and his two assistants began preparing thematic dossiers based on their research. When traveling to meet with eyewitnesses, they would bring these documents for review, along with several books, including Sereny's *Into That Darkness*, Steiner's *Treblinka*, and Hilberg's *The Destruction of the European Jews*.

The stark evolution of the filmmaker's methods is particularly palpable in the unused portion of the interview recorded with Itzak Dugin and Motke Zaidel in September 1979. Here, Lanzmann incessantly questions the two Vilna survivors in order to extract the most minute details and elicit an exemplary joint performance later chosen for the final cut. Early on in these outtakes, he even announces his demands of Holocaust representation. "It must be explained to them that ... I need their help," he tells Kaufmann, "they must understand that when you haven't lived in a ghetto it's impossible to imagine what it was like. So things that seem obvious aren't at all obvious for those who weren't there, they must have the courage to say even the obvious things."[72] While at times disclosing his frustration with the survivors and the interpreter ("For crying out loud, I am asking clear questions here," he says bluntly between two takes), Lanzmann emphasizes the veracity of their testimony, thereby revealing, three and a half years after the Garfunkel interview, his mastery of Holocaust historiography. "That's the truth, there were people who survived Ponari, who were injured and who ... who could escape the mass grave," he notes after Zaidel remembers these individuals who crawled from underneath the bodies and returned to the ghetto to warn the community of the massacres in the forest.[73]

By contrast, the distinct mise-en-scène underlying the Garfunkel outtakes exposes a method and docu-auteur still in the making. This "testimony" oscillates between Steinfeldt's translation of *The Destruction of Kovno's Jewry* and Garfunkel's factual memories of the ghetto, themselves largely centered not on his own personal experience but on that of the Jews of Kovno. The unedited material offers a significant variation to the centrality of filmed speech in *Shoah*, as well as to the excavation of deep memory practiced by the filmmaker in later years. Between 1978 and 1979, for instance, Lanzmann films Simon Srebnik's return to Chełmno, Abraham Bomba's reenactment in a Tel Aviv barbershop, and Zaidel and Dugin in the Israeli forest of Ben Shemen, a site reminiscent of Ponar. By contrast, the Garfunkel outtakes evidence not deep but common memory, not the resurfacing of a "buried self" epitomizing traumatic experience but a linear, progressive account of the past.[74] This narrative distanciation is further accentuated by the face and voice of the interpreter reading from *The Destruction of Kovno's Jewry*. In early 1976, Lanzmann does not attempt to elicit an exemplary testimonial performance from Garfunkel. Instead, what the camera captures by way of close-ups of the survivor's face—and which the domestic décor and Steinfeldt's testimonial mediation both accentuate—is the imminent passing of Holocaust survivors or the "race against death" subsequently evoked by Lanzmann in his letter to McClelland.

At the same time, in accentuating Garfunkel's frailty, the close-ups of his face displace to the off-frame the controversy surrounding the role of the *Judenrat*. Although filmed the year following the Holocaust conference in New York, this topic is broached only briefly when Lanzmann and Garfunkel discuss a dilemma the council faced in September of 1941: to follow or not follow German orders by selecting five thousand artisans to be spared during the liquidation of the ghetto. Without directly citing Arendt, Lanzmann asks Garfunkel whether the Jewish council should have refused to comply or tried to save whatever lives they could. Opting for the latter, the survivor emphasizes the tragedy of choice inherent to the role of the Kovno *Judenrat*. "It's a terrible thing, you know, when I have to decide: this man is entitled to live, this man is not entitled to live," he says to Lanzmann who, instants later, remarks succinctly: "It is an impossible dilemma." Garfunkel concludes this discussion by comparing the situation of the Jewish council to that "of a captain of a sinking ship."[75] In a passage from Czerniaków's diary cited by the filmmaker during his interview with Hilberg in *Shoah*, the president of the *Judenrat* deploys the very same image to describe his tragic position in the Warsaw ghetto.

More than a representation of "the most controversial question" in Holocaust studies in 1976, the interview with Garfunkel records a memory on the verge of disappearance: that of an elderly man in his home whom we can see, between two takes, drinking a glass of water with a trembling hand or sitting outside on his balcony, and on whose face the camera lingers when he speaks. While the interview opens with a passage from Garfunkel's monograph,

FIGURES 1.3–4. Claude Lanzmann, Leib Garfunkel, and Irena Steinfeldt; a close-up of the survivor (Created by Claude Lanzmann during the filming of *Shoah*. Used by permission of the United States Holocaust Memorial Museum and Yad Vashem, the Holocaust Martyrs and Heroes' Remembrance Authority, Jerusalem).

it closes with the black-and-white photographs of the Kovno ghetto the survivor shows to the filmmaker, and which the camera films meticulously. Given that Lanzmann claims to have known very early on that there would be no archival images in the film, this gesture further recuperates an ethics of representation and a docu-auteur still largely in the making.[76] In fact, unlike the centrality of testimony privileged in the finished film, this first interview for *Shoah* largely voiced by Steinfeldt appears entirely made out of paper. From Garfunkel's book to Lanzmann's notes to the closing shots of the black-and-white photographs, these epistemic objects articulate, three years after the filmmaker had begun his historical investigation at the archives of Yad Vashem, a narrative frame centered not on the voice of the witness but on paper knowledge.

Another documentary trace further evidences this testimonial displacement: the forty-eight-page transcript from which Lanzmann initially worked while editing *Shoah*, the annotations of which bear witness to the process of composing a film from the monumental archive he had constituted. This document contains notes in French specifying historical facts and the interview's visual details, as well as bracketed passages from both the translated excerpts of *The Destruction of Kovno's Jewry* and Garfunkel's fragmentary account. It also reveals Lanzmann's enduring interest in the testimony of a *Judenrat* member during the editing phase, as attested by a page where the impending selection of the five thousand artisans from the ghetto is described. By way of Lanzmann's scribbles representing the survivor and the interpreter, and the annotations "off" and "GP" (*gros plan* or close-up) in the margins alongside this passage of Garfunkel's book translated by Steinfeldt, these handwritten notes suggest a possible juxtaposition for the finished film between her voice-over and a close-up of his face.[77] In line with Lanzmann's relative visual absence in *Shoah*, the cropping intimated by the scribble displaces the filmmaker, along with his notes scattered on the coffee table, to the off-screen. The juxtaposition between the voice of the interpreter and the face of the elderly survivor bears witness, for its part, to the process of editing around the controversial choices of Jewish councils: namely, how—through which episode and in what form—to represent the dilemmas they faced without passing moral judgment? If Lanzmann excluded this interview from *Shoah*, the privileging of both Steinfeldt's voice and Garfunkel's book in the annotated transcript nevertheless approximates Hilberg's own reading of Czerniaków's diary, a paper memory constituting the sole representation of the *Judenrat* in the finished film.

Akin to their brief evocation in the Garfunkel interview, the Jewish councils are referred to only once in *The Patagonian Hare*. Recalling his search

this |extraordinary| passage from your book about the Lebensscheine. And how the German cracked completely the Jews with these life certificates. It was the same everywhere in the ghettos in Lithuania, in Vilna.

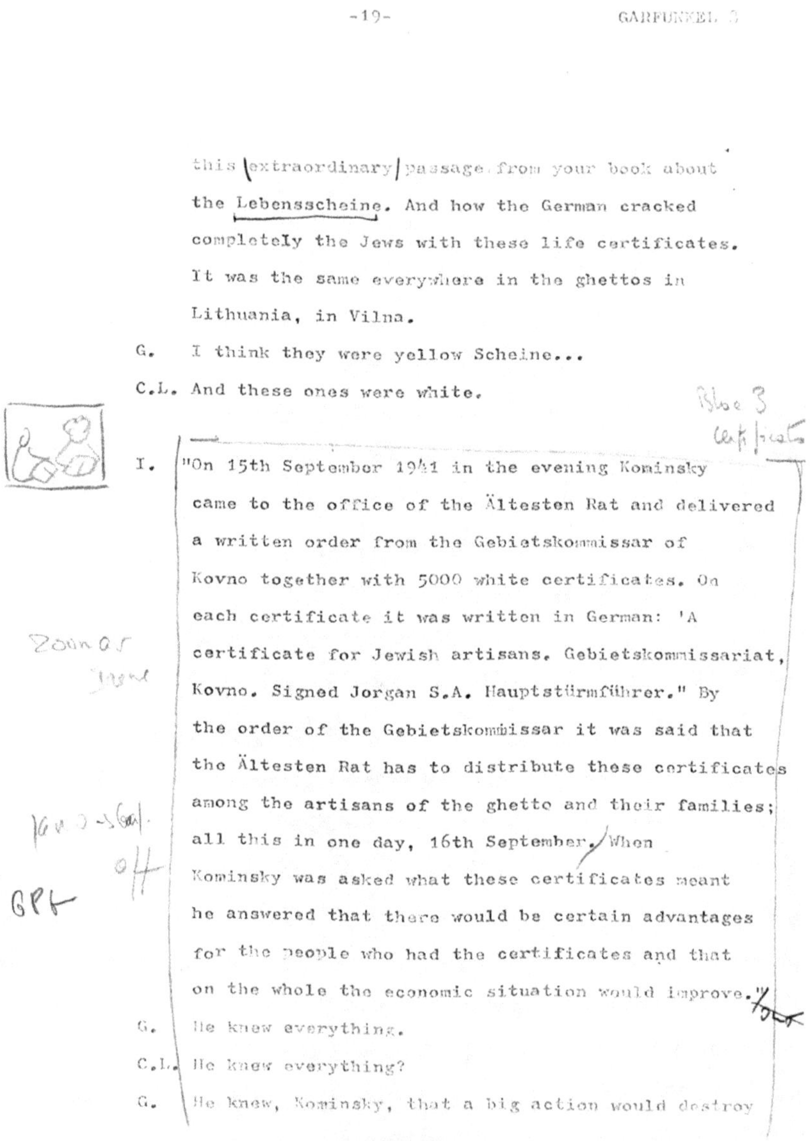

G. I think they were yellow Scheine...

C.L. And these ones were white.

I. "On 15th September 1941 in the evening Kominsky came to the office of the Ältesten Rat and delivered a written order from the Gebietskommissar of Kovno together with 5000 white certificates. On each certificate it was written in German: 'A certificate for Jewish artisans. Gebietskommissariat, Kovno. Signed Jorgan S.A. Hauptsturmführer." By the order of the Gebietskommissar it was said that the Ältesten Rat has to distribute these certificates among the artisans of the ghetto and their families; all this in one day, 16th September. When Kominsky was asked what these certificates meant he answered that there would be certain advantages for the people who had the certificates and that on the whole the economic situation would improve."

G. He knew everything.

C.L. He knew everything?

G. He knew, Kominsky, that a big action would destroy

FIGURE 1.5. An annotated page from the Leib Garfunkel transcript (Created by Claude Lanzmann during the filming of *Shoah*. Used by permission of the United States Holocaust Memorial Museum and Yad Vashem, the Holocaust Martyrs and Heroes' Remembrance Authority, Jerusalem).

for members of the *Sonderkommando*, Lanzmann proceeds to dismiss the Eichmann trial, where several of these men, including *Shoah* protagonist and Chełmno survivor Mordechai (Michael) Podchlebnik, had testified. Considering that "the trial had been conducted by ignorant people," he condemns "the shocking way in which [it] was directed [that] unjustly put much of the responsibility and the blame for the extermination on the *Judenräte*." This aspect of the trial, Lanzmann then reminds his readers, "became the subject of a bitter dispute between Gershom Scholem and Hannah Arendt, who [...] in her book *Eichmann in Jerusalem*, showed a partiality, a lack of compassion, an arrogance and a failure of comprehension for which he was right to reproach her."[78]

The filmmaker's allusion to the disagreement between Scholem and Arendt that eventually ended their friendship obscures for the reader their correspondence spanning nearly a quarter of a century. It also silences Scholem's bitter condemnation, in a letter to Arendt dated June 23, 1963, of Murmelstein, who, he writes, "deserves to be hanged by the Jews" (a phrase Lanzmann himself quotes in a segment of the outtakes found at the end of *The Last of the Unjust*).[79] Conversely, the docu-auteur never mentions in his memoir the early interviews filmed with Garfunkel and Murmelstein. The latter, along with the making of *Shoah*, resurfaces instead in *When Memory Comes*, the 1978 memoir of the Holocaust historian Saul Friedländer who also attended the 1975 conference in New York. Friedländer survived the Holocaust as a child hidden in a French monastery. At one point, Lanzmann envisaged filming him for *Shoah*. "The conversation with Claude is hard to forget," Friedländer writes in an entry dated September 20, 1977. "He told me about his film. The last sequence finished was with a former SS officer at Treblinka. [...] the notorious Perry Broad of Auschwitz tells his story in the film, too, as does Murmelstein, old Murmelstein, whom we still consider to be a traitor, the chief of the Jewish council of Theresienstadt; he, too, tells his story beneath a soft spring sky, in Rome."[80]

Murmelstein was the sole head of a Jewish council to have survived. As attested by Scholem's verdict and Friedländer's portrayal framed in terms of an unspecified collective "we" conjugated in the present tense, he remained a figure of controversy until his death in 1989. Deported in 1943 from Vienna, where he had worked in the Office of Jewish Emigration established by Eichmann in 1938, to the camp-ghetto of Theresienstadt, Murmelstein was first appointed as a member of the Council of Jewish Elders before becoming its last chairman in 1944. At the end of the war, the Czech authorities arrested him; he spent a year and a half in prison awaiting trial before all charges of collaboration against him were dropped. Exiled to Rome in 1947, he was never summoned to testify at the Eichmann trial in Jerusalem. In March 1976, he told Lanzmann his story in German over the course of a nearly twelve-hour-long interview, a length that strikingly exceeds the monumental *Shoah*.[81] Shot in a hotel near the Arch of Titus in the Italian capital, these outtakes reveal the presence of Lanzmann's second wife, the German Jewish writer Angelika Schrobsdorff. In 1974, as he worked on *Shoah*, the filmmaker translated, prefaced, and published under the title *L'Oiseau n'a plus d'ailes* (*The Bird Has No Wings*) the wartime correspondence of her half-brother Peter Schwiefert, who died in 1945 fighting for the Free French Forces.

Beyond the interview's unparalleled length and subsequent inclusion nearly forty years later in *The Last of the Unjust*, its significance is further attested by Lanzmann's brief description of this footage in "Material of 'Shoah,'" the document he drafted in 1994 when he first approached the USHMM. "One full week shooting in Rome," the docu-auteur writes about the unedited footage with Murmelstein before adding: "Unique. He never talked before and after. He is now dead."[82] Actually, Murmelstein did speak again. In 1977, he was interviewed and recorded on audiocassette by Edith Ehrlich and Leonard H. Ehrlich as part of the research they were conducting for a monograph on the dilemmas faced by Jewish leaders. In this recording, he describes having been approached by the French filmmaker, who had with him a reference letter from Yehuda Bauer. After a first meeting and a lengthy "back and forth, back and forth," Lanzmann convinced him to "represent his side of history" for the Holocaust documentary he was making, supposedly even proposing to pay him (an offer the survivor declined). At the end of the interview, Murmelstein entrusted the filmmaker with a secret manuscript from Theresienstadt to be given to Bauer—a document, he tells the Ehrlichs, he now regrets having parted with. After all, Lanzmann had agreed to send Murmelstein a transcript of his filmed testimony, which the survivor had yet to receive.[83]

If *The Last of the Unjust* exposed Lanzmann's probing of the controversy surrounding the Jewish council, the Murmelstein outtakes render visible, much like the interview with Garfunkel, a method still in the making. First, the epic length of the material and its circular structure (the unedited reels open and close with shots of Rome) give the impression of a film of its own. As the director himself observes on the final shooting day, "You know, this is very surprising, we have been talking for four days and I think I am quite mad, because I am making a film not about the Shoah, the Holocaust, but about Dr. Murmelstein."[84] Rather than the lack of historiographical and authorial mastery evidenced in the Garfunkel interview by Lanzmann's note-taking in front of the camera, these outtakes unfold in their duration his fascination with the controversial *Judenrat* chairman. They also attest to the immense gap between

FIGURE 1.6. Claude Lanzmann evidencing his "bookish [...] knowledge" during the interview with Benjamin Murmelstein (Created by Claude Lanzmann during the filming of *Shoah*. Used by permission of the United States Holocaust Memorial Museum and Yad Vashem, the Holocaust Martyrs and Heroes' Remembrance Authority, Jerusalem).

the "bookish, theoretical [...] second-hand knowledge" he had acquired during his research for *Shoah* and Murmelstein's own experiences and recollections.[85]

Comparing himself to the first-century Jewish historian Flavius Josephus and constantly referencing legends and folk tales, the survivor constructs an endless account of the past in front of the camera that reproduces the complexity of a mythological story—a narrative distanciation that further evinces the centrality of common memory in the inaugural interviews captured for *Shoah*. The distance revealed through the encounter between the filmmaker's research and the survivor's "side of history" is further evidenced by the fact that, following Murmelstein's own affectation, they often speak of him in the third-person singular as though he were, effectively, a literary figure. It is he who self-designates during the interview as "the last of the unjust," inversing the title of Schwarz-Bart's 1959 novel.

Although marked by the same urgency as the Garfunkel interview, these outtakes register a first shift in Lanzmann's approach to representing the catastrophe. Indeed, toward the end of the filmed footage, he asks Murmelstein whether it is even possible to write the history of the Holocaust solely from documents, in which case the Theresienstadt survivor would be represented as a collaborator—a question that foreshadows the centrality of eyewitness testimony to come in the finished film. Furthermore, the initial historiographical distance is progressively undone through the growing friendship between the two men, which culminates in their respective decision to wear a suit on the last day. "You are very elegant today," begins Lanzmann. "Oh, in honor...," replies Murmelstein, "because we say good-bye today."[86]

Reminiscent of the closeness forged with many of the film's protagonists, this moment of mimesis captured in 1976 crystallizes this testimony's unconventionality. Set against the backdrop of Scholem and Friedländer's judgment as well as Murmelstein's absent voice during the 1961 trial in Jerusalem, the interview takes the form of a dialogue over the course of which the survivor weaves his defense. The sheer duration of these outtakes evidences Lanzmann's growing awareness that, in capturing Murmelstein's "side of history," he could possibly rehabilitate the controversial *Judenrat* chairman and even, as he tells him in the closing moments, take him to Israel, where the Theresienstadt survivor was a persona non grata. Two decades later, a sense of guilt transpires in the interview synopsis penned for the USHMM through the evocation of Murmelstein's passing, once more calling attention to the docu-auteur's inability to compose in the editing room around the contentious choices of Jewish leaders during the Holocaust.

FIGURE 1.7. Claude Lanzmann and Benjamin Murmelstein on the last day of the interview (Created by Claude Lanzmann during the filming of *Shoah*. Used by permission of the United States Holocaust Memorial Museum and Yad Vashem, the Holocaust Martyrs and Heroes' Remembrance Authority, Jerusalem).

"A VERY FINE INVESTIGATION INSTRUMENT": THE PALUCHE
AND THE SECRET RECORDING OF PERPETRATORS (1976–1979)

In his September 29, 1977, journal entry on the making of *Shoah*, Friedländer frames his description of Murmelstein around two interviews Lanzmann conducted with perpetrators: "a former SS officer at Treblinka" who, although unnamed by the historian, is Franz Suchomel, and Pery Broad, once a functionary in Auschwitz-Birkenau. Upon being detained in a British prisoner-of-war camp in 1945, Broad wrote a thorough account of the extermination process subsequently titled "The Broad Report." He later testified as a defendant at the Frankfurt Auschwitz trials in 1964—where *Shoah* protagonists Filip Müller and Rudolf Vrba also served as witnesses—and received a four-year prison sentence. In his autobiography, Friedländer reveals the most memorable details of the Suchomel interview, the first of a dozen encounters with perpetrators that Lanzmann would film over the next three years. Anticipating the edited segments included in *Shoah*, Friedländer describes the large map of Treblinka displayed on the wall during the interview, the reenactment of the Treblinka hymn, and the memory of the Jewish women awaiting extermination. By contrast, his depiction of the footage captured with the former functionary is limited to a single sentence: "And the notorious Perry Broad of Auschwitz tells his story in the film, too."[87]

Broad, whose first name is alternatively spelled Pery, does not appear in *Shoah*. He was not actually filmed until 1979, as indicated in the opening segment of the unused interview, which shows Lanzmann and him discussing the miniseries *Holocaust* that aired on West German television in January of that year.[88] The testimony succinctly alluded to by Friedländer refers to several preliminary unrecorded conversations between Lanzmann and Broad in 1976. As recounted in *The Patagonian Hare*, Lanzmann, using the pseudonym "Dr. Sorel" and, passing as a French historian from the University of Paris working on a book about the Holocaust, attempted in vain during these initial meetings to convince Broad to grant him a formal interview.[89] Accompanied by his assistant Corinna Coulmas (who, with the exception of Suchomel, assists him during all the interviews with perpetrators), the filmmaker finally recorded Broad in the summer of 1979. He used a hidden audio recorder strapped to his chest and a tiny handheld black-and-white video camera resembling a microphone, which was called the Paluche, a slang term meaning "hand" in French. Concealed in Coulmas's handbag, this camera was equipped with an ultra-high-frequency (UHF) transmitter that relayed the images to a video monitor and recorder in a vehicle near the interview location with an antenna mounted to the roof. This unorthodox filming technique is revealed in *Shoah* in the opening segment of the Suchomel interview: while the sound of the perpetrator's voice is heard, a camera slowly zooms in on a red-and-white Volkswagen minivan parked in a residential area. It then cuts to a medium close-up shot of the moving antenna on its roof before filming the inside of the vehicle where, akin to a recording studio, two technicians work to make the images captured by the Paluche appear on the monitor.

Marketed in 1974, the Paluche was the timely invention of French engineer and cinephile Jean-Pierre Beauviala. Echoing Lanzmann's conception of *Shoah* described in his 1977 letter to McClelland, Beauviala envisaged this miniature camera as "a very fine investigation instrument."[90] In the early seventies, he founded in the southeastern city of Grenoble the camera manufacturer Aaton, whose lightweight equipment revolutionized documentary cinema and news-gathering practices, beginning with a sixteen-millimeter camera nicknamed "cat-on-the-shoulder." He conceived of the "cat" not only as a lighter and quieter alternative to the portable cameras that existed at the time but also as more discreet: its smaller ergonomic design allowed for it to be placed further back on the shoulder, thereby enabling the cameraman to move more swiftly toward and interact more freely with those being filmed.[91]

Beauviala created his film and video equipment in close collaboration with New Wave, direct cinema, and cinema verité filmmakers that included Jean-Luc Godard, Richard Leacock, D. A. Pennebaker (the three had collaborated in 1968 on Godard's unfinished film *One p.m.*), and Jean Rouch. This unique encounter between technology and aesthetics is exemplified in Beauviala's working relationship with Godard, who moved from Paris to Grenoble in 1974 and remained there until 1977. During this period, the French engineer and the New Wave director began developing a lightweight, high-resolution thirty-five-millimeter camera equipped with automatic Super-8 features; easily handled, it "was to be a *director's* camera."[92] The project resulted in the Aaton 35, a small, portable thirty-five-millimeter camera ultimately devoid of the Super-8 features. Lanzmann's cinematographer William Lubtchansky and his camera assistant on *Shoah* Caroline Champetier tested the prototype in June 1979.[93] Lubtchansky had first been introduced to Godard while working as assistant to the cinematographer Willy Kurant on *Masculin Féminin* (1966). He subsequently shot between May and June 1968 Godard's *Ciné-tracts*, eight anonymous, critical short films on current events made as part of a collective enterprise initiated by Chris Marker.

In the second half of the seventies, while working on *Shoah*, Lubtchansky assisted Godard on several of his video experiments. Their collaboration exemplifies the emergence, underlying the video revolution and its equipment, of "artist-technician couples elaborating a new relationship between conception and execution."[94] Although he opted to not relocate to Grenoble despite the filmmaker's repeated requests, the cinematographer frequently made two-week visits to work with Godard, who considered him "the most talented film technician."[95] In the summer of 1976, Lubtchansky shot Godard's first television commission (one of his earliest collaborations with Anne-Marie Miéville), *Six fois deux*, a twelve-part investigation of French society comprised of interviews. He was assisted by Dominique Chapuis, later one of Lanzmann's three primary cinematographers, along with Lubtchansky and Jimmy Glasberg, for *Shoah*. Working on a rushed shooting schedule for *Six fois deux*—the episodes aired gradually over the course of the series' making—Lubtchansky exhibited his technical prowess by transforming a minivan into a "camera car." Resembling a "mobile video studio used by television stations," the vehicle was equipped with recording gear and electrical autonomy that enabled Godard and his crew "to go film anywhere at any moment."[96]

Conceived in the summer of 1976, only a few months after Lanzmann first used the Paluche to interview Suchomel in April, Lubtchansky's "camera car" constitutes the prototype of the minivan used during the recording of perpetrators for *Shoah*. Given his frequent stays in Grenoble beginning in 1974, the year the Paluche was marketed, and given his familiarity with Beauviala's inventions, the cinematographer played a decisive role in providing Lanzmann with the technological means necessary to secretly record perpetrators. Chapuis inevitably lent his own expertise from working on *Six fois deux*, as did Bernard Aubouy, who came with expert knowledge of synchronized sound from his work on the early films of Jean Eustache.[97] Beyond its significance for these clandestine recordings, the Paluche reframes "the relationship between conception and execution" in *Shoah* by evidencing the "artist-technician couple" Lubtchansky formed with Lanzmann in the late seventies. As the filmmaker would remark more than three decades later in *The Patagonian Hare*, "Lubtchansky […] refined and deepened my cinematic education."[98] Or, as the cinematographer himself noted regarding his experience recording testimonies for *Shoah*: "Lanzmann, at the time, did not know much about directing. He let me make a lot of propositions about how to film. I would say: 'We're not actually going to shoot the entire film with people sitting down. We could go outside, to this place....'"[99]

The clapboard visible in the Suchomel outtakes confirms Lubtchansky's collaboration as cameraman for the first perpetrator testimony filmed with the Paluche. The unused portions of this interview, however, are devoid of any footage recorded either inside or outside the van parked in a residential area.

This lacuna in the April 1976 recording substantiates the hypothesis that the minivan visible in *Shoah* was conceived after Lubtchansky's work on *Six fois deux* and thus modeled on the "camera car" he had created for Godard's television series—an unexpected intersection between the two filmmakers given their subsequent dispute in 1998 over the existence (for Godard) or nonexistence (for Lanzmann) of images showing the extermination of Jews in the gas chambers.[100] The missing images in these outtakes also expose the mise-en-scène at play in the finished film: the footage of both the outside and inside of the van visible in *Shoah* was staged and recorded three years after the Suchomel interview.

The shots of the parked vehicle were captured during the secret interview with Reichsbahn official Walter Stier who appears in *Shoah*. The footage inside the minivan, for its part, bears a striking resemblance to the one found on rolls 3 and 4 of the Broad outtakes. Here, the camera slowly zooms in on the vehicle parked across from an apartment building at the corner of Eugen-Langen-Straße in Wuppertal, east of the city of Düsseldorf where the former Auschwitz functionary passed away in 1993 (given the clandestine nature of the Paluche interviews, it is highly improbable that the van was actually filmed on the street where Broad lived). As in *Shoah*, the moving antenna on the minivan's roof is then framed in a lengthy medium close-up shot. Similarly, rolls 1

FIGURE 1.8. The clapboard of the Franz Suchomel interview showing the "artist-technician couple" Lanzmann and Lubtchansky (Created by Claude Lanzmann during the filming of *Shoah*. Used by permission of the United States Holocaust Memorial Museum and Yad Vashem, the Holocaust Martyrs and Heroes' Remembrance Authority, Jerusalem).

and 2 of the Broad outtakes reveal Chapuis and sound engineer Aubouy in the back of the "camera car" as they attempt to make the interview appear on the monitor. This mise-en-scène is identical to the one included in *Shoah*—from the poor lighting inside of the vehicle to the clothes worn by the technicians to the image of Broad visible on the monitor. This excluded footage reveals that the cameraman seen inside the minivan in *Shoah* is not Lubtchansky but Chapuis.

These images of the minivan from 1979 and the ones included in *Shoah*, which show Chapuis and Aubouy attempting to make the secret recording of Suchomel appear on a monitor, were staged at the same time, a mise-en-scène substantiated by rolls 11 and 12 of the Broad outtakes. Here, during a sequence shot in the minivan the following day in which the images of the former Auschwitz functionary flicker on the monitor before disappearing, Chapuis and camera assistant Jean-Yves Escoffier can be seen and heard discussing somewhat unconvincingly the possible sources of this technical problem. This scene is suddenly interrupted by Lanzmann, who laments off-screen: "Cut, cut, that was very poor acting, Dominique [Chapuis]!"[101]

Conceived in the final year of the shooting phase and immediately following the secret recording of Broad, the importance of this mise-en-scène for the finished film is further attested by the existence of outtakes titled "*Camionnette* [minivan]," which were shot in May 1983 in Saint-Cloud by Lubtchansky (here credited, like on most of the clapboards visible in the archive, as "Bob"). In the midst of editing *Shoah*, Lanzmann and his crew filmed several takes of camera assistant Andrés Silvart driving and parking the minivan (now devoid of an antenna), one take even resulting in an unintentional fender bender with a delivery truck. Once parked, Silvart gets out, walks over to the sliding door, and looks around cautiously before entering the back of the minivan.[102] Somewhat evocative of the film technician protagonist played by John Travolta in Brian De Palma's 1981 film *Blow Out*, this thrillerlike mise-en-scène offers a reverse shot to the footage captured by the Paluche in reenacting and rendering visible the risks run by Lanzmann's crew during the clandestine recordings of perpetrators for *Shoah*.

If the staged footage involving the minivan and the technicians was not conceived until 1979, Suchomel himself was actually not filmed at his home, as was the case for all of the other eyewitnesses Lanzmann recorded with the Paluche. This first clandestine interview recorded with the former Treblinka officer took place, as Friedländer reveals in his autobiography, in a hotel room located "in Braunau am Inn, Hitler's Austrian birthplace, near the German border."[103] In 1976, Lanzmann was accompanied by his technicians

Lubtchansky and Escoffier, as well as by an unnamed male interpreter—a unique occurrence in either *Shoah* or the excluded material, where all of the interpreters are women.

In exchange for a sum, paid in Swiss francs, of nearly two thousand dollars (a financial transaction captured on camera in the final moments of the interview), Suchomel had agreed to an audio recording. Consequently, Escoffier, unseen and referred to as "Jean" by Lanzmann, is sitting across from the former Treblinka officer, using the Paluche in front of him. As French film theorist Anne-Marie Duguet remarks in her 1981 study of video aesthetics and technologies, "[The Paluche] could be confused with a microphone. The person targeted, even if warned, does not see or feel himself being filmed. [The Paluche] can be the invisible camera par excellence, the instrument of clandestinity. [...] It has even been used for instance to snatch testimonies of war criminals."[104] Four years before the release of *Shoah*, this description of the Paluche constitutes a surprising allusion to Lanzmann's film, further hinted at in a previous chapter where Duguet notes that the video monitor "can be installed [...] in the back of a minivan."[105] It also perfectly captures the process of secretly filming perpetrators and, in particular, the interview with Suchomel, the only one where Beauviala's miniature camera was not concealed in a handbag. The visibility, or clear maneuvering, of the Paluche is here attested by Lanzmann's repeated requests, made in French to Escoffier using the coded word *gros* (for *gros-plan*), for close-ups of Suchomel's face, notably when the latter cries or sings.[106] Similarly, during a moment of silence, the filmmaker asks "Jean" to speak in order to cover the noise made by the recording equipment.[107]

In these outtakes captured over the course of a single day, this moment of silence occurs when the interview resumes after a lunch break, a meal never recorded with the Paluche but which Lanzmann recalls in *The Patagonian Hare*. "We broke for lunch, to which I had also invited [Suchomel's] wife; I remember they stuffed themselves with duck, followed by whipped cream, while William [Lubtchansky, who was born in France to Polish Jewish parents], whose father had been gassed at Auschwitz, shot me murderous looks. By the time we began again, my 'teacher' had been completely won over, twice I persuaded him to sing the song [of] the Jews."[108] While Suchomel later concedes in the outtakes that he "ate too much," this moment remembered from the point of view of the docu-auteur, who successfully mediates a reenactment of the past, eclipses the malaise and silence that initially plagues the interview after lunch.[109]

Indeed, Lanzmann, seemingly exhausted and pained, is unable to resume. "Very, very complex, very, very complex, the deception...," he begins in French, as though addressing himself and the process of secretly recording a perpetrator for the first time. "*Difficile, alles ist sehr schwer* [difficult, everything is very hard]," he continues in a mix of French and German a few instants later. Over the course of the next five minutes, he proceeds to leaf through his notes of both the 1964 Treblinka trial transcript and *Into That Darkness*, sighing several times and speaking incomprehensibly in single words to a perplexed Suchomel. "*Meister Scheiße* [the master of shit]!" he suddenly exclaims, referring to the Jewish prisoner in charge of cleaning the latrines at Treblinka. "*Le maître de la merde! Scheißmeister! Le zoo également, il y avait un zoo* [The master of shit! The shit master! The zoo as well! There was also a zoo]!" he continues in French and German. These fragments intercut with silence culminate in his decision to get up from the table and go wash his hands. Once finished, but still in the bathroom, Lanzmann utters loudly in French: "*Ah, mon William…*"[110] The only time the name of his cinematographer is heard in these outtakes, this phrase serves as an apology to Lubtchansky's horrified consternation during the lunch described in *The Patagonian Hare*.

Upon recalling this 1976 interview in his memoir, Lanzmann details Lubtchansky's presence, describing the way in which he had transformed the hotel room into a recording studio and how Suchomel, upon arriving, had become agitated when he saw "William with all his equipment at the other side of the room."[111] If Escoffier is the only technician sitting near Suchomel and Lanzmann in these outtakes, the cinematographer's use of a clapboard (unbeknownst to the perpetrator) and the reflection of a window on the video monitor visible between takes suggest that Lubtchansky and his equipment are in fact in an adjacent room—an early method of secretly recording perpetrators for *Shoah* irremediably altered by the cinematographer's subsequent work on Godard's *Six fois deux*.

As noted by Lanzmann in *The Patagonian Hare*, Suchomel delivers an exemplary testimonial performance following the lunch, above all in the final hour of the interview. Here, he chants several times the Treblinka hymn included in *Shoah*, along with songs in both Polish and Yiddish, while the filmmaker presses Escoffier to make close-up shots of Suchomel's face with the Paluche. Anticipated by Gitta Sereny's remark that "recalling the details of Treblinka ha[d] become something of a passion" for Suchomel, this performance prompts Lanzmann in the final minutes of the outtakes to make the perpetrator promise he will grant him another interview.[112] Suchomel, who passed away in 1979, was never filmed again. Three years into the making of *Shoah*, however, the success of this first clandestine recording with the Paluche significantly expanded the realm of the possible for Lanzmann, who could now film other perpetrators including Broad, whom he had met the same year he interviewed Suchomel. This conjunction is evidenced in Friedländer's 1977 evocation of *Shoah* in which he casts the former Auschwitz officer as a protagonist alongside Suchomel. If the Broad outtakes were omitted, this unused interview reveals that, ultimately, the Paluche did not suffice to snatch the testimony of a perpetrator. One had, like Suchomel, to want to excavate the past.

At Broad's apartment in 1979, the "instrument of clandestinity" concealed in Coulmas's handbag captures first and foremost testimonial resistance. Over the course of several hours during which Lanzmann and Broad address each other in English, German, and French (a linguistic oscillation that itself disrupts the resurgence of the past), the latter, who declines Lanzmann's request to use a recorder, continuously reframes the interview into a "conversation," a term employed at one point in the transcript of this secret recording.[113] Offering his guests champagne halfway through the meeting and discussing the maximum speed of his new automobile, the former Auschwitz functionary largely circumvents the act of bearing witness. Six years into Lanzmann's investigation and only months before the editing began, this footage does not expose the perpetrator's testimony. Rather, it renders visible an intertextual mosaic of the archive of the catastrophe the filmmaker had already amassed.

Upon describing to Broad the book he is supposedly writing, the docu-auteur invokes, in a veiled allusion to the making of *Shoah*, "the inquiries [he] did for years."[114] In tirelessly prompting the perpetrator to recount the horrors he witnessed, he also implicitly references location shooting in former death camps and taped interviews with several of the men who became the film's protagonists: the members of the *Sonderkommando*. Lanzmann mentions having visited Birkenau, emphatically describing this non-site of memory with which he would juxtapose eyewitness testimony in *Shoah* as "terribly impressive, terribly impressive." He goes on to remark: "It is today a paradise for, uh, for rabbits—extraordinary," a comment that anticipates the title of his 2009 memoir inspired by "those hares in the extermination camp at Birkenau that slipped under those barbed-wire fences impassable to man."[115]

During the interview, Lanzmann also suggests to Broad that they draw a map of Auschwitz together, a paper memory—much like the diagram of Treblinka used in the Suchomel interview—the docu-auteur hopes will mediate the resurgence of the past. Emphasizing, as a persuasion strategy, the need to integrate in his research the perspective of perpetrators, particularly regarding the topography of the camp, Lanzmann remarks:

> When you talk to the former inmates, the people who survived, they ... whether Auschwitz or Treblinka, Sobibor [*sic*], whatever camp it is, they always talk about two camps or three camps [...]. And you have the feeling that in their memories between the place they were and the place of death there are kilometers. That it's far, far, far. You know, always this. And I see it's only their imagination and their fear.[116]

In 1979, the filmmaker's assessment of traumatic memory approximates Janet Walker's notion of *disremembering*, or "remembering with a difference," which she also identifies as "a survival strategy par excellence."[117] Analogous to this implicit evocation of interviews he had already shot prior to filming Broad, Lanzmann not only alludes several times to the testimonies of Müller and Vrba (even mentioning having met the latter) but also affirms: "I have reports of the people of the *Sonderkommando* Auschwitz."[118] While "report" stands in for "filmed testimony," the word also echoes "The Broad Report" from which Lanzmann quotes during the interview, remarking to Broad that, because he had read this document, he "saw everything" the first time he went to Auschwitz in 1978.[119] After the map of Auschwitz, the filmmaker attempts once more to use this paper memory penned in 1945 as a form of testimonial mediation. In the face of Broad's resistance, he further prompts him by citing events (without quoting his sources) he learned about from eyewitnesses already filmed for *Shoah*. He describes, for instance, the violence Czech Jews experienced for refusing to enter the gas chamber at Auschwitz, poignantly described in *Shoah* by Müller. In the outtakes, Broad does not corroborate this event.

"It is very difficult for you to communicate this world," Lanzmann concludes diplomatically in the final moments of the outtakes, concealing his fatigue and frustration after several hours in the company of the former Auschwitz officer.[120] In front of the hidden Paluche, Broad never "tells his story," nor does he excavate the past. This failure to bear witness recalls his declarations of ignorance upon testifying at the Frankfurt Auschwitz trials in 1964. "I knew nothing about it and saw nothing," he affirmed on the witness stand regarding the gassing of Jews in the extermination camp.[121] In the opening segments of the interview, Broad in fact anticipates this testimonial distance, or resistance, in remarking to the filmmaker: "If I want to dominate, to face the past, in order to avoid it [*sic*], I must go deeper, I must go down to the roots."[122] Rather than deep memory, however, Broad is referring here to a *longue durée* of anti-Semitism dating back at least 150 years. He thus reframes the past in order to displace to the off-frame the Third Reich, along with his own experience and guilt. Lanzmann counters this point by paraphrasing—without ever naming—Hilberg, whom he had filmed months before: "But the questions are so big that one can only give a small answer to big questions."[123] In *Shoah*, Hilberg affirms: "In all of my work, I have never begun by asking big questions, because I was always afraid that I would come up with small answers."

In front of the concealed Paluche, Broad resists Lanzmann's own methodological preference, to further quote Hilberg in *Shoah*, for "the minutiae or details." Such testimonial detachment diverges sharply from the nature, at once thorough and graphic, of Suchomel's account of the extermination, itself perfectly encapsulated in the final lines of Friedländer's 1977 journal entry. "'Tell me, sir,' Claude asks the officer from Treblinka, 'which burned faster, men's bodies or women's?' The SS officer calmly begins to expatiate."[124] This question, to which an immovable Suchomel retorts immediately in the outtakes, "Women better. Fatter," once again epitomizes what Sereny rightfully perceived as Suchomel's "passion" for detailing the killing process at Treblinka.

If the filmmaker's failure to elicit Broad's testimony prompted the mise-en-scène involving the minivan and the technicians in the 1979 outtakes, the exclusion of this recording from the finished film is actually intimated by Lanzmann at the very end of the footage captured by the Paluche. "What nonsense!" he exclaims bluntly in French to Coulmas upon leaving Broad's home. He then adds: "I can't take it anymore, I was at my wits' end. Anyway, I don't think we will be able to use any of this."[125] Three decades later, Lanzmann's sentiment of being "at [his] wits' end" and of having captured meaningless material contaminates *The Patagonian Hare*. As (mis)remembered by the docu-auteur, Broad's testimonial performance to come is dramatically and irremediably interrupted when the Paluche catches fire in Coulmas's handbag:

> ...suddenly, as Perry Broad was speaking, wisps of white smoke began to rise from the bag as in a fairy tale, or at the election of a pope. *Perry saw the smoke too, of course*, but his astonishment, and his Teutonic slowness, meant his reactions were not as quick as mine. I leapt to my feet, snatched up the bag, shouted to Corinna, 'Come on!', grabbed her hand and we dashed down the stairs before he caught up with us. And he never did catch us. We jumped into the minivan and took off in a screech of tires, like in a cop film.[126]

The former functionary's feigned ignorance of the extermination process at Auschwitz revealed in the outtakes is signified in a single remark: "Perry saw the smoke too, of course." Largely obscured by the quasi-cinematic projection of a burning Paluche and Lanzmann and Coulmas's abrupt exit, the memory of Broad's silence is recast in *The Patagonian Hare* as a film noir. This genre, which had only just been revived by American cinema in the early seventies, was first coined by critics in postwar France, for whom noir films not only constituted "a challenge to Hollywood conventions" but also "used unorthodox narrations [that] resisted sentiment and censorship."[127] This definition is reminiscent of the 1979 essay Lanzmann wrote as a "progress report" for the film's investors. Published the same year in *Les Temps Modernes*, the essay posits a *Shoah* still in the making as a counter-representation to the miniseries *Holocaust* and its Hollywood conventions.[128]

Coupled with the grainy black-and-white cinematography of the Paluche footage, Lanzmann's invocation of this film genre in his memoir retrospectively translates the fear, palpable in the outtakes of several of the clandestine interviews, that the concealed camera and audio recorder or the parked minivan and its moving antenna could be discovered. This fear is itself voiced in the Karl Kretschmer outtakes where, prior to visiting the former Einsatzgruppen member at his home, Lanzmann is recorded preparing for the interview in his hotel room. In front of the camera, in the summer of 1979, he tells Aubouy, who is strapping the audio recorder to the filmmaker's chest, of his "*trouille* [fear]" that the device could have shown through his shirt with his every breath when he met with Broad and then with Heinz Schubert.[129]

While the recorder remained imperceptible in both instances, the Paluche was discovered when Lanzmann, passing as the historian "Dr. Sorel" and accompanied by Coulmas, interviewed Schubert at his home. As the filmmaker recounts in his memoir and as the unused footage confirms, the Schuberts were informed by neighbors, who saw and heard the footage of the perpetrator through the ajar door of the minivan, that they were being filmed. The former Einsatzgruppen officer's sons violently confronted Lanzmann and Coulmas. Both managed to escape, leaving behind the handbag containing the Paluche.[130] It is not incidental that, immediately following this misadventure, a Paluche-less Lanzmann decided to document his unorthodox recording technique by asking to be filmed as Aubouy was strapping the recorder to his chest in preparation for his visit with Kretschmer.

If the unused Schubert outtakes encapsulate the high risks Lanzmann and his crew took at times, a sense of fear permeates this particular interview from beginning to end. "There are dogs," Lanzmann is first heard saying in a noirish tone as he and Coulmas reach the front door of Schubert's home.[131] (In the 1979 secret interview he later conducted in German with Franz Schalling, the former police guard stationed at Chełmno who appears in *Shoah*, an equally anxious Lanzmann suddenly exclaims to Coulmas in French upon hearing the doorbell: "Someone has rung."[132]) When Schubert is called into the kitchen by his wife to take a phone call halfway through the interview, Lanzmann immediately whispers to his assistant: "They spotted the minivan, I think, with the antenna. [...] I'm scared they've spotted us because of the antenna, it's quite visible this antenna, [the technicians] move it a lot"—an image that recalls the mise-en-scène with the van visible in *Shoah* and the Broad outtakes.[133] Similar anxiety is triggered by Schubert's wife, who mentions within the first minutes of the interview a certain "Irene Stein... Steinflug or something" who visited them two years prior in order to solicit an interview "for a film." She assumes that this woman was working for "Dr. Sorel." Like two actors, Lanzmann and Coulmas pretend they do not know "Irene Stein[feldt]," the filmmaker going as far as cynically remarking: "But what can one do for a film? [...] There are so many of them..."[134]

The evocation of the filmmaker's other assistant Irena Steinfeldt, along with the deception deployed by Lanzmann and Coulmas, reveal the pre- and post-Paluche methods used during the making of *Shoah*: on the one hand, the preliminary research phase when the filmmaker and his assistants visited perpetrators at their homes, concealing neither their identities nor the film they were working on; on the other hand, the shooting phase when, equipped with the miniscule camera and the minivan, Lanzmann acquired the false identity of "Dr. Sorel." During this phase, Lanzmann would first send perpetrators an introductory letter containing a questionnaire and a request for a meeting. This duplicitous method was intended to prepare the perpetrators for a secretly filmed interview. The Hans Gewecke outtakes bear witness to this method. In this footage, the elderly former regional commissioner of the Shavli ghetto in Nazi-occupied Lithuania, now seeming "more like a kindly grandfather than a killer" (as the docu-auteur accurately remembers him in *The Patagonian Hare*), reads one by one the answers to the questionnaire he diligently formulated in preparation for his meeting with "Dr. Sorel."[135]

In the clandestine recording of the former Einsatzgruppen officer, Frau Schubert's recollection of "Irene Stein" also evidences the crucial role Steinfeldt and Coulmas played in initially locating perpetrators in Germany, even conducting preliminary interviews with them, some of which they audio recorded and then transcribed. As Coulmas recalls, "[Irena and I] had to find them. Some did not want to speak, others did. I remember, for example, having interviewed [Eugen] Steimle, the Einsatzgruppen commander [...]. Ultimately, we did not film him [...]. We would have needed the Paluche and this was before we knew it existed."¹³⁶ Both Schubert and Steimle were tried in the Einsatzgruppen case at Nuremberg in 1947. Their death sentences were subsequently commuted to prison terms. In the Schubert outtakes, Lanzmann begins the informal interview by apologizing for having sent the perpetrator a letter of introduction erroneously addressed to Steimle.¹³⁷ Per Schubert's request, "Dr. Sorel" then reveals the content of the unanswered letter: a description of an oral history project on World War Two undertaken by his institute at the University of Paris, for which he was in charge of collecting audio recordings of Einsatzgruppen testimonies (in the event that the perpetrators would have agreed to an audio recording, Lanzmann could simply have used, as with Suchomel, the Paluche in front of them).

By means of the Paluche, along with the pseudonym of "Dr. Sorel" and his fictitious Paris-based institute for historical research, whose address was in fact the offices of *Les Temps Modernes,* Lanzmann secretly filmed seven perpetrators between 1976 and 1979.¹³⁸ Concurrently, he experimented with several types of mise-en-scène. Of these, the minivan and the sequence shot at a Munich beer hall where the former SS officer Josef Oberhauser refuses to answer Lanzmann's questions were the only ones to make it into the finished film. In his 1977 letter to Roswell McClelland, likening *Shoah* to an "investigation," Lanzmann observes that "the film traces the development of this investigation, [...] with all its successes and failures, its uncertainties, its contradictions, its impossibilities."¹³⁹ Exemplified in the finished film by the grainy video footage secretly recorded with the Paluche, this conception of *Shoah* penned several months after the Suchomel interview is further encapsulated in the unused color footage that was shot over the summer of 1979 with a thirty-five-millimeter camera. These remaining outtakes move away from the aesthetics of clandestinity embodied by Beauviala's miniature camera toward a literal staging of the investigation that is at times reminiscent of noir films.

The first of these recordings revolves around the search for Gustav Laabs, a former SS officer who drove gas vans at Chełmno and who is actually never filmed. This unused material captured in June 1979 in the western German village of Kaldenkirchen does not open with a secret recording but with a variation on the staged minivan scenes. After driving through the streets, the film crew parks the vehicle in front of Laabs's building. Sitting in the back but off-screen, Lanzmann begins to read the indictment of the so-called "Chełmno trial" held in Bonn between 1962 and 1963, where Laabs, found guilty of the murder of one hundred thousand Jews, received a fifteen-year prison sentence of which he served only half. As the camera slowly frames a close-up of Laabs's apartment window concealed with a curtain (intimating that he might be hiding behind it), the filmmaker's voice-over details his crimes before concluding in a detectivelike fashion: "He has dentures and suffers from hearing loss since 1934."[140]

Having revealed both the perpetrator's past and distinctive features, Lanzmann, accompanied by Coulmas, Aubouy, and Chapuis, enters the building and walks up the stairs to Laabs's apartment. As he rings the doorbell and turns the knob several times in vain, he exclaims: "We're going to need to try something else."[141] In the face of their absent subject, Lanzmann and his crew undertake a variation on the previous mise-en-scène, this time on the highway where they will later film passing trucks, notably a blue Saurer vehicle, the same manufacturer of the gas vans used in Chełmno. Sitting in the back of the minivan with Coulmas at his side, Lanzmann reads several times a letter dated May 16, 1942, in which Dr. August Becker, an SS officer and chemist, details the mobile killing process. "In order for the act to be completed as fast as possible, the driver presses the accelerator to the fullest extent," reads Lanzmann while the member of his film crew driving the minivan accelerates loudly.

Captured a few weeks before the Broad interview and the staged scenes with the parked minivan, this unused footage attests to a first attempt at integrating into *Shoah* the filmmaker's hunt for perpetrators. A few days later, in early July 1979, Lanzmann and his crew reenacted this multifaceted mise-en-scène when documenting their search for Eduard Kryshak, a former railway worker who had accompanied several transports to Treblinka. "It's widespread complicity, just like at Laabs," Lanzmann remarks. This excluded material opens with a sequence shot in the back of the moving minivan where the filmmaker, sitting next to Coulmas, reads passages from Kryshak's postwar deposition. "It's only after the war that I learned Jews had been exterminated in the camps in Poland," the filmmaker reads before interjecting a cynical "Bravo!"[142] Once the minivan arrives at Kryshak's residence, the crew records a series of takes showing Lanzmann—seeming even more like a private eye in his trench coat—and Coulmas as they repeatedly buzz the intercom and pretend to speak to Kryshak's wife. "I acted well, right?" Lanzmann asks his assistant between two takes.[143] The filmmaker and his crew then head to the hospital ("with the Paluche," suggests Lanzmann) where Kryshak is recovering from eye surgery. Having learned that he has been discharged already, they return to his residence and proceed to reenact the same scene. "Dr. Sorel is going to

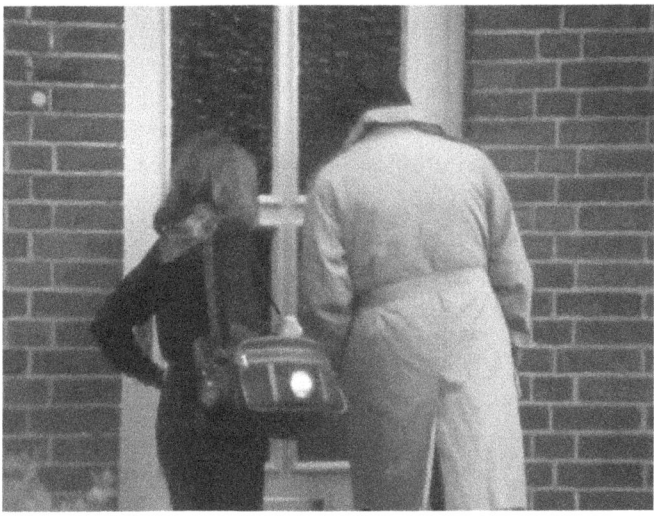

FIGURE 1.9. Corinna Coulmas, with the handbag containing the Paluche, and Claude Lanzmann outside of Eduard Kryshak's residence (Created by Claude Lanzmann during the filming of *Shoah*. Used by permission of the United States Holocaust Memorial Museum and Yad Vashem, the Holocaust Martyrs and Heroes' Remembrance Authority, Jerusalem).

ring again," Lanzmann jokes to Coulmas before he begins buzzing and yelling Kryshak's name.

Kryshak, a scar across his face attesting to his eye surgery, eventually agrees to let Lanzmann and Coulmas in and answer their questions. In this interview secretly captured with the Paluche, Kryshak notes at the outset that he is "not allowed to give testimony." He also maintains repeatedly that he "didn't get a look inside [the wagons]" of the trains he accompanied to Treblinka.[144] Similar to this excluded interview that recalls Broad's unwillingness to speak of the horrors he witnessed, the mise-en-scène inaugurated in the Laabs outtakes and reenacted in the filmmaker's search for Kryshak were ultimately left on the cutting room floor. Reframed at the LTC film laboratory through the lens of the limits of representation and through that of Lanzmann's own minimal visual presence in *Shoah*, the "investigation" of Nazi war crimes between 1976 and 1979 became in the finished film a representation *à huis-clos*. From the mise-en-scène with the technicians capturing secret footage of Suchomel inside the minivan to Lanzmann's unsuccessful attempts to properly interview Josef Oberhauser inside a beer hall in Munich, the final cut emphasizes the clandestinity of perpetrators in West Germany and of the filming process itself.

"THE POSSIBLE AND INCOMPOSSIBLE": EDITING *SHOAH* (1979–1985)

During his interview with Pery Broad in the summer of 1979, only months before the editing phase began, Lanzmann reveals the raison d'être of the monumental filmic archive of the catastrophe he had almost finished collecting. Describing the research for the "documentary book" he was supposedly writing, which stands in for the film he has been shooting, he remarks:

> You know what is the most difficult point? *The Holocaust is an abyss.* When you start to dig into this, it is unbelievable, because even if you think you know a thema [*sic*], that you know a subject, it's enough to hear somebody else who has an experience, to hear somebody else talking about, about this [*sic*], and *you have the feeling you hear the things for the first time again* even if you learn nothing new, you know. This is the most striking part, fact, the most striking point, you know.[145]

Echoing Alouph Hareven's 1973 proposal that he make "a film that *is* the Shoah," the likening of the Holocaust to "an abyss" posits the accumulation of more than 190 hours of testimonies as a signifier of the monumentality of the destruction process, of the historical magnitude of this event, and of the vastness of individual experiences. Conversely, it translates Lanzmann's own captivation as an auteur-archivist who, as though he were "hear[ing] the things for the first time again," could neither choose from the preliminary testimonies nor cut during the actual shooting of interviews—or, for that matter, when editing what became the nearly ten hours of *Shoah*.

Despite having repeatedly asserted after the release of the film, first and foremost as a rebuttal to criticisms regarding the exclusion of women survivors and French witnesses, that he knew early on the protagonists would be the all-male members of the *Sonderkommando*, Lanzmann recorded the majority of the testimonies en masse between 1978 and 1979—capturing at that time both masculine and feminine experiences of the Holocaust. This largely condensed shooting schedule calls to mind the older meaning of rushes, prior to its adoption as a film term in both English and French in the 1920s, as "the increased movement or activity of large numbers of people at a particular time" and "an eager or hasty scramble for or to do something."[146] If, in the letter addressed to Roswell McClelland, Lanzmann projects in 1977 that he would need "two more years to complete [*Shoah*]," the hurried accumulation of raw material between 1978 and 1979 foregrounds a temporal urgency: namely, to finish a film already five years in the making.[147] In turn, akin to oral history projects like the Fortunoff Video Archive for Holocaust Testimonies begun at Yale University in 1979, Lanzmann notes in the same letter "that in a few years from now it will be too late [to capture] living History." This concern for the imminent passing of survivors underlying the formation of Lanzmann's own archive of the catastrophe is movingly encapsulated in the closing outtakes of the interview with Abraham Bomba: in this mute final sequence following the reenactment in the barbershop, the survivor is filmed at dusk sitting with elderly Jews by the boardwalk in Tel Aviv.[148]

In his letter to the former War Refugee Board representative, Lanzmann already surmises *Shoah* will be "a monumental film, not only because of its length—approximately six hours, divided into three periods—but also because of the variety of its themes and the angles of research on which it is built."[149] Although the finished film was ultimately structured into two eras, this conception of *Shoah* as a doubly "monumental" work prevailed throughout the final two years it took Lanzmann to complete the shooting phase. By the end he gathered seventy interviews ranging from McClelland's rescue efforts to the highly gendered story of Ruth Elias, who, pregnant when she arrived at Auschwitz, had to kill her newborn in order to save herself from the experiments of the Nazi physician Josef Mengele. While the outtakes of *Shoah* subsist as evidence of Lanzmann's attempt to represent the Holocaust in "its entirety," this raw footage, in 1979, did not constitute a finished film. Rather, when the editing began in September that year, the testimonies amassed by the filmmaker formed a vast constellation of singular stories, themselves encompassing particular events and individual chapters of the Holocaust, from which he would have to select fragments and edit into a nine-and-a-half-hour opus.

At the LTC film laboratory in Saint-Cloud, Lanzmann and his crew were confronted over the next five and a half years with the overwhelming task of composing with incompossibles. In *Theodicy*, his 1710 philosophical investigation into the problem of evil, Gottfried Wilhelm Leibniz forged the notion of the incompossible to denote the existence of an infinite number of mutually exclusive possible worlds from which God, he argues, chooses the most just and harmonious one. Likening the divine creator to an architect, Leibniz illustrates this concept through the image of a pyramid containing an infinite number of apartments, each constituting a possible world or individual monad. Only one of these, however, the one situated at the summit, can come into existence.[150]

In the second half of the twentieth century, the concept of the incompossible became central to the work of Gilles Deleuze, a contemporary of Lanzmann alongside whom he studied the philosophy of Leibniz in postwar

Paris. There, as the French novelist Michel Tournier recalls, Deleuze and Lanzmann would meet in a bar whose "window bore the seductive words of MONAD TAKEAWAY."[151] Deleuze's formal investigation of the incompossible began as a series of lectures he gave at the University of Vincennes, in the seminar he devoted first to Leibniz during the 1979–1980 academic year and

FIGURE 1.10–11. Abraham Bomba (close-up) by the boardwalk in Tel Aviv (Created by Claude Lanzmann during the filming of *Shoah*. Used by permission of the United States Holocaust Memorial Museum and Yad Vashem, the Holocaust Martyrs and Heroes' Remembrance Authority, Jerusalem).

then to cinema in the early eighties (incidentally, the philosopher's interest in film was largely sparked by the work of Godard, including *Six fois deux*, which he discussed in an interview with *Cahiers du cinéma* in 1976).[152] Deleuze's fascination with the Leibnizian concept is encapsulated in his December 16, 1983, lecture. "Had there ever been painting in philosophy," he exclaimed, "[the incompossible] would have been the most beautiful painting philosophy had ever made."[153] His appropriation of the incompossible in these lectures informed his two major works published in 1985 and 1988, respectively: the second volume of his cinema series, *The Time-Image*, and his book-length study of Leibniz, *The Fold*.

Arguing for the *coexistence*—rather than the mutual *exclusion*—of incompossible worlds, Deleuze recasts Leibniz through the lens of both the Argentine author Jorge Luis Borges and the French philosopher Henri Bergson. In *The Time-Image* as well as *The Fold*, he cites the fictitious writer Ts'ui Pen found in Borges's 1941 short story "The Garden of Forking Paths," whose eponymous novel stages not one alternative but all the possible outcomes and ensuing bifurcations of a single event. For Deleuze, "the simultaneity of incompossible presents" crystallizes the falsifying narration manifest in modern (or time-image) cinema.[154] It also functions, as D. N. Rodowick aptly observes, to overturn—and open—the Leibnizian image of the pyramid and to transform it into Bergson's famous inverted memory cone found in his 1896 philosophical investigation into experience, *Matter and Memory*. Here, Rodowick notes, "the base still recedes indefinitely into the past and contains all of the past, but the apex is continually splitting toward an indeterminate future."[155] The Deleuzian reframing of the incompossible and inversion of Leibniz's pyramid approximate the ethics of "remaining open to excess" formulated by Eyal Peretz in his study of the off-screen. It also calls attention to the coexistence, in the case of *Shoah*, of the finished film and the excluded material—of the definitive Holocaust documentary Lanzmann created and all the other possible films that could have come into existence and that subsist today in the form of 220 hours of outtakes.

Recalling, in *The Patagonian Hare*, his postwar studies in philosophy, Lanzmann evokes Deleuze's fascination with "the possible and incompossible."[156] This notion also informs his memory of editing *Shoah*. In his memoir, the docu-auteur exposes the filming process in the final four chapters by detailing his encounters with the most memorable protagonists, including "the barber of Treblinka" Abraham Bomba, the "singing child" of Chełmno Simon Srebnik, and the SS officer Franz Suchomel.[157] By contrast, the five-and-a-half-year editing phase is contained in a single sentence. "The editing work was a long, serious, delicate, subtle process," he remarks without further detailing the selection undertaken at the LTC film laboratory.[158] Instead, the memory of cutting fragments from his vast archive of the catastrophe is displaced to an earlier chapter where a young Lanzmann visits his mother in Paris in 1942. Fittingly coinciding with the implementation of the Final Solution in January of that year and of the Vel d'Hiv roundup in the French capital the same summer, these wartime recollections penned more than two decades after the release of *Shoah* are permeated with Holocaust imagery. This narrative strategy calls to mind Alison Landsberg's notion of *prosthetic memory*: "privately felt public memories that develop after an encounter with a mass cultural representation of the past, when new images and ideas come into contact with a person's own archive of experience."[159]

This chapter of *The Patagonian Hare* set in 1942 opens with a traumatic train ride from the city of Clermont-Ferrand to Paris with false identity papers. "I remember the long wait through the night at the station Vierzon," Lanzmann writes, "the glare of the spotlights on the platforms and the trains, I remember the dogs, the thud of the boots, the brutal way the compartment doors were flung open."[160] This journey by train transports the reader to the extermination camps and to the arrival of convoys in the middle of the night, a ritual not only recounted in *Shoah* by Ruth Elias, who remembers seeing "only SS with dogs and [...] the thousands of lights," but also reenacted in fiction features such as *The Last Stage* (1948) by the Polish filmmaker and Auschwitz survivor Wanda Jakubowska in a scene Alain Resnais subsequently excerpted in his documentary *Night and Fog* (1956).[161] If Lanzmann remembers his wartime experience "through another's eyes," prosthetic memories of the Holocaust further inform this particular chapter of his memoir.[162]

When he describes visiting a Parisian shoe store in the company of his mother, an incident occurs that prompts him to unexpectedly and anachronistically reference the process of editing *Shoah*. He writes:

> We went to Chaussures André, a famous emporium—now Aryanized—on the boulevard des Capucines, with an extensive clientele, countless shop assistants and a vast selection of shoes. This, as it turned out, proved to be the source of the problem [*ce fut l'origine du drame*]. Because to choose is to kill. My mother was incapable of choosing, she wanted everything. I'm like her. The title of my dissertation for my philosophy degree was *Possibles and Incompossibles in the Philosophy of Leibniz*, 'incompossible' referring to the fact that there are things that cannot coexist. To choose one is to preclude the existence of the other. Any choice

is murder, and leaders, apparently, can be defined by their capacity to murder, we call them 'decision-makers' and we pay handsomely for it. It is no accident that *Shoah* runs to nine and a half hours. [...] Shoes and boxes piled up around the stool where I sat, trying them on.[163]

Framed in the original French as a *drame*, or tragedy, this episode once again transports the reader from Paris to the extermination camps: on the one hand, the selection ("to choose is to kill") that systematically took place when the convoys arrived; on the other hand, the pile of shoes, an iconic image of the Holocaust featured in *Night and Fog* but substituted in *Shoah* for shots of suitcases on which the names of the owners are visible. This prosthetic memory also bears a striking resemblance to Julia Kristeva's evocation of Auschwitz in her classic 1980 essay on abjection, *The Powers of Horror*. In this text contemporaneous with the editing of *Shoah*, Kristeva writes:

> In the dark halls of the museum that is now what remains of Auschwitz, I see a heap of children's shoes, or something like that, something I have already seen elsewhere, under a Christmas tree, for instance, dolls I believe. The abjection of the Nazi crime reaches its apex when death, which, in any case, kills me, interferes with what, in my living universe, is supposed to save me from death: childhood, science, among other things.[164]

In *The Patagonian Hare*, Lanzmann himself frames "the abjection of the Nazi crime" through the intertwined prosthetic memories of childhood and death—of his mother and a selection in a shoe store—just as he had in *Shoah* through the story of Czerniaków's despair in the face of the impending deportation of children from the Warsaw ghetto. As Hilberg recounts in the finished film, Czerniaków, before taking his own life, supposedly left a note that read: "They want me to kill the children with my own hands."

Coupled with the epic length of the finished film and the notion of the incompossible ("To choose one is to preclude the existence of the other"), the heap of shoe boxes in the store also conjures the innumerable reels of interviews and location filming accrued during the making of *Shoah* and the ensuing selection process at the LTC film laboratory. "To edit [a film]," writes Dominique Villain, "is to choose."[165] Or, to recast Lanzmann's own definition informed by the philosophy of Leibniz, to choose a shot, a sequence, or even a testimony is to preclude others from existing—a tragedy and finality conjured in this passage of *The Patagonian Hare* through the docu-auteur's prosthetic identification with the "decision-makers" and the likening of choice to "murder."

Yet, in the case of the *Shoah* outtakes, exclusion cannot be equated with elimination. Rather, much like the Deleuzian overturning of Leibniz's pyramid or the splitting apex of Bergson's memory cone, the finished film and the unused material *coexist*, not only producing new meanings and mobilizations of *Shoah* but also rendering visible "divergences, incompossibilities, discords, dissonances."[166] Largely displaced to the off-frame by Lanzmann, who, in his memoir, never mentions the acquisition and preservation of the excluded material by the USHMM, the omitted footage nonetheless subsists as an archive of the "forking paths" underlying the making of *Shoah*, evidencing the passage from an investigation intended to encompass the Holocaust in its entirety to a film centered on male eyewitnesses closest to the machinery of destruction.

The interview summaries and transcripts, which were annotated at the LTC film laboratory in Saint-Cloud, constitute a paper memory of the editing process that attests to the initial phase of composing with incompossibles. Faced with the vastness of the material accumulated during the making of *Shoah*, the filmmaker and his crew began in 1979 by "deciphering and typing all the speeches, everything that was said: 5,000 or 6,000 pages of text."[167] These transcripts and their accompanying summaries made from the audio reels were then used during the actual screening of the interviews where Lanzmann and his editor Ziva Postec, along with numerous assistants that included Yael Perlov, added abbreviations detailing camera movements. They also bracketed or underlined possible passages for inclusion in the film, as exemplified earlier by the transcript of the interview with Leib Garfunkel that, despite such annotations, was in the end left out.

According to Lanzmann, in this early phase of editing the rushes, they "constructed a film of four and a half hours exclusively about Chelmno [sic]," an initial entry into the vast material of *Shoah* supposedly intimated in 1978, following his first trip to Poland in March of that year, when he conducted a second preliminary interview with Simon Srebnik.[168] At home in the Israeli city of Ness Ziona, the Chełmno survivor sang for the filmmaker the same melodies he had once chanted for the Germans in the extermination camp. "At that very minute," recalls the docu-auteur in *The Patagonian Hare*, "I knew for certain that this man singing would go back with me to Chełmno, that I would film him singing on the River Ner, that this would be the opening sequence of *Shoah*."[169]

Like the four-and-a-half-hour film on Chełmno first composed by Lanzmann, the Srebnik outtakes resemble a unique documentary that, exceeding a memorable mise-en-scène, concomitantly chronicles the staged return. The footage captured in Poland in the summer of 1978 by cinematographer Jimmy Glasberg and sound engineer Bernard Aubouy opens with the car ride to the extermination camp, a silent Srebnik in the passenger seat smoking a cigarette. This silence is noted in the transcript as follows: "En route to Chełmno; no comments from Mr. Srebnik."[170] Lanzmann subsequently breaks the absence of speech by asking Coulmas, present as a Hebrew interpreter, if Srebnik recognizes anything. The decision to record the testimony in the survivor's adopted language and in the presence of an interpreter stemmed from the difficulties during the preliminary interviews when the two men communicated in German. "We talked or rather tried to talk since I barely understood anything he said," recalls Lanzmann in his memoir upon describing these inaugural encounters. "Every time he uttered the name of one of the SS officers in Chełmno, he preceded it with the title *Meister*, 'master.' It seemed to me that, though over forty, he was still the terrified child he had surely been back then."[171] This description captures the essence of Srebnik's testimony in Chełmno. There, he incessantly names the different "master[s]" in the camp who, in turn, called him "*Spinnefix* [agile spider]" because, of all the prisoners, he ran the fastest.

Upon arriving in Chełmno and walking in the direction of the camp, the filmmaker must first resolve where the interpreter will stand. Initially next to Lanzmann, Coulmas quickly moves off-screen alongside Aubouy and Glasberg. Less than fifteen minutes into the interview, however, Lanzmann suddenly exclaims: "Cut, cut, let's stop."[172] These words officially mark the end of Srebnik's testimony in Hebrew. In the following take and without any explanation given in front of the camera, the filmmaker and the survivor speak in German, thus addressing each other directly and using the informal pronoun *du*.[173] The change from Hebrew to German constitutes a return for the witness to a language learned in the extermination camp where 400,000 Jews were murdered and from which only two men returned: Simon Srebnik and Mordechai Podchlebnik. Like an echo of their incredible survival, Lanzmann remarks almost immediately when the interview resumes: "Two Jews, in Chelmno, speaking German together, that's meaningful, no?" Before the filmmaker even makes this comment, however, Srebnik notes that the German language embodied the possibility of survival in a place where all were destined to die. By understanding the "master[s]," he could obey their orders and thus survive. In the outtakes, he illustrates this point by recalling how an SS officer had once exclaimed, after having beaten to death a prisoner who had failed to comprehend his orders, "No one understands me. Only *Spinnefix* understands my German."[174]

The Srebnik footage further chronicles the staged return to Chełmno through one final interview filmed in late summer 1979 by William Lubtchansky at the survivor's home in Ness Ziona. This conversation between Lanzmann and Srebnik recorded after the staged return to Poland constitutes the only instance in all of the outtakes when a survivor comments on his or her testimony for *Shoah*. Remembering what would become, in the finished film, the famous sequence shot in front of the church where the survivor stands quietly smiling while the Polish villagers surrounding him recall his beautiful voice, the filmmaker probes Srebnik's calm demeanor. He remarks: "Some people saw this scene in front of the church with you and the Poles, and they wondered, 'Why is Srebnik still laughing?' You didn't say anything, only the Poles spoke, you didn't say anything and you were laughing. People wondered, 'Why?'" To this question, Srebnik poignantly responds: "I'll tell you. When I found myself back in Chełmno, I couldn't speak. I was so shocked, and the memory of everything that happened there came back to me. [...] So I laughed, but inside I was crying. Everyone saw the smile, but no one saw what was going on deep down inside me."[175] It is precisely this concealment of Srebnik's inner self by his smiling disposition that Lanzmann chose to include in *Shoah*.

While the viewing of the rushes in Paris appear to have prompted the post-Chełmno interview in Israel, Lanzmann's question suggests his possible intention to juxtapose in *Shoah* the return to the extermination camp and the reflection subsequently voiced by the survivor about his own testimonial performance. This unused portion of the Srebnik interview also calls attention to the fact that, beyond such conversations about the making of the film as the one recorded by Friedländer in *When Memory Comes*, the filmmaker at times screened the rushes of his collected interviews. This practice continued into the editing phase. Between 1982 and 1983, for instance, he showed the first three hours of *Shoah* not only to Bauer and Hilberg, but also to the French philosopher Raymond Aron and the Austrian-French novelist Manès Sperber, two Jewish intellectuals and contemporaries of Jean-Paul Sartre who both passed away before the film's release.[176] According to Coulmas, however, the primary external viewer and commentator throughout the making of *Shoah* was Simone de Beauvoir.[177] In the immediate postwar period, de Beauvoir had collected eyewitness accounts of the camps for publication in *Les Temps Modernes*.[178] In 1966, the interview Richard Marienstras and Lanzmann conducted with her around *Treblinka* marked the future filmmaker's first public engagement with the memory of the Holocaust in France.

A little less than two decades later, the title of Lanzmann's film would "name the event, or rather [...] impose in a part of civil society and scholarly circles (not all of them) the Hebrew word *Shoah*."[179] Concomitantly, it would displace the term "Holocaust" popularized by Marvin Chomsky's eponymous television drama. In the unused footage of *Shoah* and as late as the May 1983 recording of the minivan mise-en-scène in the Parisian suburbs, it is the word "Holocaust" that appears on the clapboard between two takes, thus testifying to the absence of another word to refer to the extermination (the Hebrew interpreter Francine Kaufmann recalls that, after being hired by Lanzmann in 1979, he told her "Holocaust" was the title he had initially chosen but could not keep after the broadcast of the American miniseries).[180] It also indicates the eventual, belated selection of the Hebrew word meaning "catastrophe" as the film's title. In *The Patagonian Hare*, after explaining that he made this decision only weeks before the premiere of the film on April 30, 1985, at the Théâtre de l'Empire in Paris, Lanzmann remarks that "'Shoah' was a signifier with no signified, a brief, opaque utterance, an impenetrable, unbreakable word."[181]

Originating from a foreign language, the title *Shoah* constitutes for the filmmaker an acoustic image that translates above all the limits of representation around which his film is constructed. Phonetically, however, *Shoah* also calls to mind the French word *choix*, or choice, a word whose importance for the making of Lanzmann's opus is twofold. On the one hand, it calls attention to the inevitable selection underlying the editing phase between 1979 and 1985. On the other hand, the word occupies a central place in narratives of the destruction of European Jewry, denoting first and foremost the selection carried out on the unloading ramp of the camp: the separation of the deported into two distinct lines, one of which was condemned to death. Echoing Lanzmann's own prosthetic framing of the incompossible ("Any choice is murder") in his evocation of editing *Shoah*, the tragedy of choice traverses the testimonies ultimately left on the cutting room floor—from the postwar controversy surrounding the decisions of the Jewish councils to the largely excluded voices of women survivors to the contentious topic of Allied inaction and indifference during the Holocaust.

CHAPTER 2

Recasting 1961

SHOAH AND THE EICHMANN TRIAL

IN 1979, while working on his autobiographical opus *Diary*, David Perlov directed for Israeli television *Memories of the Eichmann Trial*, a sixty-minute black-and-white documentary that aired only once. The film was rediscovered and restored in 2011 at the initiative of the Visual Center at Yad Vashem, which concomitantly uploaded on YouTube the entire filmed footage of the 1961 trial to mark the fiftieth anniversary of this foundational event in the globalization of Holocaust memory. Perlov's documentary constitutes his second and final engagement with the destruction of European Jewry after *In Thy Blood Live* (1962), a seventeen-minute short prompted by the largely missing representation of the genocide in Alain Resnais's *Night and Fog*, which Perlov had seen in Paris in 1956.[1]

Awarded an honorary mention at the Venice Film Festival, *In Thy Blood Live* juxtaposes images of memorials in Israel, archival photographs of victims and extermination camps, and an original score by the Hungarian-born Israeli violinist and composer Ödön Pártos. Made in the immediate aftermath of the four-month trial that opened in Jerusalem on April 11, 1961, Perlov's documentary short signifies "a new era" in Israeli society marked, on the one hand, by the centrality of Holocaust memory and its transmission (above all for the younger generation) and, on the other hand, of the witness as the very embodiment of this traumatic past (no less than 111 witnesses testified in Jerusalem in 1961).[2] *In Thy Blood Live* concludes with the Eichmann trial and the statements of survivors Zivia Lubetkin and Yitzhak "Antek" Zuckerman, two "near-mythological figures" of Jewish resistance during the Holocaust who were among the leaders of the 1943 Warsaw ghetto uprising.[3] Nearly two decades after the trial and Perlov's documentary short, Claude Lanzmann interviewed Zuckerman for *Shoah*. In October 1979, he filmed him at the Ghetto Fighters' House—the world's first Holocaust museum that holds in its collection the glass booth in which Eichmann sat during the trial—in Kibbutz

Lohamei HaGeta'ot in northern Israel before including him as the penultimate witness in *Shoah*.

Perlov's Holocaust documentary, *Memories of the Eichmann Trial*, evidences the legacy of 1961 through filmed interviews with witnesses and the so-called "generation after." The film begins with Rafael Eitan, who led the Mossad unit that captured Eichmann in Buenos Aires on May 11, 1960.[4] In front of the camera, Eitan leafs through a stack of photographs taken in the courtroom during the trial—a gesture subsequently performed by several interviewees in the film. This mise-en-scène invokes the memory of the trial as a global media spectacle, embodied by the "newspapermen and magazine writers who had flocked to Jerusalem from the four corners of the earth" and sat, day after day, in the auditorium of the recently constructed Beit Ha'am theater.[5] This cultural center had been provisionally transformed into a courtroom where, for the first time, television cameras were allowed. The four cameras installed in the auditorium recorded 350 hours of filmed footage, which was edited daily and broadcast around the world, notably on American and German television.[6]

The photographic evidence deployed by Perlov in 1979 recalls the visual memory of the Eichmann trial while foreshadowing the performance of Polish Jewish survivor and photographer Henryk Ross in the documentary. Beginning in 1940, Ross worked for the Department of Statistics of the Jewish council in the Łódź ghetto. Officially hired to take photos for identification cards as well as propaganda images, Ross clandestinely recorded scenes depicting the quotidian reality of the ghetto. During the final liquidation in 1944, Ross buried his negatives; approximately three thousand survived the war. On May 2, 1961, he testified in Jerusalem where his black-and-white images were used as evidence. In his well-known chronicle of the Eichmann trial, which first appeared in the newspaper *LaMerhav* before being published in 1962 under the title *Facing the Glass Booth*, the Israeli journalist, poet, and filmmaker Haim Gouri briefly evokes "the enigmatic photographer from Łódź, who took many, many pictures and hid the negatives, then came back from the dead, developed the pictures, and brought them to the court."[7] In 1979, in front of Perlov's camera, "the enigmatic photographer" not only recounts the story of these clandestine images but also reenacts the gesture of capturing them. Prompted by the filmmaker, Ross pulls out a camera concealed underneath his raincoat and scarf and snaps several quick photographs as he had once done in the Łódź ghetto.

In his 2011 review of the restored documentary, the *Haaretz* critic Uri Klein singles out this act of witnessing as "one of the most beautiful, moving and significant moments in the history of Israeli film."⁸ Indeed, the Łódź photographer's testimonial performance anticipates the trope of bodily reenactment exemplified by *Shoah* and, in particular, the famous staged barbershop scene with Abraham Bomba. A quarter of a century after its release, Lanzmann's work anachronistically informs Klein's privileging of reenactment as an archetype for the writing of the disaster in cinema. The critic's *parti pris* also obscures Perlov's other mode of representing trauma as established during his interview with Rivka Yoselewska, a victim of the "Holocaust by bullets" and the first survivor to appear on-screen in *Memories of the Eichmann Trial*. In Jerusalem, Yoselewska emerged as an exemplary—for her proximity to the machinery of destruction—and oft-cited witness; according to the Holocaust historian Lawrence Douglas, her statement at the Beit Ha'am theater on May 8, 1961, "gave the trial some of its greatest moments of melodrama."⁹

The following day, Gouri recalled in his daily courtroom dispatch in *LaMerhav*, "There was a murmur in the hall when she appeared. So she had made it after all. […] She had had a heart attack, but here she was, before our very eyes."¹⁰ Intimated by the heart attack she had suffered only a few days prior on the morning she was originally scheduled to testify, Yoselewska embodied what Lanzmann, in reference to his Jewish protagonists who had been touched most closely by the process of destruction, terms a "revenant"—a person

FIGURE 2.1. Henryk Ross and Stefania Ross, from the film *Memories of the Eichmann Trial*, directed by David Perlov (Israel 1979, 2011; courtesy of The Yad Vashem Visual Center and KAN 11—Israeli Broadcasting Corporation).

who has returned from the dead.¹¹ At the witness stand in 1961, Yoselewska recounted how the Einsatzgruppen, on a Sabbath in the summer of 1942, massacred the five hundred Jewish families in the Belarusian village of Zagrodski outside of Pinsk. Speaking in Yiddish (the language of the exterminated Jews) as an interpreter simultaneously translated her testimony into Hebrew (the official language of the court), she described being taken to a forest with her family, including her young daughter Marta, who wore her Sabbath dress. Stripped naked, Yoselewska stood with her child in her arms over a mass grave, watching her family members be executed one by one. When her turn came, an SS officer asked her whom he should shoot first. He then took the child from her. Yoselewska received a bullet in the head after her daughter was killed. She survived and crawled out of the pit where the bodies of her family laid.

"I never heard anything as horrible. [...] This woman moved me deeply," the French war crimes trials chronicler Frédéric Pottecher would recall a quarter of a century later while covering the Klaus Barbie trial in Lyon.¹² A similar confrontation with the horrors of the Holocaust permeates Gouri's report of May 8, 1961, which he devotes nearly entirely to Yoselewska's testimony on that day. "People started to get up and leave," he observes after having recounted the execution of her family members. "The faces of those who remained became indistinguishable. 'Who should we shoot first, you or your daughter?' the German asked. Here, I stopped taking notes. I later learned from the transcript that her turn had come after her daughter's, that she had survived and, some time later, crawled out."¹³ Beyond Yoselewska's horrific testimony, Gouri records on that day his own encounter with the catastrophe in the courtroom. Moving from the collective "we" of earlier entries to a first-person singular voice, this chapter of *Facing the Glass Booth* registers a discursive shift: rather than merely transcribe, the journalist also *receives* Holocaust survivor testimony and bears witness to his subjective position as the addressee.

"The reintegration of victims within a broader community," writes Thomas Trezise in *Witnessing Witnessing*, "can be seen to depend on the listening of nonvictims, on a reception that is not confined to the mere registration of traumatic narrative but encompasses a response to it."¹⁴ In Gouri's chronicle, the memory of Yoselewska's deposition exemplifies the emergence and integration within Israeli society of the witness as a social figure in the wake of the Eichmann trial. It also evidences a rupture into individual and collective perception of both the survivor and the catastrophe, of which the 1961 event remains emblematic. "Had it not been for her, I would not know what happened one Sabbath in a town called Povost-Zagordski [...]," Gouri remarks before repeating, thereby evidencing his own act of "witnessing witnessing": "Had it not been for Rivka Joselewska [sic], I would not know what happened on the Sabbath of the New Moon of Elul in 1942."[15] More than a decade after the Eichmann trial, Gouri would juxtapose voice-over fragments of Yoselewska's statement in Yiddish and archival images of the catastrophe in his documentary *The 81st Blow*, the first volume of a Holocaust trilogy released contemporaneously with the making of *Shoah*, between 1974 and 1985.

Memories of the Eichmann Trial constitutes Yoselewska's second and final appearance in front of a camera. A limit of representability, however, haunts in 1979 the testimony of one of the most memorable witnesses of the trial, which is here composed of four brief segments. Rather than recount the 1942 massacre in her home village, Yoselewska confronts several visual and acoustic memories of the 1961 event, including her own deposition. Similar to the opening sequence with Eitan, she is first filmed sitting in her living room, looking through a stack of photographs from the trial. While a pained expression appears on her face, she declares in Hebrew: "It's Eichmann, his face..." Another mise-en-scène utilized several times in Perlov's film frames the following segment of Yoselewska's testimony. By way of a close-up of her face, she is shown listening silently to the prosecutor Gideon Hausner's opening statement on April 17, 1961 (in another appearance a few minutes later, the

FIGURE 2.2. Rivka Yoselewska, from the film *Memories of the Eichmann Trial*, directed by David Perlov (Israel 1979, 2011; courtesy of The Yad Vashem Visual Center and KAN 11—Israeli Broadcasting Corporation).

camera remains fixated on her face while she recalls her telephone conversation with Hausner, who summoned her to testify in Jerusalem).

"I now realized I would remember this day for the rest of my life," Gouri begins his report of Hausner's famous speech in *Facing the Glass Booth*. He subsequently cites the segment Perlov plays for Yoselewska in her living room, which has the prosecutor invoking the six million dead who "cannot rise to their feet to point an accusing finger at the glass booth and shout at the one who sits there, '*J'accuse!*'"[16] In moving from photographs to an audio recording of the trial, Perlov reenacts in his documentary the memory of the medium that broadcasted the trial in Israel—the radio. Television was not going to be introduced in the country until the late sixties and newsreels of the trial were never screened in cinemas. Most Israelis followed the Eichmann trial in the streets and in their homes listening to the radio, where many of the sessions were broadcast, summarized, and discussed daily. "According to the Central Bureau of Statistics, 60 percent of the population over the age of fourteen listened to the opening-day broadcasts of the trial in full or partially," notes Hanna Yablonka in her study of the trial's legacy on Israeli society.[17] As most of the seats in the auditorium of the Beit Ha'am theater were allotted to journalists, only a tiny fraction of Israelis actually got to attend even a single session of the trial in person. An equally small number were able to watch the proceedings at the neighboring Ratisbonne Hall where the trial was concurrently shown on a large television screen.

In recovering, in 1979, the audio recording of the Eichmann trial, Perlov singularly stages the acoustic confrontation with the trauma of the Holocaust underlying public memory. By contrast, scholarship framing the trial as a transnational televised spectacle in the following decades largely displaced the significant role of the radio in Israel, particularly in the mediation and reception of Holocaust survivor testimony. As Amit Pinchevski and Tamar Liebes argue, the radio profoundly altered the prevailing perception of 1950s Israeli society that the survivor was a marginalized, traumatized, silent body:

> For it was precisely the transfiguration induced by radio of the speechless body into disembodied speech that rendered survivors' testimonies universally accessible. It is as if the logic of radio dictated a necessary trade-off: for trauma to gain voice, the body—the locus of trauma—had to be discarded. By removing survivors' voices from their bodies, radio effectively redefined the conditions by which trauma could find public articulation. The radiophonic separation between body and voice invited the return of the socially repressed.[18]

In liberating speech by displacing the survivor's stigmatized body to the off-screen, the radio mediated the emergence of the witness as a social figure in Israel. Yet, through this pivotal moment of sonic "witnessing witnessing," the broader Israeli public encountered Holocaust survivors such as Yoselewska primarily as faceless voices. Nearly two decades later, the mise-en-scène of Perlov's interview with Yoselewska not only intimates "the advent of the witness" (to cite the well-known formulation of Annette Wieviorka) as a severed voice in 1961 but also functions to reintroduce the missing face of the survivor and to reframe Israeli reception of Holocaust testimony.

In *Memories of the Eichmann Trial*, repeated silent close-ups of Yoselewska's face and its pained expression dominate the first three segments of her interview. This counter-witnessing of the traumatic past also underlies the notable recovery of her statement in Jerusalem effected by the filmmaker in her fourth and final appearance in the documentary. Here, her pained face still framed in a close-up, Yoselewska is shown listening silently to the most poignant segment of her horrific account at the trial in which she recalled the massacre of her family and the SS officer's question that Gouri subsequently included in *Facing the Glass Booth*. In 1979, this mise-en-scène by which the survivor witnesses her own act of witnessing articulates an ethics of testimony that seemingly anticipates *Shoah*: in rendering visible the survivor's face through silent close-ups nearly two decades after the Eichmann trial, Perlov reinscribes it as the site of an unspeakable trauma.[19]

"What does testimony mean," asks Shoshana Felman in her seminal analysis of *Shoah*, "if it is the uniqueness of the performance of a story which is constituted by the fact that, like the oath, it cannot be carried out by anybody else?"[20] In *Memories of the Eichmann Trial*, Perlov conveys the singularity of testimony through the staged encounter between Yoselewska's face and the acoustic memory of her deposition. This reenactment captures the exemplarity of her performance in Jerusalem, which exceeds her narrative in Yiddish. It also encompasses her appearance at the witness stand only days after having suffered a heart attack and the final revelation, prompted by the prosecution's closing question, that she had remarried and had had two sons after the war. In his concluding statement on August 8, 1961, Hausner himself returned to Yoselewska's testimony and cast her as a symbol of Jewish suffering and renewal.[21]

In 1979, Perlov thus distinctly conjures one of the most emblematic memories of the Eichmann trial. Yet, in confronting conventional modes and media of representing trauma in cinema, his mise-en-scène of Holocaust testimony simultaneously articulates a twofold limit of representation: on the one hand, the representational impossibility of reenacting through filmed testimony the uniqueness of Yoselewska's original performance in Jerusalem; on the other hand, the ethical impossibility of summoning in front of his camera a witness who had already "paid with [her] health for being called upon to testify at the Eichmann trial."[22] While, in 1961, the prosecution had brought closure to Yoselewska's statement with the question, "And now you are married and you have two children?" Perlov concludes his interview by pausing the audio recording and asking her if she can bear listening to her own testimony of the massacre. "As you see, I am still alive. But I always have this scene in front of my eyes—always... always," she responds in the final moments of the film, the camera still fixated on her face.

The Israeli television station Channel 1 aired *Memories of the Eichmann Trial* in 1979. In the fall of that same year, Lanzmann spent several weeks in Israel recording the last interviews for *Shoah*, including the testimony of the Warsaw ghetto survivor Yitzhak "Antek" Zuckerman. He had taken the stand in Jerusalem on May 3, 1961, only days before Yoselewska. In addition to Zuckerman, two other witnesses of the Eichmann trial appear in *Shoah*: Mordechai Podchlebnik and the "child singer" Simon Srebnik. Survivors of the Chełmno extermination camp, both men immigrated to Israel after the war, where they testified on June 5 and 6, 1961, respectively. In the finished film, the sole reference to the landmark trial is made by Podchlebnik, who laconically alludes to his courtroom testimony.

Unvoiced and unseen in the finished film, the legacy of 1961 in the making of *Shoah* subsists in the vast archive of Holocaust testimonies ultimately left on the cutting room floor of the LTC film laboratory, where Perlov recorded Lanzmann for *Diary*. Indeed, Lanzmann confronts in the outtakes manifold memories of the Eichmann trial: the *Judenrat* polemic prompted by Hannah Arendt's coverage of the 1961 event, the controversial negotiations between Rudolf (Rezső) Kasztner and Eichmann that resulted in the rescue of nearly 1,700 Jews in the midst of mass deportations from Hungary to Auschwitz in 1944, and the heroic deeds of Jewish resistance fighters, notably evidenced by the excluded testimony of the poet Abba Kovner who, in the Vilna ghetto in 1942, had urged Jews not to go to their deaths "like sheep to their slaughter."

In *The Patagonian Hare*, Lanzmann bitterly dismisses the court proceedings, as well as Arendt's attack on the Jewish council. Describing the preliminary research for *Shoah* undertaken between 1973 and 1974, he concludes: "The Eichmann trial would be of no use to me."[23] The memory of 1961, however, tacitly resurfaces in the following chapter through the unexpected evocation of Yoselewska, the only woman survivor to be mentioned in his memoir. Remarking on the unfortunate absence of members of the Einsatzgruppen in the finished film (epitomized, for Lanzmann, in the lost footage with Heinz Schubert that he secretly recorded in the summer of 1979), he recalls his attempt to interview a survivor of the "Holocaust by bullets" for *Shoah*—Yoselewska. "Not prepared to give up entirely," he writes,

> I hoped I might be able to film one of the Einsatzgruppen's victims whom I had located in Israel, a woman named Rivka Yossilevka [*sic*]. She was a tall, very thin woman with a deeply sorrowful face, her whole being was pain. With several bullets in her body, she had found herself still alive, buried under a pile of bloody corpses in a mass grave [...]. Nothing in the world would persuade her to tell her story in front of my camera, she did not have the strength and would not give in to my pleas.[24]

Never invoking her deposition in Jerusalem, Lanzmann posits himself as a docu-auteur, having "located in Israel" the woman who nevertheless, as an exemplary witness of the Eichmann trial, imparts the uncharted legacy of 1961 in the making of *Shoah*.

By her sheer proximity to death, Yoselewska embodies the missing feminine counterpart in the finished film to the male members of the *Sonderkommando*, the so-called revenants whom Lanzmann persuaded "to speak in front of a camera and [...] relive it all."[25] Juxtaposed with her contemporaneous appearance in Perlov's documentary, Yoselewska's refusal to be interviewed by the French director evidences the friction produced through the encounter between the finished film and the unused (or, in this case, unrecorded) interviews: namely, the surfacing of alternative testimonial scenes that resist the trope of reenactment universalized by *Shoah*. In Lanzmann's archive of the catastrophe, the unedited interview of Ada Lichtman, who was the first witness of the years of extermination to take the stand in 1961 before being filmed for *Shoah* in the late seventies, poignantly recovers such intersecting modes of survival and remembrance.

REFRAMING REENACTMENT: ENTER ADA LICHTMAN

On April 26, 1961, Gouri sat in the Beit Ha'am auditorium recording the words of Morris Fleischmann. Fleischmann had asked to testify in German. In the courtroom, he recalled the quotidian humiliation and suffering of Jews in Vienna. In Gouri's chronicle of the trial, the statement of "this broken little man" displays a first rupture in the journalist's reception of Holocaust testimony.[26] It also evidences the concurrent "welcoming back [...] into the larger community" of survivors in Israel.[27] Just as he would later do in his report of Yoselewska's narrative, Gouri records his own reaction to Fleischmann's words on the witness stand. "I did not want to see him, and I did not want to hear him," he writes and continues,

> I would have preferred to go today to the military parade at the stadium, to see Jews at their strongest and most beautiful. But with an uncanny force, this Morris Fleischmann grabbed hold of us by the scruff of our necks, as if to say, 'Sit still and hear me out.' [...] These, too, are your own flesh and blood, I said to myself.[28]

In contrast to the mythic figure of the Sabra or native-born "New Jew" who—like Gouri himself—had fought from a young age for the existence of Israel, survivors were largely perceived in the newly founded state as passive victims who had been led "like sheep to their slaughter." This leitmotif persisted in the courtroom through Hausner's oft-repeated question to the witnesses—"Why didn't you resist?"—for which Arendt condemned the prosecutor in the first pages of *Eichmann in Jerusalem*. In the aftermath of Fleischmann's statement, Gouri himself critically returns time and again to the subject of passivity, concluding eight days later in his account of Yoselewska's testimony: "But they could not run away."[29]

In *Facing the Glass Booth*, Fleischmann is the ultimate witness of the period preceding the extermination to be mentioned by Gouri. Absent from the courtroom for several days, the Israeli journalist neither heard the remaining depositions on the persecution of European Jewry nor attended the various presentations of documentary evidence that, according to Lawrence Douglas, failed to grab the attention of the audience at the Beit Ha'am auditorium. More importantly, Gouri was not present on the morning of April 28, 1961, when, following such a presentation, the survivor of the Sobibór death camp Ada Lichtman (née Fiszer) entered "a largely empty courtroom," took the witness stand, and rendered audible through her Yiddish testimony "the first murmurs of the voiceless dead."[30]

Inaugurating the chapter on the years of extermination for the court, Lichtman's narrative begins on September 12, 1939. On that day, the Germans entered the town of Wieliczka near Kraków where Lichtman lived with her family. They rounded up the Jewish men, took them into the forest of Taszyce, and executed them. In her statement, Lichtman described how she ran after the truck. When she arrived in Taszyce, she saw the men lying in rows of five, already dead; among them was her father. "I kissed my father," she told the court. "He was already cold, ice-cold although it was only one hour since they had taken them."[31] In front of Lanzmann's camera almost two decades later, Lichtman would recall how, at that very moment, she had also addressed her father: "I fell on the ground to kiss him. He was completely cold and covered with blood. So I said: 'Mister, look at me, I am covered with blood.'"[32] Echoing her statement in 1961 where, literally tainted by the atrocities she had witnessed, Lichtman concealed her eyes behind a pair of sunglasses, the evocation of her voiceless father also captures the gendered dimension of her Holocaust testimony. At the witness stand, the survivor punctuated her narrative with memories of Jewish men systematically murdered by the Germans—from the older men "slaughtered and shot" in the synagogue of Mielec to the young men in Dubienka whose "mutilated bodies" Lichtman helped bury.[33] Conversely, summoned in 1961 to testify on "the period of small-scale terror in the occupied areas in Poland," she never told the story of her deportation to Sobibór and subsequent participation in the revolt that broke out at the extermination camp on October 14, 1943.[34]

In the decades following the trial, and in contrast to Yoselewska's horrific account of the Holocaust, Lichtman emerged as an exemplary witness less for her experience during the Shoah than for her performance at the stand. "The testimony of Ada Lichtman is rarely remembered," writes Wieviorka in *The Era of the Witness,* where she decries her absence in Gouri's chronicle.[35] The statement of the first witness of the catastrophe nevertheless engendered a rupture in 1961. According to Douglas, the impact of her deposition was first and foremost acoustic. In light of the radio broadcasts of the trial in Israel and of Lichtman's request to testify in Yiddish, her voice filled the courtroom, the streets, and the homes of listeners with "the language of the exterminated Jewish population of Europe."[36]

The Sobibór survivor was actually not the first witness to testify in Yiddish in the courtroom. Just a few days before, Shmuel Grynszpan, whose son assassinated the German diplomat Ernst vom Rath in Paris in 1938, had also testified in Yiddish. At the time, Gouri had duly noted this linguistic shift in his daily dispatch for *LaMerhav,* pointedly remarking while first describing Grynszpan: "He was speaking Yiddish."[37] Yet, whereas Grynszpan was assisted by an interpreter, the judges and prosecution unprecedentedly accommodated Lichtman's request by addressing her directly in Yiddish instead of Hebrew. In addition to this momentary silencing of the official language of the court, the survivor's singular demeanor at the witness box also marked a defining moment in the 1961 trial. As Douglas additionally observes, Lichtman refused to be seated during her statement and never removed the sunglasses that she wore as though she were "consumed by the trauma of what she [had] seen."[38]

On the morning of April 28, 1961, the charged imagery of both Lichtman's Yiddish deposition and her sunglasses signified the destruction of European Jewry, of which she was the first to bear witness at the Eichmann trial. Yet, more than the embodiment of traumatic memory, her performance in the Beit Ha'am auditorium also articulates a certain resistance to and concomitant reframing of institutionalized testimony. "I can stand," the Sobibór survivor answered the judge who suggested that she sit down.[39] By choosing to remain standing, to speak in Yiddish, and to conceal her eyes, Lichtman affirmed linguistically and corporeally her singularity. She also redefined the act of bearing witness: rather than the prosecution merely eliciting her statement, she imposed her own terms of testimonial performance. In asserting herself as "a subject with a will," she ultimately reclaimed in the witness box and after the catastrophe her dignity.[40]

Nearly two decades later, Lanzmann recorded Lichtman for almost three hours at her home in the city of Holon near Tel Aviv. In front of the camera, he never mentions the Eichmann trial. Yet the memory of her 1961 deposition largely defines this omitted interview. Reminiscent of Lanzmann's brief evocation of Yoselewska in *The Patagonian Hare*, these outtakes unfold a gendered perspective on the Holocaust and a counter-performance that ultimately resists the reliving of the past elicited by Lanzmann. Despite Lichtman's exclusion from the finished film, the transcript of her testimony used during the editing phase contains numerous bracketed and underlined passages, as well as annotations suggesting possible juxtapositions with three male witnesses who

FIGURE 2.3. Ada Lichtman at the witness stand during the Eichmann trial (accessed at the United States Holocaust Memorial Museum, courtesy of the Steven Spielberg Jewish Film Archives of the Hebrew University of Jerusalem).

appear in *Shoah*: the SS officer Franz Suchomel, the Treblinka survivor Richard Glazar, and the Polish switchman at the Sobibór train station Jan Piwonski. However, whereas the transcript of Lanzmann's interview with Bomba signals the famous staged barbershop scene by means of the heading "*Chez le coiffeur* [At the barbershop]," the paper memory of Lichtman's testimony never reveals the exceptional reenactment of her traumatic past, which the preservation of the outtakes renders visible.[41]

Over the course of a narrative beginning in September 1939 and ending before the 1943 revolt, Lichtman describes in a mix of German and Yiddish not only events that she had recalled at the witness stand in Jerusalem but also her extraordinary situation as a woman following the selection on the ramp of the death camp. "We were three women out of an entire convoy of nearly 7,000 people—we were three to remain," she says, describing to Lanzmann her arrival at Sobibór in the summer of 1942 (the uniqueness of her situation is rendered even more palpable in the transcript, where this sentence is the only one underlined on that particular page).[42] At the extermination camp, Lichtman would work as a laundress and seamstress mending dolls (*Puppen*) found in the trains, which the German officers then gave to their own children. In her staged testimony for *Shoah*, the Sobibór survivor repeats the very gestures associated with this traumatic experience: alternatingly holding a pair of scissors, a sewing needle, and a thread, she narrates her story while mending dolls scattered over a coffee table.

The reenactment of the past visible in these outtakes immediately calls to mind Bomba's famous testimonial performance at the barbershop, which was the first interview Lanzmann filmed when he returned to Israel in September of 1979 to complete *Shoah*. In the Lichtman outtakes, he wears the same shirt visible in the portion of the Bomba footage captured on the terrace in Jaffa overlooking the Mediterranean. Recorded shortly after Bomba, who also lived in Holon, Lichtman embodies the missing feminine counterpart to his exemplary reliving of the past that, contrary to her interview, made it into the finished film. The Lichtman material also reveals an intriguing symmetry between the two testimonies that exceeds this shared physical reenactment centered on the repetition of gestures performed in the camps. Bomba, who was selected at Treblinka to cut the hair of women before they were gassed, had been a barber in his Polish hometown of Częstochowa. After the war, he continued to cut hair professionally until his retirement in 1978 (in *Shoah*, his testimony is doubly staged insofar as Bomba no longer worked as a barber when Lanzmann filmed him). Prior to her deportation to Sobibór, Lichtman had worked with young children. In the outtakes, she recalls the deputy commandant of

Sobibór, Gustav Wagner, asking her on the ramp what her profession was. "Kindergarten teacher," she responded.[43] Following her immigration to Israel in 1950, Lichtman taught kindergarten until her retirement.[44]

In her unedited testimony filmed for *Shoah*, the dolls she is mending implicitly gesture to her profession, which in turn permeates her memory of new convoys at Sobibór—a memory itself bracketed in the transcript of the

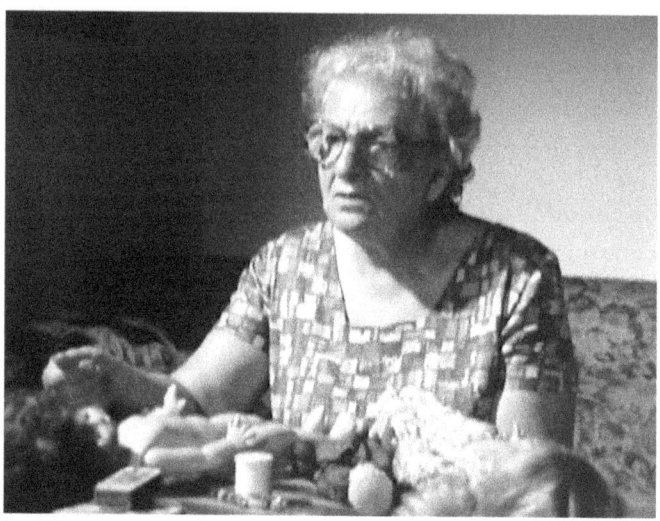

FIGURES 2.4–5. Ada Lichtman mending dolls during her filmed interview with Claude Lanzmann (Created by Claude Lanzmann during the filming of *Shoah*. Used by permission of the United States Holocaust Memorial Museum and Yad Vashem, the Holocaust Martyrs and Heroes' Remembrance Authority, Jerusalem).

interview. "You knew that transports were arriving?" Lanzmann asks her. "We looked at the window and saw different things," she explains. "For example, we saw... Once a transport arrived with small children [*kleine Kinder*]. They got them on their feet and chased them out of the wagons. [...] Once we saw how they threw out from the wagons... this was later, in winter time... they threw out naked newborns [*Geburtskinder*]." A few instants later, Lichtman returns to the memory of these transports when she remembers the "very many dolls, different ones, beautiful and big ones, broken ones," which the children brought with them and which she had to clean, mend, and dress for the Germans.⁴⁵

While being filmed giving a haircut to a man in a Tel Aviv barbershop, Bomba describes and demonstrates how he cut women's hair in Treblinka. Prompted by Lanzmann's insistence (captured in his oft-cited phrase "You must go on"), he finally breaks down and starts crying when remembering a group of women from his hometown being herded into the gas chamber. In *The Patagonian Hare*, which never so much as mentions Lichtman, the docu-auteur details the staging of this scene. "It was I who thought of using a barbershop," he writes. "Bomba was no longer a barber [...]. But the idea appealed to him and he set about finding a salon himself. This immediately posed an ethical problem: it couldn't be a ladies' hairdressing salon. We both realized that would be horrendous and obscene."⁴⁶ *Horrendous and obscene*: with these words, Lanzmann once more affirms his familiar revulsion at and prohibition of a certain way of representing the catastrophe, whether through fiction, archival images, or, even, an attempt at comprehension.⁴⁷ A gender bias, however, transpires in his invocation of an ethics of representation, which is here recast through the lens of both the supposed agreement, or mutual identification, between the (male) survivor and the (male) filmmaker *and* Lichtman's excluded testimony. "The changing of the customer's gender hardly takes care of the problematic nature of this setting," Agnieszka Piotrowska observes in her reading of this passage from *The Patagonian Hare*.⁴⁸ Equally perplexing is Lanzmann's imperative refusal to film Bomba in a women's salon while deploying a number of dolls—a feminized object par excellence—as a medium of reenactment during his interview with Lichtman.

What is it that distinguishes on an ethical scale a women's hair salon from a pile of mostly girl dolls scattered on a coffee table, particularly since the latter constitutes an equally literal rendering of the traumatic past? Despite the literality of Lanzmann's staged reenactment, Lichtman's narrative effectuates a gender reversal: whereas Bomba recalls the women in the gas chamber, memories of men permeate Lichtman's account of the catastrophe. The evocative mise-en-scène of her interview thus extends beyond the dolls she remembers mending for the Germans to conjure the memory of the mute and inert body of her father, whom she addressed one last time in the forest of Taszyce. This vivid recollection originating in her 1961 testimony and bracketed in the interview transcript marks the beginning of the extermination in Lichtman's narrative. Similarly, upon describing the moment she learned of the reality of the death camp, she details the memory of a prisoner at Sobibór who had seen the destruction but could not speak. "They were building a barn," she explains to Lanzmann,

> and a worker climbed on the roof. He saw it from the roof, what they were doing with the people. He came back and told us. He was a mute [*ein Stummer*], he did not speak. His brother who was a cobbler spoke for him. They conveyed to us that he had seen people lying dead and being... being buried. During the first period of the existence of Sobibor [*sic*], people were only buried.[49]

Evoking the dolls on the coffee table, the figure of the male witness remembered in this testimony emerges as a voiceless body whose own muteness frames the traumatic past through the lens of the unspeakable. This Sobibór prisoner who has seen the horrors that remain off-frame for Lichtman calls to mind the silence of mute characters in cinema. For Michel Chion, this voiceless protagonist—and polar opposite of the disembodied voice—born with the advent of the talkies constitutes "a secondary character [...] somehow positioned intimately close to the heart of the mystery [...] presumed to see all, as if the deprivation of speech were a payment for something he wasn't supposed to have seen."[50]

The mute character, who has witnessed the secret of the extermination in Lichtman's filmed testimony, is personified through the presence of her husband, never named in front of the camera. Himself a survivor of the Sobibór uprising (the husband and wife met in the death camp), Itzhak Lichtman resembles the "secondary character" described by Michel Chion: comparable to the dolls visible in this interview, he sits silently at Lichtman's side with a pained expression during her Holocaust narrative. "What did you do in Sobibór?" Lanzmann suddenly asks him (at that very moment, the disembodied voice of an unnamed woman interpreter, who remains off-screen for the entirety of the interview and does not appear in *Shoah*, is heard for the first time translating this question into Yiddish). Itzhak Lichtman begins a fragmented narrative intertwining memories of his family, of the Jewish council, and of the death camps of Bełżec and Sobibór. Lanzmann interrupts him after only a few minutes.⁵¹ In the closing moments of the interview, the camera lingers on the taciturn face of this man, whose largely missing voice accentuates the gender reversal underlying the Lichtman material.

In his reading of the staged barbershop scene in *Shoah*, the French critic Jacques Mandelbaum likens Bomba's performance to the final speech act of the Jewish barber in *The Great Dictator* (1940).⁵² Akin to this fictional character and parody of Hitler in Charlie Chaplin's first talkie, the *Puppen* in Lichtman's filmed testimony are themselves evocative of other dolls in the history of Nazi Germany. In

FIGURES 2.6–7. Ada and Itzhak (close-up) Lichtman (*The Four Sisters*, 2017).

these outtakes, the pile of dolls on the coffee table strikingly conjures the cadavers at execution sites and death camps, dehumanized by the euphemistic SS designation *Figuren*. "The Germans made us refer to the bodies as *Figuren*, that is, as puppets, as dolls," the Vilna ghetto survivor Itzhak Dugin explains at the beginning of *Shoah*. In the outtakes, he adds that the prisoners who pulled the bodies from the pits were called *Figurenzieher* and the ones who carried them *Figurenträger* (in German, the word *Figuren* also refers to inanimate chess pieces).[53]

In 1979, Lichtman performing doll mending in front of the camera is also reminiscent of the famous *Puppen* made of wood and metal by the German-born Surrealist Hans Bellmer in the wake of Hitler's rise to power. Between 1933 and 1935, Bellmer constructed two life-size, adolescent girl dolls whose body parts he dismantled and rearranged incessantly. He documented the process of decomposing and recomposing these depersonalized feminine bodies by means of black-and-white photographs staged indoors and outdoors, a series of which were first published in German in 1934 under the title *Die Puppe* and translated two years later into French at the initiative of Paul Éluard (one the leading figures of the Surrealist movement, Éluard was also the friend of the Serbian poet Monny de Boully, Lanzmann's stepfather).[54] While Bellmer conceived of the dolls as a *détournement* of the idealized Aryan body aesthetic, the manipulation of *Puppen* by the male artist is equally suggestive of the Surrealist imagery of dislocated body parts and, in particular, of "the violated female form."[55]

Reframing the director's mise-en-scène through the lens of the famous *Puppen* intimates a gendered history of the Holocaust that remains mostly untold in the Lichtman outtakes: the sexual violence against Jewish women in ghettos and camps. Lichtman never recounted her experience at Sobibór during the Eichmann trial, but her testimony was later collected by Miriam Novitch and published, along with thirty other accounts of the death camp, under the title *Sobibór: Martyrdom and Revolt*. The book appeared concurrently in French and Hebrew in 1978, a year before Lanzmann filmed Lichtman at her home in Holon. The work of "the indefatigable Miriam Novitch" (to borrow the words of Samuel Moyn), herself a Holocaust survivor and one of the founders of the Ghetto Fighters' House, where Lanzmann filmed the heroes of the Warsaw uprising, did not escape his attention during the making of *Shoah*. As early as 1946, Novitch began gathering and publishing survivor testimony in French, including, in the late sixties, a volume on Greek Jewry (a decade later, Lanzmann would film the Jews of Corfu). She was also an important voice during the French controversy surrounding Jean-François Steiner's *Treblinka* in 1966 and edited a "counterdossier" a year later.[56]

"Among the testimonies [Novitch] collected," Sharon Geva observes, "were stories of women who had lost their children in the Holocaust."[57] Memories of violence against women and children pervade the testimony Novitch collected from Lichtman for *Sobibór: Martyrdom and Revolt*. This gendered perspective, which is largely unvoiced in the filmed interview with Lanzmann, specifically emerges in the survivor's description of her arrival at the death camp. While recounting almost identically the question posed to her by the SS officer, to which she answered, "Kindergarten teacher," and the transport of seven thousand people from which she was selected with only two other women, she concludes her published testimony with a vivid recollection of sexual violence: "I remember that first night. I heard screams, and opened the door, but received lashes of a whip across my face. [...] Later I learned that these screams came from young girls who were raped before being gassed." Lichtman also remembers "a young woman in labor" whose newborn was "floating in the ditch" before concluding her account of the extermination camp with the memory of "convoys [that] often carried children who were frozen to death" and of the SS officer Wagner who "piled up the little bodies."[58] In the Lichtman outtakes, these unspoken memories strikingly subsist in 1979 through the imagery of dolls, a mise-en-scène already objectionable and here rendered "horrendous and obscene."

"It's unbelievable to dress a doll in a death camp, right?" Lanzmann asks Lichtman, whom he addresses directly in German throughout the interview. In this excluded footage, the director of *Shoah* never broaches the reenactment staged at the survivor's home in Holon. "*Du arbeitest* [you work]," he orders the Sobibór survivor off-screen when the camera begins to roll. Omitted from the transcript, this first audible sentence in Lichtman's excluded testimony approximates the voice of an SS officer in the camp, a role Lanzmann immediately assumes in order to prompt the reliving of the past. Recorded shortly after the Bomba interview, Lanzmann still appears to be playing his role at the barbershop as a pressing disembodied voice that Piotrowska likens to "the voice of the master" who affirms "the right to break the silence of the other—because testimony is called for."[59]

In *Shoah*, the voice of the "master" is also the voice of the docu-auteur who exhibits complete control over the survivor's testimonial performance while imprinting onto this scene his stern directorial dictum, aptly summarized by Michael Rothberg: "the event cannot be explained or represented, but it can be reexperienced!"[60] Rather than merely listen to Holocaust testimony, he appropriates the speech and process of remembrance of the other as his own to elicit and mold accordingly. "*We* have to do it," Lanzmann famously tells Bomba off-screen when the latter falls silent upon describing the women from Częstochowa. His use of the first-person plural pronoun finds echo in both his recollections of the Treblinka survivor in *The Patagonian Hare* and the unused segments of the interview.

Akin to the "we" audible in the finished film, an immediate closeness frames his memory of spending a weekend with him at his cabin in the Catskills in 1975, over the course of which he listened with "thoughtful and companionable attention" to the testimony of Bomba, who is described here as "a magnificent speaker."[61] In her reading of this passage from *The Patagonian Hare*, Piotrowska calls attention to Lanzmann's language of "love and desire," creating "a scene in which two people get very close to each other indeed, one giving a most intimate account of his pain and the other listening like 'no one else.'"[62] Four years later, on the day before the staged barbershop scene, Lanzmann and Bomba reenact an equally close personal encounter in the excluded portions of the interview recorded on the terrace in Jaffa. While Bomba details in front of the camera his deportation to and escape from the death camp, this first shooting day also functions as an emotional rehearsal for the reenactment to come. "It's difficult, I know," Lanzmann tells Bomba when he begins to choke up trying to describe his arrival in Treblinka with his wife and child whom he never saw again. "It is because, you know, we have to go through this thing all over again, and it is very painful," Bomba responds, here alluding to their 1975 weekend in the Catskills when he had first told him his story. "Yes, but you have to do it," Lanzmann declares. "You have no choice."[63]

Anticipating the infamous words he will utter in the barbershop the next day, the docu-auteur affirms at once emotional and ethical demands of Holocaust representation: in front of *his* camera, the only testimony possible will be a testimony in which the trauma is revived and relived. However, in a marked visual contrast to his disembodied voice in *Shoah*, Lanzmann is sitting next to Bomba on the terrace, holding his hand at different moments of the interview as though he were effectively preparing the survivor to restage the past (a few instants later, Bomba actually describes—albeit briefly—cutting the hair of women in the gas chamber of Treblinka).[64] In these outtakes, the cinematographer William Lubtchansky accentuates the physical closeness between the two men by effecting a close-up of their clasped hands. While this camera movement bears witness to the interview process, it also emphasizes an ethics of care ultimately excluded from the finished film. The docu-auteur is here reframed as an attentive, if not exemplary, listener and receiver of Holocaust testimony. This self-representation underlies Lanzmann's own memory of the interview in *The Patagonian Hare*, where he recalls, in an attempt to counter criticisms of the staged barbershop scene, how "Bomba hugged [him] for a long time" when they finished the reenactment.[65]

Beyond attesting to the personal relationship Lanzmann and Bomba first forged in 1975, the closeness exhibited in this excluded material calls the viewer's attention to the gendered mode of eliciting and receiving Holocaust testimony forged over the course of making *Shoah*. As a rebuttal to criticisms concerning the exclusion of women survivors from the final version, Lanzmann

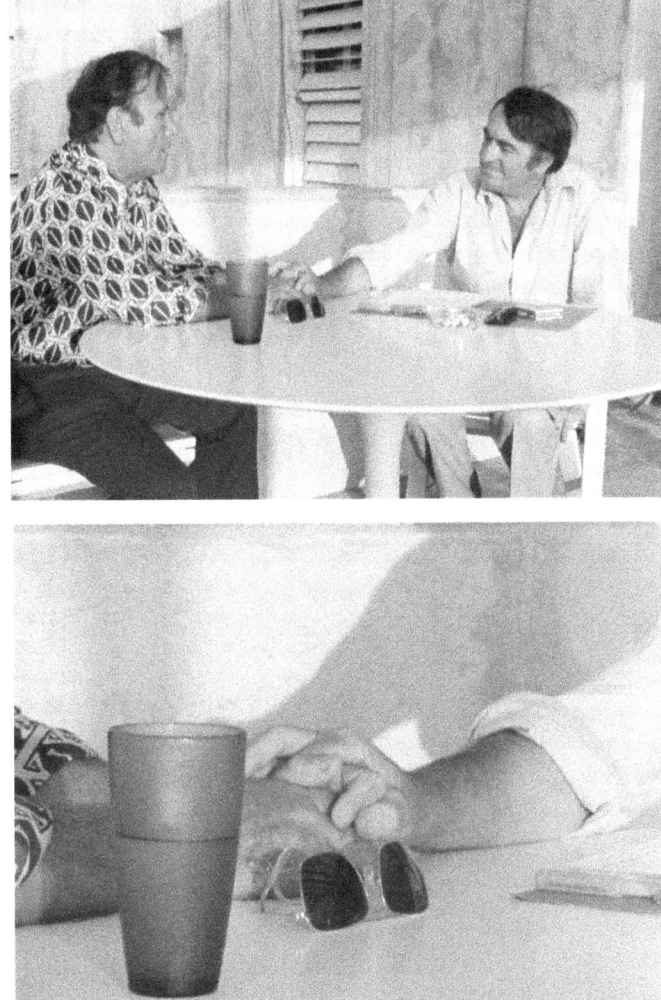

FIGURES 2.8–9. Claude Lanzmann holding Abraham Bomba's hand the day before the reenactment in the barbershop (Created by Claude Lanzmann during the filming of *Shoah*. Used by permission of the United States Holocaust Memorial Museum and Yad Vashem, the Holocaust Martyrs and Heroes' Remembrance Authority, Jerusalem).

stated time and again that he knew early on that the male members of the *Sonderkommando* would be the protagonists of the film. After all, they had witnessed the process of destruction most closely. Yet these men were also the witnesses whom Lanzmann himself could be closest to and even identify with in order to undertake the joint endeavor of excavating deep memory. The close-up of the clasped hands thus underscores the dynamics, recovered by the archive, of the relationship between the male filmmaker and the male survivors who appear in the finished film: that of a fraternal bond or pact between two men (the "we" used by Lanzmann in the barbershop) who will mutually lean on each other over the course of the interview. Indeed, while his grasping hand foreshadows his appropriation of the survivor's traumatic experience in the barbershop, it also stages the docu-auteur's own difficult confrontation with the process of eliciting testimony.

The unused segments of Lanzmann's interview with Mordechai Podchlebnik, whom he filmed in Israel in May 1979, further displays the gendered dynamics and charged physical proximity underlying the demands of Holocaust representation in *Shoah*. In the finished film, where Lanzmann's partially visible hand rests on Podchlebnik's shoulder, the Chełmno survivor and witness of the Eichmann trial breaks down like Bomba when describing how he had to unload the corpses of his wife and two children from a gas van. Comparable to this frame of reception, Lanzmann's hand often grips Podchlebnik's shoulder or arm in the excluded material, at once providing support over the course of his testimonial performance *and* pressing him to carry on with his account of the extermination. Yet, unlike the idyllic close-up of clasped hands in the Bomba interview, a certain tension transpires in the Podchlebnik outtakes, evidenced in the relative brevity of the testimony (a mere two hours) and in the respective body language of both men.[66] At the beginning of take 7, a seemingly reticent Podchlebnik, sitting with his arms folded, shrugs Lanzmann's hand off his shoulder. In turn, when the two later broach the chapter of Podchlebnik's deportation in the minutes preceding the traumatic memory of his wife and children, a momentary close-up of the filmmaker's face reveals his frustration at the survivor's persisting reluctance.

"Ask him if he wants to tell this story or not," Lanzmann says to the Yiddish interpreter Fanny Apfelbaum while glancing up several times at Lubtchansky to ensure the camera is on him. In *Shoah*, he exposes the survivor's testimonial ambivalence through similar questions: "Does he think it's good to talk about it? [...] why is he talking about it?" he asks. "Because you're insisting on it," Podchlebnik answers. With the same pained smile visible in the finished film and as tears well up in his eyes, the Chełmno survivor reaffirms in the excluded material a reluctant sense of duty. "If he has to, he will do it," the interpreter tells Lanzmann, who is now off-screen. Responding with an exasperated, disembodied voice, the docu-auteur explains that Podchlebnik "must tell this story in a more detailed manner." He then adds, speaking over the interpreter at this very moment: "I cannot keep asking him questions—it's like pulling teeth! [*Je ne peux pas lui poser des questions tout le temps pour lui sortir les vers du nez!*]."[67]

Countered by the softness of the voice of the interpreter, who survived the Holocaust in France as a young girl in hiding, the lack of empathy and patience encapsulated in the emphatic "It's like pulling teeth!" recalls at that moment Lanzmann's disembodied voice in the barbershop.[68] As with Bomba, his insistence engenders the resurgence of deep memory, epitomized in the finished film by a weeping Podchlebnik (even though it is not entirely clear, upon viewing the outtakes, whether the latter is emotionally overwhelmed by the past or by Lanzmann's incessant probing). Yet tensions subsist in the excluded portions of the interview. Immediately following the emotional reliving of the past included in *Shoah* and rendered all the more poignant through a close-up of Podchlebnik's face, the camera pulls back into a medium shot of the two men. While Lanzmann's right hand is still gripping Podchlebnik's arm, the fingers of his left hand are clenched tightly to a fist at his side. Invisible in the finished film, this gesture captures the extenuating process of eliciting an

FIGURE 2.10. Mordechai Podchlebnik with Claude Lanzmann, whose left hand is clenched to a fist (Created by Claude Lanzmann during the filming of *Shoah*. Used by permission of the United States Holocaust Memorial Museum and Yad Vashem, the Holocaust Martyrs and Heroes' Remembrance Authority, Jerusalem).

emotional reexperiencing of the past while inscribing an ethics of ambivalence onto Lanzmann's own demands toward Holocaust representation.

Referencing in *The Patagonian Hare* the testimonial performances of survivors at the Eichmann trial, where Podchlebnik testified on June 5, 1961, Lanzmann deplores the way in which "the tearful witnesses gave a kind of show, making it impossible to recreate what they had truly experienced."[69]

FIGURES 2.11–12. Gideon Hausner during the testimony of Mordechai Podchlebnik, here sitting at the witness stand (accessed at the United States Holocaust Memorial Museum, courtesy of the Steven Spielberg Jewish Film Archives of the Hebrew University of Jerusalem).

Anachronistically measured against his own representational dictum, this assessment of the Eichmann trial intimates the friction between two modes of bearing witness underlying the Podchlebnik outtakes: the judicial deposition and an emotional reliving of the past. The tensions that run through this interview, once again illustrating the legacy of the Eichmann trial, arise from a conflicting—or incompossible—approach to filmed testimony.

Rather than a sheer reluctance to speak, Podchlebnik exhibits in the excluded footage a willingness to bear witness in the same way that he had in Jerusalem: namely, in the form of questions and answers and in maintaining a safe distance to the past—a distance embodied during the trial by the relative isolation of the witness box.[70] In 1961, Podchlebnik was the first survivor of the Chełmno extermination camp to be called to the stand. Dressed in a suit jacket and speaking Yiddish, he recalls in his filmed deposition unloading corpses from the gas vans, finding the bodies of his wife and children, and escaping from the death camp. Podchlebnik, who is prompted by specific questions from the prosecutor, grows visibly more and more uncomfortable as he nears the traumatic memory of his family in his chronological account of deportation and escape.

Like Lichtman before him, Podchlebnik was questioned directly in Yiddish by Hausner; like Yoselewska, his horrific proximity to the destruction process as a member of the *Sonderkommando* made a deep impression on Gouri. "Among the billions of people who inhabit the planet that is home to the human race," the journalist begins his report of June 5, 1961, "there is one named Michael Podchlevnik [*sic*] who works in a chocolate-wafer factory and lives in Benei Brak [a suburb of Tel Aviv]. This man removed bodies from gassing vans at Chełmno. Through these vans passed all the people of his hometown." Following the eerie juxtaposition between the past at the death camp and the present at the chocolate-wafer factory, Gouri proceeds to transcribe and comment on the exchange between the prosecutor and the witness that engenders Podchlebnik's deeply personal recollection of Chełmno:

> Prosecutor: "And in the third van you saw someone you knew?"
> Witness: "Everyone I knew in the town turned up in the vans."
> Prosecutor: "Including whom?"
> Witness: "My wife and two children..."
> The heavyset man was grimacing as people do when they cry.[71]

Thus Hausner, leaning over a table where his notes were piled, posed questions to which he already had the answers in order to lead the survivor to this one memory that, on June 5, 1961, encapsulated the horrors of the extermination for Gouri. Eighteen years later, Lanzmann would sit, his own notes in front of him, at a table with Podchlebnik, leading him again to the same memory of which he would demand in front of the camera an intense emotional reexperiencing. Sometime later while editing his footage, he would single out for *Shoah*, like Gouri before him in *Facing the Glass Booth*, the same memory from Podchlebnik's filmed testimony and the same face with its perpetual pained smile framed in a close-up.

In their important books on Holocaust trials where they observe that the two Chełmno survivors also testified in *Shoah*, Wieviorka and Douglas both emphasize the novel way in which Lanzmann, contra Hausner, pressed Podchlebnik not only to recount the past but also to reflect on the act of bearing witness.[72] Yet what is the significance of this testimonial repetition and its difference in *Shoah*, that is, of Lanzmann's decision to include in the finished film the act of rendering new the repetition of the 1961 memory? In the finished film and in the outtakes, Lanzmann recasts the most memorable testimonies of the Eichmann trial by abolishing the distance between the past and the present, the prosecution and the witness, the filmmaker and the survivor. More than opening a space of reflection, Lanzmann's authorial inscription, by means of which he demarcates *Shoah* from the Eichmann trial, lies in his directorial insistence or demand (both of which have proven objectionable for many) that the past not only be recounted factually in front of the camera, but that it also be reexperienced. Or, to borrow Dominick LaCapra's formulation from his critique of the reenactment staged with Bomba, the disembodied voice of the auteur audible in *Shoah* requires survivors to "*both* play *and* [be] themselves."[73]

The sheer immediacy with which Lichtman "plays" her past self in the outtakes offers a striking contrast to Lanzmann's exasperation at "pulling teeth" in the excluded footage with Podchlebnik and the emotional rehearsal with Bomba on the terrace in Jaffa the day before the famous reenactment. This testimonial immediacy also bears witness to the gendered mode of eliciting and receiving Holocaust testimony employed by Lanzmann during the making of *Shoah*. Lichtman solely reenacts the past in front of the camera and never reflects on the process of bearing witness. Moreover, her unused interview is itself devoid of either physical proximity (Lanzmann and Lichtman sit across from each other) or an ethics of care (illustrated most acutely in Lanzmann's opening command "*Du arbeitest*"). Yet, despite the immediacy of her testimonial performance, and in further contrast to both Bomba and Podchlebnik, Lichtman's excluded testimony ultimately unfolds not the resurgence of but a resistance to the deep memory Lanzmann as a docu-auteur is highly invested in eliciting in front of the camera. This tension transpires most explicitly when, in an attempt to solicit an emotional response beyond the mere repetition of gestures once performed in the camp, he asks Lichtman to sing different melodies from her time in Sobibór.

Akin to the disembodied "voice of the master" in the barbershop, Lanzmann prompts the survivor several times to remember and perform the same melodies she had once sung during the Holocaust. In the outtakes, Lichtman begins to sing in Yiddish. "*Kein taten, kein mamen, kein schvester, kein brider...* [No father, no mother, no sister, no brother...]," she chants, recalling the performance in *Shoah* of Gertrude Schneider and her mother, whom Lanzmann filmed in November of 1978 singing a melody in Yiddish. Unlike the two women who were included in the finished film, Lichtman continuously reframes her testimonial performance, notably dismissing Lanzmann's request with humor. "I'm afraid everyone will run away," she jokes after having first sung. When Lichtman resumes singing and stumbles over the words, the cameraman anticipates a possible resurfacing of the traumatic past in effecting a close-up of her face. But rather than cry as Schneider's mother does in *Shoah*, Lichtman punctuates the melody she sings with facial expressions of incredulity. Finally, interrupting her own singing to comment on the lyrics, she concludes (at that very moment, emphatically speaking over an insistent Lanzmann who affirms, "Again!"), "It is when one *has to* that one cannot remember."[74]

Encapsulating Lichtman's self-affirmation and Lanzmann's failure to mold her process of bearing witness, the survivor's response bracketed in the interview transcript calls attention to the cuts and choices later made in the editing room. "To choose one is to preclude the existence of the other": thus Lanzmann summarizes the Leibnizian concept of the incompossible in his memoir, deploying it as a metaphor for the selection process between 1979 and 1985.[75] In including the silencing performances of Bomba and Podchlebnik (among others) and in excluding Lichtman's striking verbal resistance to recreating for the camera an emotionally charged return of the past, the author of *Shoah* effectively produced a universalizing—and overwhelmingly masculine—representation of trauma and its aftermath. In this sense, Perlov's contemporaneous documentary *Memories of the Eichmann Trial* presents a striking counterpoint to *Shoah*. Instead of displacing diverging experiences of survival and witnessing to the off-screen, the Israeli filmmaker incorporates multifarious frameworks of remembrance, from the reenactment of the Łódź photographer to the testimonial silence willed by Yoselewska. The reception of Holocaust testimony visible in *Memories of the Eichmann Trial* strikingly approximates Trezise's recent paradigm shift away from "a silencing reenactment" underlying a certain tendency of trauma theory since *Shoah*. Instead, Trezise calls for an ethics of listening to survivors "not only to support their recovery of speech but to respect their singularity, to recognize that their experience, however deeply it may affect us, is not our own."[76]

Although initially left out, the preservation of Lichtman's unedited interview now allows for the coexistence of incompossibles and the recovery beyond the finished film of other unique scenes of memory and mourning. "It is when one *has to* that one cannot remember." With these words, Lichtman refuses the silencing reenactment and revictimization Lanzmann demanded of the film's protagonists, thereby once more reclaiming her dignity and difference in front of the camera. With these words, she also reveals her own awareness of the mediated and even deceitful nature of her staged testimony, an awareness that, in turn, recasts the immediacy with which she repeats the gestures of the past in the opening take of the interview. Perhaps more than Lanzmann could see or hear, Lichtman was in fact "playing" the role she herself had once played at the death camp. There, she had been made to participate in the German strategy of deception by mending the dolls of Jewish children murdered at Sobibór. "It lay heavy on our hearts," she tells Lanzmann while describing her work as a seamstress.[77] All the while performing these gestures for the Germans, Lichtman nevertheless countered deception with deception by helping organize the revolt. As she explained in her 1965 testimony collected by an Israeli judge for the Sobibór trial held that year in Hagen (West Germany), "women played an active role in the revolt in Sobibór. I was also one of those who were introduced to its secrets. I knew the general outline of the plan for the revolt. [...] The women who worked in the laundry were assigned the task of stealing as many rifle bullets as possible."[78]

In the *Shoah* outtakes, Lanzmann largely limits Lichtman's testimony to her experience as a seamstress, a gendered reenactment of the past that eclipses, once again after the 1961 trial, her untold tale of revolt and escape. More than perform these gestures in front of the camera in 1979, Lichtman inscribes difference in repetition upon disrupting Lanzmann's attempt to elicit an emotional reexperiencing. Emerging as an interlocutor in the midst of a silencing reenactment, Lichtman ultimately embodies what Trezise terms "the possibility of a survival beyond revictimization."[79]

"THE LAST REMNANTS OF THE *REVOLT*"

In *The Patagonian Hare*, Lanzmann concludes his account of the staged barbershop scene by likening Bomba to "an unforgettable hero" whose tears captured on camera embodied "the seal of truth, its very incarnation."[80] For his exemplary reliving of the past and for embodying the director's representational dictum, Bomba did in fact become one of the protagonists of *Shoah*, that is, one of its "unforgettable hero[es]." Beyond the reenactment included in the finished film, however, this characterization gestures toward Bomba's heroic escape from Treblinka in January 1943, only three months after his arrival. Untold in *Shoah*, this story is recounted during the interview shot on the terrace in Jaffa. Immediately after having briefly recalled cutting women's hair in the gas chamber, Bomba details his escape in front of the camera at Lanzmann's request. Indeed, following the brief traumatic memory that would be reenacted the next day, Lanzmann tells Lubtchansky to cut; without any transition and as though he were anticipating how courageous Bomba will have to be the following day at the barbershop, he suddenly turns to the chapter of his escape. "Do you know how many people succeeded in escaping from Treblinka [...]?" he asks when the interview resumes.[81]

With this question, Lanzmann replicates the narrative structure found in the filmed testimonies of members of the *Sonderkommando* and other male survivors: namely, an account of the catastrophe that moves beyond the destruction process to also encompass their respective heroic tales of survival through either escape or revolt. Thus, in the outtakes, Richard Glazar details the Treblinka revolt in the summer of 1943, Filip Müller the uprising at Auschwitz in the fall of 1944, and Rudolf Vrba his famous escape from the same camp a year earlier (in *Shoah*, both Müller and Vrba provide the details of the camp's resistance movement leading up to the prisoner revolt). Podchlebnik also recounts, shortly after the emotional memory of his wife and children, his own escape from Chełmno in the winter of 1942. Lanzmann's deep interest in the heroic deeds of these male revenants transpires most vividly in the outtakes captured with the Vilna ghetto survivors Itzhak Dugin and Motke Zaidel in mid-September 1979, shortly after the Bomba interview.

At the beginning of *Shoah*, the two men describe exhuming and burning the bodies of Jews massacred by the Einsatzgruppen in the Ponar forest. In the excluded footage, they recount at length having dug a tunnel with members of the *Sonderkommando* for seventy-six days in the spring of 1944. Dugin and Zaidel were among the eleven men, out of a total of eighty, who managed to escape on the last evening of Passover and to survive the war. "Can he say now, *can he tell that extraordinary story*, when the idea of escape came to them?" a fascinated Lanzmann asks Zaidel during the second part of the interview filmed at the survivor's home in Petah Tikva (central Israel) in the presence of his family.[82] This question prompts Dugin and Zaidel to detail their escape for almost half of the four-hour interview. Their narrative encompasses the memory of the earth's texture in the tunnel, the moment they saw the sky and the stars outside, and, immediately after, the armed German officers who were waiting for them.[83] Lanzmann's fascination with their tale of escape and survival subsists a decade after the release of the film in his description of the *Shoah* material drafted for the USHMM. Under the names of the two Vilna survivors, he writes, echoing the outtakes: "<u>Extraordinary</u>: the whole story of their escape from Ponar, digging for months a tunnel. A fascinating and untold account of courage and fighting spirit."[84] Akin to the testimonies of the other male survivors who appear in the finished film, the story of heroic survival narrated by Dugin and Zaidel remained on the cutting room floor, only to be revived in 2016 when researchers finally discovered the tunnel they had dug by hand.[85]

After *Shoah*, Lanzmann never returned to the stories of the male *Sonderkommando* members whom, in the face of accusations of collaboration sparked by Steiner's *Treblinka*, he had redeemed and rendered the "unforgettable hero[es]" of his film. Instead, he chose to retrieve from his archive of the catastrophe the four-hour-long interview he had shot in Jerusalem on October 11, 1979, with Yehuda Lerner, one of the leaders of the Sobibór revolt. Lerner was first deported at the age of sixteen in July 1942 from the Warsaw ghetto to Treblinka, from which he was immediately sent to work in Belarus. During the following six months, he escaped from eight different camps before being sent to Sobibór in 1943. Lanzmann used segments of Lerner's excluded testimony to make *Sobibór, October 14, 1943, 4 p.m.* in 2001. This documentary filled two narrative lacunae in *Shoah*: the absence of survivors from this specific death camp and the untold story of heroic revolt and escape.

In the film's prologue, Lanzmann explains having "extensively recorded not only Ada Lichtman and her husband, who also survived the uprising, but especially Yehuda Lerner, its emblematic hero." This memory of making *Shoah* recovers the gendered representation of the hero in the outtakes where, unlike the male protagonists, Lichtman is never asked on camera to recount her participation in the revolt and her subsequent escape from the extermination camp. "Heroic virtues tend to be the province of men," remarks Tzvetan Todorov in *Facing the Extreme* (1991), approximating here the absence of a narrative of the revolt in Lichtman's filmed testimony.[86] Calling to mind the physical proximity visible in the Bomba and Podchlebnik interviews, Lanzmann's fascination with heroism recovered in the excluded footage also evidences a gendered generational identification with men who were his direct contemporaries. Like him, many of the male survivors filmed for *Shoah* were born in the 1920s; like him, they experienced the war as teenagers and young adults. In the remaining outtakes of the Lerner interview, this generational connection transpires by way of a shot reverse shot of both men's facial close-ups.[87]

In his critique of the staged barbershop scene, LaCapra calls attention to the objectionable way in which reenactment engenders a "full identification" of the filmmaker with the survivor, whereby the former is able to "act out the trauma vicariously in the self as surrogate victim."[88] The heroic narratives left

FIGURES 2.13–14. Close-ups of Yehuda Lerner and Claude Lanzmann in 1979 (Created by Claude Lanzmann during the filming of *Shoah*. Used by permission of the United States Holocaust Memorial Museum and Yad Vashem, the Holocaust Martyrs and Heroes' Remembrance Authority, Jerusalem).

out, however, unfold not only an appropriative but also *affiliative* identification. In her important work on postmemory, Marianne Hirsch discerns a horizontal transmission of the Holocaust from the second generation to its own contemporaries, which she terms "affiliative memory." Although devoid of the generational remove, the dynamics at play in the excluded *Shoah* footage echo Hirsch's discussion of photographs of both child and, more broadly, adolescent victims. The adult subject of postmemory, she argues, sees "through the eyes of his or her own child self," a form of projection and identification prompted by the "it could have been me" scenario.[89] Fittingly, rather than the off-screen voice of the docu-auteur he largely embodies in the finished film, Lanzmann positions and projects himself in the outtakes with male survivors as a masculine subject within a shared generational space that is defined by resistance and spans from west to east.

When listening to their tales of revolt and escape, the docu-auteur encounters and identifies with his male protagonists through his own experience fighting the Germans in the armed French Resistance—a personal narrative that he, somewhat prosthetically appropriating the deeds of the Jewish men filmed for *Shoah*, heroically frames in *The Patagonian Hare*.[90] In the outtakes, the memory of Lanzmann's own wartime activities unexpectedly surfaces during the interview shot with Simha "Kazik" Rotem and Yitzhak "Antek" Zuckerman at the Ghetto Fighters' House in early October 1979. After having filmed Rotem and Zuckerman at the museum, Lanzmann interviews the former separately in his apartment. In the midst of the survivor's account of the Warsaw ghetto uprising, Lanzmann asks him to reflect on his feelings and impressions as an eighteen-year-old member of the resistance.

"Another question," Lanzmann tells his Hebrew interpreter Francine Kaufmann. "When he looks back on this today, does he think that he was fully aware of what he was living? He was 18 years old, wouldn't he have liked to have been ten years older?" After Rotem answers that he "lived these things with enough intensity," Lanzmann reframes the question through his personal experience in the French Resistance. "The reason that I ask this question is that it matters to me personally. *I am the same age as him and I was in the Resistance*—I know that one must not compare. I always told myself that later, I was not fully aware of this at the time, I would have liked to experience this with a little more awareness," he observes.[91] Openly identifying through generational affiliation with one of the Warsaw ghetto fighters, Lanzmann as a subject bearing witness to his own past momentarily displaces the auteur he embodies in *Shoah*. This autobiographical moment also marks the curious intrusion of France into a narrative of the destruction that, in the finished film as well as in the outtakes, largely omits the Vichy regime.

"Without a story to exalt him, the hero ceases to be heroic," Todorov further observes in *Facing the Extreme*, where he devotes a dozen pages to the mythic status the Warsaw ghetto revolt acquired after the war, particularly in Poland and Israel.[92] On April 19, 1948, a date marking the fifth anniversary of the uprising, Nathan Rapoport's Warsaw ghetto monument was erected on the empty square where the ghetto had once been located (the POLIN Museum of the History of Polish Jews, which opened its doors in 2013, today faces the monument). Dedicated to "The Jewish People—Its Heroes and Martyrs," the two-sided monument depicts on one side the deportation of Jews and, on the other, seven figures incarnating the revolt. The latter are characterized by James Young in his classic study of Holocaust memorials as "heroically sculpted men and women […] transformed from skeletal to legendary proportions."[93] In 1975, the monument was recast and installed at Yad Vashem (in *Shoah*, Lanzmann juxtaposes parts of Rotem's testimony with shots of the monument first in Warsaw and then in Jerusalem). Akin to the Rapoport monument with its twofold depiction of the catastrophe, Israel had chosen in 1953 the date of April 19 as its Holocaust and Heroism Memorial Day, thereby framing the memory of the catastrophe through the heroic wartime deeds of the Jewish diaspora. In the newly founded State of Israel, the figure of the "Old Jew," the victim born in exile perceived as feminine and passive, was largely displaced in favor of heroes of the resistance such as the legendary commander of the uprising, "Antek" Zuckerman. Through generational and Zionist affiliation, these heroes of the Holocaust emerged as the counterpart to the native-born "New Jew" or Sabra, a stereotypically masculine and young kibbutznik who had partaken in Jewish resistance movements in Palestine and fought for the founding of the state.[94]

At the Ghetto Fighters' House in 1979, Lanzmann momentarily interrupts the story of the famous revolt to address the relation between heroism and narrative exemplified by memory practices in Israel immediately after the war. Speaking directly to Zuckerman, whom he calls in the outtakes by his *nom de guerre* "Antek," he asks: "And why, according to him, do we write books? Is it not inevitable? […] Why is it that the ghetto revolt has become almost a legend?" Rather than respond to this specific question, the commander of the uprising affirms that "it is absolutely unfair that two or three bear the laurels from the work of the hundreds," here referring to his own status as an Israeli national hero and to the lesser-known heroic deeds of Rotem.[95]

The "two or three" unnamed mythic figures in Zuckerman's filmed testimony call to mind Gouri's chronicle of the Eichmann trial where, upon introducing the depositions of "the last remnants of the *revolt*" on May 3 and 4, 1961, he specifies: "Two or three I knew personally, as friends"—namely, the Warsaw ghetto fighters "Antek" and his wife Zivia Lubetkin as well as the poet and partisan leader of the Vilna ghetto Abba Kovner.[96] Summoned by Hausner, all three heroes came to the courtroom with prepared statements and remained standing while testifying. In the witness box, Lubetkin narrated the 1943 uprising, which Gouri admiringly characterizes in his report as "the story that has no parallel in the annals of war." In their statements, Kovner and Zuckerman each bring up the Ponar forest where the Jews of Vilna were massacred (a story told in *Shoah* by Dugin and Zaidel). In the auditorium of the Beit Ha'am theater, Kovner recalled the moment when he realized in 1941 that "Ponar mean[t] death"; Zuckerman, who "nearly broke down," remembered having played in the forest as a child. "This same Ponar! The Jews of my beloved Vilna were being murdered in Ponar!" Gouri recalls "Antek" exclaiming at the witness stand in early May 1961.[97]

At the Eichmann trial, Kovner also submitted to the court the well-known manifesto he had penned in December 1941 and read aloud at a Zionist youth group meeting on January 1, 1942, following which the first organization of fighters was established in the Vilna ghetto. Calling on the Jews and, in particular, the youth to resist and take arms, Kovner had declared: "We will not be led like sheep to the slaughter!" Already aware of the destruction, he had also affirmed, as he would later in 1961: "All the roads of the Gestapo lead to Ponar. And Ponar means death.... Hitler plans to destroy all the Jews of Europe."

In France in 1966, this manifesto served as the catalyst for Steiner's *Treblinka*.[98] The issue of Jewish passivity also pervaded scholarly debates in the sixties and seventies, notably evidenced by Kovner's participation in the international conference, "The Holocaust—a Generation After," held in New York in March 1975 and which Lanzmann attended. There, Kovner gave a personal account of the underground activities, quoting throughout his testimony from the various proclamations he had authored, including the famous 1942 manifesto.[99] Four years later, in the final days of September 1979, Lanzmann interviewed Kovner at Kibbutz Ein HaHoresh, where the national hero lived from 1946 until his death in 1987 (he is today buried in the kibbutz cemetery). Over the course of four hours captured by Lubtchansky, all of which were left out of *Shoah*, the Vilna ghetto fighter delivers in Hebrew a poignant account of resistance and destruction. If his voice is punctuated with grief throughout his filmed testimony, sadness is also visible on his face as he gazes downward when the camera begins to roll.

"I want you to explain my problem to Abba Kovner, it is to arrive to … the famous proclamation of January 1, 1942, […] the extraordinary … prescience of this proclamation," Lanzmann begins the interview, speaking to his interpreter Francine Kaufmann and referring to the affirmation in the manifesto that "Hitler plans to destroy all the Jews of Europe." In his response, Kovner intuits the filmmaker's frame of representation in *Shoah*: the destruction process itself. "Factually, your question places me immediately in the center of a difficult maze … you do not allow me the possibility to arrive to the doors of the ghetto, you force me to penetrate immediately into the heart of this maze," he answers, before beginning to recount the days leading up to the arrival of German troops in Vilna.[100]

A single question, which permeates the outtakes of the archive as a whole, underlies Lanzmann's return to the manifesto: when exactly did the Jews know that sites such as Ponar, Auschwitz, and Treblinka meant death? Accordingly, Kovner's filmed testimony moves from the initial impossibility of imagining the destruction process in 1941 to the moment when the rare survivors of Ponar returned to tell of the atrocities they had witnessed. In this footage, he conveys this initial impossibility and concomitant lack of resistance through the vivid description, bracketed in the eighty-nine-page transcript of the interview, of the bundle each Jewish family was allowed to bring with them when they were resettled to the ghetto. "Well, so, you are at the window," he begins,

FIGURE 2.15. Abba Kovner at Kibbutz Ein HaHoresh in the opening moments of the interview (Created by Claude Lanzmann during the filming of *Shoah*. Used by permission of the United States Holocaust Memorial Museum and Yad Vashem, the Holocaust Martyrs and Heroes' Remembrance Authority, Jerusalem).

> you see... the thousands of people coming down into the street with a pack, a bundle for the whole family [...]. If one of the bundles... falls in the street, and the... cloths open, and you see two silver candlesticks come out of the bundle, it's because people think they're going to the ghetto to live there... and there will be holidays when you will light the candles. [...] you go down to the street, you are carrying... a babe in arms, the baby falls, you pick it up; your first thought isn't to flee; it's to pick up the baby to stop its crying.[101]

This affecting scene of seemingly uninterrupted Jewish life in the Vilna ghetto encapsulates the chapter of persecution in Kovner's narrative. In turn, the chapter of extermination opens with the story of a young girl, also singled out in the interview transcript, who survived an Einsatzgruppen massacre at the Ponar forest. "One day," Kovner recalls, "I was called and told to go to the hospital of the ghetto, that there was a young girl, injured, who wanted to talk to me, and only to me." He continues:

> From her I got the first direct evidence about what was happening at Ponari. She had been... executed, and fell like all the others inside the ditch, covered by... many cadavers, but... finally, being only injured, she was able to get out of the ditch, to drag herself, and return at the end of the day, to Vilna.[102]

This first memory of the destruction of Vilna Jewry calls to mind Yoselewska's 1961 deposition and Gouri's own changing perception of the catastrophe described in *Facing the Glass Booth*. During his interview with Lanzmann, Kovner posits himself as the direct addressee or receiver of this story of the atrocities committed by the Germans, a moment of "witnessing witnessing" that engenders in the Zionist youth leader in 1941 the realization that "Ponar means death" and only organized resistance remained.

The ensuing 1942 manifesto and its "extraordinary prescience" of the destruction of European Jewry occupies a central place in the second half of the interview where Lanzmann and Kovner, who each have a copy of the document, discuss at length its making and meaning. If the annotated interview transcript used during the editorial process evidences an enduring interest in this testimony, the interview mise-en-scène suggests that, in 1979, the docu-auteur envisioned including the famous proclamation and, in particular, a discussion of its infamous phrase "We will not be led like sheep to the slaughter!" into the finished film. When Kovner proposes to read several key sentences of the proclamation, an off-screen Lanzmann interrupts him and explains that *he* himself will read a few passages, which the ghetto fighter will then comment on in front of the camera. Affirming and imposing his authorial intention, he specifies: "I would like to read it myself in French as not the whole text will be read ... And it is done another way in the film." Lanzmann begins reading, but the camera remains fixated on Kovner's now-perplexed face as he listens, awaiting the interpreter's translation of his own text. "Appeal to the resistance in the Vilna Ghetto, dated 1 January 1942. Do not let us be conducted as sheep to the slaughterhouse. Jewish youth," Lanzmann recites before stopping to comment: "*It is addressed to the Jewish youth*," here evidencing generational affiliation and emphasizing the heroism to come of individuals who were in fact still children (an observation he also makes several weeks later during his interview with Rotem and Zuckerman).[103]

Here, after having interviewed Bomba and Lichtman, Lanzmann strikingly deviates from his representational dictum: rather than demand that Kovner reenact the past by reading the text as he had once done in front of a Zionist youth group in Vilna, the docu-auteur appropriates the manifesto and momentarily embodies a survivor considered at the time to be "a living symbol of Jewish resistance to the Nazis."[104] While calling to mind the open identification with a hero that the camera captured a few weeks later at Kibbutz Lohamei HaGeta'ot, Lanzmann's reframing of the famous proclamation through his own voice and language arises from a point of contention underlying both these outtakes and postwar controversies: that of the supposed passivity of victims.

When he interviewed Kovner in the final weeks of shooting *Shoah*, Lanzmann had already amassed the near entirety of more than 190 hours of filmed testimonies. This archive of the catastrophe from which he would compose a film about the Final Solution informs his refutation of passivity claims and retrospective perception that Kovner had assumed a critical stance vis-à-vis his own people in 1942. "Jews could have with great difficulties resisted [...]," Lanzmann affirms before he begins to read the manifesto. "I think I understand [victims and survivors] well and that ... I do not see what could have been done differently. The text of the appeal is ... very violent, and it is a condemnation of the Jews."[105] This accusation confounds Kovner, who asks him to clarify which part of the manifesto he is referring to. At that moment, Lanzmann begins to read the appeal in French before exclaiming a few instants later: "Ah, this is where ... where ... I find ... when I speak of condemnation, this is it, this is what I want you to translate: 'but the anguish of this terrible misfortune is even bigger in view of the disgraceful conduct of Jews today.'" While Kaufmann translates the passage into Hebrew, Kovner interrupts her. "No need to continue this… I have never written something like this. [...] Where… where did you find this text, where was it printed? Who gave it to you?" he asks, visibly upset and shaking his head. A surprised Lanzmann then learns that he is reading an altered version of the manifesto. This revelation prompts him to inverse the mise-en-scène. In the following take, Kovner begins by stating, "I have in my hands the printed text of the appeal," thereby reappropriating his authorship.

More than an unofficial version of the manifesto, this French translation accentuates the supposed lack of resistance on the part of the Jews. It also calls attention to Lanzmann's own reception of the 1942 manifesto through the lens of decades of debates and controversies centered on the issue of passivity. More precisely, his abrupt condemnation of Kovner and decision to read the manifesto in French appear as a belated response to Steiner's *Treblinka* and its distortion of survivor narratives, to which Lanzmann could effectively retort in September 1979 with his archive of audiovisual testimonies. The enduring legacy of the "Treblinka affair" in France recovered by the outtakes is further revealed in Lanzmann's subsequent editing choices. He opted to leave out Kovner, who had inspired Steiner. Instead, he used the testimonies of the Jewish male survivors whom the author of *Treblinka* deemed collaborators. In excluding from the finished film "a living symbol of Jewish resistance," he instead rendered the members of the *Sonderkommando* "unforgettable hero[es]." Only after *Shoah* would Lanzmann explicitly address the question of passivity and resistance upon retrieving from the cutting room floor the Lerner outtakes and affirming in the prologue of *Sobibór, October 14, 1943, 4 p.m.*: "One must do justice to a double legend, the one that claims the Jews let themselves be led to the gas chambers without premonition or suspicion, that their death was 'gentle,' and the other according to which they offered the perpetrators no resistance."

Beyond *Sobibór* and the Kovner outtakes, the remaining unused footage attests to Lanzmann's original intention to refute in the finished film claims of passivity encapsulated in Kovner's infamous phrase—a phrase in fact never uttered in the nine-and-a-half-hour-long opus. In the archive, Lanzmann's questions prompt, for instance, *Shoah* protagonist Filip Müller to affirm of the Jews murdered at Auschwitz: "it's not true when they say they went like sheep."[106] Similarly, during the final shooting phase in Israel, the postwar accusations frame Lanzmann's reception of Dov Shilansky's excluded testimony.[107]

Lanzmann interviewed the fighter of the Lithuanian Šiauliai ghetto in Jerusalem at the Knesset, to which Shilansky had been elected in 1977. Born in 1924, the Revisionist Zionist had unsuccessfully attempted to organize a revolt in the ghetto; he was later deported to Dachau. After the Holocaust, he fought successively in the War of Independence in 1948, the Six-Day War in 1967, and the Yom Kippur War in 1973, thus exemplifying the ideological bridge between wartime resistance and the creation of the State of Israel underlying memory politics at the time.

While interviewing Shilansky in 1979, Lanzmann never openly identifies with the Šiauliai ghetto fighter as he later would with the unsung hero of the Warsaw ghetto, Simha Rotem. Instead, in this presumably improvised or partially lost interview (no transcript exists for the forty-five-minute testimony conducted in English and Hebrew that ends midsentence, parts of which are inaudible), he reveals an agenda informed by the *Treblinka* controversy. "What interests me because Mr. Shilansky was a fighter," Lanzmann explains early on to his interpreter, "is not so much to have him speaking about the resistance but speaking about the Jews in general: how they behaved, everything that was told about the Jews being led like sheep to the slaughterhouse." Akin to the reversal effectuated in the representation of the *Sonderkommando* from "collaborators" to "heroes" in *Shoah*, Lanzmann here inverses the perspective of Steiner. Instead of glorifying the activities of the resistance fighter, he probes the ways in which the conditions in the ghetto rendered any sort of revolt difficult, if not altogether impossible. While Shilansky shares Lanzmann's understanding of the Holocaust, he nevertheless comments on his choice of words, specifically when exclaiming: "The expression like sheep to the slaughter is very unfair and very degrading." In this moment, Lanzmann reveals his viewpoint and agenda. "I don't believe in the expression myself," he explains to Shilansky. "It was an expression used by Abba Kovner in the ghetto of Vilna in the proclamation of January 1942."[108]

This deliberately provocative tone adopted in order to gauge the legacy of Kovner's infamous phrase also permeates a post-screening debate with military students at Yad Vashem recorded on October 12, 1979—one day after the interview with Yehuda Lerner—and later left out. After having watched a Holocaust film, whose title is never provided in these outtakes, Shalmi Barmore, then director of education at Yad Vashem, mediates a discussion centered above all on the issue of passivity and resistance. Assisted by Kaufmann, who simultaneously translates into French, Lanzmann does not directly participate. He listens intently to the debate unfolding in front of the camera. Yet Barmore's questions bear the docu-auteur's imprint and intention to engage with postwar controversies.

Evocative of the Kovner and Shilansky outtakes, Barmore deploys the expression used by the Vilna ghetto fighter in 1942 several times over the course of the fifty-minute class. Seemingly cued by Lanzmann beforehand to steer the discussion toward the Israeli legacy of the phrase, he asks the students at the beginning of the debate: "Is this question—namely, that the Jews were led to the slaughter like sheep—is this question still the question that preoccupies the youth [...]?" A few instants later, he reiterates: "I want to know if this question still concerns you, this concern about sheep going to the slaughterhouse, or, after thirty-five years, has this problem ceased to interest you [...]?"[109] Reminiscent of Shilansky's own reluctance to use the same expression in front of the camera, only two students repeat Barmore's wording during the debate. While one concedes that the majority were in fact "led to the slaughterhouse like sheep," the other affirms that "we will never be able to comprehend" the situation of the Jews during the Holocaust.[110]

In 1979, the relative omission of the infamous phrase on the part of the military students gestures toward the enduring effect of the Eichmann trial on Israeli youth. Duly documented through interviews and questionnaires reminiscent of the classroom discussion recorded by Lanzmann, the 1961 trial engendered for them a marked shift in the perception of the supposed passivity during the genocide. As Yablonka reveals in her study of the Eichmann trial, "The main question with which they wrestled related to ways in which the Jews had died and their apparent lack of resistance." Accordingly, for many, the Eichmann trial "furnished answers to their questions about Jews who had gone to their death without resistance."[111]

In Lanzmann's archive of the catastrophe, the debate recorded at Yad Vashem shifts the focus from the testimony of ghetto fighters such as Shilansky and Kovner to the second generation. Much like Hanna Zaidel, daughter of the member of the *Sonderkommando* at Ponar and the only child of a survivor to appear in *Shoah*, the majority of students present during the post-screening discussion embody what Hirsch terms not affiliative but *familial* postmemory. Toward the end of class, in a rare intervention translated by Kaufmann, Lanzmann asks students who are children of survivors to raise their hand. Off-screen, he and his interpreter express their surprise at the sheer number of hands suddenly in the air. "Unbelievable! In packs!" Lanzmann exclaims. As though to ensure his cameraman captures this scene, he then asks Kaufmann, herself the daughter of survivors who, years later, would remember having identified with Hanna Zaidel while serving as the interpreter for the filmed testimonies of the Ponar revenants, "Have them keep their hands up!"[112]

Despite his astonishment, however, Lanzmann later excluded this debate from the finished film, once more setting aside—after the unused testimonies of Kovner and Shilansky—the 1942 manifesto. He also limited the second generation to Hanna Zaidel who, curiously anticipating the relentless filmmaker at the barbershop, affirms in *Shoah*: "I never stopped questioning [my father], until I got at the scraps of truth he couldn't tell me. It came out haltingly. I had to tear the details out of him." In the unused portion of her very short and seemingly improvised interview, this young woman embodies the postmemory generation Lanzmann sought to capture at Yad Vashem. Describing herself as a Sabra, she mentions her exposure to the genocide through Holocaust and Heroism Memorial Day and several recent films of which she names only Gouri's *The 81st Blow*. Never uttering the infamous phrase penned by Kovner, she nevertheless indirectly condemns postwar accusations of passivity. She remarks in the outtakes: "I think that the attitude we have in Israel toward the people who went through, who lived those events, I think that that attitude isn't good."[113]

In the final months of the shooting phase, Lanzmann envisioned a possible juxtaposition between the youth of the past and the youth of the present, between resistance fighters and the second generation, between Holocaust

FIGURE 2.16. The children of survivors raise their hands during a film course at Yad Vashem (Created by Claude Lanzmann during the filming of *Shoah*. Used by permission of the United States Holocaust Memorial Museum and Yad Vashem, the Holocaust Martyrs and Heroes' Remembrance Authority, Jerusalem).

testimony and Israeli postmemory. While he would eventually compose a representation of the catastrophe largely devoid of national specificity, the interviews he captured in late 1979 recover an explicit engagement with the memory politics of the State of Israel, who had originally commissioned *Shoah*. The closing scene of the Yad Vashem outtakes, staged by the filmmaker, further captures this engagement: immediately following the debate, Barmore speaks to the military students in front of the Warsaw ghetto uprising memorial situated at the foot of the museum.

The replica of Rapoport's iconic sculpture appears briefly in *Shoah* when an off-screen Rotem narrates the aftermath of the 1943 revolt. Yet, in line with the exclusion of the post-screening debate, the representation of Yad Vashem, a national institution established in 1953, is largely displaced in *Shoah* in favor of the Ghetto Fighters' House. Whereas *Israel, Why* ended in the archives of Yad Vashem, the concluding joint testimony of *Shoah* leads us to Kibbutz Lohamei HaGeta'ot (Hebrew for "ghetto fighters"), an equally symbolic site founded during the Passover holiday in 1949 by Warsaw ghetto survivors, including Zuckerman and Lubetkin. That same year, and well ahead of Yad Vashem, which would open to the public in 1957, Kibbutz Lohamei HaGeta'ot set up a Holocaust exhibition and archive; the museum where Lanzmann filmed Rotem and Zuckerman for *Shoah* was, for its part, inaugurated in 1955. Together, the kibbutz and museum exemplify the ideological bridge between Jewish resistance

FIGURE 2.17. The military students in front of the Monument to the Ghetto Heroes at Yad Vashem (Created by Claude Lanzmann during the filming of *Shoah*. Used by permission of the United States Holocaust Memorial Museum and Yad Vashem, the Holocaust Martyrs and Heroes' Remembrance Authority, Jerusalem).

and the founding of the State of Israel, further bound by the heroic Zionist youth, underlying national politics of memory in the postwar period. Hausner himself visited the Ghetto Fighters' House shortly before the Eichmann trial began, writing in the visitor book: "On the eve of the trial of the tyrant, I passed through [the museum] and soaked up its atmosphere, so that I can be the mouthpiece for the martyrs of the Jewish nation."[114]

In 1979, two years before "Antek" passed away, Lanzmann interviewed him alongside Rotem in the same museum Hausner had once visited. Prior to being recorded for *Shoah*, Zuckerman was filmed at least twice at Kibbutz Lohamei HaGeta'ot. In 1961, he briefly recounted the ghetto uprising in Erwin Leiser's documentary *Eichmann and the Third Reich*. In 1968, he was featured in Mira Hamermesh's short film about the kibbutz, *Fighters of the Ghetto*, in which he is shown speaking to a group of soldiers visiting the museum.[115] Following the Yom Kippur War, Zuckerman was urged by friends to record his testimony. He agreed under the condition that the audiocassettes not be transcribed until after his death.[116]

Five years later, "Antek" was sitting in the exhibition space of the Ghetto Fighters' House in front of Lanzmann's camera: for the first hour, he remains next to Rotem—the unsung hero of the 1943 revolt who largely assumes the role of the witness in this joint testimony—both in the outtakes and the finished film. Zuckerman then moves off-screen, interjecting intermittently for the remainder of the interview. During the editing phase, the filmmaker retained only a fragment of Zuckerman's words. Moreover, he reframed the legendary commander of the revolt as a man broken by the Jewish tragedy. "I began drinking after the war," he affirms in *Shoah*. "It was very difficult... If you could lick my heart, you would be poisoned." Similarly, Lanzmann cut Rotem's testimony through the lens of destruction: while he describes wandering alone through a now-defeated and decimated ghetto, he concludes by recalling the words he had uttered to himself at the time: "I am the last Jew. I'll wait for the morning and the Germans." Editing this material, the docu-auteur chose to silence the well-known and oft-recounted story of the revolt. Yet the inclusion of the Ghetto Fighters' House and of the national hero "Antek" at the end of *Shoah* spoke for itself, at the very least in Israel, where the film premiered in June 1986 at a packed Jerusalem Cinematheque. The invited audience members included Rotem.[117]

Lanzmann's decision to select, among the seventy interviews he recorded for *Shoah*, Rotem and Zuckerman as the last witnesses is not insignificant: shot on October 4, 1979, the joint testimony of the ghetto fighters was one of the last captured by the filmmaker and his crew. If the position of this joint testimony in the finished film can be read as an homage to the late Zuckerman and his legacy at Kibbutz Lohamei HaGeta'ot, the outtakes operate an extraordinary reframing of both the hero and the auteur. In his memoir, Lanzmann recalls "Antek" as "a drinker with a puffy drunkard's face," from whom he heroically "managed the amazing feat of getting a few words." He describes in particular the reluctance of the other kibbutz members. He remembers having had to fight "them every inch of the way, promising [he] would not make [Zuckerman] talk but insisting that he be present, even if only in the background." Implicitly remembering the docu-auteur that he had become over the course of making *Shoah*, Lanzmann affirms that it had been a triumph to enter the Ghetto Fighters' House. "But I had no intention of keeping my word," he writes in *The Patagonian Hare*, "I knew that I would do everything in my power to get Antek to speak, realizing that once he began it would be impossible to stop him."[118]

Similar to this memory of an initially taciturn "Antek," the excluded footage begins with Rotem sitting alone, as he does in *Shoah*, in front of a wall-sized photo of the Warsaw ghetto (accordingly, the transcript used while editing the footage is labeled "Interview with Mr. Rotem"). Half an hour later, he is joined by his comrade. As though to mark the entry of the hero ("a towering giant," as Gouri once described him) and of the auteur, the camera captures the staged entrance, requiring two takes, of Rotem, Zuckerman, and Lanzmann.[119] Immediately invoking generational affiliation, this scene is also reminiscent of the Podchlebnik outtakes: as the three men arrive in the exhibition space, the somewhat fatigued filmmaker is walking next to "Antek," clinging to his arm and leading him to the interview.

Over the course of the next hour, Zuckerman and Rotem are sitting on a bench in the museum. "Antek," whose face is often framed in a close-up, speaks intermittently while drinking cognac between takes, a bottle and glass at times visible behind him. In front of the camera, he references early on the alcohol's effects on his ability to bear witness. "I think that Claude Lanzmann, aside from all his other talents, [...] must also work for a cognac distributor because, thanks to this [drink], he has succeeded in tearing from us words that I did not think I was capable of saying." When Kaufmann finishes translating the survivor's words, the docu-auteur laments: "He hasn't spoken much yet..."[120] Yet, a few instants later, seemingly finishing his thought, "Antek" pronounces the famous lines later included in *Shoah*. Shortly after, he once again alludes to the effect of the cognac, insisting that the influence of alcohol on his testimony be known. "I want my last sentence to be translated, namely, that your cognac is doing wonders, you have succeeded in tearing from me what I didn't want [to say]," he tells Kaufmann. "It's not the cognac," Lanzmann responds, implicitly affirming the authorial influence he would describe decades later in his memoir. "Tonight, most definitely, it's the cognac," Zuckerman maintains. "No," the docu-auteur insists. "It's something other than the cognac; or, rather, it's the cognac and something else," he then concedes while reiterating his directorial control over Zuckerman's words.

Rather than provoke or mediate his filmed testimony, as retrospectively suggested in *The Patagonian Hare*, the exchange between the hero and the docu-auteur reveals Lanzmann's failure to mold Zuckerman's process of remembrance for *Shoah*. Often deferring to Rotem, who remains the principal addressee of these outtakes, "Antek" poignantly calls attention to the existing testimony of his late wife when Lanzmann asks that the two men describe the revolt day by day. Zivia Lubetkin passed away on July 11, 1978, that is, as Zuckerman specifies in front of the camera, exactly "one year, three months, one week" before the interview. Inversing the gendered perspective Lanzmann would adopt in *Shoah*, "Antek" urges him to read the final chapter of her memoir, published at her request posthumously in 1979 under the title *In the Days of Destruction and Revolt*.[121]

In what constitutes one of the final interviews recorded for *Shoah*, the memory of Lubetkin prompts Lanzmann, in a rare on-camera moment, to reflect openly on the Holocaust film he is making. First explaining that he needs not a memoir but "human faces," he exclaims, visibly exhausted and referring to his unfinished opus, at that point six years in the making, "I have undertaken a crazy endeavor." He then attempts to lead the survivors back to the interview, asking them whether it is possible to represent the Holocaust. "He answers that he is very sad," Kaufmann states, translating Zuckerman's words. "I am sad too. Why is he sad?" Lanzmann responds, in a moment of identification and empathy. Zuckerman then embarks on a long monologue, largely untranslated, in which he first describes the "millions" of ghosts—that is, the victims of the catastrophe—that haunt him to this day. His voice is still audible during the few minutes it takes Lubtchansky to recharge the camera. When the image resumes, Lanzmann is now standing next to "Antek."

In an unprecedented reversal of roles that offers a striking contrast to the famous disembodied voice in the barbershop captured just a few weeks earlier, the hero takes the auteur in his arms. Calling to mind the legendary and heroically sculpted figures of the Rapoport monument, "Antek" holds Lanzmann in silence for almost a minute, during which the latter, suddenly turning away from the camera and his own Holocaust documentary, buries his head in the survivor's chest. Aware that a *grand moment de cinéma* is transpiring, Lubtchansky, the great cinematographer of the French New Wave,

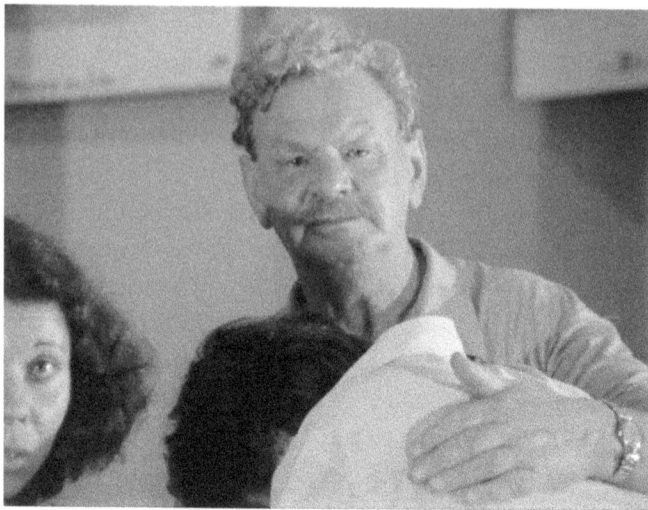

FIGURE 2.18. Francine Kaufmann, Itzhak "Antek" Zuckerman, and Claude Lanzmann at the Ghetto Fighters' Museum (Created by Claude Lanzmann during the filming of *Shoah*. Used by permission of the United States Holocaust Memorial Museum and Yad Vashem, the Holocaust Martyrs and Heroes' Remembrance Authority, Jerusalem).

continues filming—unbeknownst to the hero and the auteur who each ask that the camera stop rolling.

The collapse of the French director in the midst of accumulating the last fragments of his archive of the catastrophe anticipates the exhaustion Lanzmann would describe eight years later during a PBS interview with Roger Rosenblatt following the release the *Shoah*. "I don't feel myself in particularly good shape, to tell the truth [...]," he explains, "I am proud of what I have achieved, definitely, yes, but it didn't release me from the anguish—I think it's the other way around."[122] This anguish briefly described in 1987 calls to mind the image of his tightened fist during the Podchlebnik interview, which revealed the conflicting process of excavating deep memory for *Shoah*. At Kibbutz Lohamei HaGeta'ot several months later, the footage furtively captured by Lubtchansky marks the auteur's momentary impossibility to continue "witnessing witnessing" and impose onto survivors his demands of Holocaust representation. In fact, Zuckerman's heroic gesture marks the end of his filmed testimony. When the interview resumes a few instants later, he sits silently offscreen for the remainder of the excluded footage and listens to Rotem narrating the story of revolt and destruction.

Akin to the reframing of the auteur, the ghetto fighter is recast in these outtakes as the hero he remained until his death. Haunted by the ghosts of the six million victims he has just evoked, "Antek" cannot look away from the catastrophe: he stares into the camera while Lanzmann turns away, while Kaufmann, the second-generation interpreter and testimonial mediator, joins the survivor in confronting the Shoah. As though emerging from the ruins of the Warsaw ghetto once more, the hero assumes a form calling to mind Walter Benjamin's famous Angel of History. "His eyes are wide," Benjamin tells us in 1940 with extraordinary foresight. "His face is turned toward the past [...], *he* sees one single catastrophe, which keeps piling wreckage upon wreckage and hurls it at his feet. The angel would like to stay, awaken the dead, and make whole what has been smashed."[123]

A HISTORIAN AT THE WITNESS STAND

On February 13, 1979, several months before Lanzmann captured the final interviews for *Shoah*, Marvin Chomsky's award-winning miniseries *Holocaust* premiered on French television. Reminiscent of his intention, detailed in the 1977 letter to Roswell McClelland, to direct a film encompassing the major chapters of the catastrophe, the four-part series took the form—to borrow Peter Novick's apt phrasing—of "a mini-survey course" that included landmarks such as Auschwitz, Theresienstadt, the Warsaw ghetto uprising, and the Jewish council.[124] In the midst of filming his opus, Lanzmann retorted in June of the same year with an article published in *Les Temps Modernes*. In it, he condemned Chomsky's chronological and fictionalized account of the event before formulating the ethics of representation, reiterated innumerable times after the release of *Shoah*, underlying his own Holocaust film. As a docu-auteur, he shifts the emphasis from content to form, effectively displacing to the offframe the specific chapters of the Holocaust represented in Chomsky's nineand-a-half-hour miniseries, as well as his own archive of the catastrophe. He only seemingly alludes to the interview captured with McClelland months before in late November 1978 when he brings up the world's indifference to the plight of the Jews and the failed attempts at rescuing Hungarian Jewry. Similarly, he cites a passage on anti-Semitism from the interview he recorded with the historian Raul Hilberg in January 1979.[125]

If he neither names the author of *The Destruction of the European Jews* as a protagonist of his film nor provides the source of this quotation, he also omits Hilberg's counter-representation, in the filmed interview, to Chomsky's account of the Jewish council in the Warsaw ghetto and of its chairman Adam Czerniaków. In *Holocaust*, the Weiss brothers Josef and Moses both become members of this very same *Judenrat*. When the Germans demand that the council draft deportation lists, they refuse to decide who shall live and who shall die. In contrast to the chairman Dr. Kohn, a character based on Czerniaków who urges the members of the *Judenrat* to continue cooperating with the Germans, the two brothers join the resistance, helping to prepare the 1943 uprising. As Omer Bartov remarks, in moving from the Jewish council to the armed revolt, *Holocaust* not only refutes claims of passivity but also "strives to dispel th[e] widespread prejudice about the Jewish willingness to collaborate in their own murder," a prejudice epitomized in the accusations leveled against the *Judenrat* by Arendt during the Eichmann trial.[126]

In *Shoah*, Lanzmann himself strives to dispel the condemnation of the *Judenrat* through his representation of Czerniaków. More specifically, he reframes the chairman of the Warsaw ghetto as a tragic figure who, summoned by the Germans to draft deportation lists in July 1942 for "resettlement" in the East (a euphemism for the death camps), chose to take his own life rather than cooperate. Lanzmann brings into play a distinct mise-en-scène to represent the Jewish council: rather than filmed testimony, he draws on the diary Czerniaków left behind, a unique Jewish record of the catastrophe that enables him to adopt an eyewitness perspective at once contemporaneous with the events and devoid of postwar controversies. Concurrently, he calls on Hilberg to incarnate the late *Judenrat* leader by reading and commenting on the diary in front of the camera (unseen in either *Shoah* or the outtakes, Czerniaków appears in the propaganda footage shot by the Nazis in the Warsaw ghetto that Yael Hersonski used in her 2010 documentary, *A Film Unfinished*).

In 1961, the Eichmann trial marked the first time a historian—Salo Baron, then professor of Jewish history at Columbia University, whose lectures Hilberg attended as a graduate student—had taken the stand. More or less two decades later, Lanzmann features the author of *The Destruction of the European Jews* as an expert witness. Hilberg, however, does not narrate history as Baron had in the witness box, where he provided a rich panorama of Jewish life in prewar Europe. According to Shoshana Felman, Hilberg's role in *Shoah* is first and foremost "to take part in a cinematic vision which Lanzmann has defined as crucially an 'incarnation' and a 'resurrection.'"[127] As a reader of the diary, Hilberg embodies in the finished film the deceased leader of the Warsaw ghetto and Lanzmann's demands of Holocaust representation. Yet, more than bearing the imprint of the docu-auteur, the performance of the historian in *Shoah* stages his own identification with Czerniaków as it is revealed in the excluded portions of his interview.

When he was filmed by Lanzmann in early 1979, Hilberg had just completed the English edition of *The Warsaw Ghetto Diary*. In the introduction penned with Stanislaw Staron, he quotes several passages that he also reads in *Shoah* as well as in the unused footage. Prompted by the filmmaker in the outtakes to address claims of collaboration made against the *Judenrat*, Hilberg remarks that such judgment stems from a lack of rigorous historiographical engagement, to which he contrasts the years he spent preparing the diary for publication. "I think it's necessary to put oneself to some extent into somebody else's place," he tells Lanzmann. "Invariably, inevitably I did this, living five years with this diary and beginning to think somewhat the thoughts which Czerniaków had."[128] In *Shoah*, Lanzmann does not so much mold the performance of the historian as capture his literal identification with Czerniaków, along with his admiration for a diary that, in its depth and breadth, appears as a micro-version of *The Destruction of the European Jews*. As the camera lingers in these outtakes on books and documents scattered over a table, Hilberg's answer also calls attention to the historian's and the filmmaker's respective parallel methods. While the former spent half a decade with Czerniaków's diary and, before that, years gathering archival documents to compose his 1,300-page magnum opus ("Your master book," as Lanzmann calls *The Destruction of the European Jews* in the excluded footage), the latter would devote twelve years to making his equally monumental film.

Evocative of the closeness underlying the testimonies of the male Jewish survivors, the excluded six hours of Hilberg footage evidences Lanzmann's own generational and authorial identification with the great Holocaust historian. By contrast, the two-and-a-half-hour unedited interview recorded in English with the renowned Israeli scholar Yehuda Bauer does not recover the same affiliative frame of reception. Symptomatic of its relatively short duration, the Bauer footage is omitted from the list of outtakes Lanzmann drafted in 1994 for the USHMM, where he describes instead the material captured with Hilberg as "strong and brilliant."[129] While the Hilberg interview opens with a discussion of his landmark study that immediately intimates Lanzmann's admiration, the excluded footage captured at Bauer's home in the fall of 1979 begins as a testimony. Bauer, a native of Prague born the same year as Hilberg, describes his upbringing in a Zionist family in Czechoslovakia, his immigration to Palestine in 1939, and his intellectual trajectory, which was marked by a decisive encounter with the Vilna partisan and poet. "I think what made me deal with the Holocaust was a long discussion I had with Abba Kovner in 1964 or 1965," observes Bauer, who then shifted his work from Zionist history to the issues of Jewish compliance, resistance, and passivity during the war.[130]

Reminiscent of the Hilberg footage, Bauer and Lanzmann discuss at length the role of the *Judenrat*. The historian argues that it is impossible to generalize about the behavior of the council members during the Holocaust. He proceeds to describe the divergent decisions made by each chairman in ghettos such as Vilna, Łódź, and Minsk. In a move to individualize these Jewish leaders, he reads and comments in front of the camera a short speech made by Jacob Gens, the head of the Vilna ghetto *Judenrat*. In stark contrast to Czerniaków's unwillingness, never mentioned by either Bauer or Lanzmann, to compromise and send people to their death, Gens willingly deported the elderly in the hopes of saving the majority. He later admitted his responsibility in the destruction of his own people in the speech Bauer reads to Lanzmann.

Although evocative of the diary utilized in the Hilberg interview, the historian neither "incarnates" nor exhibits any identification with this Jewish leader who was assassinated by the Gestapo in 1943. Rather than partake in or mirror Lanzmann's cinematic vision, Bauer serves as an expert witness who uses documents to counter postwar generalizations and controversial claims. Emphasizing that "the possibilities of [resistance] were very limited" for the *Judenrat* members, the historian establishes a key distinction between ideological collaboration and administrative cooperation. In the interview transcript used in the editing room, this distinction is underlined, suggesting a possible refutation in the finished film to accusations made against the Jewish council.[131]

"I don't like this word [collaboration]," Lanzmann tells Hilberg in a portion of the interview left on the cutting room floor (in a French context, the word immediately connotes the Vichy regime).[132] Just like Kovner's infamous phrase that is audible in numerous outtakes, the word "collaboration" is entirely omitted from the finished film. Conversely, Lanzmann silences the equally controversial assertions found in the first edition of Hilberg's book: on the one hand, the compliance of Jewish councils in the destruction process; on the other, the lack of Jewish resistance (narrowly conceived by the historian as armed resistance). For these assertions, Hilberg was bitterly criticized in 1961 and for many decades thereafter. "Did you change your mind since you wrote *The Destruction of the European Jews* on this particular point?" Lanzmann asks him in the outtakes regarding the *Judenrat* leaders. "Because I have the feeling that you were much more harsh, severe, towards these people, when you were writing the book, than you are now." While contending that the ghetto chairmen were in fact victims, the historian does not so much refute as reiterate his 1961 stance in front of the camera. He only concedes that new archival documents such as Czerniaków's diary enable him to now substantially detail this chapter of the catastrophe. "We can see how, step by step, the Jewish councils, not only the Germans, propelled themselves into a situation which became the Final Solution," he maintains in January 1979 (in the transcript of the interview, this sentence summarizing the historian's enduring perspective is underlined).[133]

In his memoir, Hilberg explains that his treatment of the *Judenrat* in 1961 stemmed from his unwillingness—contra the main current in Holocaust studies at the time—to systematically posit Jewish victims as "heroic."[134] The historian Saul Friedländer, however, provides a biographical reason for the radicalness of Hilberg's position vis-à-vis the Jewish council. Hilberg was brought up in a Revisionist Zionist family, the right-wing movement founded by Vladimir Ze'ev Jabotinsky, one of whose call to arms was "Jewish youth, learn to shoot!" According to Friedländer, the author of *The Destruction of the European Jews* "could not bear the thought that there had not been more resistance or combat" during the Holocaust.[135] Attested by his narrow definition of resistance as armed resistance, Hilberg's Revisionist background subsists in the subsequent editions of his opus published in 1985 and 2003, respectively, where he leaves his conclusions regarding Jewish resistance untouched. Conversely, he made "small but significant changes in language concerning the Jewish councils"—a modification the historian Christopher Browning attributes to Hilberg's edition of the Czerniaków diary in 1979.[136]

Beyond this document, Lanzmann's interview with Hilberg the same year surely played an equally determining role in the historian's decision to revise and reframe more neutrally his treatment of the *Judenrat*. Indeed, in the second edition of *The Destruction of the European Jews*, which appeared the same year as *Shoah*, he substituted the word "collaboration" for "compliance."[137] Fittingly, the docu-auteur himself edited around the January 1979 interview in order to recast Hilberg as an empathetic figure and redeem him despite his 1961 claims. At the same time, he appropriated the neutralized and authoritative voice of the historian reading the diary to reframe the contentious issue of Jewish leadership as "tragic rather than accusatory."[138] Hilberg himself posits the chairman of the Warsaw ghetto as a tragic figure in his introduction to the English edition of the diary, which he concludes in the same way he does in *Shoah*: he recounts Czerniaków's utter despair. "It has been reported that after Czerniaków made the last entry in his diary on July 23, 1942, he left a note to the effect that the SS wanted him to kill the children with his own hands."[139] These words are rendered even more tragic in the finished film through Hilberg's use of direct speech: "'They want me to kill the children with my own hands.'"

If the mise-en-scène centered on the diary effaces postwar controversies in *Shoah*, Hilberg's role cannot simply be aligned with the director's ethics of representation, as Felman affirms in her seminal text where she adds that Lanzmann chose Hilberg to embody Czerniaków even though he had filmed "someone alive who had been a director of the ghetto."[140] The unnamed chairman in question is Benjamin Murmelstein, the only leader of a *Judenrat* to have survived. Rather than evidence the cinematic vision of the auteur, the invocation of Murmelstein calls attention to the process of selection and omission underlying the finished film: namely, Lanzmann's ethics of editing around the generalized accusations leveled against Jewish leaders. In choosing to include only the story of Czerniaków, Lanzmann individualized, as Bauer reckons necessary, the Warsaw ghetto chairman. Yet in order to rehabilitate Czerniaków, perhaps the most tragic of the *Judenrat* leaders, did Lanzmann not have to exclude all the others, whether Gens who publicly admitted to "having blood on his hands" or Murmelstein, whom Gershom Scholem thought should be hung? Lastly, in choosing Hilberg to impart or "incarnate" the only representation of the Jewish council in the finished film, Lanzmann as an auteur minimized his own fascination—unabated throughout the making of *Shoah*—with one of the most controversial issues of both the Holocaust and the postwar period.

"I have dwelt on this chapter of the story, which the Jerusalem trial failed to put before the eyes of the world in its true dimensions," writes Arendt in her report of the Eichmann trial regarding the "collaboration" of the *Judenrat*.[141] In search of a counter-representation, which he ultimately found in Hilberg's "incarnation" of the deceased chairman, Lanzmann himself dwelt extensively between 1973 and 1985 on this tragic chapter of the catastrophe. In 1976, he first recorded the vice chairman of the Kovno ghetto Leib Garfunkel and, after him, Murmelstein. Similarly, when he interviewed Kovner in September 1979, he concluded by asking the poet and partisan to share his views on the *Judenrat*. In front of the camera, a visibly pained Kovner answers, "I knew that this question was coming," before asserting that he "refuse[s] to judge" the Jewish leaders.[142] In these final weeks of filming *Shoah*, Lanzmann also posed the question to Shilansky, who explained that the members of both the resistance and the *Judenrat* were right but that "only history will be able to judge who of us was correct."[143] When he interviewed Bauer, as well as the Israeli economist and politician Ya'akov Arnon, whose uncle had been chairman of the *Judenrat* in Amsterdam, Lanzmann also probed the legacy of hostile attitudes toward the Jewish councils in Israel.

In March 1979, while filming the Warsaw ghetto fighter Gustaw Alef-Bolkowiak only weeks after the French broadcast of *Holocaust*, Lanzmann explicitly posits the Jewish council as a major chapter of his film still in the making. "There is a point that fascinates me and which is very, very important in this film—it's the question of the Jewish councils, the *Judenräte*," he begins before asking Alef-Bolkowiak if, thirty-five years after the events, his opinion on this matter has changed. Akin to Bauer, the resistance fighter, who speaks French with the filmmaker, declares that he cannot generalize. Taking the Warsaw ghetto as an example, he provides a striking counter-representation of the *Judenrat* chairman. "With Czerniaków, there are problems," he affirms before explaining that he committed suicide without warning the resistance that "resettlement" meant death.[144]

The ambivalence voiced by Alef-Bolkowiak in these outtakes is echoed by Todorov's assertion in *Facing the Extreme* that "Czerniaków acted with dignity but without real concern for others."[145] Similarly, Leonard Tushnet notes in his portrait of the Warsaw ghetto chairman, "Ghetto opinion, then and later, was divided about the meaning of Czerniaków's suicide." He illustrates this point by quoting the divergent opinions of a number of Warsaw ghetto personalities, including the poet Itzhak Katzenelson who delivers the harshest judgment. "Czerniaków, the traitor," he writes in his epic poem "The Song of the Murdered Jewish People" composed in 1943–1944, "knew the Angel of Death was waiting for the deportees and he kept his mouth shut."[146] Not only during but also long after the war was Czerniaków subject to accusations leveled against the *Judenrat*—as the excluded 1979 testimony of Alef-Bolkowiak attests in Lanzmann's archive of the catastrophe. Nevertheless, Hilberg's edition of the diary the same year would begin to neutralize the contentious topic of Jewish leadership. In 1985, his "incarnation" of the deceased chairman in *Shoah* would operate an unprecedented rehabilitation of Czerniaków.

Through the mise-en-scène with Hilberg in *Shoah*, Lanzmann defies the classical figure of the hero embodied in the Rapoport monument by forcefully shifting heroism within the highly symbolic Warsaw ghetto from the 1943 uprising to the despair and death of Czerniaków. In so doing, he moves away from postwar politics of memory that simultaneously exalted the resistance while condemning the Jewish council. "I think that to emphasise [*sic*] too much the contrast between the resistance and the *Judenrat* can lead to a completely distorted picture of what was the real situation," Lanzmann observes in the Bauer outtakes.[147] Editing his footage between 1979 and 1985, he effaced this binary opposition through omission, setting aside the many testimonies of resistance fighters and Jewish council officials or their descendants, such as Arnon who, evocative of Arendt, condemns the compliance of the *Judenrat* in front of Lanzmann's camera.

Intent on rehabilitating Czerniaków and reframing traditional heroism, Lanzmann notably excluded the highly cinematic testimonial performance of Hersh Smolar, the Yiddish writer and leading member of the Jewish underground in the Minsk ghetto. The unused testimony of this heroic figure of resistance offers an important counterpoint to the widely known narratives of Warsaw and Vilna. These two ghettos and their "living symbols" of resistance, Zuckerman and Kovner, largely overshadowed the unique story of Minsk, of which Smolar served as the primary storyteller, offering a detailed account in two Yiddish memoirs. In the Minsk ghetto, resistance was widespread. Similarly, rather than organize a revolt, the underground assisted Jews in escaping to nearby forests and joining partisan units. An estimated ten thousand Jews thus reached the forests from the ghetto between 1941 and 1943.[148]

In 1979, Smolar tells this extraordinary tale in front of Lubtchansky's camera over the course of two hours at his home in Tel Aviv. Closeness and admiration permeate this interview devoid of an interpreter (only Corinna Coulmas is present) during which Smolar and Lanzmann sit across from each other at a table, the former speaking in Yiddish—and, at one point, even singing—and the latter in German. "Ah, my son... You are my son!" Lanzmann exclaims mysteriously in a humorous tone when the camera begins to roll. Smolar retorts immediately: "*You* are my son!" Much like this opening performance, Smolar embodies throughout this interview a lively *dertseyler* (storyteller in Yiddish), reminiscent of Eastern European Jewish life and unparalleled in the *Shoah* outtakes. "Performing in Yiddish," writes Jeffrey Shandler in his analysis of language in audiovisual testimonies, "animates not only the survivors but also the language and all that it had come to represent a half century after the Holocaust."[149] In these outtakes, Yiddish functions as an exceptional act of remembrance, staged as much by the survivor as by the filmmaker, who contributes to the performance. He requests that Smolar wear his eyeglasses while telling specific stories. He also joyfully exclaims, "That's fantastic!" when Smolar lays on the table the medals he received after the war. These relics evocative of the unused portion of Richard Glazar's testimony encapsulate Smolar's extraordinary account of heroism and survival.

More than a moving portrait of the Minsk ghetto resistance leader whose face and medals the camera—in homage—frames in close-ups, this excluded testimony distinctly refutes generalized postwar condemnations of collaboration made against the *Judenrat*. "I would like to understand [...] why did these things happen in Minsk and not in Warsaw?" Lanzmann asks the survivor in the middle of the interview regarding the widespread resistance in the ghetto. From the moment the ghetto was established in

FIGURE 2.19. The resistance hero Hersh Smolar displaying his medals (Created by Claude Lanzmann during the filming of *Shoah*. Used by permission of the United States Holocaust Memorial Museum and Yad Vashem, the Holocaust Martyrs and Heroes' Remembrance Authority, Jerusalem)

1941, Smolar explains, the Jewish resistance defined as its primary goal not revolt but escape. Similarly, unlike the Warsaw ghetto, the members of the first Minsk *Judenrat* under the leadership of Ilya Mushkin worked closely with the underground movement until 1942. To further illustrate the cooperation of the resistance and the *Judenrat*, Smolar relates the tragic story of the Purim pogrom: amid the murder of six thousand Jews on March 2, 1942, Jewish council members were hanged in the street. The Germans, he adds, then proclaimed that "the role of the *Judenrat* in Minsk is such that the council is actively an organization of the Jewish resistance." In fact, Mushkin's council had not only assisted the underground in the ghetto, but it also systematically refused to hand over its own people to the Germans for destruction—as Czerniaków would also do in Warsaw in July 1942.[150]

In Lanzmann's archive of the catastrophe, the fantastic performance of the decorated Minsk hero invokes the excluded testimony of Tadeusz Pankiewicz, the legendary Polish pharmacist of the Kraków ghetto later featured in *Schindler's List*. Between 1941 and 1943, Pankiewicz witnessed from the window of his pharmacy the quotidian ghetto brutality, including the first deportations in June 1942. From the day it became enclosed in the ghetto, the Apteka Pod Orłem (Under the Eagle pharmacy), located at Plac Bohaterów

FIGURE 2.20. Tadeusz Pankiewicz with Claude Lanzmann (Created by Claude Lanzmann during the filming of *Shoah*. Used by permission of the United States Holocaust Memorial Museum and Yad Vashem, the Holocaust Martyrs and Heroes' Remembrance Authority, Jerusalem).

Getta 18, served as a hideout for wanted Jews and a secret meeting place for intellectuals, artists, and members of the underground. Immediately following the war, Pankiewicz recounted the two years he spent in the ghetto in a memoir titled *The Kraków Ghetto Pharmacy* (1947).

Nearly two decades later, he retold his story during a one-hour-long interview with Lanzmann in which he exclaimed: "One can't describe in words what I saw there." Left out of the final cut, the testimony of the heroic pharmacist resurfaced in 1994 following the French release of *Schindler's List*. Like *Holocaust* before it, Lanzmann retorted with a bitter critique published, this time, in *Le Monde*. Denouncing in particular Spielberg's decision to focus on the rescue of 1,300 Jews when millions had died, he also reiterated the impossibility of representing the catastrophe through fiction. In the midst of his article, however, he confirms the veracity of Spielberg's fictional reconstruction of the famous Apteka Pod Orłem. "At one point we see a pharmacy in the Cracow ghetto. The pharmacist is called Pankiewicz [...]. Now, that very long-established Polish pharmacy was still there in 1981, when I did my last batch of shooting in Poland. I filmed in the pharmacy and met the pharmacist Pankiewicz himself. So Spielberg has done a proper job. But that's not the real point."[151]

Almost a decade after the release of *Shoah*, the docu-auteur invokes the distinct reenactment he elicited from Pankiewicz in a Kraków pharmacy months before he captured Bomba's exemplary performance in a barbershop in Tel Aviv. Lanzmann interviewed the famous pharmacist not in 1981 but in March 1979. Pankiewicz had retired five years earlier; the Apteka Pod Orłem, for its part, had been closed since 1967. Converted into a bar, this site of memory would eventually be renovated and transformed into a museum that opened in 1983 amid national efforts at reviving the memory of the Holocaust in Poland.[152] Accordingly, Pankiewicz's testimonial performance is entirely staged: Lanzmann elicited a reenactment from him in a rented or borrowed pharmacy in Kraków.

In these outtakes, the interview begins with Lanzmann and Pankiewicz addressing each other directly in German and sitting on a bench in the square where the Apteka Pod Orłem once stood. After fifteen minutes, the footage cuts to a shot of Pankiewicz, now dressed in a white pharmacist's jacket, in front of Plac Bohaterów Getta 18. In the next take, he is standing in a pharmacy where he resumes his eyewitness testimony.

In March 1979, Lanzmann does not elicit an emotional reliving of the past from Pankiewicz as he would from the "barber of Treblinka" months later in

FIGURE 2.21. The reenactment in the pharmacy (Created by Claude Lanzmann during the filming of *Shoah*. Used by permission of the United States Holocaust Memorial Museum and Yad Vashem, the Holocaust Martyrs and Heroes' Remembrance Authority, Jerusalem).

Israel. If these outtakes retrospectively appear as the inspiration for the famous staged scene in *Shoah*, the reenactment captured in Kraków cannot be reduced to the auteur's demands of Holocaust representation. Evocative of Smolar's medals recovered in the archive, Pankiewicz's testimony suggests Lanzmann's intention to pay homage to the heroic pharmacist who would be honored as Righteous Among the Nations by Yad Vashem a decade before being featured in *Schindler's List*. "There were a lot of Jews who built a legend around me," Pankiewicz observes in the closing moments of the interview.[153] In the editing room, the docu-auteur would go on to exclude the well-known story of the Apteka Pod Orłem pharmacist. He would include, instead, the unknown "barber of Treblinka," who subsequently became, by performance alone, "an unforgettable hero" in *Shoah*.

In the end, there would be neither medals nor sites of memory in Lanzmann's narrative of the catastrophe. Rather, the docu-auteur chose to recast heroic action through the eyes of the tragic *Judenrat* chairman whose diary captured between 1939 and 1942 quotidian acts of bravery amid unspeakable horrors. In *Shoah*, Hilberg thus recounts the poignant tale of a woman singer that Czerniaków recorded on January 10, 1940. While redefining courage and resistance in the Warsaw ghetto, the evocation of this anonymous heroine momentarily inverses Lanzmann's gendered *parti pris* in the finished film where women—and their experiences of trauma—remain off-screen:

> There was a lady somewhere in Warsaw in love with a man, and the man was hit, grievously wounded, with his insides coming out. This woman stuffed the insides back with her own hands. She carried the man to a first-aid station. He died. He was buried in a mass grave. She disinterred him and buried him.

CHAPTER 3

Off-Frame

TRAUMA AND THE FEMININE

TEL AVIV, 1979. In the late afternoon, the cinematographer William Lubtchansky stands on a sidewalk filming without sound passersby and cars near the intersection of Ben Yehuda and Gordon Streets in the city center. After a few instants, the camera pans left to slowly reveal a row of shops, then stops in front of a lighting store where a woman is leaning against the open entrance door. By means of a medium long shot lasting almost a minute, Lubtchansky introduces the protagonist and décor of a testimony seemingly improvised in the final weeks of shooting *Shoah*. Devoid of a clapboard, in lieu of which crew members Corinna Coulmas and Bernard Aubouy use their hands, this twelve-minute interview filmed outside of 83 Ben Yehuda Street strikingly omits the name of the survivor. Never uttered in front of the camera, her name only appears in the original work print list used in the editing room: "GOLDBERG, MALKA."

Akin to this omission, Malka Goldberg very briefly alludes to her traumatic experiences during the Holocaust when questioned by Claude Lanzmann. "How is business?" the filmmaker begins in German while the camera fixates in a medium close-up on the survivor, whose smile calls to mind the face of Mordechai Podchlebnik in *Shoah*. Her husband, whom she addresses as Jacob, has joined her in the shop doorway. "Ah, good. [...] It's better than inside the ghetto, than inside the concentration camp," she responds in Yiddish, pointing to the number tattooed on her left arm, which an off-screen Lanzmann asks Lubtchansky to ensure he includes in the frame.[1] "I was [...] in the ghetto, in Majdanek, in Auschwitz, in Ravensbrück, in Malchow," Goldberg then elliptically explains. Instead of probing the extraordinary tale of survival hinted at in these few words, Lanzmann reveals his agenda. "And you were in Warsaw, in the uprising?" he asks, thereby steering the survivor's testimony toward Jewish resistance during the Holocaust and, in particular, the famous 1943 revolt. "Yes, I was in the uprising—a partisan!" Goldberg answers proudly.

In these outtakes, this exclamation marks the end of her first-person account of the catastrophe. The cinematographer cuts in order to reload the camera. When the interview resumes, however, at least an hour has elapsed. Night has fallen and a second (nameless) man now stands behind the couple in the doorway. "You sing!" Lanzmann orders in German, dictating his demands of Holocaust representation in a disembodied voice reminiscent of the Ada Lichtman material. Similar to the taciturn husband of the Sobibór survivor, Jacob Goldberg remains silent while his wife and the other man begin to chant in Yiddish "Undzer shtetl brent! (Our Town Is Burning!)." Composed in 1936 by the poet and native of Kraków Mordechai Gebirtig in response to the growing persecution of Jews in Poland, "Undzer shtetl brent!" (also known as "Es brent") was appropriated in ghettos and camps as a hymn of resistance. After the war, it became a famous commemorative song.

On Ben Yehuda Street in 1979, the staged Yiddish performance of "Undzer shtetl brent!" which calls to mind the testimony of Hersh Smolar, recasts the memory of the Warsaw ghetto through the voices and faces of anonymous survivors, themselves defiant, like the language in which they sing.[2] This mise-en-scène negotiated between two takes captures, as well, the auteur's indefatigable intention to reframe Holocaust testimony through his

FIGURE 3.1. Jacob and Malka Goldberg, as Malka points at the number tattooed on her left arm (Created by Claude Lanzmann during the filming of *Shoah*. Used by permission of the United States Holocaust Memorial Museum and Yad Vashem, the Holocaust Martyrs and Heroes' Remembrance Authority, Jerusalem).

representational dictum. "Again, again!" Lanzmann exclaims in his customary disembodied voice immediately after they finish singing. When they refuse to continue performing in front of the camera, the docu-auteur unexpectedly enters the frame, pleading: "One more time [...] one more time, [...] the same song!"[3] Malka Goldberg and the unnamed man deliver another performance of "Undzer shtetl brent!" before falling silent. The camera continues to roll for a short moment; the interview ends as inexplicably as it began.

A sense of urgency permeates this improvised material in the final weeks of the shooting phase. Epitomized by Lanzmann's anxious insistence and on-screen appearance, the rushed nature of this excluded testimony is further evidenced by the gaps and silences underlying its making. How did Lanzmann find Malka Goldberg? How did he know she would sing in front of the camera? What was said, but never recorded, during the lengthy pause separating her laconic testimony and the staged performance of "Undzer shtetl brent!"? In the editing room, this exceptionally brief footage would, in a way, be forgotten: the interview was never transcribed and the tin can containing the reel was labeled "*Coupes Varsovie* [Warsaw cuts]" and not "Goldberg, Malka." While further evidencing Lanzmann's persisting interest in recasting Jewish resistance in the famous ghetto, the can label gestures toward the very *cut* at play in these

FIGURE 3.2. Claude Lanzmann enters the frame, insisting that Malka Goldberg and the two men perform "Undzer shtetl brent!" again (Created by Claude Lanzmann during the filming of *Shoah*. Used by permission of the United States Holocaust Memorial Museum and Yad Vashem, the Holocaust Martyrs and Heroes' Remembrance Authority, Jerusalem).

outtakes: namely, the way in which his agenda and demands of Holocaust representation displace Goldberg's personal trauma to the margins or periphery of the interview.

"Producing a cut," writes Eyal Peretz in his investigation of the off-frame, "means, at the most basic level, being able to interfere in the composition, directionality, and meaning of something, to expose it to a complete indeterminacy of direction and be able to reorient it, assign it a new meaning."[4] Between two takes, Lanzmann effectively redirects the testimony of the survivor toward the momentary reliving of the past that he, as a docu-auteur, is highly (if not obsessively) invested in eliciting for *Shoah*. At the same time, he silences Goldberg's testimony within the frame: while she remains on-screen for the entirety of the interview, her narrative of the catastrophe is now off, largely consigned to the inaudible beneath the famous lyrics of Gebirtig's song.

Décadrage (deframing): forged by Pascal Bonitzer, this concept designates camera angles and cinematic frames that cut objects and bodies on-screen. In fragmenting and decentering them, *décadrage* pulls the eye to the limits of the frame, to the concealed or unrepresented—the off-screen. Bonitzer thus equates the deframed image to "the place of a mystery, of a suspended, interrupted narrative, of a question eternally without an answer." At the same time, in disrupting stories and points of view, the strategy of *décadrage* evidences "the arbitrariness of the directorial gaze."[5] In the Goldberg outtakes, the docu-auteur's insistence on strictly eliciting a reenactment of "Undzer shtetl brent!" despite the brevity of the interview inadvertently engenders a *décadrage* of its own: while the camera remains fixated on the survivor (and the two men who successively join her), her testimony is irremediably "suspended, interrupted."

Four decades later, Malka Goldberg emerges from the *Shoah* archive as "a messenger of the off-frame" whose displaced tale of survival and process of remembrance encapsulate the deframing of women's narratives in the finished film.[6] This excluded material also calls attention to the myriad ways in which the outtakes, albeit always incompletely, "fill the hole, the *terra incognita*, the hidden part of representation" in recovering missing gendered memories—and in ultimately offering "new arrangements," beyond the trope of reenactment and the exemplary performances of male protagonists, for representing trauma in cinema.[7]

In an influential article published in 1993, Marianne Hirsch and Leo Spitzer duly noted the absence of a feminine perspective in Lanzmann's nine-and-a-half-hour Holocaust opus. Indeed, only five women survivors were included in *Shoah*: Paula Biren, Inge Deutschkron, Ruth Elias, and Gertrude Schneider and her unnamed mother. While they each appear once in the finished film, unlike the majority of the male protagonists who bear witness several times, their combined testimonies amount to a mere ten minutes.⁸ The outtakes of these four interviews, however, exceed ten hours. If the brevity of the unused Goldberg footage anticipates the fleeting presence of women survivors in *Shoah*, the cut effected between two takes outside of 83 Ben Yehuda Street calls attention to the ensuing cuts or choices made by Lanzmann in the editing room between 1979 and 1985: namely, gendered narratives of the Holocaust "suspended, interrupted" in the finished film and recovered in the archive. More than muted voices, however, the most outstanding feature of these unedited interviews is the tragedy of choice—or the incompossible—at the heart of the women's tales of survival that, unseen and unvoiced in *Shoah*, point to the ever-unstated, yet always present choices that constitute the film as it stands.

CHOICE AND SURVIVAL IN THE ŁÓDŹ GHETTO: PAULA BIREN

Panama City, winter 1978–1979. Rather than a close-up of the "survivor of Auschwitz" Paula Biren, as she appears in *Shoah*, the excluded material of her two-hour interview opens with a deframed image reminiscent of Super 8 footage that offers a brief glimpse onto what remains unseen in the finished film. A clapboard that reads "Bob [Lubtchansky]" covers the face of the survivor who sits across from Lanzmann on a Floridian beach where a parked station wagon, at the back of which a crew member is standing, is partially visible. The arms of an unidentified woman holding the clapboard enter the image from the right while her hair is inadvertently blown into the frame by the wind. The scenery revealed in these outtakes bears the imprint of Lubtchansky, who suggested during the making of *Shoah* that they film the interviewees outside. During the same trip to Florida, the cinematographer not only filmed Biren on a beach, but also the Holocaust theologian Richard Rubenstein on a small boat in the wetlands, as well as the former State Department refugee specialist Robert Borden Reams golfing and fishing with Lanzmann. Lubtchansky's directorial influence is hinted at in the unused Biren footage when he makes a rare appearance in front of the camera between takes.

The opening image of this testimony further evidences its making: while the caption in the finished film indicates the location of the interview, reading "Cincinnati," the archive reveals that it actually took place in Panama City. The Auschwitz survivor did in fact live in Cincinnati and remained there until her death on June 26, 2016. According to Biren, Lanzmann asked her to come to Florida after waiting in vain with his crew for a (male) German eyewitness he was scheduled to interview.⁹ Like the Goldberg outtakes, her filmed testimony in the Florida Panhandle was not planned. Yet, in contrast to the footage shot outside of 83 Ben Yehuda Street and never inside the couple's shop, a certain closeness between Lanzmann and Biren, who were born three years apart, permeates the outtakes captured in Panama City.

"Be quiet, nothing happened, we didn't start yet [silence]... I want to make you nervous," Lanzmann begins in an amicable tone when the camera starts rolling. "You want to make me nervous? Thanks... a million!" Biren retorts,

FIGURE 3.3–4. Seeing the making of *Shoah*: the filmmaker, the survivor, and the crew; the cinematographer William "Bob" Lubtchansky (Created by Claude Lanzmann during the filming of *Shoah*. Used by permission of the United States Holocaust Memorial Museum and Yad Vashem, the Holocaust Martyrs and Heroes' Remembrance Authority, Jerusalem).

laughing. Throughout this testimony that takes place first on a beach and then in a hotel room, Lubtchansky emphasizes this sense of closeness with frequent shot-reverse shots of their faces that render the director of *Shoah* much more visible than usual. Twenty minutes into the interview, he also films Biren and Lanzmann speaking and walking side by side along the water. This moment calls to mind the testimony of Benjamin Murmelstein, which Lubtchansky shot two years earlier: after the interview, the cinematographer captured Lanzmann and the sole surviving head of a Jewish council walking together near the Titus Arch in Rome. The similarity between these two moments in the archive is further accentuated by the fact that Lanzmann wears the same sunglasses in the company of Murmelstein and Biren.

In the Murmelstein outtakes, the closeness between the two men progressively emanates over the course of an epic interview nearly twelve hours in length. In the case of Biren, it predates the footage shot in Panama City. The Auschwitz survivor first met Lanzmann at the 1975 Holocaust conference held in New York where Raul Hilberg and Abba Kovner, among others, presented. Rather than Lanzmann finding her for *Shoah*, Biren introduced herself during this conference, which was largely devoted to the question of Jewish councils. When Lanzmann explained that he was searching for survivors, she told him: "You're talking to one."[10] This initial meeting, during which Biren told him her story for the first time ("You once told me...," he says to her toward the end of the filmed interview), informs the dynamics of the outtakes.[11] In front of the camera, the eloquent survivor, who smokes Lanzmann's French cigarettes, largely dictates the terms of her testimony, at times refusing, despite his customary insistence, to answer some of his questions. If the survivor and the filmmaker appear as equals in the excluded material (as Lubtchansky's mise-en-scène and camera movements themselves suggest), the director of *Shoah* explicitly identified with Biren during a 1985 interview with *Cahiers du cinéma*. Explaining that he did not go to Poland until five years into the filming process, he remarked: "I thought much like one of the women in the film who, when I asked her, 'Haven't you ever returned to Poland?' responded, 'What would I see there? Nothing is left.'"[12]

As the transcript used in the editing room reveals, the part of Biren's interview included in *Shoah* is taken from the very end of her two-hour testimony shot at the hotel room (her words audible in the finished film constitute a mere eleven lines in the forty-nine-page annotated transcript). During her brief appearance, as the first woman survivor to speak in the film, she explains her inability to return to Poland upon evoking her grandparents who "died in the ghetto" and "are buried in Łódź." As she tells Lanzmann: "I heard from somebody that visited Poland that they want to level off the cemetery, do away with the cemetery. How can I return to visit then?" As her face is framed in a close-up, the on-screen caption reads, "survivor of Auschwitz." If Auschwitz is silenced in Biren's brief testimony in the finished film because of Lanzmann's editorial decisions, it also displaces the name of the ghetto mentioned by the survivor. More specifically, the extermination camp evoked in numerous testimonies in *Shoah* deframes at this particular moment the

FIGURES 3.5–6. Claude Lanzmann listening to the testimonies of Benjamin Murmelstein in the spring of 1976 and of Paula Biren in the winter of 1978–1979 (Created by Claude Lanzmann during the filming of *Shoah*. Used by permission of the United States Holocaust Memorial Museum and Yad Vashem, the Holocaust Martyrs and Heroes' Remembrance Authority, Jerusalem; *The Four Sisters*, 2017).

memory of the Łódź ghetto and its highly controversial *Judenrat* leader, Mordechai Chaim Rumkowski, whose infamous cooperation strategy consisted in providing forced labor to the Germans and drafting deportation lists.

The caption visible in the finished film actually inverses Lanzmann's investigation in the Biren outtakes: the excluded material focuses almost entirely on the Łódź ghetto into which the Biren family was forcefully moved in February 1940 and where they remained until the very last deportations in August 1944. "We will come to Auschwitz later on," Lanzmann tells her ninety minutes into the two-hour interview, during which the survivor only reveals unsolicited fragments of her traumatic experience in the death camp.[13] By contrast, she provides a vivid and factual testimony of daily life in the Łódź ghetto under "King Chaim," as the Jews nicknamed the head of the Jewish council who perceived himself as their savior. Rumkowski notably created a ghetto currency, whose coins bore his signature, and a Jewish police force comprised of 1,200 individuals in charge of implementing Nazi orders, whether in arresting Jews for petty crimes, such as stealing bread, or in assisting in the deportations.

Although nearly entirely left out of the final cut, Biren's testimony constitutes an extraordinary account of the Łódź ghetto's uniqueness and of the extent to which Rumkowski complied with the Germans. The second largest Polish ghetto after Warsaw and the last one to be liquidated, the Łódź ghetto was "the longest lasting, best organized, and most cut off from the world," as Biren aptly observes in front of

FIGURE 3.7. Claude Lanzmann interviewing Paula Biren in a hotel room (*The Four Sisters*, 2017).

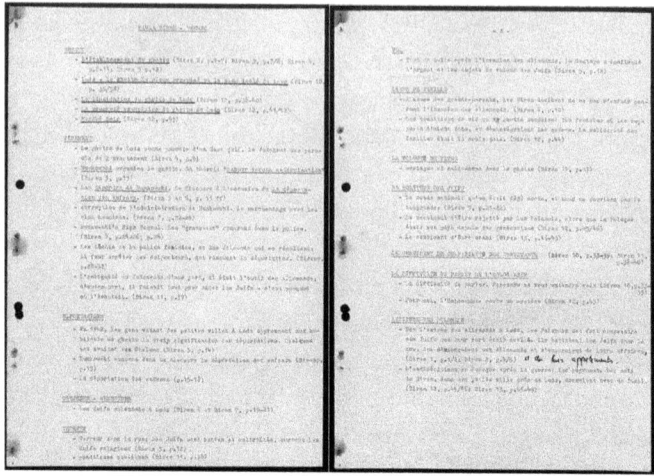

FIGURE 3.8. The two-page list of themes included in the transcript of Paula Biren's interview (Created by Claude Lanzmann during the filming of *Shoah*. Used by permission of the United States Holocaust Memorial Museum and Yad Vashem, the Holocaust Martyrs and Heroes' Remembrance Authority, Jerusalem).

the camera. This sentence is itself bracketed in the transcript of the interview, which contains significant underlining and annotations, including comparisons between Rumkowski and the equally controversial Murmelstein. Unlike other interviews, however, this paper memory of the editing phase is supplemented with a two-page document in French titled "Paula Biren—Themes."[14]

While summarizing Biren's account, this document evidences the intersecting themes of the survivor's testimony and the filmmaker's investigation of varied perspectives on the catastrophe, above all the *Judenrat*, "The difficulty of speaking about the Holocaust," and the "Attitude of the Poles." Unique in Lanzmann's paper archive of thousands of pages of transcripts, this document encapsulates the deep impression the survivor made on the docu-auteur as an exemplary eyewitness of the Łódź ghetto. The significance of her testimony during the making of *Shoah* is further intimated in the existence of a single roll of location filming in Łódź captured several months later, with which the filmmaker could have intercut Biren's testimony in the finished film. This material largely comprised of tracking shots in this non-site of memory strikingly opens with a series of archival images of the ghetto where Biren and her family had been imprisoned.[15]

"Did it happen to you that you occupied, you, in these four years a privileged position?" Lanzmann asks Biren halfway through the interview while discussing acts of corruption within the ranks of the *Judenrat*, the most prominent theme in the two-page document. "Oh, in a way yes," she answers in the outtakes before explaining how, in 1941, she spent her last year of high school on a kibbutzlike farm situated on the outskirts of the ghetto in the Marysin suburb. There, students received agricultural training for a future life in Palestine and enough food, while the rest of the ghetto faced starvation. "So one felt guilty about it," she remarks at that moment, revealing another important theme of her filmed testimony singled out in the two-page document prepared in the editing room.[16] Biren's experience in the early years of the ghetto bears witness to Rumkowski's involvement in Zionist politics, as well as to his genuine interest in working with children and the youth. Before the war, the childless Rumkowski had directed for several years an orphanage in the suburbs of Łódź, to which the farm was attached; in the ghetto, he established schools where the children received a meal a day. Tragically, children could not be protected under Rumkowski's policy of salvation through work, which he had established in 1939—in the period of persecution—following his appointment by the Germans as leader of the Jewish community in Łódź.

When the deportations began in January 1942, his cooperation, to this day controversial, would entail selecting and sacrificing the unproductive members of the population in the hopes of saving the rest. "Either Rumkowski did not realize that the fate of the Jews was sealed or he wished to pretend to himself that there was yet some avenue of salvation open to them," Filip Friedman, whose work Lanzmann consulted during the research phase, observed in a 1954 article, where he likened the *Judenrat* leader to a "dictator."[17] In 1961, Hilberg used the same term in *The Destruction of the European Jews*; for the historian and future protagonist of *Shoah*, Rumkowski's rescue strategy exemplified the tragic compliance of the Jewish councils. In 1986, Primo Levi, too, called attention to Rumkowski's "dictatorship," while concluding his reflection on moral ambiguity and compromise during the Holocaust with no other than Rumkowski's story, which, for him, "sums up the entire theme of the gray zone."[18] Two decades later, Rubenstein, whom Lanzmann filmed in Tallahassee, refuted Levi's attempt at rehabilitating the *Judenrat* leader, declaring: "In Rumkowski the gray zone had turned black."[19]

The two hypotheses put forward by Friedman in the immediate postwar period encapsulate an unanswered question regarding the cooperation of the head of the *Judenrat* in Łódź: In 1942, had Rumkowski become aware of the Germans' genocidal intent? Did he know that "resettlement to the East" entailed deportation to the death camp of Chełmno? In the outtakes, Lanzmann probes this point of contention upon asking Biren what the Jews knew in the ghetto when the deportations began. "This is a very important question," he begins. "We know today that people were killed, they were killed either in Chełmno in the gas vans or in other extermination camps and in Auschwitz too. [...] When did you know?" According to Biren, the inhabitants of the ghetto (herself included) gained knowledge of the extermination in 1942 following the influx of Jewish deportees from western Poland that knew people were being sent to Chełmno. "And Rumkowski himself knew very well," Lanzmann observes in response. "I think he knew, but he wouldn't say it," Biren specifies, exhibiting her testimonial ethics by refraining on several occasions from speaking in the place of another eyewitness.[20]

To illustrate her point, she recalls the darkest chapter in the history of the Łódź ghetto ("the worst moment I lived through," she notes): the "resettlement" of children in September 1942. Evoking Rumkowski's oft-quoted speech—in which he declared, "Fathers, mothers, give me your children!"—Biren remarks: "It was never stated that [the children] will be killed."[21] At this moment of the interview, Lanzmann asks her to detail this tragic episode that resulted in the deportation of twenty thousand "unproductive" Jews, principally the children and the elderly. After they discuss Rumkowski's speech of September 4, 1942, he returns to the critical question of what the Jews knew. "And I would like to know, were there people—I don't say many—who knew, who knew this wasn't the truth [...], that it was to destroy [the children]?" he asks. In her response, Biren reframes this epitome of Rumkowski's compliance through the memory of an unnamed woman:

> Well I had a neighbour [...]. She came I think towards the end of 41 or so, and ... from a little town where ... they liquidated the little town. Her husband was a member of the *Judenrat*. He was killed in [front of] her eyes. She and her little girl that was ten came into the ghetto. [...] She told me everything that happened there. [...] She knew [...]. That they were killing. [...] So, we were collected in the yard and I was next to her, to my friend and her little girl. [...] And then the Germans started to pull out the children. Well, first they started: "All children, talala, come, step out." And many did already. [...] That little girl also made a step forward. [...] And the mother pulled her back and said: "No, you stay here." And a German came to the woman and said: "Put the child." And she says: "No." In German she said: "Nein." And he said: "You better do it or else I shoot you." So she says: "Go ahead and shoot me." So he grabbed her by the neck, turned her around and shot her. So she fell next to me.[22]

In Biren's testimony, the woman's defiance approximates the courage of the "lady somewhere in Warsaw" recorded in Adam Czerniaków's diary and recounted in *Shoah* by Hilberg. At the same time, her refusal to give up her own child accentuates the compliance of Rumkowski who, in his speech, had justified his decision to "perform this bloody operation" (namely, the selection of the children for deportation) by invoking the ultimatum given to him by the Germans—"If you don't do it, we will."[23] Finally, this woman's tragic act of resistance calls to mind the Warsaw ghetto and Czerniaków's refusal, as Hilberg relates in *Shoah*, "to kill the children with his own hands" despite Nazi orders. Contemporaneous with Biren's testimony, Lanzmann's 1979 interview with Hilberg sheds light on his later selection of footage for the final version of his film. No greater contrast exists than that of the willingness of "King Chaim" and the unwillingness of the *Judenrat* leader of the Warsaw ghetto: that is, between a Rumkowski that complied and decided who shall live and who shall die and a Czerniaków who, confronted with an incompossible or the tragedy of choice, took his own life. The latter's rehabilitation in the finished film ultimately demanded the former's exclusion and, inevitably, the exclusion of Biren's recollections of the Łódź ghetto.

When Biren recalls having stood next to her neighbors the day the Germans came to arrest the children, Lanzmann interrupts her and asks: "The Jewish police did not participate?" "I don't recall," she says. "My attention was, you know, paid to the Germans. I saw the Germans." Rumkowski had in fact deployed the Jewish police to conduct the "action" against children and the elderly between September 5 and 12, 1942. However, as Biren's memory of the traumatic event accurately suggests, the ghetto police could not cope with the resistance they encountered from parents. After two days, they arrested so few individuals that the Germans took over and finished the "action" themselves.[24]

The surprise in Lanzmann's question reveals his underlying agenda in choosing to interview the Łódź ghetto survivor for the film he was making: namely, to probe the highly controversial role of the Jewish ghetto police and possibly redeem, contra such scholars as Hilberg, the policemen who, after the war, had been accused of "collaboration" and even tried in Courts of Honor. In *The Destruction of the European Jews*, Hilberg denounced the complicity of the Łódź ghetto police ("the office [of the *Judenrat*]," he writes, "that was most openly destructive in its function").[25] For his part, Isaiah Trunk concludes the section on Łódź in his extensive study of the *Judenrat* by noting, "the fact remains that the Jewish police everywhere, to a larger or lesser degree, participated in the 'deportations' and in the horrid events that went along with them."[26] During the liquidation of the ghetto in the summer of 1944, Henryk

Ross, "the enigmatic photographer from Lodz" (to quote Haim Gouri once more), himself photographed the police escorting Jews for deportation to Auschwitz.²⁷

A somewhat unique and lesser-known component of the Jewish police in the Łódź ghetto was the women's squad. Established by Rumkowski in October 1942, its primary duty consisted in arresting and jailing street vendors.²⁸ As Biren reveals in the excluded portion of her filmed testimony, after having first worked in a factory that made raincoats for the Wehrmacht, she was assigned to work in the administrative office of the female police following its creation by the *Judenrat* leader. "But what was the need for... for a women's police force?" Lanzmann asks in the outtakes. After the survivor details their responsibilities, the docu-auteur reframes his question through a gendered lens. "I ask why women. There were not enough men in the police?" According to Biren, Rumkowski simply found it "neat" to incorporate women within the ranks of the ghetto police. "He was a pioneer, as a matter of fact!" Lanzmann responds, laughing.²⁹ This brief exchange intimates his relative inability to situate—as the survivor nevertheless suggests doing—the women of the Jewish police alongside its male members and to integrate them as complementary voices within his narrative of the catastrophe.

The two-page document subsequently drafted in the editing room includes an entry titled "The tasks of the feminine police and the ensuing dilemmas" under the broader theme of the *Judenrat*. Yet the outtakes reveal a deframing of Biren's own experience and survival in the ghetto. Rather than receive her Holocaust testimony on the women's squad of the Jewish police, Lanzmann attempts several times during the interview to recover the missing voices of the male members. As though anticipating the possible inclusion, in the finished film, of his failed investigation of the Łódź ghetto police, he explains in two back-to-back takes how he tried in vain to record the testimonies of these men who, unlike police squads from other ghettos, "refused categorically to talk [...] as if there would be a big secret."³⁰

The silence encountered by the filmmaker is not surprising. If Rumkowski remains to this day a figure of controversy, the Łódź ghetto police was stigmatized both during and after the war for having chosen compliance. In his investigation of choice and survival during the Holocaust, Evgeny Finkel remarks that those who cooperated with the Germans in ghettos "had few reasons to leave substantial paper trails, to volunteer testimonies, or to agree to oral history interviews. Unlike the other [survival] strategies, most of the evidence here comes *not* from the people who chose this course of action, but from other, often hostile survivors."³¹ A rare published account is the memoir Calel

Perechodnik penned in hiding in 1943, a year before his death, detailing his activities as a member of the Jewish police in the Otwock ghetto near Warsaw. Haunted by guilt and the tragedy of choice, this confessional text includes an affecting account of the liquidation of the ghetto when "the policemen lead their own fathers and mothers to the cattle cars" and Perechodnik brings his wife and daughter to the square where the two are loaded onto a train and deported to Treblinka.[32]

During the making of *Shoah*, Lanzmann sought to interview former policemen of the Łódź ghetto in order to redeem them in his film. "I didn't want to accuse them at all—it's the other way around," he explains in the Biren outtakes.[33] The silence of these men, whom the docu-auteur could not convince to speak in front of his camera, prompts him to ask her several times to elucidate their choices and feelings. Categorically refusing to speak for someone, Biren evokes instead the moral dilemmas faced by the members of the women's squad. In particular, she relates how she learned after patrolling the streets one night with a friend that the same peddlers they were supposed to arrest faced deportation. "So after that night," Biren tells Lanzmann, "I resolved, I am getting out. I can't take that. I had to get out. The other... agony is that if I get out, I have no job. I'll be deported. [...] I didn't need to agonize over that because within a week or so the police was dissolved. But I don't know what I would have done. Stay on or not?" In the excluded material, Lanzmann does not provide a response to Biren's words. Rather, he immediately repositions the policemen at the center of his investigation. "Yes, and do you know something about the feelings of the... of the men, of the Jewish police or not? Did they feel guilt in one way or not?" he asks, silencing the question of choice and survival that defines Biren's own experience in the Łódź ghetto.[34]

When Lanzmann interviewed Biren during the winter of 1978–1979, scholars had yet to integrate feminine voices in their research. The first major conference on women and the Holocaust would be organized by Esther Katz and Joan Ringelheim in New York in 1983. Ringelheim, who had begun collecting oral histories of women survivors in the late seventies and subsequently interviewed Biren in 2005 for the USHMM, published her influential article "The Unethical and the Unspeakable: Women and the Holocaust" shortly after the conference. In this essay, she called for a greater emphasis on and exploration of women's survival strategies in the ghettos and camps.[35] It was not until the late 1980s and early 1990s that a new generation of feminist scholars began to reverse the assumption "that men's experiences were normative and that women were either an addendum or that their specific experiences can shed no broader light onto the Holocaust."[36]

The Biren outtakes evidence this premise underlying Holocaust scholarship in the seventies: rather than deploy the experience of this woman "survivor of Auschwitz" to advance his investigation, Lanzmann returns time and again to the experiences of the Jewish policemen. The docu-auteur would himself have been "a pioneer" (as he jokingly refers to Rumkowski in these outtakes) had he listened and responded to Biren's firsthand account and effectively integrated it into his own narrative of the catastrophe. Ultimately, her excluded memories capture the tragedy of choice that largely defines the history of the Łódź ghetto. Selected for a special transport in the summer of 1944, she opted to hide with her parents and sister. When they were discovered, the entire family was deported to Auschwitz; only Biren survived. "I did find out later, much later," she tells Lanzmann in the final moments of the outtakes, "that a special transport did go to Theresienstadt, and that was a much better way to go ... than to Auschwitz. So you can imagine […] what I went through. It was my decision not to go there. […] what would be if I decided differently? Maybe somebody would survive."[37]

CHOICE AND SURVIVAL IN THE RIGA GHETTO: GERTRUDE SCHNEIDER

New York, November 1978. In an auditorium, members of the Society of Survivors of the Riga Ghetto are gathered for their annual meeting. Lubtchansky films the attendees, the buffet, and the American and Israeli flags hanging on the wall. Lore Oppenheimer, who founded the society in 1970, appears on stage. Upon addressing the crowd to make several announcements, she first asks that they welcome "Mr. Lanzmann from Paris and his film crew." In the next take, the director of *Shoah* is standing in the auditorium, smoking and speaking in English with survivors of the ghetto. The annotated transcript of the event reads: "Interview with three members of the Jewish police in Riga."[38]

Calling to mind the Goldberg outtakes, the unnamed men remain standing during the twenty-minute improvised group testimony. Filmed only weeks before the Biren interview, this footage centered on the Riga ghetto once more conjures narratives haunted by the tragedy of choice. In late November and early December 1941, all but 3,800 Latvian Jews of the thirty thousand incarcerated in the ghetto were massacred. At the same time, twenty thousand Jews from Germany, Austria, and Czechoslovakia were deported to the Latvian capital. They remained in the ghetto until its liquidation in 1943; only eight hundred survived the war. On camera in 1978, the unnamed men recall having been assigned to work in the ghetto police in 1942 in order to replace the Latvian Jews. The latter, who had been spared during the horrific 1941 "action," were

FIGURE 3.9. Claude Lanzmann (right) speaking with three Jewish policemen of the Riga ghetto (Created by Claude Lanzmann during the filming of *Shoah*. Used by permission of the United States Holocaust Memorial Museum and Yad Vashem, the Holocaust Martyrs and Heroes' Remembrance Authority, Jerusalem).

murdered by the Germans in October 1942 in retaliation for their involvement in the ghetto resistance.[39]

At the annual meeting, the three survivors' amicability and willingness to share recollections in front of the camera offers a stark contrast to the silence of the Łódź ghetto policemen Lanzmann would later evoke in Panama City. Similarly, these men who recall having had neither uniforms nor weapons do not appear haunted by the same moral dilemmas. When asked whether they had been "forced to accomplish some unpleasant tasks," one man describes having had to accompany the SS to the cemetery where they executed Jews. Reminiscent of Biren's memory of her neighbor, he recalls an old woman from Berlin who had stolen a piece of bread. In the cemetery, she asked if she could put her coat back on while awaiting execution. As the Jewish policeman helped the woman with her coat, the SS shot her. "I was standing there, holding up the coat," he tells the filmmaker.[40] When Lanzmann later asks the Riga policemen if they "have the slightest guilt feeling," they respond in the negative. First observing that they were given "no choice" upon being assigned to the Jewish police, they then explain that they helped others and also smuggled food into the ghetto.[41]

As this excluded interview suggests, the actions of the Jewish police (and the judgment of other survivors), like those of the Jewish council, differed from one ghetto to the next. Indeed, in a short section of his study *Judenrat* titled "Compassion Among Ghetto Policemen," Trunk notes that memoirs of Riga ghetto survivors "give positive evaluations of the behavior of individual policemen or the police as a whole."[42] In 1978, when interviewing the three Riga policemen, a somewhat puzzled Lanzmann suddenly mentions the making of *Shoah* and the testimonial resistance of the male members of the Łódź ghetto police. "It is the first time, since I am making this enquiry and making this film, that [...] I find people who admit that they were in the Jewish police and who agree to talk. For instance, I have found people of the Lodz ghetto, [...] they are in Israel, they are in America. They don't want to talk," the docu-auteur tells the three policemen before asking, to no avail as he would in Panama City, "Can you explain me why?"[43]

How did Lanzmann know a group of policemen from the Riga ghetto would attend the society's annual meeting? Did the filmmaker and his crew walk around the auditorium in hopes of finding these men? If the group testimony was itself improvised, Lanzmann's presence at the meeting was not. The remaining footage of these outtakes contains a planned interview, notably evidenced by his customary pile of preparatory notes on the table, with the society's founder and president, Lore Oppenheimer, and vice president, Hermann Ziering.[44] This nearly two-hour-long testimony in English recovers a mise-en-scène that is doubly unique in Lanzmann's archive of the catastrophe: neither in the finished film nor in the excluded material do we find another interview where a man *and* a woman appear on-screen as equal eyewitnesses of the catastrophe.

Evoking Vilna survivors Itzak Dugin and Motke Zaidel in *Shoah*, Oppenheimer and Ziering take turns recounting their respective narratives of the years of persecution and extermination. In the finished film, Dugin and Zaidel first tell their story in the Israeli forest of Ben Shemen, where Lanzmann had asked local woodsmen to burn branches in the background in order to invoke "the pyres of burning corpses in Ponari."[45] In the outtakes of the society's annual meeting, however, it is Oppenheimer and Ziering who dictate the limits of representation underlying the mise-en-scène: while they sit across from each other at a table, Ziering speaks with his back turned to the camera in order to conceal his face. His testimonial performance, which offers a poignant counter-representation to the facial close-ups of survivors in *Shoah*, is accentuated by Lubtchansky, who pivots the camera around the witness and tightly frames his face in profile throughout the interview. "You don't want to say why you... you don't want to show your face?" Lanzmann asks Ziering in the closing moments of this excluded footage. "I don't think a face is important,"

Ziering answers in a pained voice. As the camera moves into a close-up of the back of his head and slightly visible profile, he adds with difficulty: "I don't think I... I could give you the... a real explanation how... I... I feel. It's... It's very hard. It's very hard."[46]

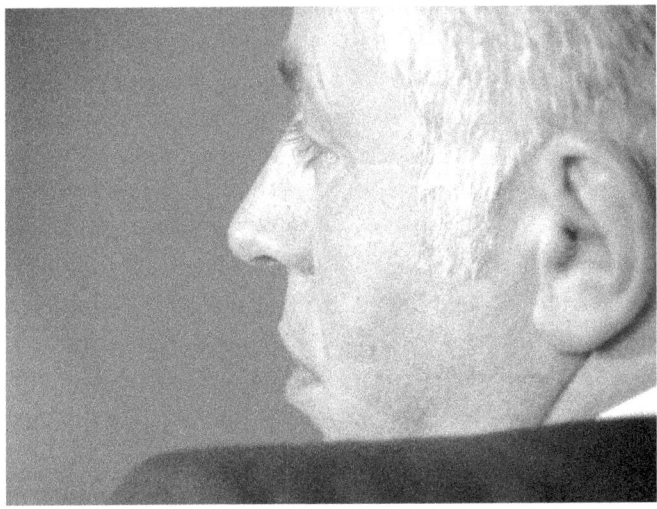

FIGURES 3.10–11. Lore Oppenheimer and Hermann Ziering (close-up) with his back to the camera (Created by Claude Lanzmann during the filming of *Shoah*. Used by permission of the United States Holocaust Memorial Museum and Yad Vashem, the Holocaust Martyrs and Heroes' Remembrance Authority, Jerusalem).

The material captured at the society's annual meeting recovers an investigation, during the making of *Shoah*, of the destruction of the Latvian Jews by the Einsatzgruppen in 1941 and the concomitant deportation of German Jews to the Riga ghetto. In the last half hour of their interview, Oppenheimer and Ziering bear witness to their arrival in early December 1941 as well as to the ensuing revelation that the Latvian Jews had been massacred only days before. "You see a table, you see a table-cloth on it, you see food on the table, you see a shoe on the left hand side, you see a pair of pants on the right hand side, you see blood stains there. And suddenly you come from far away and [the Germans] say: 'This is your home,'" Ziering poignantly recalls, describing their first intimation of the extermination.[47]

Beyond Riga, which was the birthplace of Lanzmann's paternal grandmother Anna, Oppenheimer and Ziering provide a detailed joint testimony of the years of persecution in Germany evocative of Saul Friedländer's concept of an "integrated" history of the Holocaust: namely, "an account in which the Nazi policies are indeed the central element, but in which the surrounding world and the victims' attitudes, reactions, and fate are no less an integral part of this unfolding history."[48] In tandem, Oppenheimer and Ziering recall their memories—many of which are underlined and bracketed in the interview transcript—of the compulsory Jewish star, of Kristallnacht, of the *Kennkarte* (identification card) marked with a capital *J* for Jew, of the adoption of the additional name "Israel" for men and "Sara" for women, of the children's transports to England and Holland, of the deportation of foreign and stateless Jews (including German-born Ziering, whose parents were Polish), and of the suicides leading up to the deportations ("A dozen a day," Oppenheimer specifies in front of the camera).[49] Throughout the interview, Lanzmann demonstrates a deep interest in what he would remember, years later when drafting his description of the unused material for the USHMM, as "fascinating and vivid accounts of the harassment of German Jews before and after the Kristall Nacht [*sic*]."[50] While annotating the transcript in the editing room, he left out the material gathered at the society's annual meeting in 1978 upon reframing his cinematographic investigation through the lens of the extermination.

Eight months before interviewing Oppenheimer and Ziering in November 1978, Lanzmann had traveled to Poland for the first time. This decisive experience is palpable in the outtakes with the Riga survivors when Lanzmann, turning to the chapter of their deportation, mentions his film's "theme of the East." As though projecting his own apprehension of the East he later described in the interview with *Cahiers du cinéma*, he asks twice, "What was the meaning of the East?" before adding: "It was frightening the East?" When neither of the two Riga survivors provide a satisfactory answer, Lanzmann interjects to reveal his agenda. "Yes, no, but [...] for me, it's a difficult question. Because this is what I call in the film the *Ostthema* because, as a matter of fact, the people were not resettled to the west. It was to the east," he explains. Unconvinced, Oppenheimer affirms, "I don't think we gave it much thought," and reminds him that they were still children at the time of their deportation.[51]

In September 1978, several weeks before he headed to New York with his film crew, Lanzmann traveled again to Poland, this time with Simon Srebnik, "the child singer of Chełmno" and native of the Łódź ghetto. (That same month, the docu-auteur also filmed the Jews of Corfu singing in a synagogue.) In *Shoah*, Srebnik relives the traumatic past by returning to the extermination camp and singing the melodies he had once sung for the Germans. Traces of this verbal reenactment subsist in the outtakes with the Riga survivors when Ziering recalls having had to report daily as a boy to the police station in Kassel following the invasion of Poland in September 1939. It was at this moment that Ziering, along with his Polish-born family, became "the enemy of the Reich." As he explains to Lanzmann, every morning at the station, a police sergeant demanded that he repeat his full name, which by then included the mandatory "Israel." "Can you say it in German how... how you had to do it every day?" the docu-auteur asks, prompting the survivor to momentarily reexperience the past through this linguistic change. "*Ich bin der Jude Hermann Kempinsky* [I am the Jew Hermann Kempinsky]... No... Hermann Israel Kempinsky," he first says. At Lanzmann's request, he repeats the phrase several times over two different takes, while also suddenly detailing this episode in German. Bearing the imprint of the docu-auteur, this entire exchange is bracketed in the interview transcript.[52]

This moment in the excluded testimony of Oppenheimer and Ziering anticipates the reenactment captured by the camera only days later during Lanzmann's interview with Riga survivors Gertrude Schneider and her (unnamed) mother in New York. In *Shoah*, the testimony of these two women takes the form of a Yiddish song titled "Azoy muss sein (That's the Way It Has to Be)." This exclusively verbal reenactment engenders an emotional reliving of the past for the mother, who cries and buries her face in her hands. "As you can see, my mother doesn't remember the words, but she remembers the songs all right," Schneider observes in the outtakes immediately after they finish singing. She then provides the origin of this melody that, untranslated in the finished film, recounts the end of a love affair and the moment two lovers part. "This was from the Latvian Jews and was very, very poignant—it meant a lot to all of us," she explains to Lanzmann, here invoking the 3,800 Latvians Jews, among them three hundred women, who had been spared during the massacre of November and December 1941.[53]

In his 1995 description of the excluded material, Lanzmann grouped the three Riga survivors under one and the same entry: "Gertrud [sic] Schneider, Mrs. Oppenheim [sic], Mr. Ziering." If he only remembered the daughter and not her mother, the numbered reels of the interviews shot in New York in October and November 1978 reveal that he captured with Schneider two different testimonies, both in English, which amount to nearly two hours of unused material. The first, with her alone, took place a few weeks before the annual meeting organized by the society; the second was recorded after the interview with Oppenheimer and Ziering. The latter includes Schneider's mother, Charlotte Hirschhorn, who passed away in 1982, as well as her younger sister Rita Wasserman, who remains off-frame in the finished film (her voice, however, remains audible in *Shoah* when the women sing "Azoy muss sein").[54]

In the first recording with Schneider, Lanzmann begins the interview in the same way he would weeks later when filming Hilberg in Vermont. Just as he first discusses with the historian his published study of the Holocaust, he starts by asking "Dr. Schneider," as he refers to her in these outtakes, why she chose to write a book on the Riga ghetto. This opening question reveals Schneider's dual perspective on the catastrophe underlying her writings as a whole and unique in Lanzmann's archive of filmed testimonies: that of a historian-eyewitness. When interviewed for *Shoah*, Schneider had just completed a book manuscript based on her doctoral dissertation, *Journey into Terror: Story of the Riga Ghetto* (1979), which incorporated archival documents, survivor testimonies, and the diary she had kept as a thirteen-year-old girl in the ghetto. "There was no actual book on this most unique ghetto," she first observes, here alluding to the fact that, following their deportation, Jews from the Reich formed a community of their own. Unlike in other ghettos in Eastern Europe, they were physically isolated from the Latvians Jews who were housed in a separate section of the Riga ghetto.

In front of the camera, Schneider details the tragedy of choice that defined their arrival: "[*Journey into Terror*] brought to light certain of the things that had bothered me already then, as an inmate, and bothered me later, when I started to learn more about the Holocaust itself. Like why we were selected to live, and for instance, the Latvian Jews were killed." Asked to elucidate the nature of her book ("Do you think it is an exemplaire [sic] book, a classical book about the Holocaust, about this particular theme...?"), she defines *Journey into Terror* as "a minute detail of the vast theme of the Holocaust." Her phrasing calls to mind how Lanzmann would eventually edit *Shoah* so as to turn it from a broad investigation of the catastrophe into a minutely detailed depiction of the extermination process (Lanzmann's and Schneider's parallel approach is further accentuated in the excluded footage by the fact that they consulted some of the same archival documents for their respective research).[55]

In these outtakes, Schneider provides a vivid and exhaustive account of the German Jews' arrival and their life in the ghetto, which likely influenced the director's decision to center his interview with Oppenheimer and Ziering on the years of persecution in Nazi Germany instead of on their deportation to Riga. His interest in Schneider's testimony and her twofold perspective as a historian-eyewitness is evidenced in the transcript: in addition to extensive underlining and bracketing of entire pages, this document also contains highlighted sentences, beginning with the inaugural exchange around *Journey into Terror* (the summary of the transcript in French, which is several pages long, also contains annotations and highlighting). Akin to the excluded portion of Biren's interview, however, Lanzmann edited out almost the entirety of the Schneider footage. Effacing, as he did with Łódź, his investigation into the "unique" case of Riga (in the finished film, an unspecific caption for Schneider and her mother reads "survivors of the ghetto") and the historian-eyewitness's unparalleled intertwining of public and private memory, Lanzmann only retained his authorial imprint in *Shoah*—the reenactment of "Azoy muss sein" during his second interview with Schneider and her family. In this footage, much like in the Biren material, the story of the women's survival beyond the Riga ghetto is never told in front of the camera.[56]

Unlike the testimony captured in Panama City, Lanzmann does not appear on-screen in the Schneider outtakes. Sitting across from the historian-eyewitness, his presence from beginning to end takes the form of a disembodied voice reminiscent of the barbershop scene with Abraham Bomba. Schneider is seated in the same place in both interviews; she knits while being filmed with her mother and sister. Calling to mind Ada Lichtman's needle and thread, this gesture encapsulates the movement of memory or weaving of testimony. It also accentuates the intimacy underlying this "family frame" (to borrow the title of Marianne Hirsch's influential book on photography and postmemory).[57] At the same time, it foreshadows Schneider's role throughout this second interview where, sitting in the center, she literally holds the threads of familial memory, particularly by singing a total of seven songs, sometimes twice.

Her mother, visibly upset at different points of the interview, remains for the most part silent: sometimes briefly singing and smiling, sometimes waiving her hand in disbelief at the lyrics being sung, sometimes covering her face with her hands, she interjects at different moments in order to mention the world's indifference or her deceased husband, who perished at Buchenwald in the final

FIGURES 3.12–13. Gertrude Schneider (center), Charlotte Hirschhorn (right), and Rita Wasserman (close-up) singing "Azoy muss sein" in the outtakes; in the finished film, Wasserman remains off-frame (Created by Claude Lanzmann during the filming of *Shoah*. Used by permission of the United States Holocaust Memorial Museum and Yad Vashem, the Holocaust Martyrs and Heroes' Remembrance Authority, Jerusalem).

days of the war. Schneider's sister, Rita Wasserman, sits apart from the rest of the family and often observes the film crew, all the while readily answering Lanzmann's questions about their life in the ghetto. Yet when solicited, along with her mother and sister, to perform songs from the ghetto, she sings in a quiet voice with a sad expression on her face, at times only mouthing the words she clearly remembers. "And so we sang, and so we suffered…," Schneider declares after finishing the last of the seven songs that, combined, encompass nearly two-thirds of the entire interview. "… And so we died," Rita Wasserman immediately adds.[58]

If these outtakes recover a distinct portrait of two generations of women survivors, they also capture the docu-auteur at work. Unbeknownst to the three women, who resume their testimony after the first song only to be immediately prompted to strike up another melody from the Riga ghetto, this excluded material suggests that Lanzmann had intended to solicit a specific testimonial performance during his second interview with Schneider. Following a discussion on forced abortions in the ghetto, Lubtchansky cuts in order to recharge the camera; when the footage resumes, two cameras are now filming, a rare technical change that is even recorded in the interview transcript. "But tell me about the songs, you used to sing in the ghetto in which circumstances?" Lanzmann begins, steering, twenty minutes into the interview, the women's testimony toward a reenactment reminiscent of Srebnik's performance in Chełmno he had captured weeks before.[59]

In *The Patagonian Hare*, Lanzmann recalls that, during a preliminary meeting at Srebnik's home in Ness Ziona, he learned that the Chełmno survivor had once sung for the Germans. "*Mały biały domek w mej pamięci tkwi…*[A little white house sticks in my memory…]," Srebnik began to sing in Polish. The docu-auteur then decided to take the survivor back to Chełmno in order to film him performing songs in a boat on the river (in the opening moments of *Shoah*, Srebnik can be heard and seen singing this same Polish song).[60] In his memoir, Lanzmann never mentions Schneider nor how he learned that she had sung in the Riga ghetto. Perhaps he inquired after reading the manuscript of *Journey into Terror* where she devotes a chapter to cultural activities, including songs composed and concerts performed in the ghetto.[61] Schneider's musical memory, however, precedes her traumatic experience in Riga. In the preface to her 2000 edition of Mordechai Gebirtig's songs, she recalls having learned Yiddish melodies as a child from a Jewish Polish housekeeper who, every fall for several weeks, visited family in her native Kraków. Upon returning to Vienna, she would bring back with her new songs. "The last such absence occurred in the fall of 1937," writes Schneider. "She taught me a new song, and while it seemed quite sad to me, it had an interesting effect on her. Whenever she sang it, she stopped whatever she was doing and grew thoughtful. The name of that new song was '*Es Brent.*'"[62]

In front of the camera in November 1978, Schneider never sings the Yiddish melody Lanzmann would ask Malka Goldberg to perform on Ben Yehuda Street the following year. Rather, she limits her repertoire to melodies the three women had intoned in the Riga ghetto, beginning with a moving adaptation of the famous German resistance song "Die Moorsoldaten" ("The Peat Bog Soldiers"), which was originally composed in the thirties by concentration camp inmates. In the cinema verité classic *Chronicle of a Summer* (1961), a film Michael Rothberg considers "an unacknowledged predecessor of *Shoah*," the Holocaust survivor Marceline Loridan-Ivens briefly chants "Die Moorsoldaten" in French in the midst of her filmed testimony.[63]

"I consider [it] really, very, very much the ghetto-song," Schneider tells Lanzmann in the outtakes, before explaining that in Riga they had modified the final lines of "Die Moorsoldaten" to capture their deportation: "*Denn uns hat man verbannt / In ein fernes Land / Als Juden* [Then we were banished / To a foreign place / As Jews]." Momentarily lapsing into German, thereby revealing his intention to engender an emotional reliving of the past, the docu-auteur interrupts the survivor. "*Können Sie*....Could you sing it? [...] *Aber* [but]...from the beginning!" he exclaims in an imposing tone. As Schneider sings, the two cameras carefully frame this first performance by capturing close-ups of Charlotte Hirschhorn and Rita Wasserman. The former initially murmurs the words before burying her face in her hands as she does in *Shoah* while singing "Azoy muss sein." Visibly pained, the latter looks down silently. When Schneider stops singing, Lanzmann's asks that she continue. "I would like.... your mother [to sing]!" he declares emphatically, a hint of impatience in his tone. "And you too, please!" he says to Rita Wasserman, further affirming his authorial intentions.[64] Schneider's singing prompts the same emotional reaction from her mother who, when hearing the line, "*Heimat, du bist wieder mein* [Homeland, you are once again mine]," waives her hand in disbelief.

In these outtakes, the two performances of "Die Moorsoldaten" serve as a rehearsal—both for the survivors and the film crew operating the two cameras—for the reenactment of "Azoy muss sein" that immediately follows. In the finished film, Lanzmann excluded the famous German song of resistance and included instead the unknown Yiddish melody composed by the Latvian Jews whose story of destruction he had originally envisaged as a chapter of

obligée de se faire avorter, même au 8ème mois. L'avortement était fait par un
Juif letton, Dr. Josef, qui devait en même temps stériliser la femme. Il a es-
sayé de ne pas toujours le faire, mais souvent il n'avait pas le choix. Une
femme allemande avait demandé de se faire tuer avec son bébé, mais on ne l'a
pas fait. Souvent, les bébés étaient vivants - alors on les jetait dans les
toilettes; p.30à32 Quant aux rapports sexuels, le Hausvertrauensmann était
un soir venu leur lir lire la déclaration - les gens au ghetto faisaient des
blagues à ce sujet. Comme les sexes n'ont jamais été séparés, cet ordre n'a
jamais été appliqué. Il n'y avait pas de contrôles. Schneider pense que c'était
fait pour leur montrer à quel point ils étaient des soushommes. p.33/34
Malgré l'interdiction, quelques enfants sont nés dans le ghetto, par exemple
le fils d'une Juive lettonne, qu'elle appela Moshe ben Ghetto. Elle l'a ca-
ché pendant une longue période, mais finalement les Allemands l'ont trouvé
et tué. p.35/36 Il y avait, au ghetto, un autre endroit où les femmes pou-
vaient se faire avorter, sans contrôle allemand et donc sans risque de se
faire stériliser. On appelait une grossesse, dans le jargon du camp, une apen-
dicite avec mains et pieds. p.36 Il y avait ux aussi des cours préventifs con-
trei les maladies vénériennes - autre prétexte pour la stérilisation. p.36/37

Bobine 256 et 256A (deux caméras)x, NY 94 et 94A
Les chansons.
Moorsoldaten; Asoi muss es sein; p.37 à 40
Ein Mädchen liegt im Spital p.41
Chanson sur le troc à la gare de Schirotawa p.42/43
Chansons de Vilna: In der Hejm. p.44

Bobine 258 et 258 A, NY 96 et 96A
Schneider: Le 25 Septembre 1943, un transport de Vilna est arrivé à Kaiserwald
avec beaucoup de jeunes. Quelques jeunes filles d'un grand talent chantaient
toutes ces chansons, et nous avions la nostalgie pas seulement de chez nous,
mais aussi du ghetto, parce que Kaiserwald était beaucoup plus dur: mainte-
nant, hommes et femmes étaient séparés, et nous avions très peu d'espoir. p.45
Explique le contenu d'une chanson où une fille en prison pense à la vie libre.
La mère dit: Et tout le monde le savait et a laissé faire. On nous a abondonné
- c'est une honte. p.46
Schneider chante la chanson. p.46/47
Chanson russe - un soldat dit Au revoir. p.47
MALE BIALE DOMEK p.48 C'était une chanson que les filles de Lodz avaient em-
menéexxx de chez elles. p.48

FIGURE 3.14. A page from the French summary of the Gertrude Schneider interview with "Les chansons [the songs]" highlighted and an arrow pointing to "MALE BIALE [sic] DOMEK" at the bottom (Created by Claude Lanzmann during the filming of *Shoah*. Used by permission of the United States Holocaust Memorial Museum and Yad Vashem, the Holocaust Martyrs and Heroes' Remembrance Authority, Jerusalem).

his Holocaust opus. From these outtakes, Lanzmann also omitted a poignant coincidence that further accentuates the cinematographic filiation between the testimonial performance of Srebnik in Chełmno and that of Schneider, her mother, and her sister in New York. Asked if they know any Polish songs, Schneider begins to sing the very melody with which *Shoah* would open: "*Mały biały domek...*" When she sees Lanzmann's astonished (off-screen) face, she interrupts herself and exclaims with surprise: "You know it? [...] Why, when did you hear it?" Rather than reveal that he had just recorded Srebnik singing this melody in Chełmno, the familiar disembodied voice of the docu-auteur simply replies: "Please, go on, sing it."[65]

CHOICE AND SURVIVAL IN AUSCHWITZ: RUTH ELIAS

Theresienstadt, March 1979. One late afternoon, Lubtchansky films out the rear left window of a moving car as it traverses the largely deserted fortress town. These tracking shots revealing the occasional child and soldier walking the streets also catch glimpses of the railroad tracks—framed in a close-up—leading to the former camp-ghetto of Theresienstadt (Terezín in Czech). These tracks call to mind the non-sites of memory or places of extermination devoid

FIGURE 3.15. A tracking shot of Theresienstadt in 1979 (Created by Claude Lanzmann during the filming of *Shoah*. Used by permission of the United States Holocaust Memorial Museum and Yad Vashem, the Holocaust Martyrs and Heroes' Remembrance Authority, Jerusalem).

of traces of the past with which Lanzmann juxtaposes in the finished film the voices of survivors. With the exception of the crematorium on the outskirts of town and the large menorah-shaped memorial in the Jewish cemetery that Lubtchansky later captures, nothing remains of the Nazi era on this single roll of location filming in Terezín that was eventually left out.[66]

"In my eyes, the case of Theresienstadt was capital, both lateral and central, in the genesis and process of the Final Solution," Lanzmann declared nearly four decades later in the prologue of *The Last of the Unjust*, in reference to the Benjamin Murmelstein interview. With these words, he also intimates his broader investigation, while making *Shoah*, of the camp-ghetto, an assembly area for western Jews en route to the East and a tool of deception used by the Germans who described it as a "spa town" where the elderly would retire. They also featured this "model ghetto" in the 1944 propaganda movie *The Führer Gives the Jews a City*. In this film, scenes of children playing and inmates happily working had been staged for the visit, in June of that year, of representatives from the Red Cross, among them Maurice Rossel, the protagonist of Lanzmann's documentary *A Visitor from the Living*, who "saw nothing" of the Nazi propaganda. Akin to the exclusion of Murmelstein and Rossel from the finished film, only mere traces of the docu-auteur's investigation of the camp-ghetto subsist in *Shoah*.

In the finished film, Ruth Elias briefly recounts her deportation from Theresienstadt to Auschwitz in December 1943. Rudolf Vrba, for his part, describes the "family camp" established three months earlier at Auschwitz. Two separate transports of Czech Jews from Theresienstadt—including Elias—had been regrouped in the extermination camp without any selection. They were even allowed to keep on their civilian clothes. Vrba relates in *Shoah* the tragic story, reminiscent of Czerniaków in Warsaw, of Fredy Hirsch. Already in the Youth Welfare Department in Theresienstadt, Hirsch had attempted to remove children from deportation lists.[67] Aware that the children, for whom he organized classes and activities in the "family camp," would likely perish during the 1944 prisoner revolt at Auschwitz, he committed suicide. Weeks later, in March 1944, the deportees of the first transport from Theresienstadt were exterminated. In *Shoah*, the Czech native and member of the *Sonderkommando* Filip Müller recalls in tears how these same Jews began singing the Hatikvah and the Czech national anthem after having entered the gas chamber. In her largely unedited testimony, Elias evokes a similar memory: in the "family camp," which was situated only four hundred meters from the crematorium, the remaining Czech Jews from Theresienstadt could hear their compatriots. "The moment we heard the Hatikvah being sung we knew these people were going to die," she tells Lanzmann in the outtakes.[68]

The investigation of Terezín during the making of *Shoah* is further evidenced in the excluded testimony of Andre Steiner, a Czechoslovakian-born architect and member of the Bratislava Working Group, an underground organization established in 1942. Filmed over two days in Atlanta during the fall of 1978, this interview centers on Steiner's rescue operations, in particular the so-called "Europa Plan," which he undertook alongside the group's coleaders Gisi Fleischmann and Rabbi Michael Dov Weissmandl. The "Europa Plan" included negotiations with the Germans between 1942 and 1943 to halt deportations in Europe in exchange for two million dollars. In this unused footage, Steiner describes, as well, their attempt to rescue from the death camps a thousand children from Białystok and send them to Palestine—a story Murmelstein had himself recounted at length during his 1976 interview.[69] Instead of being "resettled" to the East, the children were deported to Theresienstadt in August 1943 where, taken to the showers after their arrival, they reportedly began to scream, "Gas! Gas!" (as Lanzmann remarks in the Murmelstein outtakes, it would appear that, in Białystok in 1943, people knew of the extermination). In the camp-ghetto, they were separated from the rest of the population and cared for by specifically selected counselors, among them Franz Kafka's sister Ottla. Two months later, when the rescue organization failed to gather the sum promised to the Germans, the children and their counselors were sent to their death.

Steiner's recollection of this specific rescue mission engenders a rare moment in the archive where the filmmaker turns the camera on himself, as he would decades later in *The Last of the Unjust*. When Steiner finishes the story of the Białystok children, a seemingly annoyed Lanzmann, off-frame at that moment, turns to Lubtchansky and exclaims in French: "*Coupe! Ça ne va pas du tout!* [Cut! This isn't working!]." Once the interview resumes, the camera has shifted from a medium close-up of Steiner to a medium shot of the two men who sit facing each other around a coffee table where their respective notes are scattered. As if he were envisaging, in these final weeks of 1978, that he might include the Terezín investigation into the finished film, Lanzmann references on-screen the making of *Shoah*. He strikingly reveals having visited, in the winter of 1975 and long before he would go to Poland for the first time, the camp-ghetto—a detail that further attests to his conception of this site as "capital" in the destruction process. "I went myself to Theresienstadt," he tells Steiner. "I was there with a Czech Jew who was a former inmate […] and he told me that a transport of children came from Białystok. This means from the

FIGURE 3.16. Claude Lanzmann telling Andre Steiner about the making of *Shoah* and his investigation of the transport of children from Białystok to Theresienstadt (Created by Claude Lanzmann during the filming of *Shoah*. Used by permission of the United States Holocaust Memorial Museum and Yad Vashem, the Holocaust Martyrs and Heroes' Remembrance Authority, Jerusalem).

East and generally the transports were all going from West to East and not from East to West."[70]

Reminiscent of the "theme of the East" referenced in the footage with Oppenheimer and Ziering that permeates many of testimonies filmed for *Shoah* ("It was frightening, the East?" Lanzmann asks Elias in the outtakes), his fascination with this transport and its unique destination westward is further attested in Saul Friedländer's 1978 autobiography, *When Memory Comes*.[71] In the few pages dedicated to the making of *Shoah*, the historian evokes the "unknown" story of the Białystok children, noting, as Lanzmann might have upon telling him about the Murmelstein interview: "an unusual movement, from east to west, from centers of rapid extermination to a more merciful transit camp."[72] In the finished film, Lanzmann would structure his investigation of the catastrophe around the "theme of the East," omitting not only the children's journey westward but also the West more broadly, including his native France.

He retained, however, the leitmotif of children during the Holocaust—a leitmotif invoking what Julia Kristeva identifies in *The Powers of Horror* as the apex of "the abjection of the Nazi crime."[73] He thus included not only the testimonial performance of the "child singer of Chełmno" Srebnik as the opening sequence of *Shoah* but also the parallel choices of Czerniaków in Warsaw and

Fredy Hirsch in the "family camp" at Auschwitz. In the largely unedited testimonies of women survivors, this leitmotif permeates Biren's memories of the Łódź ghetto; the experiences of a young Schneider and her sister in Riga; and, even, the mise-en-scène of the Lichtman outtakes. It also encapsulates the tragedy of choice—or the incompossible—in Elias's testimony, which was filmed by Lubtchansky at her home in Tel Aviv during the final weeks of the shooting phase.

In their important essay on the absence of a gendered perspective on the Holocaust in Lanzmann's film, Hirsch and Spitzer observe that the Jewish women included in the final cut are largely off-frame. "They themselves appear onscreen on only a few, and extremely brief, occasions. And even when they do appear, even when their voices are heard, the camera seems to shy away from sustained focus on their faces."[74] In *Shoah*, Elias's voice describing her deportation to Auschwitz is at first juxtaposed with evocative footage of a moving train. "In Theresienstadt," she begins off-screen, "this time it reached us, the transport to the east, we were loaded into these wagons for cattle, and it went for two days and one night." She only then appears on-screen, the camera slowly moving from a medium shot showing her sitting outside at a table to a close-up of her face while she details her arrival at Auschwitz.

If her face is not immediately visible in *Shoah*, the outtakes reveal that her appearance in this segment is dictated by Lanzmann's meticulous editing around her testimony. Seamless and evidencing the "theme of the East," her off-screen description is in fact truncated in order to omit her gendered trauma: shortly before her deportation from Theresienstadt to Auschwitz, Elias discovered she was pregnant; unable to obtain an abortion, she arrived in the death camp expecting a child. The following crossed-out text renders visible Lanzmann's gendered editorial choices. "~~So~~ this time it reached us, the transport to the East, ~~and I knew I was pregnant and could not do anything.~~ We were loaded into these wagons for cattle," Elias recounts in the outtakes before detailing the horrific conditions, also omitted from *Shoah*, during the journey (the first two words of her testimony included in the film, "In Theresienstadt," are taken from an earlier section and circled in the noticeably largely unannotated transcript of her interview).[75] The exclusion of her pregnancy during her brief appearance in *Shoah* also entailed the exclusion of her gendered firsthand account of the "family camp" at Auschwitz: rather than detail how the prisoner revolt was organized (like Vrba would do), or how exactly the Czech Jews were exterminated (like Müller would remember), Elias chronicles her efforts to conceal her growing belly in order to survive.

The first take of Elias's largely unedited testimony opens with silence. While the camera captures a medium shot of the survivor, a German shepherd by her side and sheets of paper in front of her (two details deframed in *Shoah*), an off-screen Lanzmann, who smokes his customary Gitanes cigarettes, remains quiet for nearly ninety seconds. Suddenly, exhaling, he emits a long sigh. Reminiscent of Bomba's mid-interview affirmation at the barbershop, "I told you it's going to be very hard today," this audible apprehension, much like the largely unannotated interview transcript, is indicative of the difficult narrative to come: namely, a gendered version of survival centered—to borrow a phrase deployed by Lawrence Langer in his analysis of testimonies from the Fortunoff Video Archive—on "maternity infected by atrocity."[76]

As Elias reveals in front of the camera, she had to kill her own child days after having given birth at the death camp. This episode approximates the notion of "choiceless choice" coined by Langer in his earlier examination of Holocaust literature, which he defines as "a crisis [...] where crucial decisions did not reflect options between life and death, but between one form of abnormal response and another, both imposed by a situation that was in no way of the victim's own choosing." In fact, he illustrates this concept through the story of a woman at Auschwitz who witnessed another woman killing the newborn of an inmate in order to save her.[77] Revealed in the final half hour of Elias's nearly three-hour-long interview, the death of her child also emerges as the culmination of horror—or apex of "the abjection of the Nazi crime"—in an

FIGURE 3.17. Ruth Elias during the silent opening moments of her testimony (Created by Claude Lanzmann during the filming of *Shoah*. Used by permission of the United States Holocaust Memorial Museum and Yad Vashem, the Holocaust Martyrs and Heroes' Remembrance Authority, Jerusalem).

extraordinary narrative that spans from her prewar childhood in Czechoslovakia to her postwar exile in Israel. Hers is a narrative that encompasses the "capital" site of Theresienstadt, the unique "family camp" at Auschwitz, and the selections and experiments undertaken by Josef Mengele.

Further evidencing Lanzmann's investigation, Elias devotes nearly half of her testimony to her imprisonment in the camp-ghetto between April 1942 and December 1943. On camera, she never relates the tragic story of the Białystok children recounted before her by Murmelstein and Steiner (in her memoir first published in 1988, however, Elias reveals that she had briefly been assigned to care for these children, recalling their screams in the showers).[78] Rather, she first describes her work as a nurse in the geriatric department for several months where she cared for the dying elderly at night. "I was confronted with death for the first time, and I was not even twenty," she explains. "It was not one death a night; it fell on me, 2 or 3 people, and I had to pick them up and carry them away to the '*Leichenhalle* [morgue].'"[79]

Elias describes her experience at the request of the filmmaker who appears particularly intent on representing the Nazi strategy of deception deployed in Theresienstadt. "It's funny because I have just written here: 'the old people,' because I wanted you to talk about this," an off-screen Lanzmann first asks, audibly leaning over his notes on the table. As Elias begins to answer that she only briefly worked in the geriatric department, he interrupts her and discloses his agenda: "Could you describe how they lived? Because they came with illusions to Theresienstadt. They were even told you can rent a room in the sun, and so on." Over the course of the next ten minutes, he repeatedly returns to this question, hoping that the survivor, who finally changes topics, can bear witness to the experiences of the elderly dying en masse in the camp-ghetto.[80] In her depiction of Theresienstadt, Elias focuses instead on her work in the kitchen. There, she not only cooked but also sang in the company of other women. She reenacts these memories in the excluded footage by singing several songs in Czech. In contrast to the Schneider outtakes where the three Riga survivors are prompted repeatedly to perform melodies from the ghetto, Elias integrates these songs as part of her filmed testimony. "I will sing," she tells Lanzmann before adding, "if you allow, I will take the accordion and accompany myself, ok [*sic*]?"[81]

Elias concludes her detailed account of working in the camp-ghetto kitchen with an anecdote that functions as a momentary screen memory of her pregnancy, which she reveals immediately after. Remembering, her voice animated, how the women would steal pieces of dough and hide them behind their aprons, she relates that, one day, the dough behind her own apron began to rise from the heat of the kitchen. "I was growing and growing and all the kitchen was laughing," she says, amused.[82] The image of both her growing belly and the women at her side anticipates the female solidarity that defines her subsequent account of survival as a pregnant woman in Auschwitz. In this narrative, the men of her family—her father who had been deported to the East from Terezín before her and her husband, Koni, who had been deported with her to the "family camp"—disappear entirely. "And where was your husband?" Lanzmann suddenly interjects, when Elias describes her first winter at Auschwitz. "In the '*Familienlager*' it was like this: on one side were women and on the other side were men. We saw each other, we talked together. In the evening it was allowed for one hour," she explains, never mentioning again in these outtakes her husband, who we are left to assume did not survive.[83]

In her testimony, the image of a clear separation between the two sexes in the "family camp" communicates the irremediably gendered isolation the survivor felt as a pregnant woman at Auschwitz. A silence, however, haunts Elias's response in front of the camera. During a preliminary interview with Lanzmann, she had described her sense of alienation from her husband. Recovered by the archive, this unrecorded story surfaces not in the Elias footage but in the closing moments of the Schneider outtakes. Turning to the traumatic memory of their deceased father who perished in Buchenwald and their perception of this event as children, Lanzmann asks Schneider and her sister: "How does one experience this, when one is a child or an adolescent, to … to feel that your parents are completely powerless? […] was [sic] there … among the children reactions of … hatred or despise against the parents?" "No, no," Rita Wasserman exclaims, somewhat perplexed by the question. She then adds: "one loved them even more." In order to elucidate his reasons for posing the question, Lanzmann evokes an interview he conducted with a woman survivor living in Israel who had had such a reaction. "It was [against] the husband … [Paula] Biren," his off-screen assistant Irena Steinfeldt corrects him at the moment. "Biren? Yes, she was in Lodz. She said that," Lanzmann affirms. At once incredulous and intuitive, Schneider's sister responds: "She must have some other reason, maybe something happened there, that she didn't say."[84]

The woman survivor remembered by the director of *Shoah* and his assistant is in fact not Biren but Elias, whose pregnancy he does not disclose to Schneider and her sister. In turn, everything Elias herself does not say in the outtakes she discloses in her memoir, *Triumph of Hope*. Evoking the one-hour evening meetings with her husband in the "family camp," she writes: "After a while we scarcely had anything to say to each other. Even though it was his child that I was carrying, Koni didn't seem at all interested in my condition. Why didn't he have a single word of encouragement for me, a little consolation? How I longed for some understanding and sympathy. His indifference was hard to bear."[85] In 1979, Lanzmann's question "And where was your husband?"—which he asks with his preparatory notes in front of him—suggests an attempt to capture on camera what Elias had once told him, which he misremembered during his interview with Schneider and her sister. Concomitantly, Elias's silencing response conveys her painful isolation as a pregnant woman in the death camp, all the while bearing witness to a narrative of the extreme centered on the individual will to survive. "I have got a very long story," she tells Lanzmann in the middle of the interview, "but you will see how the will to live is so very strong."[86]

One male figure does loom over Elias's account: the infamous camp physician Mengele. "How was he? How was Mengele?" Lanzmann asks her when she describes a selection in the *Frauenlager* [women's camp] to which she had been transferred shortly after the liquidation of the "family camp" in July 1944. "How did he look?" he specifies. "I will tell you a little later, ok [*sic*]?" she responds, unwilling to interrupt her narrative of survival. In Lanzmann's archive of the catastrophe, Elias is the only survivor to bear witness to Mengele's selections and experiments at Auschwitz. While this unique testimony remained unused, other outtakes suggest that Lanzmann might have envisioned including an account of the atrocities committed by the Nazi physician who, after the war, escaped to South America. On July 5, 1979, while filming former SS officers in West Germany using the Paluche, Lanzmann improvised interviews with anonymous workers at the Mengele family factory, an agricultural machinery firm located in Bavaria. This twenty-minute-long footage consisting of three short conversations was shot two days—as the filmmaker tells a worker—after the Bundestag had abolished the statute of limitations for Nazi crimes. Lanzmann asks the men if they know of Mengele and his horrific medical experiments. Captured several months following the screening of the miniseries *Holocaust* in West Germany, an oft-cited turning point in the Germans' awakening conscience, which also incited the debate on whether the statute of limitations should be abrogated or not, this excluded material emphasizes a persistent denial.[87]

Over the course of these brief interviews during which Lanzmann evokes twice the children killed in Mengele's experiments (in the transcript, the first mention of the children is bracketed), one by one the workers claim to not know anything of the crimes perpetrated by the Nazi doctor. The first worker observes, in regard to the persecution and extermination of the Jews, that "it's over"; the second one tells Lanzmann that Auschwitz was "partly good, partly bad."[88] This excluded material that was recorded only weeks before Elias would be filmed in Israel evidences a search for a form: namely, a possible montage in *Shoah* between the survivor's memory of Mengele and the collective German silence at the factory. Left out, the unused factory footage was retrieved shortly after the release of *Shoah* to be edited into a sequence possibly intended for French television. Dated June 17, 1985, this first unreleased short film made from *Shoah* outtakes coincides with the exhumation and identification earlier that same month of Mengele's body in Brazil, where he had drowned in 1979.

In the Elias outtakes, the survivor's first memory of the Nazi physician known as the "Angel of Death" revolves around the selection process in the *Frauenlager*. Here, he was standing, she recalls, "making 'Right! Left!' waving with his hand." Eight months pregnant, Elias managed to escape his gaze by standing among a group of young women. "Several beautiful girls were in front of me, and Mengele waved me to the side with these beautiful girls," she tells Lanzmann. She adds: "I wanted to live, I was so young."[89] Elias was sent to Hamburg as forced labor; from there, she was deported to Ravensbrück and then back to Auschwitz. Placed in the infirmary of the *Frauenlager*, she encountered Mengele a second time. "How was he?" Lanzmann asks Elias again. "He was tall or small? [...] He was young?" he continues, further revealing his intention to elicit a portrait of Mengele, who managed to disappear after the war and was never tried. Elias responds to these questions before describing how, after she gave birth to a baby girl, Mengele ordered that she not feed the child. "Every day Mengele came to see me and make his research, how long a baby can live without food." One day, he declared that Elias and her dying child were to be sent to the gas chamber the following morning. That night, as she lay crying and screaming, a Jewish woman doctor came to her and listened to her story. She left and returned with an injection of morphine. "She told me, 'Give this to your child.' [...] I told her, [...] 'How can I be the murderer of my child?' She told me, '[...] You are young and I must save your life.' [...] I didn't want to, and she started to talk to me, into me. The more she talked, the less I had any '*Widerstand*' [resistance] ... until I made it. I gave the injection to my child," Elias recounts in front of the camera.[90]

In *Shoah*, a limit underlies the representation of death mediated by the male Holocaust survivors whom Lanzmann posits as unique witnesses of the extreme. In narratives permeated by the memories of women, the men recount a moment that immediately precedes or follows the destruction: the arrival of women at the gas chambers at Auschwitz (Filip Müller) and Treblinka

(Abraham Bomba); the opening of the mass graves in Ponar (Motke Zaidel and Itzak Dugin) and Chełmno (Mordechai Podchlebnik) where the men recognize their mothers, wives, sisters, and children. While Lanzmann has repeatedly posited these male protagonists as those closest to the extermination, the excluded Elias footage unfolds a narrative of trauma wherein the distance between life and death is abolished and a mother—the giver of life—is rendered "the murderer of [her] child."

In recovering a proximity to the catastrophe that remains off-frame, this voice from the margins calls attention to the gendered limit underlying Lanzmann's ethics of representation. Akin to Levi's contemporaneous framing of the gray zone—to his suspension of moral judgment through the stories of male protagonists including the Jewish prisoners of the *Sonderkommando*—Lanzmann recasts these men likened to collaborators in the postwar period as morally redeemable. In fact, he humanizes them in *Shoah* by eliciting from them an emotional reliving of the past. At the same time, he reintegrates them into the broader community of Holocaust survivors by extensively including their testimonies in the finished film. Beyond these two strategies, his gendered editorial ethics is encapsulated in the figure of Czerniaków, who, in a striking resonance to Elias's own words, *refuses* to "kill the children with [his] own hands." By contrast, her omitted narrative of trauma centered on the incompossible is effectively relegated to the morally intolerable and inassimilable: namely, another kind of proximity to death and a gendered version of survival.

Despite her exclusion, Elias does speak in the archive. She is the only woman survivor interviewed by Lanzmann to recount her story in its entirety and to have her notes laid out in front of her on the table, adjacent to his. In recounting the past, she evidences a survival that, in Freudian terms, "is not restricted to what trauma has made of its victims but includes what, in colloquy, victims make of their trauma."[91] Equally strong as Elias's will to survive is her will to bear witness and to integrate her traumatic experience into a personal history forever altered by the catastrophe. Beyond her account of Theresienstadt, of the "family camp" at Auschwitz, and of Mengele, she relates her depression in the immediate postwar period in Czechoslovakia as well as the birth of her first child in Israel. Upon seeing a nurse take the baby, she remembers, she began to scream, "Don't take my child away, you will kill my child!"[92] Reclaiming, by words alone, her dignity in these outtakes, Elias ultimately situates her gendered account of trauma as part of the main narrative of the Holocaust. "It is a story," she poignantly affirms in the final moments of the interview.[93]

FIGURE 3.18. Ruth Elias's notes adjacent to Claude Lanzmann's on the table (*The Four Sisters*, 2017).

CHOICE AND SURVIVAL IN BERLIN: INGE DEUTSCHKRON

Berlin, late spring 1979. After recording Inge Deutschkron near the Grunewald railway station, the filmmaker, the survivor, and the crew drive to the suburb of Wannsee in the red-and-white minivan used during the making of *Shoah* to capture clandestine interviews. Once in the Berlin outskirts, Lanzmann and Deutschkron walk to the villa located at Am Großen Wannsee 56–58, where the 1942 conference on the Final Solution was held. In this last year of the shooting phase, the lakeside villa subsists as a non-site of memory: transformed into a school after the war, this plaqueless building only became a memorial in 1982. Standing in front of the closed school gate, Lanzmann presses on the intercom. While Deutschkron remains silent, he explains in German that he has come from Paris and would like to visit the villa. Told it is not possible, he insists. "*Es tut mir leid* [I am sorry]," a man's voice heard through the intercom repeats several times. A noticeably upset Lanzmann, who would otherwise conceal his Jewish identity with the pseudonym "Dr. Sorel" whenever he secretly filmed perpetrators in West Germany, makes a rare autobiographical plea. "No, no, no," he protests in German. "A very important decision for me and my people was taken inside this building." The man on the intercom has hung up, marking the end of take 23 in the unused Deutschkron material.[94]

Neither image nor sound remain of this affecting dialogue—only the transcript. When the footage resumes with the next take, it partially reveals this non-site of memory in Wannsee. At the foot of the villa garden, the camera moves from the lakefront replica, erected in 1938, of the Flensburg Lion statue (dubbed "Lion of Goebbels" on the film can label) to locals eating and drinking at a snack bar. The parked red-and-white minivan is faintly visible in the background.[95] Deutschkron remains off-frame for the entirety of this take, during which Lanzmann proceeds to interview an unidentified man in German who, seemingly in his late thirties, could have been born the year that Nazi officials gathered in Wannsee to implement the systematic extermination of the European Jews. The man, his anachronistic beard invoking the Bismarck era, begins by detailing the history of the original 1862 statue commemorating a Danish victory over Prussian troops. The lakefront replica, he specifies, was commissioned by "Herr Professor [Wilhelm] Conrad."[96] When the director of *Shoah* steers the conversation toward the Wannsee villa, the interviewee evokes postwar plans to turn it into a memorial "for the Jews." In sharp contrast to his interest in Prussian history, however, he is unable to tell Lanzmann what, exactly, took place inside of the building in January 1942. "I don't know," he affirms before alluding to the "persecution of the Jews." At that moment, Lanzmann interjects: "Persecution or extermination?" The man responds: "That I also don't know…"[97]

In the Deutschkron interview transcript, this exchange reminiscent of the workers at the Mengele factory is followed by one final take: a conversation between the filmmaker and the survivor directly prompted by the man's supposed ignorance of the Wannsee conference and attempt at minimizing the catastrophe. "*Son seuls* [sound only]," the transcript specifies at the top of the page, thereby indicating that no visual component ever existed for this improvised addendum to Deutschkron's testimony, which was most likely captured near the villa or in the minivan on the way back to Berlin. Spanning five pages and invoking the theme of *Vergangenheitsbewältigung*, a distinctly German concept forged in the 1950s denoting the process of coming to terms with and, even, superseding the past, the conversation centers on the population's attitudes toward the Jews during the war as well as the current state of Holocaust remembrance, several months after the broadcast of Marvin Chomsky's miniseries. Lanzmann specifically refutes the claim that "Germans awakened to their past, to their history" after watching *Holocaust*. "It's a big lie, it's not true," he declares toward the end of the interview following which he would spend weeks attempting to secretly record perpetrators reluctant to speak of the past (although not immediately palpable in the spring of 1979, *Holocaust* nevertheless served as a catalyst in Holocaust memory culture in West Germany during the following decade).[98]

In this final take of her three-hour-long testimony, Deutschkron also provides a critical counter-representation to national narratives of *Vergangenheitsbewältigung*, which Lanzmann retained in the finished film. Asked at the beginning of this improvised audio recording, "What do you feel when you are here in Berlin?" she utters, off-screen, the poignant sentences with which her brief account in *Shoah* opens. "This is no longer home, you see? And especially it is no longer home when they start telling me that they didn't know, they didn't know. They say they didn't see. Yes, there were Jews living in our house and one day they were no longer there. We didn't know what happened."[99]

In 1979, the words of Deutschkron, who survived the Holocaust in hiding with her mother for over two years in her native Berlin, strikingly echo those pronounced in 1959 by Theodor Adorno in a famous conference lecture (and, subsequently, radio address) titled "The Meaning of Working through the Past." Critical of the postwar catchphrase *Aufarbeitung*, or "working through the past," which he likens to the process of doing away with rather than confronting the memory of the catastrophe, he notes: "A very great number claim not to have known of the events at that time, although Jews disappeared everywhere […]. Surely one may assume that there is a relation between the attitude of 'not having known anything about it' and an impassive and apprehensive indifference."[100] These remarks are further illustrated in the final take of the unused Deutschkron material. Here, the survivor observes that it was impossible to *not* witness "the people being torn out of their houses" in Berlin, where Jews did not live in a ghetto but throughout the city. Immediately after having made this remark, she substantiates the correlation between postwar denial of knowledge and wartime indifference put forward by Adorno in his lecture. Evoking the day the city became *judenrein* (cleansed of Jews) in February 1943, she recalls the Germans who "hastened in the streets" and "didn't want to look."[101]

This description was included in *Shoah*. It calls to mind Deutschkron's earlier memory, recounted on the first day of her interview, but left out of the final cut, of Kristallnacht, a euphemism for the November 1938 anti-Jewish pogroms that Adorno deems "almost good-natured" (because it obscures the traumatic events) and that the survivor herself reluctantly uses in her filmed testimony. Bracketed in the interview transcript, her memory of the destroyed Jewish businesses and synagogues is indissociable from the reactions of Germans who, here as well, "hasten" in the streets unwilling to confront the evidence of Jewish persecution. "And we saw on the Wiesenstraße the synagogue burning. We also saw the German people hastening along the street, not stopping by and just looking away from what happened." At that moment, she recalls a German barber who, having identified Deutschkron and her parents as Jewish, began to shout: "Get out of here, quit Germany, you Jews!" Anticipating her gendered story of survival in hiding, she remembers her father standing there terrified while her mother, "a very brave woman," walked up to the barber and shouted back: "You dirty swine."[102]

Over the course of a filmed testimony largely centered on the "very slow process [...], step by step, gradual," of persecution, Deutschkron details the coexistence and, at times, connection between what Marion Kaplan terms, in her study of Nazi Germany, the ongoing "normality" of daily life for Germans and the growing "abnormality" underlying the quotidian experiences of their Jewish neighbors.[103] In her narrative of survival, this twofold perspective culminates in her life in hiding beginning in 1943 (as the caption for her testimony in the finished film reveals), during which she relied on courageous Germans willing to risk their lives by providing shelter for Jews. Her account of the years of persecution offers a nuanced window into the non-Jewish population's response: indifference exemplified during Kristallnacht and the deportations; eagerness to make a bargain whenever a Jewish family was forced to sell their possessions in order to fund their attempt at emigrating; overt anti-Semitism such as that of the barber;[104] but also daily gestures of resistance, including a man in the subway car that, upon seeing her yellow star, offered her his seat (which, she immediately observes to Lanzmann, as a marked Jewess she could not take), and a friend of her mother's, Frau Gurms, who made them promise they would not let themselves be deported to the East where, as she had heard from a soldier living next door, horrible things were being done to the Jews.[105]

In this largely excluded testimony captured a year after the German publication of her memoir *Outcast*, Deutschkron emerges as an exemplary witness—for her proximity to the defining stages of the years of persecution—in Lanzmann's archive of the catastrophe. Indeed, the docu-auteur rarely interrupts her. Instead, he can be seen taking notes while she speaks, a gesture emphasizing the importance of her testimony for his investigation. Deutschkron, meanwhile, provides a vivid and precise account of the years of persecution in Berlin spanning from the 1933 boycott of Jewish-owned shops to the last deportations in 1943. "But was there a fear of the East?" Lanzmann, in keeping with his custom, asks her, when she evokes these transports from the Grunewald station. "We did not think that this meant death," Deutschkron answers.[106]

FIGURE 3.19. The filmmaker takes notes while the survivor narrates her account of the years of persecution (Created by Claude Lanzmann during the filming of *Shoah*. Used by permission of the United States Holocaust Memorial Museum and Yad Vashem, the Holocaust Martyrs and Heroes' Remembrance Authority, Jerusalem).

Filmed months after the Riga conference in New York, these outtakes once more document Lanzmann's initial conception of *Shoah* as a film that would retrace the disintegration of Jewish daily life in Nazi Germany leading to the deportations and the extermination. "What always strikes me about these events is that there was a first period before the war, when everything was in the open, this persecution," he tells Deutschkron in the outtakes.[107] Beyond the shooting phase, the possible representation of the gradual exclusion of Jews from the public sphere is further evidenced in the interview transcript. Significantly annotated, it contains references to Ziering's account of the persecution, as well as bracketed passages labeled with a number or letter that suggest the respective passage's possible inclusion into a montage or a sequence of testimonies for the finished film.[108] In the end, Lanzmann retained only a fragment of Deutschkron's integrated history of Nazi policies emphasizing the attitudes and reactions of both Germans and their Jewish neighbors—a unique twofold perspective that distinguishes her narrative of 1933–1939 from the joint testimony of Oppenheimer and Ziering. Evocative of Friedländer's assertion that the voices of survivors "reveal what was known and what *could* be known" by the local population, Lanzmann's decision in the editing room to limit Deutschkron's narrative to her memory of German indifference functions, for its part, as a critical response to the reception of *Holocaust* as a catalyst for *Vergangenheitsbewältigung* in West Germany.[109]

In the finished film, Deutschkron's edited testimony forms a counterpoint to the voices of two nonparticipating female eyewitnesses to the Final Solution: Helena Pietyra, a citizen of the town of Auschwitz (Oświęcim in Polish) and Martha Michelsohn, a German native who volunteered to resettle to Chełmno during the war and lived directly across from the church where Jews were loaded into gas vans. In contrast to the women survivors, Pietyra and Michelsohn appear several times in *Shoah*. Similarly, Lanzmann mentions both

FIGURE 3.20. A transcribed page from the Inge Deutschkron interview whose annotations are accompanied by the letter *C* and the number 7 (Created by Claude Lanzmann during the filming of *Shoah*. Used by permission of the United States Holocaust Memorial Museum and Yad Vashem, the Holocaust Martyrs and Heroes' Remembrance Authority, Jerusalem).

of them in his memoir where he recalls, on the one hand, the complacency of Pietyra as she explains, regarding the town's Jewish cemetery, "They don't bury there anymore," and, on the other hand, the "terrible words" of Michelsohn, who could not remember whether four thousand, forty thousand, or four hundred thousand Jews had been murdered in Chełmno ("I knew there was a four in it," she exclaims in the film upon being told it was four hundred thousand).[110]

In the twenty-five-minute outtakes of the interview recorded in March 1979 at Pietyra's home, which had belonged to Jews before their deportation in 1940, she reveals that she had been relocated to this apartment after the land on which she had lived before became part of the death camp.[111] This detail omitted in the final cut is indicative of her proximity to the Holocaust. Unlike the Germans in Deutschkron's testimony, who claim to have neither known of nor seen the persecution and the deportations, Pietyra asserts that she had knowledge of both the selections in the camp and the extermination itself. One could smell the odor of the burned bodies, she specifies, "when there was a wind blowing from the west."[112] In keeping with her appearance in *Shoah*, she remains unmoved by either her wartime knowledge or the disappearance she witnessed firsthand: that of the Jewish community of Oświęcim. If, in these outtakes, the significant presence of Jews before the war is encapsulated in the supposedly Jewish but ostensibly anti-Semitic proverb "The streets belong to you, the buildings are ours," the eradication of this community is embodied in the image of the town's only synagogue, which was destroyed and never rebuilt.[113]

"Witnessing, we are reminded if we contemplate women's less visible roles in the Holocaust, is not passive," Doris Bergen observes. "A person who sees terrible things is also involved in and changed by the experience."[114] In front of the camera, Pietyra involuntarily bears witness to the fate of Jewish property from which she directly benefited and to the fact that she herself remained inactive—despite having known of the extermination. She bears witness, finally, to a life seemingly unchanged, much like the town of Oświęcim, by the catastrophe. "Good, very well, to return to the city, the city where we find ourselves today, the marketplace, all that, it is intact, that has not changed much?" Lanzmann asks her at the end of the outtakes. "In principle it stayed as before," she answers, just as indifferent as she had been during the war to the fate of the Jews, who once constituted 80 percent of the town's population.[115]

Pietyra is one of several Polish bystanders Lanzmann chose to include in the final cut. By contrast, Michelsohn, as Dominick LaCapra observes, is the sole German in *Shoah* "who did not participate in some official capacity during the Holocaust, although, given her views, she might just as well have."[116] The "wife of a Nazi schoolteacher in Chełmno," as the caption in the finished film indicates, she was born in the small town of Lage in central western Germany. Her husband, Erhard Michelsohn, was an ethnic German, or *Volksdeutscher*, from Riga, who testified at the postwar Chełmno trials held in Bonn, where the gas van driver Gustav Laabs received a fifteen-year sentence.[117] Lanzmann interviewed Michelsohn for nearly two hours at her home in her native Lage in the late spring of 1979, the year, he first remarks in these outtakes, following his trip to Chełmno, where he had filmed Srebnik.

It is impossible to know how, exactly, the docu-auteur found the "wife of a Nazi school teacher in Chełmno." The caption in the finished film, along with Lanzmann's mention of a teacher named Michelsohn and his postwar testimony in the clandestinely captured footage with Franz Schalling, the former police guard at Chełmno, suggest that he interviewed her in lieu of her deceased husband (Corinna Coulmas, who sits off-frame to Lanzmann's left during the Michelsohn interview, once recalled having conducted extensive research for *Shoah* in the German Federal Archives, where she had access to all the postwar trial files).[118] In 1979, his presence is further intimated in the opening moments of excluded take 7 where Lubtchansky moves from a close-up of Erhard Michelsohn's photograph to a wide shot of Martha Michelsohn, Lanzmann, and the framed picture on the wall.

Unseen in the finished film, this photograph reminiscent of postwar political portraiture depicts Erhard Michelsohn as an honorable German citizen rather than a *Mitläufer* (fellow traveler). This postwar term was used as part of denazification efforts to classify supporters of the Third Reich who, to varying degrees, had not played an active role in promoting the regime. A member of the NSDAP since 1941, Erhard Michelsohn, like his wife, constituted a literal "fellow traveler" who had willingly resettled to Poland as part of Hitler's plans for a significantly enlarged German nation-state. As a schoolteacher, he also partook in the indoctrination of German children in the classroom.[119] While the Berliners in Deutschkron's narrative turned a blind eye to the persecution, the Michelsohns witnessed, with indifference, the systematic mass killing of Jews in Poland. Rather than "ordinary" Germans, all were in fact exemplary eyewitnesses given their proximity to either the years of persecution or the years of extermination.

The photograph visible in the outtakes provides a stark, if not gendered, contrast to Lanzmann's cinematic treatment of Martha Michelsohn in *Shoah*. In choosing to exclude both the portrait and himself from the finished film, the docu-auteur reorients and limits our gaze to the horrifying "wife of a Nazi school teacher," who calls to mind the Hitchcockian figure of the terrible mother, above all the Nazi matriarch Madame Sebastian in *Notorious* (1946). As suggested by LaCapra's likening of Michelsohn to a Nazi criminal or, even, director Marcel Ophüls's singling out of her "terrible words" as "one of the most truly horrible moments in *Shoah*," Michelsohn embodies by words and demeanor alone an incomprehensible, monstrous indifference.[120] This representation is accentuated in the excluded material where, unlike Pietyra, she

FIGURES 3.21–22. Martha Michelsohn, Claude Lanzmann, and the photograph of Erhard Michelsohn (close-up) at her home in Lage (Created by Claude Lanzmann during the filming of *Shoah*. Used by permission of the United States Holocaust Memorial Museum and Yad Vashem, the Holocaust Martyrs and Heroes' Remembrance Authority, Jerusalem).

repeats time and again, "I never saw anything"—despite her detailed testimony. Similarly, when asked, "Did you have guilt feelings?" she immediately asserts, without remorse, "No, because we were not guilty."[121]

In the finished film, Lanzmann also excludes his own moral difficulty at interviewing her. Michelsohn, as the transcript reveals, pronounces, in a culmination of horror, her oft-cited "terrible words" only at the very end of her testimony.[122] The final takes are themselves punctuated with silence and unfinished phrases, as well as shots of Lanzmann resting his head on his hand. In looking for the "Nazi schoolteacher of Chełmno," he unexpectedly found in Martha Michelsohn an exemplary witness: a *Mitläuferin* who, in keeping with the *Ostthema*, resettled to the East to where Jews would be forcefully deported and exterminated. "Were you afraid of the East?" Lanzmann asks her, while Lubtchansky effectuates the close-up of her husband's photograph. "No," she responds matter-of-factly.[123]

One can only wonder whether her seemingly righteous late husband pictured on the wall would have appeared as monstrous had he been interviewed for *Shoah*. Gender nevertheless shaped the reception of Michelsohn's testimony. On the one hand, at a time where historians, as Claudia Koonz notes in her 1987 groundbreaking feminist study of the Third Reich, "dismissed women as part of the timeless backdrop against which Nazi men made history, seeing men as active 'subjects' and women as the passive 'other,'" Lanzmann's decision to include the "wife of a Nazi schoolteacher" in his Holocaust opus renders him somewhat of a "pioneer."[124] On the other hand, in a nine-and-a-half-hour film that posits men as the "active subjects" of history, Michelsohn's representation evidences what Sara Horowitz, in her reading of Ophüls's cinematic treatment of French female collaborators, terms "a special horror at something seen as particularly monstrous": namely, a woman in whom supposedly "naturally female" attributes such as care and compassion have been utterly corrupted.[125]

Michelsohn's testimonial gaze as a former settler in Chełmno is turned, like the finished film itself, toward the East and toward the extermination. If Lanzmann's decision to render her the only German-speaking bystander in his film inevitably accentuates her presence, the archive reveals that very little material was in fact captured with so-called "ordinary" Germans who witnessed firsthand the persecution and deportation of Jews. In West Germany, Lanzmann focused his investigation on perpetrators, several of whom he filmed, or attempted to film, in the summer of 1979. His contemporaneous interview with Deutschkron, however, belatedly prompted an interest in capturing the voices of the German population—as the improvised and ultimately excluded interviews near the Wannsee villa and at the Mengele factory both attest.

This material, recorded in highly symbolic locations, bears the trace of the richly evocative mise-en-scène revealed in the Deutschkron outtakes. Like Srebnik in Chełmno, Deutschkron returns to Berlin from Tel Aviv, where she had been living since 1972, in order to be filmed for *Shoah*. Centered on three non-sites of memory, each designating a decisive stage in the process of destruction (persecution, deportation, extermination), her largely unedited testimony constitutes a film or "documentary of return" in its own right in Lanzmann's archive of the catastrophe.[126] Conversely, whereas Hirsch and Spitzer argue that her survival in hiding "emblematizes the position of women in the film as a whole," the mise-en-scène in the excluded portions of her interview bears witness to an authorial intention to render her *visible* in Berlin, a city once encompassing 160,000 Jews in which, of the five to seven thousand who went into hiding, only 1,400 survived.[127]

In the finished film, Lanzmann juxtaposes the opening segment of her testimony with tracking shots of the West Berlin city center. Captured at night and thus evocative of her survival in hiding, these images show the famous Gedächtniskirche on Kurfürstendamm. This church, severely damaged during the Second World War, is located only steps away from the iconic Café Kranzler, where Lanzmann interviews Deutschkron on the first day. "It's not so easy to speak in this coffeehouse," she observes when the camera starts to roll (indicative of a certain reliving of the past, she initially begins in German, her native tongue, into which she inadvertently lapses several times over the course of her testimony). "I have not been here for many, many years, because this reminds me very much of the years when there was a signboard downstairs saying: '*Juden unerwünscht*—Jews unwanted.' Now, this signboard appeared not at once in all the coffeehouses, it appeared gradually, one after the other."[128] In these opening remarks, which are underlined and bracketed in the interview transcript, Café Kranzler emerges as a non-site of memory signifying the years of persecution in Nazi Germany and, more particularly, in Berlin, a city seen during the first day of the interview through the large glass window where Deutschkron and Lanzmann are sitting.

The docu-auteur's clear intent on rendering Deutschkron visible in a place from which she had once been excluded, where she had had to hide in order to survive, is further evidenced by the presence of two cameras (and of two cinematographers, Lubtchansky and Chapuis). Beyond capturing countershots showing Lanzmann attentively listening to Deutschkron, the second camera permits a

FIGURE 3.23. Inge Deutschkron narrating the years of persecution at Café Kranzler with West Berlin visible behind her (Created by Claude Lanzmann during the filming of *Shoah*. Used by permission of the United States Holocaust Memorial Museum and Yad Vashem, the Holocaust Martyrs and Heroes' Remembrance Authority, Jerusalem).

unique mise-en-scène that further posits Café Kranzler as a non-site of memory. Positioned on a rainy afternoon at a busy intersection, it remains fixated on the two streets signs of Kurfürstendamm and Joachimstaler Straße as if to provide clues for future researchers, before slowly beginning to pivot. It first reveals the Gedächtniskirche, which it will film again that evening, then traverses the intersection and finally arrives at the café facade, its large golden letters visible beneath the rotunda. In what could have been a poignant opening to her testimony in the finished film, the camera moves very slowly from a wide shot to a close-up of the café window showing Deutschkron and Lanzmann speaking.

Although calling to mind Srebnik's testimony, Lanzmann stages in these outtakes a negative return insofar as Deutschkron is filmed in a café that had banned Jews from entering. Similarly, he records her at the Grunewald railway station the next day where transports to ghettos and camps had once departed (devoid of traces of the past at the time of the making of *Shoah*, a monument was erected in 1991 near track 17 where most of these trains left). Lanzmann would include a significantly edited segment of Deutschkron's testimony into the finished film, which is devoid of his own questions and observations, from this second shooting day. Spanning three pages in the transcript, but reduced to several lines in the final cut, Deutschkron recalls the day Berlin became *judenrein*. Concomitantly, she describes her own guilt at choosing to defy Nazi deportation orders and going underground. As she concludes in *Shoah*, she thereby escaped the tragic fate of her people (these moving last lines in the finished film mark the end, in the interview transcript, of her testimony at the Grunewald station).[129]

FIGURES 3.24–25. The facade of Café Kranzler, and a close-up of Claude Lanzmann and Inge Deutschkron sitting by the window (Created by Claude Lanzmann during the filming of *Shoah*. Used by permission of the United States Holocaust Memorial Museum and Yad Vashem, the Holocaust Martyrs and Heroes' Remembrance Authority, Jerusalem).

"You and your mother were the last Jews left in Berlin," Lanzmann remarks in these closing moments of her testimony.[130] Strikingly echoing the famous last words of *Shoah*, as pronounced by Simha Rotem, "I am the last Jew," Lanzmann's remark effectuates a gendered reversal in the excluded material. While, as Hirsch and Spitzer aptly observe, male witnesses in *Shoah* "make devastatingly clear [that] in the Holocaust mothers cannot protect or nourish their children," these outtakes unfold a narrative of the catastrophe, reminiscent of Schneider and her family, in which a mother and a daughter do survive.[131] At the Grunewald railway station, Lanzmann thus reenacts Deutschkron's fate as "the last Jew" by transposing her to this non-site of memory from which the Berliner Jews disappeared. Beyond the bench on the platform where she appears alone in *Shoah*, she is also filmed from several angles sitting by herself on a moving train with a pained expression as she looks out the window.

A single French comment to his cinematographer, omitted from the transcript and containing the coded word *gros* for close-up, encapsulates Lanzmann's authorial intention at the Grunewald station and on the moving train. "I hope you stayed *gros* this whole time," he suddenly says to Chapuis in reference to Deutschkron's face in the closing moments. "You swear? If it's not the case, I am going to throw you on the tracks. Really... you're not lying?"

FIGURE 3.26. Inge Deutschkron, "the last Jew of Berlin," on a train departing from the Grunewald railway station (Created by Claude Lanzmann during the filming of *Shoah*. Used by permission of the United States Holocaust Memorial Museum and Yad Vashem, the Holocaust Martyrs and Heroes' Remembrance Authority, Jerusalem).

he adds, bearing witness to his own reception of Deutschkron's Holocaust testimony as irreplaceable material for *Shoah*.[132] A similar anxiety surfaces weeks later when he attempts in vain to convince the former Einsatzgruppen member Karl Kretschmer to be interviewed. Walking back, after several minutes of pleading, with Coulmas to the minivan where the cinematographer has secretly been filming the whole scene, Lanzmann suddenly exclaims in a jovial tone: "In the event that you, Dominique [Chapuis], did not film us, I am going to strangle you!"[133]

From the Grunewald station where Deutschkron concludes her testimony with the day Berlin became *judenrein* in 1943, the survivor and the filmmaker travel directly to Wannsee, a non-site of memory signifying the extermination where he had possibly envisioned filming her in the villa. Akin to Biren and Schneider before her, Deutschkron never recounts her story in its entirety in front of the camera. The "cut" produced at the railway station displaces to the off-frame the most gendered portion of her narrative: her survival in hiding. In April 1939, after her father immigrated to England, Deutschkron and her mother were, to borrow her words, "left behind" in Berlin.[134] In January 1943, the two women went underground, hiding together throughout the war in the homes of at least twelve different Germans.[135] If, in 1979, Lanzmann possibly considered Deutschkron's story in hiding too evocative of the paradigmatic tale of Anne Frank, her untold account of choice and survival subsists in the outtakes through his authorial design to render her visible in the very city from which she had once disappeared. Captured only shortly before he would traverse West Germany attempting to film "underground" with the Paluche, this excluded material further suggests a deep admiration for Deutschkron's courage. "You see, I was brought up a fighter and therefore I accepted what was my fate," she tells him early on in front of the camera, in anticipation of her defiance of Nazi orders and survival at the periphery of the extermination.[136]

CHOICE AND SURVIVAL IN BUDAPEST:
HANNA MARTON AND HANSI BRAND

Jerusalem, October 1979. Toward the end of the three-and-a-half-hour Hebrew interview with Hanna Marton at her home, Lubtchansky captures a medium-long shot reminiscent of the Michelsohn outtakes. Lanzmann sits with his habitual preparatory notes spread out before him while Marton is holding in her hands the 1944 diary of her late husband, Dr. Ernst Marton, whose portrait is visible on the bookshelf behind them. Earlier, the cinematographer had captured close-up shots of the diary and of the year "1944" printed in gold

FIGURE 3.27. Claude Lanzmann, Dr. Ernst Marton (photograph), and Hanna Marton at her home in Jerusalem (Created by Claude Lanzmann during the filming of *Shoah*. Used by permission of the United States Holocaust Memorial Museum and Yad Vashem, the Holocaust Martyrs and Heroes' Remembrance Authority, Jerusalem).

letters on the cover. In this document, which the survivor reads in front of the camera in lieu of its deceased author, Dr. Marton chronicled what Lanzmann terms halfway through the interview "a unique matter in the history of the Holocaust."[137]

During the spring of 1944, Rudolf (Rezső) Kasztner, the director of the Jewish Aid and Rescue Committee in Budapest (also known as the Vaada), bargained with Adolf Eichmann for the release of one million Jews in exchange for ten thousand trucks. This "Blood for Goods" deal failed. The negotiations, however, resulted in a special transport, which carried 1,684 Jews to safety in Switzerland. Kasztner and the committee had to select those who would escape. Among the passengers were a dozen of his own family members and several hundred individuals from his hometown of Cluj in northern Transylvania, including the Martons. Concurrently, between May and July 1944, the Germans deported approximately 440,000 Jews from Hungary to Auschwitz, the majority of whom were exterminated. In *Shoah*, Vrba evokes twice "the expected murder in a very short time of a million Jews from Hungary," which he attempted to warn the world about following his escape from Auschwitz in April of that year. In late May 1944, two SS men captured nearly two hundred photographs today known as the "Auschwitz Album." These images show Hungarian Jews arriving in the camp, awaiting selection on the ramp, and walking to the gas chambers. The survivor Lili Jacob found this album in the Dora-Mittelbau concentration camp shortly after it had been liberated by American troops. She donated it to Yad Vashem in 1980. That same year, Serge Klarsfeld, the Nazi hunter and child survivor of the Holocaust in France, published a limited first edition of the album.[138]

In 1944, the negotiations with Eichmann forced the Vaada director to choose who would live and who would die. After the Holocaust, the tragedy of choice underlying Kasztner's rescue efforts fueled a controversy, equaled in scope and violence only to that surrounding Benjamin Murmelstein. This controversy also marked a first turning point, several years before the Eichmann trial, in the emergence of the memory of the catastrophe in Israel, where Kasztner had settled in 1947. In a pamphlet published in 1953, Malchiel Gruenwald, a Hungarian Jew who had immigrated to Palestine before the war, accused Kasztner of having collaborated with the Germans while keeping silent about the fate that awaited the Jews of Hungary at Auschwitz. Kasztner sued Gruenwald for defamation, but the libel case became known as the "Kasztner trial" since the defense sought to prove that Kasztner was in fact guilty of collaboration. This "first great Holocaust trial held in Israel" opened in early January 1954 in the small Tel Aviv courtroom of Benjamin Halevy, who would go on to serve as one of the three presiding judges of the Eichmann trial. A few months later, as "crowds began to flock to the doors, including reporters from Israel and overseas," the "Kasztner trial" was transferred to a larger courtroom and received extensive news coverage.[139]

In this high-profile case, Shmuel Tamir defended Gruenwald and famously cross-examined Kasztner, who took the stand eleven times, detailing the steps leading up to the destruction of Hungarian Jewry. Intent on proving his collaboration, the young defense attorney argued that Kasztner had concealed his knowledge of the extermination in exchange for the transport to Switzerland. Tamir also placed significant emphasis on how the passengers of this special train had been chosen. "Kasztner," Tom Segev writes of this trial in *The Seventh Million*, "[…] now looked like the 'doctor' who had stood on the train platform at the death camps and, with a wave of his finger, performed the selection—who would be sent to work, who to the gas chamber."[140] As Hilberg remarks in an excluded segment of his filmed interview, Kasztner was never forgiven for "playing God"—a formulation that echoes Leibniz's notion of the incompossible.[141]

On June 22, 1955, Halevy delivered his verdict: finding Gruenwald innocent of the majority of the libel charges, he ruled that Kasztner had collaborated with the Germans and, even, "sold his soul to the devil"—a dramatic verdict that would reverberate throughout Israeli society beyond the making of *Shoah* and well into the late eighties.[142] In Lanzmann's archive of the catastrophe, the legacy of Halevy's phrase is evidenced in the excluded interview he filmed in 1979 with Tamir, who likens in his closing words the director of the Vaada to "a man whose soul was burned in Auschwitz."[143] Following the trial, Kasztner appealed the verdict, which the Supreme Court eventually overturned in early 1958. The Court's decision came too late: in March 1957, Kasztner was assassinated in front of his home in Tel Aviv. In the outtakes, Hilberg effectuates a parallel between the fates of Czerniaków in Warsaw and Kasztner in Budapest: both men witnessed the destruction as it was unfolding and tragically paid with their lives.[144] This comparison encapsulates Lanzmann's parallel investigation throughout the filming phase of these two men's choices, only one of whom he retained as a protagonist of *Shoah*.

"The question of the rescue of the Hungarian Jews will be one of the major topics of my film," the docu-auteur declared in his 1977 introductory letter to Roswell McClelland, the representative of the War Refugee Board in Switzerland who had been informed of the "Blood for Goods" deal in 1944.[145] In the editing room years later, he chose to leave out this unique episode in the history of the Holocaust, which, beyond epitomizing the leitmotif of the tragedy of choice underlying the outtakes of women survivors, also bears witness to memory politics in Israel as well as to Hannah Arendt's controversial *Eichmann in Jerusalem*. During the 1961 trial where, as Haim Gouri aptly observed, "the heroism of the Warsaw Ghetto cast a shadow over Hungary," Arendt extended her criticism of Jewish leadership to the Vaada.[146] In her report, she bitterly summarized the incompossible underlying the selection of passengers for the special convoy. "Dr. Kasztner," she writes, "[…] saved exactly 1,684 people with approximately 476,000 victims."[147] In 1961, two members of the Budapest committee had been called to the witness stand to recount the rescue efforts: Joel and Hansi Brand. Joel Brand ("a broken man now," Gouri observes in his chronicle) had traveled in the midst of the "Blood for Goods" negotiations to Turkey, where he desperately appealed for help from the Jewish Agency in Istanbul in saving a million Jews. Arrested by the British authorities, he never returned to Hungary. Hansi Brand, who "initially refused to testify" at the 1961 trial, played an active role in the Vaada: serving as the committee liaison after her husband's departure, she partook in the negotiations with Eichmann, sometimes alone, sometimes with Kasztner, and in the selection of the train's passengers.[148]

Nearly two decades after the trial, Lanzmann recorded Hansi Brand at her home in Tel Aviv during the final weeks he spent shooting *Shoah*. First evoking her reluctance to be interviewed for his film, he quickly reveals his intention to speak with her in lieu of the director of the Vaada and her late husband, who had passed away in 1964. "Hansi Brand was the wife of Joel Brand and the collaborator of Rudolf Kasztner, the two men who were the most important in the negotiations about the fate of the Hungarian Jews," he explains to the Hebrew interpreter in the opening moments of the interview, thereby silencing her participation in the negotiations with Eichmann.[149] Despite this introduction, Hansi Brand bears witness throughout her testimony to the significant role she played as the committee liaison, even remarking: "I want to add, that some people on our committee protested against [my role], saying that a woman can't represent Jewish concerns by herself."[150]

In Lanzmann's archive of the catastrophe, the excluded interview with the former Jewish Aid and Rescue Committee liaison recovers, in 1979, a sense of urgency in capturing for *Shoah* the moral dilemmas faced by the Jewish leaders in Hungary. "Hansi," Lanzmann says halfway through the interview, suddenly addressing her by her first name, "really now, you have to help me. I want to

FIGURE 3.28. Hansi Brand during her filmed interview (Created by Claude Lanzmann during the filming of *Shoah*. Used by permission of the United States Holocaust Memorial Museum and Yad Vashem, the Holocaust Martyrs and Heroes' Remembrance Authority, Jerusalem).

understand and to see [the situation] and not just for myself, but for the people who will see this film. What was your situation from a human point of view, and the situation for Kasztner?"[151] Despite this intimation of familiarity, the dynamics between the filmmaker and the survivor in these outtakes offer a stark contrast to Lanzmann's first filmed interviews with members of the *Judenrat*, above all Murmelstein. Unlike the chairman of Theresienstadt, who weaves his defense over the course of four days, Hansi Brand's unedited testimony is marked by brevity, totaling a mere one hour and forty-two minutes. In this unused footage contemporaneous with the Tamir interview, Lanzmann's questions are reminiscent of the ones the defense attorney had posed during his famous cross-examination in the 1954 trial where "Kasztner lost his temper, shouted, became flustered."[152]

Not surprisingly, the conversation with Brand quickly shifts to a confrontation unparalleled in any of the unused material. The tensions permeating the footage and echoing the enduring legacy of Halevy's verdict in Israel are first evidenced by the linguistic change that, unexpectedly and without any explanation on camera, occurs early in the interview. Aided by an interpreter, Brand begins in Hebrew and Lanzmann in English. In take 5, they abruptly switch to German, their sole common tongue, which they speak for the remainder of the interview. More than the language in which Brand had negotiated with Eichmann and later asked to testify at the witness stand in 1961, this linguistic change permits the interviewer and interviewee to address or, rather, confront each other directly.

Echoing the "Kasztner trial" and Arendt's verdict in *Eichmann in Jerusalem*, Lanzmann probes the contentious rescue efforts that resulted in the special convoy by way of three questions: First, given that Kasztner was accused of not having warned the Hungarian Jews about Auschwitz, had people in fact known of the extermination in 1944? Second, was it fair that Kasztner had included his own family among those selected for the transport to Switzerland? Last, how were the remaining passengers chosen? In answering the first question, Brand evokes Vrba's report following his escape from Auschwitz, which detailed the extermination process. Unbeknownst to the former liaison of the Vaada is the fact that Lanzmann had discussed with Vrba in November 1978 the negotiations that resulted in the "Kasztner train." Akin to his silence in the Brand interview, Lanzmann carefully edited around Vrba's testimony for the finished film in order to exclude the segments pertaining to the committee's rescue deal with Eichmann. In the unused footage, Vrba deems Kasztner a "traitor" who, rather than warn Hungarian Jewry, preferred to carry on with his negotiations in order to ensure not only his survival but also that of "a small community of his own choice."[153]

Brand cites Vrba's report as proof that "people knew" of the reality of Auschwitz when the deportations began. She also observes that, even prior to his report, knowledge of the extermination was widespread in Hungary where many Polish and Slovak refugees were living. "For God's sake, how can anyone maintain that in 1944, that [sic] no one knew what was going on in the German areas?" she tells Lanzmann, who nonetheless continues to probe the question of whether "ordinary Jews" had knowledge of the extermination. Brand, however, ultimately interrupts him by shouting: "People knew [*Man hat gewusst*]!"[154] Then, turning to the selection of the passengers and, in particular, the inclusion of Kasztner's family members, she once more reframes the interviewer-interviewee dynamics by posing the question to Lanzmann. "I ask you, if you were in the same situation, wouldn't you be thinking about your own family?" "That's a very good answer," the docu-auteur is forced to concede.[155] The filmed interview with Brand differs from the one Tom Segev conducted with her a decade later when the controversy had begun to subside in Israel. "After almost fifty years, Hansi Brand is no longer angry," he writes in *The Seventh Million* after recounting their exchange in which she evokes the twofold incompossible, unvoiced in the *Shoah* outtakes, that ultimately defined the 1944 rescue deal. If Kasztner was never forgiven for having chosen several hundred Jews for survival, "those who were on the train never forgave him either [...]. Every morning, when they woke up, they knew that they were living at the expense of those who had not boarded the train."[156]

Recorded by Lubtchansky in 1979, Marton herself describes how she lives with the guilt, unabated, of having been selected for the transport, which Kasztner had nicknamed "Noah's Ark." After Tamir and Brand, Lanzmann attempts to capture the perspective, past and present, of a passenger chosen in 1944. Assisted by the interpreter Francine Kaufmann, Marton narrates her story of choice and survival in an accented Hebrew evidencing her postwar immigration to Israel. At the same time, she translates excerpts from her late husband's diary. The mise-en-scène centered on a document concurrent with the events is evocative of Hilberg's methodology. In discussing with Lanzmann the controversial rescue deal, the historian declares: "I only try to understand from the writings left behind, from the diaries and the reports and the testimonies of these people, what it is that they were thinking."[157] The Marton material calls to mind, as well, the filmed testimony of the former *Judenrat* member Leib Garfunkel. In this interview, an on-screen Irena Steinfeldt translates out loud the survivor's monograph, based on his own wartime diary, detailing the destruction of Kovno Jewry. The mise-en-scène at the very beginning of the shooting phase in March 1976 and again at the very end in October

1979 evidences Lanzmann's privileging of paper memory as a framing device for postwar debates surrounding the choices of Jewish leaders during the Holocaust—of which, in the finished film, Czerniaków's diary read by Hilberg subsists as the single trace.

Unlike the Garfunkel outtakes where the survivor seldom bears witness to his personal experience, Marton's testimony renders visible a shift from the paper memory embodied by the diary to the present-day testimony of a woman rescued as a result of Kasztner's deal with Eichmann. As a passenger removed from the negotiations, her account differs from Brand's, particularly regarding the crucial question, in Lanzmann's investigation, of what the Jews in Hungary knew in 1944. Marton claims to never have heard of Auschwitz when the deportations began that year. She then adds that, even if people had known, it was too late to escape. Paradoxically, one of the episodes chronicled in Ernst Marton's diary suggests that those selected for the "Kasztner train" had in fact known of the extermination camp. During the journey, one of the passengers mistakenly heard that the convoy was headed to Auschwitz—instead of the Moravian town of Auspitz—and caused everyone aboard to panic. Despite this anecdote, Marton affirms that the word "Auschwitz" did not signify death in 1944. On camera, she has to acknowledge, though, that such ignorance was perhaps a defense mechanism, which allowed the passengers of "Noah's Ark" to not admit to themselves that, unlike the Jews who were being deported en masse to Auschwitz, they had been chosen to survive.[158]

Similar to the excluded footage with Brand, these outtakes reveal that it is impossible to discuss this unique episode in the history of the Holocaust without evoking the ethical implications of Kasztner's "selection," which fueled accusations of collaboration for decades in Israel. In the final moments of the interview, as Marton's testimony moves beyond the memory of the special convoy to address its present-day legacy, she remarks that the "Kasztner trial" was one of the worst events she had to live through after the Holocaust. For her, in portraying the Vaada director as a collaborator, the trial minimized his rescue of 1,684 Jews and erased the very context out of which these negotiations arose. "What bothers me in this story," she explains, "it's that one always forgets the origin of this horror, that is to say the Nazi horror; it's the Nazi system which forced people to choose, rather than those who were put in the position of being forced to choose who should live and who should die."[159] Marton's invocation of both choice and culpability in front of Lanzmann's camera strikingly approximates Primo Levi's metaphor of the gray zone. If, as Debarati Sanyal observes, Levi distinctly conveys "this coerced mimesis between executioner and victim" through the anecdote of a soccer match opposing the SS and the

Sonderkommando at Auschwitz, Marton's own remark articulates and problematizes a similar kind of "passing" of guilt from the Nazis to the Jews—and from Eichmann to Kasztner—in Israel during the postwar period.[160]

In this excluded interview, Lanzmann reframes Marton's poignant observation and indirect refutation to Arendt's controversial claim through a paradigm intended to encapsulate the Holocaust as a whole: the tragedy of choice. "The dilemma of Kasztner," he remarks, "the tragedy of Kasztner, the tragedy of choice, [...] it was not the case only with Kasztner, I mean, this happened generally throughout the Holocaust."[161] Seemingly prompted by his confrontation, after Tamir and Brand, with a survivor of the "Kasztner train," this nuanced conclusion to his extensive probing of the 1944 negotiations obscures his own difficulty, evidenced throughout the making of *Shoah*, in coming to terms with the fact that Kasztner had accepted the Faustian bargain of selection. "I would never dare to judge, but we are obliged to ... to go on with this question," he tells Hilberg during their discussion of "Noah's Ark."[162]

A single question raised in the immediate postwar period permeates his investigation in the late seventies: should there have been an ethical limit to negotiations with the Nazis and should this limit have been to not choose who would live and who would die?[163] Beyond the Hilberg material, Lanzmann went "on with this question" in several filmed testimonies, notably opposing in his 1978 interview with Andre Steiner the "Kasztner train" to the "Europa Plan," an attempt to rescue Jews as a whole "without choosing who could be saved."[164] Similarly, when filming Tamir the following year, he concedes in anticipation of his own paradigm voiced in the Marton material, "I agree with you the tragedy is the selection."[165] In the end, Lanzmann produced a "cut" that inscribed an ethical limit into the finished film: the one separating Czerniaków's suicide and decision *not* to choose in Warsaw from Kasztner's survival and selection in Budapest. "Do you think Czerniaków would have behaved like him?" Lanzmann asks Hilberg toward the end of their discussion. "No," the historian responds. "Different person. Different personality."[166]

Recorded on October 10, 1979, the excluded Marton footage was one of the very last testimonies the docu-auteur captured for *Shoah*. As his observation in the closing moments of the interview suggests, he had already accumulated the near entirety of an archive of the catastrophe that would, time and again, bear witness to the tragedy of choice—above all in the testimonies of women survivors whose narratives of trauma remained, in the end, at the margins of his Holocaust opus. In this excluded interview, the tragedy of choice anticipates the notion of the incompossible deployed four decades later in *The Patagonian Hare* as a metaphor for the selection Lanzmann undertook between 1979 and 1985 when composing the final version of the film. "Because to choose is to kill," he writes, framing his own choices in the editing room through the prosthetic memory of the "Kasztner train." The destruction of Hungarian Jewry and the question of the knowledge of the extermination in 1944 underlying the Brand and Marton outtakes surface paragraphs before in his memoir through the invocation of the "Auschwitz Album." In *The Patagonian Hare*, Lanzmann singles out and recasts as a prosthetic memory the photograph of one woman—the supposed double of his maternal aunt Sophie—awaiting the selection on the ramp. "She *is* Sophie," he writes, "her beautiful face stamped with suspicion and anguish; she knows she is going to die and she cannot, does not want to believe it."[167]

CHAPTER 4

The Question of Rescue and Refugees

> In 1944 Rabbi Michael Weissmandl and Mrs. Gisi Fleischmann smuggled a letter out of Nazi-occupied Hungary to the Allies pleading for the rescue of European Jewry. It said: "And you, our brothers in all free countries: and you, governments of all free lands, where are you? What are you doing to hinder the carnage that is going on?"
> —Laurence Jarvik, *Who Shall Live and Who Shall Die?* (1982)

WRITTEN ON MAY 15, 1944, the day the mass deportations of Hungarian Jewry began, the excerpted letter of the two coleaders of the Bratislava Working Group serves as the epigraph to Laurence Jarvik's documentary on the wartime inaction of Jewish leaders and the American government. The words of these messengers of the catastrophe, both of whom were deported to Auschwitz in the fall of 1944 (Fleischmann was murdered upon arrival and Weissmandl survived by jumping out of the moving train), constitutes a final plea to the Allies at a time when the largest remaining Jewish community in German-occupied territory was still alive.

Jarvik, whose Jewish mother fled from the Netherlands during the war, utilizes in this film the tragic voices of Fleischmann and Weissmandl in order to reorient our gaze toward the West and its own "bystanders," to borrow the nuanced category first proposed by scholars Michael Marrus, Raul Hilberg, and Deborah Lipstadt.[1] In *Perpetrators Victims Bystanders* (1992), for instance, Hilberg moves from "Helpers, Gainers, and Onlookers" in German-occupied Europe to "The Jewish Rescuers," "The Allies," and "The Churches." A chapter dedicated to "Messengers" mediates this passage from the "bystanders" of the East to those of the West. These are individuals—among them *Shoah* protagonist Jan Karski, the famous underground courier for the Polish Government-in-Exile in London, to whom the historian devotes three pages—who were intent on revealing the destruction of European Jewry to the outside world.

Their message or mission, Hilberg carefully observes, ultimately depended "on the extent to which their listeners were prepared to absorb and accept the substance of the information itself."[2]

The historian illustrates this intimacy between knowledge and belief through the figure of Moishe the Beadle, with whom Elie Wiesel's *Night* opens. "They called him Moishe the Beadle, as if his entire life he never had a surname," Wiesel begins, immediately positioning the first character of his classic Holocaust memoir at the margins of the Jewish community in his native Transylvanian town of Sighet.[3] Yet what distinguishes Moishe the Beadle in these opening pages is primarily the knowledge he imparts: on the one hand, the traditions of the Kabbalah, which he transmits to a young Wiesel; on the other, his account of the massacres committed by the Einsatzgruppen in Poland at the end of 1942, which he miraculously survived. After returning to Sighet and relating the atrocities he had witnessed, the messenger Moishe the Beadle encountered only disbelief from a community that now considered him a madman. "Thus passed the year 1943," writes Wiesel in *Night*.[4] In the spring of 1944, following the German occupation, the Jews of Sighet were among the hundreds of thousands deported from Hungary to Auschwitz.

Who Shall Live and Who Shall Die? also opens with a messenger of the catastrophe. Following the words of Fleischmann and Weissmandl, the first interviewee to appear on-screen is Gerhart Riegner. In 1933, Riegner fled to Switzerland from Nazi Germany; during the war, he directed the World Jewish Congress (WJC) in Geneva. "On August 1, 1942, history thrust a terrible burden upon Gerhart Riegner," writes Arthur D. Morse in the opening chapter of *While Six Million Died*, his best-selling journalistic account of "American apathy" during the Holocaust, first published in 1967. "On that day," he continues, "Riegner [...] learned from a leading German industrialist that many months before, Hitler had ordered the extermination of all the Jews in Europe."[5] Weeks later, Riegner dispatched the first news of the Final Solution to the West. In New York, his cable reached Stephen Wise, an American Zionist leader and political supporter of Franklin D. Roosevelt, and the cofounder of the WJC. Wise rushed to the State Department to relay the German plan of systematic extermination. In Washington, he was asked to not render the "Riegner telegram" public until the government had gathered more evidence on the crimes committed by the Nazis. Only in late November did Wise finally receive permission to release the information, which now included confirmation from varied sources, notably in Switzerland and Britain, that two million Jews had already been murdered (earlier that same month, Karski had arrived in London and detailed to government officials, as he would decades later during his five-hour-long interview filmed for

Shoah, the horrors he witnessed firsthand in the Warsaw ghetto and at a site near the Bełżec extermination camp).[6]

On November 25, 1942, the *New York Times* infamously reported on Wise's press conference only on page 10. A young Hilberg, who had immigrated with his family to Brooklyn, via Cuba, from Vienna in 1939, telephoned the American Jewish leader. "What are you going to do about the complete annihilation of European Jewry?" he asked Wise, who hung up.[7] In Washington, the news of the extermination reached Peter Bergson (born Hillel Kook), a young Revisionist Zionist and follower of Vladimir Ze'ev Jabotinsky. Beginning in 1940, Bergson campaigned for the creation of a Jewish army to fight alongside the Allies; following the press conference, he shifted his focus to the plight of European Jewry. Working with Samuel Merlin, he established the Emergency Committee to Save the Jewish People of Europe and campaigned tirelessly to rally public and congressional support. In *Who Shall Live and Who Shall Die?*, an emotional Bergson pounds his fist on the table as he deplores the failure of American Jewish leaders, including Wise, to unite and lobby to save the Jews. Merlin, who also appears in the film, maintains that the Zionist leadership was ideologically uninterested in rescuing the Jewish masses of Eastern Europe.

In front of Jarvik's camera, Bergson recounts how the committee's campaign contributed, exactly one year after Wise's press conference, to the introduction of the "Rescue Resolution" in Congress that called on Roosevelt to establish a government agency dedicated to saving European Jewry. The president created the War Refugee Board (WRB) in January 1944 and appointed John Pehle as executive director. While being interviewed in *Who Shall Live and Who Shall Die?*, Pehle describes the actions of the board, which resulted in the rescue of an estimated two hundred thousand Jews, as "little and late."[8] Six years had passed since the international refugee conference, which Roosevelt convened in July 1938 in the French town of Évian, near the Swiss border. In Jarvik's documentary, Nahum Goldmann, the cofounder of the WJC, recalls his participation in the Évian Conference where, in the end, world leaders remained reluctant to accept refugees. "It was one of the most tragic experiences of my long life," Goldmann declares on screen. By 1944, the Germans had murdered millions of Jews in Europe. In the spring of that year, Roosevelt's agency turned to negotiations in Hungary. Roswell McClelland, the WRB representative in Switzerland who had previously partaken in rescue efforts in Vichy France, soon received details of the "Blood for Goods" deal.

McClelland worked alongside the Swiss Jewish leader Saly Meyer to negotiate with the Nazis and delay deportations to Auschwitz; he also appears in *Who Shall Live and Who Shall Die?*. He was approached by Jarvik only weeks before being filmed for *Shoah* in late November 1978. "I am currently making a documentary film about the policy of the United States towards refugees from Hitler," Jarvik announces in his first letter to the former WRB representative dated October 12, 1978.⁹ In his own introductory letter written a year and a half earlier, Lanzmann posits the "bystanders" of the West as protagonists of his cinematographic endeavor. "The reasons for which it seems to me primordial to meet you are obvious," he writes to McClelland in February 1977. "The attitudes of the governments and international organizations faced with, first persecution, then, later, with the process of destruction, are clearly one of the major themes for any work dealing with the holocaust [*sic*]."¹⁰ Throughout his investigation of Allied responses to the catastrophe, Lanzmann recorded not only McClelland but also Riegner, Bergson, Merlin, Pehle, and Goldmann. In addition to these excluded testimonies contemporaneous with the ones featured in *Who Shall Live and Who Shall Die?*, the *Shoah* outtakes include several interviews with tertiary witnesses who recount the rescue efforts, as well as the despair, of Weissmandl, some by reading his wartime letters in front of the camera.

"Through the books of Henry Feingold, Arthur Morse, Raul Hilberg and Phillip [*sic*] Friedman," Lanzmann continues in his letter to McClelland, "I am very much aware of the personal action you took while with the WRB and before—in France, and the priceless results you have achieved. Such a stand shows and implies *what might have been done*."¹¹ The filmmaker's use of the past conditional tense reflects a critical trend in Holocaust studies, intent on exposing the failure to save the Jews of Europe despite Allied—and, in particular, American—knowledge of the destruction. Comprised in the late seventies of only a handful of publications (including the account penned by Morse, whom Lanzmann met at the 1975 Holocaust conference in New York also attended by Feingold and Hilberg), research on rescue and refugee policy would evolve into an important field of study by the time of the release of *Shoah*.¹²

In the decade following Friedman's classic volume on righteous gentiles, *Their Brothers' Keepers* (1957), Hilberg broached the topic in the penultimate chapter of his magnum opus in which he describes "the functional blindness" of the Allies, who prioritized defeating Nazi Germany over saving Jewish victims. "The Jews of Europe," he writes in 1961, "had no allies. In its gravest hour Jewry stood alone, and the realization of that desertion came as a shock to the Jewish leaders all over the world" (Hilberg's assessment of Allied indifference remains unchanged in the subsequent editions of *The Destruction of the European Jews*).¹³ The sixties specifically saw a shift toward scholarship that condemned the Roosevelt administration. In *While Six Million Died*, Morse raised the question, precisely, of "what might have been done," denouncing in particular the anti-Semitism and inaction of the State Department. Several books followed suit, beginning with Feingold's more nuanced study, *The Politics of Rescue* (1970), whose critical stance vis-à-vis American policy between 1938 and 1945 accounts for the limited rescue possibilities in the face of the Nazi machinery of destruction. During the making of *Shoah*, Lanzmann's initial intention to incorporate this historiographical trend within his narrative of the Holocaust is further evidenced through the unedited interview he captured with Feingold in New York, shortly after having recorded Hilberg. In his archive of the catastrophe, these outtakes subsist as a reverse shot to the perspective offered by the author of *The Destruction of the European Jews* in the finished film: that not of the East but of the West—that not of destruction but of rescue.

In 1973, Alouph Hareven had supposedly commissioned Lanzmann to make a film "that *is* the Shoah."[14] Throughout much of the shooting phase, the docu-auteur envisaged a vast cinematographic work that would span from the East to the West and "treat the [Holocaust] in its entirety, in all its gigantic dimensions and its consequences."[15] In the editing room between 1979 and 1985, however, Lanzmann progressively limited the Shoah to the years of extermination and to the *Ostthema* invoked in the excluded testimonies of the Riga survivors Lore Oppenheimer and Hermann Ziering. Encompassing ghettos and killing centers in Poland, the finished film centered in the end on a proximity to the extermination mediated by the testimonies of eyewitnesses closest to the machinery of destruction: the victims, the perpetrators, the "bystanders"—themselves by and large Polish—of the East. In excluding the testimonies of Riegner, Bergson, Merlin, Pehle, Goldmann, and McClelland, *Shoah* abolished the tolerable distance to the catastrophe underlying the perspective of "bystanders" situated in the West.

Over the course of making his opus, Lanzmann recorded fifteen interviews, totaling almost thirty hours of footage, on the question of rescue and refugees.[16] As this chapter reveals, his investigation is noticeably steeped in contemporaneous historiographical debates. Devoid of the proximity of eyewitnesses that would come to define his demands of Holocaust representation, it offers in form and content a striking contrast to both the finished film and the rest of the archive of testimonies he amassed. Accordingly, at the LTC film laboratory between 1979 and 1985, the docu-auteur produced a drastic cut: of these fifteen interviews, he excluded all but Karski and his eyewitness account of the Warsaw ghetto, omitting in the final version the Polish courier's mission to inform world leaders of the destruction, among them Roosevelt.

Silenced in *Shoah*, the question of rescue resurfaced in 1994, following the French release of *Schindler's List*. In his oft-cited review first published in *Le Monde* in March of that year, Lanzmann reaffirms—fifteen years after the miniseries *Holocaust*—the impossibility of representing the event through fiction. Retrospectively, he posits *Shoah* as an anti–*Schindler's List*, even though, as Michael Rothberg aptly argues, the two films "share certain representational techniques and, to some extent, each manipulates survivors and survivor testimony."[17] Nearly a decade after the release of his opus, Lanzmann also faults Steven Spielberg for exclusively focusing on the Jews saved by the German industrialist Oskar Schindler. Yet, more than impose his demands of Holocaust representation, he recasts *Schindler's List* through the memory of undertaking *Shoah* and, more specifically, of composing with incompossibles in the editing room.

In the opening paragraph of his critique, Lanzmann begins by recounting his reaction when he first heard about the *making* of Spielberg's film. "I told myself he was going to be faced with a dilemma. He could not tell Schindler's story without also saying what the Holocaust was. And how could he do that by telling the story of a German who saved 1,300 Jews, since the overwhelming majority of Jews were not saved. [...] In Treblinka or in Auschwitz, the question of rescue was not even on the agenda."[18] In 1994, Lanzmann anachronistically projects onto Spielberg the very dilemma with which he himself had been confronted at the LTC film laboratory: how to compose from his monumental archive of interviews a film about death *and* survival—about the East *and* the West?

MESSENGERS OF THE CATASTROPHE

"*La Solution.*" Thus reads the red label on the three tin canisters containing the negatives of the interview with Nahum Goldmann captured for *Shoah* at his Jerusalem apartment in late January 1975. The hundreds of film cans shelved in the editing room were color-coded according to filming location by Lanzmann and his crew: red for Poland, yellow for Israel, white for Greece, blue for the United States, green for Germany and Switzerland. The red label "*La Solution*" affixed to the Goldmann canisters situates, at once geographically and thematically, this footage within the East. In front of Lanzmann's camera, however, the excluded testimony of the Zionist leader moves only westward.

Following his recollections of Nazi Germany where, in speeches delivered as early as 1932, he "warned that the greatest attack on the existence of the Jewish people is being prepared," Goldmann details a life in exile, first in Switzerland during the years of persecution and then in New York and Washington during the years of extermination. Shortly after having arrived in the United States in 1940, he publicly declared in a speech that "half of

European Jewry may be annihilated" during the war. Two years later, he received Riegner's cable regarding the Final Solution and rushed, alongside Wise, to the State Department. In the *Shoah* outtakes, Goldmann emerges as the first messenger of an impending catastrophe whose magnitude he himself could not have envisioned. "One has to have the imagination of a Hitler to foresee the possibility of Auschwitz," he tells Lanzmann in 1975.[19]

Subsequently labeled "*La Solution*," this early interview footage typifies the theme of systematic destruction found in the excluded material. Yet in *Shoah* no trace remains of prophets such as Goldmann. Rather than the foresight of messengers in the West who, ultimately, could not impede the catastrophe, the finished film privileges the eyewitness accounts of victims, perpetrators, and bystanders in the East—among them the testimony of Franz Suchomel, the officer at the Treblinka killing center where, from July 1942 to November 1943, the Germans murdered an estimated 900,000 Jews. The canisters containing the Suchomel footage secretly recorded with the Paluche in 1976, too, were given the red label of "*La Solution.*" This label was a shortened version of "*La Solution Finale*," a tentative title Lanzmann gave to the film after recording the first interviews with Goldmann and Suchomel.[20]

"Raul Hilberg, Gerhart Riegner and Nahum Goldmann, whom I have already interviewed [...], have agreed to take part in my film as protagonists (I have already been shooting with Riegner and Goldmann)," Lanzmann writes to McClelland in 1977.[21] In the archive, nothing is left of the Riegner material, neither negatives in a tin canister possibly labeled "*La Solution*" nor an annotated interview transcript. A trace of this other messenger of the catastrophe merely subsists in the excluded Goldmann material. In front of the camera, the Zionist leader suggests that Lanzmann meet Riegner who, he specifies, is scheduled to arrive in Jerusalem on that day, seemingly to attend the Sixth Plenary Assembly of the WJC held there February 3–10, 1975.[22] One can only wonder if Lanzmann in fact met with Riegner, in the company of a film crew, during the latter's stay in Jerusalem. Indeed, in the letter to McClelland, his ambiguous wording, "I have already been shooting with Riegner and Goldmann," suggests an early and short-lived interview method abandoned by the time he would record the *Judenrat* members Leib Garfunkel and Benjamin Murmelstein the following year: that of filming his protagonists more than once, over an unspecified period of time, rather than in one sitting or during several consecutive days.

Chronologically, the January 1975 outtakes, for which no transcript exists, were the first to be recorded during the making of *Shoah*. Rather than the inaugural interview in Lanzmann's archive, however, the Goldmann footage constitutes a filmed preliminary meeting or rehearsal in preparation for the opus he would then devote the following decade to. "Claude Lanzmann, who made the excellent *Why Israel?* [*sic*] has asked me to take part in a film he wants to make about the Holocaust," recounts Goldmann in *The Jewish Paradox*, a series

FIGURES 4.1–2. The cans containing the Nahum Goldmann interview negatives; color-coded film cans, including the footage with the historian Raul Hilberg (in blue), the survivor Inge Deutschkron (in green), and the SS officer Franz Suchomel (in red and also labeled "La Solution") (Created by Claude Lanzmann during the filming of *Shoah*. Used by permission of the United States Holocaust Memorial Museum and Yad Vashem, the Holocaust Martyrs and Heroes' Remembrance Authority, Jerusalem).

of autobiographical essays first published in French in 1976. "I asked him what he wanted from me and he replied: 'No other Jew can be the pivot of this film. You lived in Germany before Hitler, you fought against the Nazis for ten years, you got away during the war and did your utmost to save other Jews, you know about the Allies and their shameful attitude."[23]

The material recorded with a protagonist whom Lanzmann once supposedly deemed "the pivot" of *Shoah* offers a striking contrast to the vast archive of filmed testimonies collected thereafter. First, the three tin canisters labeled "*La Solution*" contain a black-and-white work print, thereby rendering the Goldmann outtakes the only ones not in color (the clandestine footage of perpetrators, originally filmed in black and white with the Paluche, aside).[24] Second, unlike the epic length of the interview shot in Rome with Murmelstein in the spring of 1976, the meeting with the Zionist leader and "pivot" of *Shoah* lasts merely an hour and a half—a striking brevity in the filmmaker's archive of the catastrophe. Last, and perhaps most importantly, the familiar film crew that would accompany Lanzmann everywhere between 1975 and 1979 is noticeably absent. Here, an anonymous crew records the Goldmann material. Comprised of a sound engineer, briefly on-screen while holding the clapboard, and a cameraman, they are never seen again in the *Shoah* outtakes.

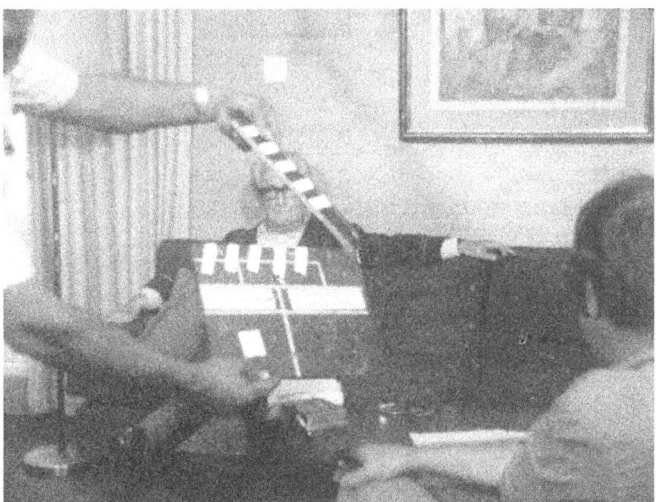

FIGURE 4.3. An anonymous technician holding the clapboard appears briefly on-screen during the interview with Nahum Goldmann (Created by Claude Lanzmann during the filming of *Shoah*. Used by permission of the United States Holocaust Memorial Museum and Yad Vashem, the Holocaust Martyrs and Heroes' Remembrance Authority, Jerusalem).

Hired for that specific shooting day, the ephemeral presence of the two technicians further accentuates the rehearsal quality of this footage, all the while calling attention to the significant role played by Lanzmann's permanent crew in the making of *Shoah*. Beginning with Garfunkel, who is filmed the following year by William Lubtchansky, himself visible and audible in the first minutes of the interview, a handful of collaborators—cinematographers, sound engineers, research assistants—surround Lanzmann during the entirety of the shooting phase. Although largely off-screen in both the finished film and the outtakes, their presence informs and permeates each testimony recorded for *Shoah*. "Incidentally, I love your crew—all of them," a rather taciturn Robert Borden Reams of the State Department suddenly exclaims in the final moments of the interview captured at his home in Panama City in the winter of 1978–1979. "Me too," Lanzmann replies, "I love them very, very much."[25]

Conducted in English, the shared language of the filmmaker and the crew, rather than French, which Goldmann spoke fluently, the 1975 meeting commences with a still shot showing a wall of books and a desk covered with several piles of paper. This opening frame intimates the initial research phase over the course of which Lanzmann determined the contours of his investigation of the Shoah. Accordingly, he starts the interview by referencing Goldmann's memoir, published in 1969. "In your autobiography, where you write in retrospect about the Holocaust, you condemn severely and with very harsh words, not only the non-Jewish world for the appeasement policy, but mostly, too, the Jews themselves," begins Lanzmann, while the camera slowly pans to the right side of the room where he sits across from Goldmann. "You talk about the total failure of what might be called the Jewish leadership," he continues, "you accuse them of miopie [sic], shortsightedness [...] and you say they were unable to foresee the catastrophe."[26]

An unusual distance from the destruction process underlies these inaugural words. In marked contrast to the opening images of Chełmno that are coupled with Simon Srebnik's testimonial performance in the finished film, Lanzmann oscillates here between *before* and *after* the catastrophe—between the early years of persecution and the postwar years of accusation. Similarly, the question of the unseen expressed by Goldmann in harsh denunciatory terms subsequently became an aesthetic and ethical dilemma in *Shoah*: how to represent in cinema an unprecedented disaster of which no images exist? Rather than "a film that *is* the Shoah," this very first footage gathered by Lanzmann constitutes a portrait of a leading public figure haunted by his failure to convince the Jews of the atrocities to come and, ultimately, to save them. Much like Moishe the Beadle in Wiesel's *Night*, Goldmann's repeated warnings went unheard. As he tells Lanzmann, he was accused during the years of persecution of being a madman: of having "the imagination of hysterical Jews" and of acting as "a prophet of gloom."[27]

"Did you meet personally in New York with [Szmul] Zygielbojm?" Lanzmann asks Goldmann in 1975, invoking another messenger of the catastrophe whose despair and tragic fate calls to mind the story of Adam Czerniaków.[28] In October 1939, Czerniaków appointed Szmul "Artur" Zygielbojm, a prominent leader of the Bund, to the Warsaw ghetto *Judenrat*. Advocating not compliance but resistance to German orders, Zygielbojm fled Poland in February 1940 with the mission of revealing to the world the persecution of the Jews.[29] After several months in Belgium and France, he reached the United States and unceasingly appealed to Americans to rescue Polish Jewry. In New York, Goldmann never encountered Zygielbojm, who left for London in the spring of 1942. There, he served as one of the two Jewish members of the National Council of the Polish Government-in-Exile, along with the Zionist leader and WJC member Ignacy Schwarzbart. Reports of the annihilation, including from the Bund in Warsaw, soon reached him. Then, on December 2, 1942, Zygielbojm met with Karski. The courier had just begun

FIGURE 4.4. A close-up of the "prophet of gloom" Nahum Goldmann (Created by Claude Lanzmann during the filming of *Shoah*. Used by permission of the United States Holocaust Memorial Museum and Yad Vashem, the Holocaust Martyrs and Heroes' Remembrance Authority, Jerusalem).

his mission to inform the Western Allies of the unfolding catastrophe in occupied Poland that he had seen with his own eyes and detailed in a written report (after reading Karski's account, Schwarzbart cabled the information to the WJC in New York, pleading in the last line of his telegram: "BELIEVE THE UNBELIEVABLE").[30]

Several weeks earlier in Warsaw, two men of the Jewish underground, unnamed in *Shoah* but identified by Karski in the outtakes as the Bundist Leon Feiner and the Zionist Adolf Berman, had smuggled the courier into the ghetto following the mass deportations to Treblinka between July and September 1942.[31] They had also entrusted him with a final request for the Jewish leaders in exile: to start hunger strikes outside the offices of British and American authorities in order to shake the world out of its indifference. In London, Karski relayed the demand of the two leaders to Zygielbojm—a memory he reenacts in the outtakes of his interview with Lanzmann. "Let them stay outside. Let them refuse drink. Let them refuse food. Let them die. Let them die a slow death. Let humanity see it. Perhaps it will move humanity," the courier repeats in front of the camera in 1978, his eyes closed as they had been when he had addressed Zygielbojm.[32] Several months later, following his meeting with Roosevelt, Karski met with Goldmann and Wise in Washington, DC. During his interview with Lanzmann, Goldmann never recounts the 1943 meeting with the Polish courier. Yet when he describes his own guilt at not having done enough to rescue the Jews of Europe, he recalls how the underground in Warsaw had urged them to start a hunger strike outside of the White House. "We didn't do it," he tells Lanzmann. "Even we were lacking such a daring imagination."[33]

As Karski recalls in *Shoah*, during his meeting with the two Jewish leaders in Warsaw, Berman had alluded to a future revolt in the ghetto for which they were requesting weapons. On April 19, 1943, months after the courier's clandestine visit, the Warsaw ghetto uprising began. That very day, American and British delegates gathered in Bermuda for a conference on the Jewish refugee question. On this island, inaccessible to the press and located thousands of miles away from Warsaw, neither government offered any concrete plan for the rescue of European Jewry. "The conference was held and of course it goes down in my book as the mockery of the Bermuda Conference," the historian Henry Feingold explains to Lanzmann in the outtakes. "The irony is of course that precisely while the conference was being held the Warsaw ghetto uprising is occurring."[34]

This tragic multidirectional memory, or shot reverse shot of the catastrophe, is evoked in several excluded interviews with "bystanders" of the West. It also haunts the story of Zygielbojm with which Morse, in *While Six Million Died*, ends the book's third chapter titled, precisely, "Warsaw Bermuda." On the night of May 11–12, 1943, in the final days of the suppression of the Warsaw ghetto revolt, during which Zygielbojm's wife and youngest child perished, the Bund leader took his life in London, after months of pleading for Allied action to save the remaining Jews of Poland. "By my death I wish to make my final protest against the passivity with which the world is looking on and permitting the extermination of the Jewish people," Zygielbojm wrote in his farewell letter to the Polish Government-in-Exile.[35]

In *Shoah*, the narrative of the Warsaw ghetto unfolds entirely in the East, from Czerniaków's suicide to Karski's visit to the end of the uprising recounted by Simha Rotem in the final moments of the film. In the outtakes, however, it encompasses Zygielbojm's despair in the West, which the messenger Karski details in the excluded segments of his filmed testimony—as he had already done in the pages of *Story of a Secret State*. In this 1944 bestselling memoir, even before detailing his mission in the West, he concludes the chapter succinctly titled "The Ghetto" with a description of his meeting with Zygielbojm in London and the news of his suicide.[36]

Following the publication of *Story of a Secret State*, Karski ceased to speak of his wartime experiences until Lanzmann contacted him in 1977. In a short testimonial account published in 1992, recalling how the filmmaker finally convinced him to be a protagonist of his Holocaust opus, Karski bitterly explains that his silence in the immediate postwar period originated in the "hypocrisy" of political, military, and religious leaders who had been informed of his report between 1942 and 1943. When the war ended, he watched as they went to Germany and Poland to see the atrocities for themselves. "They saw, and all of them were shocked. All of them, without exception. [...] Hypocrisy. They knew. And if some didn't know, it was because they didn't want to know. Human beings have this capacity to disregard. For over thirty years I never mentioned to anyone that I was in the war." In 1977, the first letter he received from Lanzmann went unanswered. The filmmaker then telephoned him. "I told him, 'I saw terrible things in Poland concerning the Jews which I don't want to remember.' He replied, 'That is why we should not let humanity forget.'"[37]

After a preliminary interview conducted a few months before Lanzmann's first trip to Poland, Karski was filmed for *Shoah* in October 1978 over the course of two days at his home in Washington, DC. His wife, Pola Nirenska, a native of Warsaw who lost most of her family in the Holocaust, appears briefly toward the end of the footage captured on the first shooting day. "Unable to bear it," the courier later recalled while describing the filming process, "[she] left the house."[38] During this first day, Karski describes in detail his visit to both the Warsaw ghetto and a transit camp located in the vicinity of Bełżec. In the final cut, Lanzmann solely retained the account of his mission in the ghetto. "Now... now I go back thirty-five years. No, I don't go back," the witness first exclaims in *Shoah* before breaking down and leaving the room. Evocative of Abraham Bomba's testimonial performance in the barbershop, these tearful opening words precede Karski's poignant reenactment of the past in the finished film. "Now I go back in my memory to another world," he declares a few instants earlier in the outtakes, affirming his intention to relive his mission for the film.[39] Anticipating his own role in the barbershop the following year, Lanzmann tells Karski in the footage captured on that first day: "I just want you to know that I know how difficult it is."[40]

In a letter dated July 7, 1978, Lanzmann had suggested that Karski prepare for the interview by rereading *Story of a Secret State* and perusing his wartime papers.[41] Accordingly, rather than the emblematic gestures of either Bomba in *Shoah* or Ada Lichtman in the archive, Karski "goes back" to the traumatic past by delivering his filmed testimony in the very manner he had delivered his report to the leaders in the West thirty-five years earlier: from memory, and with precision and detachment, his gaze often lowered or to the side, breaking down only in the final moments of his description of the Warsaw ghetto. This testimonial performance encapsulates his description, excluded from the finished film, of the very method he deployed as a messenger of the catastrophe. "Precision, no comments unless I was asked for some personal comments," he remarks in the outtakes captured on the second shooting day, during which he details his meetings with leaders and officials in England and the United States. "I understood my mission: I was not supposed to have any feelings. I was a camera. And I did not have any feelings for some time."[42]

In the excluded footage, the framing of the interview participates in the reenactment of Karski's wartime mission. While only Lubtchansky's name appears alongside Lanzmann's on the clapboard, two cameras were in fact used to record this testimony in October 1978. The presence of another camera, operated by Dominique Chapuis and duly noted throughout the portions of the interview transcript corresponding to the second day, effectively stages the transmission of knowledge of the catastrophe. Instead of a reverse shot of Lanzmann listening to the eyewitness—a shot commonly used in the *Shoah* outtakes but omitted from the finished film—the two men appear together in the frame, thereby rendering Lanzmann the receiver of Karski's testimony, both past and present.

The Question of Rescue and Refugees   189

FIGURE 4.5. A second camera films Claude Lanzmann and Jan Karski sitting across from each other during the interview (Created by Claude Lanzmann during the filming of *Shoah*. Used by permission of the United States Holocaust Memorial Museum and Yad Vashem, the Holocaust Martyrs and Heroes' Remembrance Authority, Jerusalem).

"When once in your life you have been the bearer of a message, you remain its bearer forever," writes Yannick Haenel in *The Messenger*, here approximating the reenactment at play in Karski's testimony for *Shoah*.[43] Originally published in French in 2009 under the title *Jan Karski*, Haenel's fictionalized portrait of the famous courier recounts his wartime mission from the East to the West in three distinct parts: the first describes, and at times comments on, his testimony of the Warsaw ghetto in *Shoah*; the second summarizes *Story of a Secret State*; the third, which is the only one narrated in the first-person singular, imagines Karski's life haunted, in the decades following his mission, by the indifference of Allied governments during the Holocaust. "No one believed me because no one *wanted* to believe me," declares Karski's character in the opening paragraph of his monologue.[44] These words encapsulate the *parti pris* of the French writer in this section of the novel: a severe condemnation of the leaders in the West, first and foremost Roosevelt, whom the courier remembers, under the pen of Haenel, as bored during his report and generally more interested in his secretary's legs than in the atrocities being described.[45]

The publication of *The Messenger* in France spurred controversy. During the so-called "Karski affair," the historian Annette Wieviorka labeled the novel a "false testimony" and criticized Haenel's vilification of the Western Allies, as well as his fictionalization of the events by reconstructing and distorting—despite existing historical accounts—Karski's meeting with Roosevelt on July 28, 1943.[46] Lanzmann also condemned *The Messenger*, which he called a "false novel." He deplored that Haenel chose to rewrite history, seemingly unaware of the excluded *Shoah* footage in which Karski recounts his meeting with Roosevelt. Although never invoking the transfer of the outtakes to the USHMM nor the fact that the Karski interview, one of the first to be preserved, had been available for viewing since 2000, Lanzmann affirms the necessity of reestablishing the truth by making the voice of the courier heard again.[47]

The Karski Report, a fifty-two-minute documentary made from the unused portions of the 1978 footage, aired on French television in March 2010. Concomitantly, this newly edited version of the interview appeared in print in *Les Temps Modernes*. In this third film using *Shoah* outtakes, the docu-auteur deploys the words of the Polish courier to offer a counter-representation of Haenel's fictionalized account. Karski nevertheless acknowledges on camera that Roosevelt did not ask any questions about either his visit to the ghetto or the transit camp. At the same time, as Richard Golsan emphasizes in his critical assessment of the "affair," he reminds Lanzmann that the fate of German-occupied Poland, rather than the plight of the Jews, was the main objective of his mission as messenger for the Polish Government-in-Exile.[48] The courier does praise the American president for arranging meetings with several prominent Jewish officials during his mission, including Goldmann and the Supreme Court justice Felix Frankfurter.

In his critique of *The Messenger* as a "false novel," Lanzmann notes that the making of *Shoah* coincided with a certain historiographical trend epitomized in Feingold's *The Politics of Rescue* and David Wyman's *The Abandonment of the Jews* (1984), which consisted of retrospectively denouncing, much like Haenel, the supposed passivity of the Allies during the Holocaust.[49] A quarter of a century after the release of *Shoah*, the docu-auteur never reveals that he had considered integrating this perspective into his own narrative when he interviewed Feingold several weeks after Karski (incidentally, reminiscent of Haenel's portrayal of Roosevelt, Lanzmann reprimands Feingold on-camera—and supposedly Hilberg before him—for staring at the female crew members instead of looking at him during the excluded interview).[50] Rather, he summarizes American rescue efforts, specifically mentioning the creation of the WRB in 1944, which Roosevelt "unfailingly supported," and the important work of men like Pehle and McClelland. He fails to divulge, however, that these two men were also recorded for *Shoah*. "It was very late," Lanzmann concedes in passing in 2010 regarding the WRB, here echoing Feingold, who affirms in the outtakes: "It came too late."[51]

At the same time that he retrieves the Karski outtakes to refute a manipulation of history in *The Messenger*, Lanzmann displaces to the off-frame his own investigation of what he initially termed, according to Goldmann, the "shameful attitude" of the Allies. Haenel, however, insinuates this investigation in the first part of his novel. Invoking the image of the Statue of Liberty with which the courier's testimony is juxtaposed in *Shoah*, he asks: "Does Claude Lanzmann want [...] to highlight the difference [...] between the suffering of Europe's Jews, as expressed in Jan Karski's voice, and what America actually did to save them?"[52] In his analysis of this passage from *The Messenger*, Golsan expresses skepticism about this reading of Lanzmann's editing strategy. He writes: "Given Lanzmann's reaction to [the novel] and his rejection of Haenel's interpretation of history and the role of the Allies and especially the United States during the war, this speculation as to the filmmaker's intent in *Shoah* seems doubtful, to say the least."[53] Yet, much like the outtakes used in *The Karski Report*, which, Remy Besson reminds us, "have undergone an editing process every bit as elaborate as that of *Shoah*," Lanzmann's published critique of *The Messenger* carefully edits out his own investigation of Allied indifference and inaction during the making of the film—of which the footage in *Shoah* of not only the Statue of Liberty but also the White House subsists as a trace.[54] Although he chose to leave out this contentious chapter of the Holocaust from the finished film, the outtakes recast the "Karski affair" in a very different light. Akin to the "surprising hypothesis" put forth and pertinently argued by Rothberg that "*Schindler's List* and *Shoah* themselves almost converge," *The Messenger* and the excluded footage with "bystanders" of the West also overlap significantly.[55]

The filmmaker's probing of the question of Allied indifference, which Haenel revived in 2009, is evidenced by the inclusion of several "bystanders" of the West filmed for *Shoah* in *Who Shall Live and Who Shall Die?*, a documentary that also met a controversial reception. Following its release in 1982, Lucy Dawidowicz published a rebuttal denouncing both Jarvik's failure to represent rescue efforts during the war as well as his condemnation of American Jewish leaders.[56] Beyond this article, and contra the contemporaneous historiographical trend, Dawidowicz systematically refuted in her work accusations against the Western Allies. For her, these accusations overshadowed the extent of the machinery of destruction and what in fact had been done to save the Jews of Europe. Accordingly, in her correspondence with McClelland, she suggests that the former WRB representative consider focusing his memoir entirely on his wartime rescue efforts.[57]

In *The Messenger*, Haenel posits Zygielbojm as the unique counterpoint to the supposed indifference of leaders and officials in the West to whom Karski delivered his report. "I thought of Szmul Zygielbojm, who had just committed suicide," the author-narrator writes upon describing the fictional Karski's insomnia, following his mission. "When I arrived in London, he was the first person, and probably the only person, who really listened to me, because he *wanted* to know—and because, in a sense, he already did know."[58] In *Story of a Secret State*, which was written a little over a year after the Bund leader's suicide, the courier concludes the chapter on the Warsaw ghetto by juxtaposing the messenger's death and the world's silence. "Since then I have often thought about Szmul Zygielbojm," Karski writes. "Of the deaths that have taken place in this war, surely Zygielbojm's is one of the most frightening, the sharpest revelation of the extent to which the world has become cold and unfriendly, nations and individuals separated by immense gulfs of indifference, selfishness, and convenience."[59]

In the *Shoah* outtakes, Zygielbojm embodies a tragic figure whom Lanzmann, like Haenel, sets apart from the other "bystanders" of the West in Karski's testimony. In the letter dated July 7, 1978, suggesting that the courier reread his memoir and papers, Lanzmann divides the filmed interview to come into six topics that move from the East to the West. The courier's mission to inform the world of the annihilation encompasses two distinct points by means of which Lanzmann differentiates the Bund leader from all the other officials, including Roosevelt: "(4) Your meeting with Zygielbojm, his reactions to your report and your personal opinion about him; (5) The reactions of the people in England and America to whom you delivered your report: Roosevelt, Justice Frankfurter [...], Dr. Goldmann, Rabbi Wise etc. etc."[60]

Contrary to these "bystanders" of the West, Zygielbojm occupies the twofold position of witness *and* messenger. Like Karski, he saw with his own eyes the persecution of Polish Jewry and informed Allied governments of the impending destruction. Like Karski, he was a protagonist in the narrative of the Warsaw ghetto, a site of memory of capital importance for Lanzmann. If Zygielbojm's suicide in May 1943—duly reported at the time by newspapers around the world—invokes Czerniaków's tragic fate in the ghetto, this messenger's story ultimately remained on the cutting room floor, alongside the many other testimonies of "bystanders" of the West recorded for *Shoah*. In the finished film, Lanzmann retained only the *Judenrat* leader who took his life behind the ghetto walls in July 1942, unbeknownst to the Allied governments, whose silence and indifference Zygielbojm denounced months later in his farewell letter.

"Who bears witness for the witness?" Haenel asks in the epigraph of his novel, freely translating the oft-cited final line of Paul Celan's poem

"Ash-aureole."⁶¹ In *Shoah*, Hilberg bears witness for Czerniaków in reading excerpts from the English edition of his diary. In the outtakes, a similar mise-en-scène underlies the footage with the Bund leader's brother, Faivel Zygielbojm, at his home in Tel Aviv in 1979. Faivel also bears witness for the witness in translating from Yiddish to English excerpts from Szmul's wartime letters, including his farewell note to the Polish Government-in-Exile. As he reads in front of the camera, the famous portrait of his brother, taken in London sometime between 1942 and 1943, hangs on the wall behind him. In marked contrast to the finished film, where Lanzmann omits all archival images, including of Czerniaków, Lubtchansky effectuates in the opening moments of the interview a close-up of Szmul's black-and-white photograph. More striking is the closing shot of this excluded material, evidencing an ethics of representation still in the making in 1979: an extreme close-up of an archival image, thought to have been taken in Treblinka, showing a pile of corpses at the center of which a woman's face is visible. The most explicit representation of the destruction of European Jewry in all of the *Shoah* outtakes, this photograph is juxtaposed with Faivel's now-off-screen voice. The woman pictured, he tells Lanzmann, is believed to be Rivka (Rivkele) Zygielbojm, Szmul's daughter from his first marriage, who was deported with her mother from the Warsaw ghetto.⁶²

Whereas the expert witness Hilberg, who imparts historical knowledge of the catastrophe as much as he mediates the representation of Czerniaków, was filmed for over six hours, the footage with Faivel Zygielbojm lasts merely forty minutes. Rather than interview him, Lanzmann remains off-frame and directs his performance. Once an actor in Warsaw and later in Johannesburg where he survived the war, Faivel Zygielbojm merely lends his voice in front of the camera. Never revealing his own trajectory during the Holocaust, he mentions in passing *The Strength to Die: A Family Book*, which he published in Yiddish in 1976. Evocative of a *yizkor* book, this memoir centered on the Zygielbojm family includes some of the letters penned by the late Bund leader during the war.⁶³

Calling to mind Lanzmann's question in the Goldmann outtakes ("Did you meet personally in New York with Zygielbojm?"), the first letter from which Faivel quotes is dated "New York, 4th June 1941" (further enacting this paper memory reminiscent of Czerniaków's diary in *Shoah*, the camera films this document at the end of the interview, lingering in particular over the Yiddish handwriting). The Bund leader describes a life in exile in the shadow of the horror he witnessed in the Warsaw ghetto. "I feel torn apart by homesickness and restlessness about my dear ones who have remained there," Faivel Zygielbojm reads in two different takes. "[…] I cannot free myself of the thousands of images of terrifying fear and terror, from the destruction of countries, the tragedies of thousands of individuals which I have seen with my own eyes."⁶⁴ The second letter, "dated April 7th 1943 from London, over a month before his suicide" and

FIGURES 4.6–7. A close-up of Szmul Zygielbojm's portrait in the outtakes captured at the home of his brother Faivel (Created by Claude Lanzmann during the filming of *Shoah*. Used by permission of the United States Holocaust Memorial Museum and Yad Vashem, the Holocaust Martyrs and Heroes' Remembrance Authority, Jerusalem).

nearly half a year after his meeting with Karski, is the last one Faivel Zygielbojm received from his brother.

In remarkable proximity to Czerniaków ("The survival of the children was the ultimate test of his efforts in the ghetto," write Hilberg and Staron in the closing paragraph of their introduction to the diary), the Bund leader is here haunted by the fate of the children, including his daughter.[65] More precisely, in this letter permeated with guilt and despair, Szmul Zygielbojm recalls the news he received in November of the murder of the children in the Bund-run Medem Sanatorium near Warsaw, where his wife Manie worked (the children were deported to Treblinka on August 22, 1942). He then mentions Rivkele, whose fate is unknown to him, before asking: "What right did I have to save myself? Why did I not share everybody's fate? *I did not even have the satisfaction of saving a single child.*"[66] In these outtakes, the parallel representation of Czerniaków and Zygielbojm's tragic fates is rendered even more explicit when the camera captures a shot of Faivel's bookshelves where the 1968 Hebrew version of *The Warsaw Ghetto Diary* is displayed.

On May 11, 1943, the night the Bund leader took his own life, the Jewish underground in Warsaw sent him a telegram titled "What have you accomplished?" In front of the camera, Faivel Zygielbojm reads the condemnation of the West—reminiscent of *The Messenger*—written in the final days of the

FIGURE 4.8. The 1968 Hebrew edition of the diary kept by Adam Czerniaków in the Warsaw ghetto (Created by Claude Lanzmann during the filming of *Shoah*. Used by permission of the United States Holocaust Memorial Museum and Yad Vashem, the Holocaust Martyrs and Heroes' Remembrance Authority, Jerusalem).

revolt. These words from the East never reached his late brother in London. "World of freedom and justice remains silent and inactive [stop] Astonishing [stop] This is the third cable in the last two weeks [stop] Wire immediately what you have done [stop]."[67] Months earlier, when Karski had relayed the message from the Bundist and Zionist leaders in Warsaw, Szmul Zygielbojm had ultimately answered: "I will do everything I can. Believe me, Mr. Karski, believe me. I will do everything they demand."[68] After repeatedly pleading to the Allied governments and even appealing to the world on the BBC ("we shall bear most of the moral responsibility for what is happening," Faivel reads on camera, quoting from the radio broadcast), Szmul took an overdose of sleeping pills.[69] In *Story of a Secret State*, as well as in the excluded portions of his interview with Lanzmann, Karski inaccurately recalls, as though haunted by the catastrophe, Szmul Zygielbojm having taken his own life by turning on the gas in his London apartment.[70]

In the *Shoah* outtakes, the memory of Zygielbojm's suicide casts a shadow over Karski's mission to inform the world of the annihilation. "Do you think that the requests you made to him from the Jews in Poland had a direct influence on his suicide, which he committed exactly six months later?" Lanzmann asks Karski in two different takes in the excluded footage.[71] This question is indicative of a certain sense of guilt that, already expressed in *Story of a Secret State*, continues to burden the courier in 1978. If, in the decades following his mission, which he spent teaching at Georgetown University, Karski condemned himself to silence ("I disciplined myself," he declares during the interview), he reveals that the story of Zygielbojm constituted the sole exception.[72] "You forced me into this interview about the ghetto and Bełzec, I don't go there when I have free will. I do go to Zygielbojm. I did not have one single class in twenty years of teaching […] where, when I come to the war situation, I did not tell my students, 'There was Zygielbojm!'" he exclaims with tears in his eyes while the camera effectuates an extreme close-up of his face.[73]

Evocative of his opening words in *Shoah*, as well as of his tears in the final moments of his description of the Warsaw ghetto, Karski once again "goes back" and bears witness for the witness. The first meeting in the West he describes to Lanzmann is the meeting with the Bund leader. While denoting the importance accorded to Zygielbojm by both the courier and the docu-auteur, the primacy of this encounter largely effaces—with the exception of Roosevelt and Justice Frankfurter—his other meetings. "You remember Zygielbojm but you cannot remember Wise," Lanzmann remarks after having asked how the American Jewish leader reacted to his report of the transit camp near Bełzec.[74]

The emotionally charged memory of the Bund leader seemingly informs the entirety of the courier's testimonial performance on this second shooting day entirely omitted from *Shoah*. Perhaps from having "gone back" the day before to the atrocities he witnessed in German-occupied Poland after decades of silence, perhaps still haunted by Zygielbojm's despair and suicide—or perhaps both—the courier bears witness in an agitated manner to how the "bystanders" in the West received his testimony. He quite literally incarnates his interlocutors, like an actor on stage, at times even jumping from the sofa in order to add dramatic effect while he details their respective reactions. In *The Karski Report*, he suddenly stands up as he recalls the words of Justice Frankfurter, who exclaimed after hearing the details of the unprecedented horrors unfolding in the East, "I did not say that you are lying; I said that I don't believe you!" Lanzmann duly notes this altered testimonial performance in the introductory crawl text of the documentary. In fact, it retrospectively serves as a justification for his editorial decisions at the LTC film laboratory between 1979 and 1985. "For properly artistic reasons of dramatic tensions," he declares in *The Karski Report*, "at this point of the construction of [*Shoah*]—because it would have been too long, because Karski himself acted very differently on the second day of shooting compared to the first—I decided not to include the second day."

Beyond the meeting with Roosevelt, with which he refuted Haenel's fictional reconstruction in 2010, Lanzmann also left out Karski's encounter with Zygielbojm. In lieu of the portrait visible on the wall behind Faivel, Lanzmann prompts the courier to first describe him. "How did he look?" he asks, as he would months later while questioning Ruth Elias about her encounters with Dr. Mengele at Auschwitz. "Rather smallish, not tall at all," Karski replies. "Not fat, physically. Nervous. Agitated."[75] Intertwining mimesis and remembrance, an equally nervous and agitated Karski details how Zygielbojm, "disintegrating" in front of his eyes and already "lost in helplessness," had pressed him to "Talk! Talk!" He kept him so long that Karski feared he would miss his next meeting. At the same time, because he already knew, Zygielbojm appeared unmoved by the atrocities being described. "He said 'I know everything,' and he was keeping you," Lanzmann aptly remarks, hinting at Zygielbojm's despair.[76] Beyond despair, could there have also been a certain identification on the part of Zygielbojm with Karski, this other messenger of the catastrophe who, like him, would inform the world of the atrocities he had witnessed in the Warsaw ghetto?

In the unused material, Karski's act of bearing witness for the witness culminates in a poignant minute-long reenactment of Zygielbojm's reaction when he relayed the request of the Warsaw Jewish leaders. Suddenly and quite theatrically—and in stark contrast to his calm reenactment of the day before—he jumps up from the couch and proceeds to pace around the room yelling, as though he were Zygielbojm, "Madness! Madness! Madness! They are mad! They are mad! The whole world is mad! Madness! Madness! They are crazy! They don't understand anything! They will not let me die! They will send two policemen, they will arrest me! They will take me to an asylum!"[77] After the Bund leader sat down again, Karski remembers, he proceeded to ask the courier—possibly in a moment of identification—how *he* was coping. "Then I left him," Karski recalls in the outtakes, concluding his memory of the encounter.

In his critique of *The Messenger*, Lanzmann begins with the making of *Shoah* and his search for Karski, whom he deemed "a capital witness" of the catastrophe. Karski, after all, had seen the atrocities in the East and informed the West. He had also met with Roosevelt and Zygielbojm. Yet for the docu-auteur Lanzmann would become between 1973 and 1985, the Polish underground courier was "capital" insofar as he had rediscovered him. Unlike Goldmann or Zygielbojm, Karski and his memoir (once a "Book of the Month," the courier remarks in the outtakes) had been all but forgotten by 1977 when Lanzmann first wrote to him.[78] Calling to mind Czerniaków, whose memory

FIGURE 4.9. Jan Karski incarnating Szmul Zygielbojm reacting to the request for a hunger strike (Created by Claude Lanzmann during the filming of *Shoah*. Used by permission of the United States Holocaust Memorial Museum and Yad Vashem, the Holocaust Martyrs and Heroes' Remembrance Authority, Jerusalem).

Hilberg revived in myriad ways, "the release of *Shoah*," Lanzmann affirms in his critique of *The Messenger*, "resuscitated Karski for each one of us, allowing him to enter History."[79]

Crediting his Holocaust opus for making the voice of the courier once again heard, Lanzmann never evokes Karski's own decision or even his reasons to stop bearing witness after the war. He omits, as well, the methods deployed to convince Karski to tell his story. "I consider it fair to compensate the people who participate in my film," Lanzmann writes in his 1978 letter. "Would you agree, dear Professor Karski, upon the sum of 500 Dollars for each shooting day?"[80] By contrast, in *The Patagonian Hare*, Lanzmann affirms that Karski had asked to be paid for his testimonial performance, as a result of which they signed a contract. Per this agreement, Karski would refrain from giving any additional on-camera interviews until the release of *Shoah*.[81] A contract was in fact drafted in 1982 when, in the midst of the editing phase, Karski wrote to him asking if the film would ever be finished (in this contract, "Death in the Fields" is the provisional title of Lanzmann's opus still in the making).[82]

Having broken his silence for the film, Karski was now willing to tell his story again in front of other cameras. In order for the auteur to resuscitate this "capital witness," however, the courier's postwar silence needed to be maintained. Much like this silence, Lanzmann would also edit carefully around the interview, retaining Karski's "capital" account of the Warsaw ghetto, but omitting the West and its indifference. "The public opinion, as well as the Governments, of the Allied nations cannot say that they did not know": thus Karski concludes his testimony on the second shooting day, echoing with these last words not only the reason for his postwar silence but also Haenel's *The Messenger*.

After the release of *Shoah*, Lanzmann repeatedly affirmed having decided in the early stages of making the film that his protagonists would be the Jewish victims who had witnessed the destruction process most immediately—the members of the *Sonderkommando*. During the editing phase, between 1979 and 1985, the docu-auteur transposed this selection criterion to the category of perpetrators and "bystanders" alike, thereby rendering proximity to the horror the defining feature of all the testimonies in *Shoah*. Not only did he exclude American and British indifference to the fate of European Jewry, but also he solely retained the indifference of the "bystanders" in the East. In the finished film, the faces, voices, and gestures of Poles in towns and villages near killing centers, who passively watched as the Jews arrived in cattle cars and disappeared behind barbed wire, alone encompass the broad category of "bystander" in *Shoah*.[83]

In reframing his investigation through the lens of the destruction, Lanzmann concomitantly left on the cutting room floor the counter-perspective of rescue. If he excluded the WRB representatives' testimonies recorded in Washington, he opted during the filming phase to *not* record Polish rescuers—among them, Władysław Bartoszewski, the leader of Żegota, the Polish Council to Aid Jews in Warsaw. In his 1978 letter to Karski, Lanzmann mentions his first trip to Poland during which he met with Bartoszewski, whom he intended to film (years later, following the release of *Shoah*, the docu-auteur revealed that Bartoszewski, unlike the courier, had been "unable to relive the past," thereby recasting his decision to not film him through the lens of his demands of Holocaust representation).[84] In 1978, he writes: "I was very impressed during this inquiry in Poland, when I discovered how many Poles endangered their lives in order to save Jews. As you know, *this question of rescue will be one of the major items of my film*."[85] As though remembering Lanzmann's words, Karski, in his short text on *Shoah* published in 1986, deplored Bartoszewski's eventual absence and that of other Polish rescuers. For the courier, this missing page of history in Lanzmann's narrative of the catastrophe would have revealed to the world—as could be said about the excluded story of Zygielbojm—that, while "the Jews were abandoned by governments, [...] [t]hey were not abandoned by mankind."[86]

IMAGINING TREBLINKA FROM WASHINGTON OR NEW YORK

On the tin canisters containing the footage captured with Robert Borden Reams in Panama City during the winter of 1978–1979, the blue label cryptically reads "Fish." The title found on the transcript only deepens the mystery: "Fishing Party." The excluded one-hour-and-forty-minute interview with Reams, once a refugee specialist at the State Department, begins as a road movie with noirish, enigmatic undertones. At the wheel of a Pontiac also visible in the Paula Biren outtakes, Lanzmann drives down a road in the Florida Panhandle. His crew, including sound engineer Bernard Aubouy, whom the filmmaker addresses several times, remains off-screen. After three takes, they finally arrive at the Bay Point resort community. "Excuse-me, [the house of] Ambassador Reams—I don't remember the road," Lanzmann asks the security officer at the front gate. Invoking the name of his protagonist for the first time, the docu-auteur reveals that he visited him before for a preliminary interview. As he drives through Bay Point in search of the Reams residence, he then declares somewhat cynically, "What a nice place!" A few instants later, recognizing the

FIGURE 4.10. Claude Lanzmann driving to the Bay Point resort community (Created by Claude Lanzmann during the filming of *Shoah*. Used by permission of the United States Holocaust Memorial Museum and Yad Vashem, the Holocaust Martyrs and Heroes' Remembrance Authority, Jerusalem).

red roof, he heads slowly toward the house, outside of which Reams can be seen. "He's there, *waiting for us*," Lanzmann exclaims in a slow sardonic tone, as though concealing a plan.[87]

More than three decades later in his critique of *The Messenger*, Lanzmann recalled this shooting day with just as much cynicism, describing Reams as "a retiree living the good life on a golf course in Panama City and proud of his mastery of the dry martini."[88] At the State Department, Reams had served as principal advisor on Jewish questions under Assistant Secretary of State Breckinridge Long. In 1943, he had also been part of the American delegation at the disappointing Bermuda Conference. In scholarship concurrent with *Shoah*, Reams and Long epitomized the State Department's anti-Semitism, which hindered humanitarian efforts during the Holocaust. As revealed first by Morse in *While Six Million Died* and, subsequently, in the books of Feingold, Friedman, and Wyman, both men worked during the war "to curb any special efforts on behalf of the Jews," above all by suppressing reports of the genocide, increasing visa restrictions, and propagating the idea that most refugees were subversive agents.[89] Long emerged as the principal culprit, having misled the president and, to quote Feingold in the outtakes, "single-handedly taken upon himself to stop the entrance of Jews into the United States."[90]

Long's anti-Semitic attitudes and actions culminated in his inaccurate testimony in Congress, in the midst of the campaign to pass the "Rescue Resolution" in late 1943. In an attempt to refute accusations that the State Department had mishandled refugee matters, he grossly inflated—by as much as 250 percent—the numbers of asylum seekers who had actually entered the United States since 1933.[91] Tragically, as John Pehle observes in his unused testimony for *Shoah*, not only were the quotas not filled during these years but "the amount of refugees that the US could and should have received goes up till one million and a half people."[92] Long resigned from the State Department a year later. He passed away in 1958, leaving behind diaries archived at the Library of Congress. In preparation for his investigation of the rescue and refugee question, Lanzmann read these diaries, which tarnished Long's anti-Semitic legacy only further.[93] Reams, for his part, pursued his diplomatic career after the war, serving as ambassador in several West African countries. In the unused interview, the camera documents this unhindered career by filming the diplomatic certificates on his living room wall that he received from Presidents Eisenhower and Kennedy.[94]

In *While Six Million Died*, Morse notes that Reams retrospectively cast himself as a "master sergeant" who had merely followed orders from his superiors at the State Department—a perspective that he also adopts during his

FIGURE 4.11. Ambassador Reams and his wife Dotty "living the good life on a golf course in Panama City" (Created by Claude Lanzmann during the filming of *Shoah*. Used by permission of the United States Holocaust Memorial Museum and Yad Vashem, the Holocaust Martyrs and Heroes' Remembrance Authority, Jerusalem).

interview for *Shoah*. "It was my duty to do what I was told to do," he says on camera.⁹⁵ If his words echo the Nuremberg defense, these outtakes call to mind the varied means deployed by Lanzmann to record perpetrators during the making of the film. Indeed, the first three takes showing him driving and looking for the Reams residence in Bay Point are reminiscent of the footage of the red-and-white minivan in which the docu-auteur and his crew traversed West Germany to clandestinely capture footage with Nazis. There, he tried either to persuade perpetrators such as Karl Kretschmer into being interviewed or to elicit their testimony in secret—as would be the case, for instance, with Pery Broad during the summer of 1979. Indicated by his sardonic tone when arriving at Reams's house, Lanzmann also has a hidden agenda in Panama City: to trap—like a fish—one of the State Department's "villains" into his auteuresque net and break his silence.⁹⁶

Reams had in fact agreed to be filmed. At the same time, he had told Lanzmann beforehand that he would not discuss his wartime activities in the Roosevelt administration. In stark contrast to the grainy black-and-white images recorded with the Paluche, the tin canisters labeled "Fish" not only contain sixteen-millimeter color footage but, more specifically, forty-minute-long outtakes of Lanzmann, Reams, and his wife Dotty fishing and golfing beneath a bright blue Floridian sky.

Fitting the sarcastic transcript title "Fishing Party" (*partie de pêche* in French), this décor strikes the viewer as somewhat obscene, albeit intentionally so. Lanzmann suggested this mise-en-scène to Reams with a view to revealing and denouncing in the finished film the latter's pleasant retired life in the aftermath of the catastrophe. Accordingly, Lubtchansky captures a panoply of shots showing Reams—sometimes alone, sometimes with the filmmaker—fishing and golfing in Bay Point. This material includes a silent minute-long take reminiscent of a film noir: standing in the woods behind the lake where the "fishing party" takes place, the camera slowly moves from a wide shot showing the décor and the protagonist to a mid-shot of him with his back turned to the French cinematographer, as though unaware that he is being recorded.⁹⁷

Never referenced in *The Patagonian Hare*, this excluded material approximates Lanzmann's memory of Dov Paisikovic, the *Sonderkommando* member at Auschwitz sent to the extermination camp in May 1944, in the midst of en masse deportations from Hungary. "He was the most taciturn man I have ever met, a slab of silence," Lanzmann recalls in his memoir before describing how, after having learned that Paisikovic loved to fish, he had envisioned integrating the survivor's silence into *Shoah* by way of a distinct mise-en-scène. "We won't speak, we'll fish together in silence and I will tell his story in voiceover."⁹⁸ The outtakes captured at Bay Point during the winter of 1978–1979 suggest that Lanzmann intended to show the former advisor of Breckinridge Long enjoying leisurely pastimes and simultaneously denounce in voice-over his disingenuous handling of the refugee question.

FIGURES 4.12–13. The filmmaker fishing and golfing in Panama City with Ambassador Reams (Created by Claude Lanzmann during the filming of *Shoah*. Used by permission of the United States Holocaust Memorial Museum and Yad Vashem, the Holocaust Martyrs and Heroes' Remembrance Authority, Jerusalem).

Much like the description of Paisikovic, Reams emerges in this unused footage as "the most taciturn" of all the "bystanders" of the West interviewed for *Shoah* (not surprisingly so given that he is the only "villain" in Lanzmann's cast of characters). The docu-auteur seemingly arranged this mise-en-scène in the hopes that Reams's on-camera gestures would—like Bomba cutting hair in a barbershop or Lichtman mending dolls in her living room—engender a testimonial account. However, in the face of the former refugee specialist's obstinate silence, itself reminiscent of the footage with Pery Broad, Lanzmann is forced to concede during the "fishing party," whispering in French to his crew: "It's harder to catch him than it is to catch a fish..."[99] The equally obstinate docu-auteur nevertheless persists in trying to elicit a testimony from Reams. "Tell me what to do. You are my master," he exclaims during their golf game, visibly reversing the power dynamics and actively resorting to flattery. In *The Patagonian Hare*, he would remember telling the perpetrator Suchomel at the beginning of the secretly filmed interview: "I am your pupil, you are my teacher, you will instruct me."[100]

A certain self-reflexivity accompanies Lanzmann's on-screen performance: punctuating his poor fishing and golfing skills with a despairing "*Oh la la la*," he jokingly warns an apparently very amused off-screen Lubtchansky and Aubouy in French: "Making fun of me is not an option!"[101] In turn, while filming Reams and his wife in their living room that same evening (where the former refugee specialist showed him, off camera, his martini-making skills), Lanzmann evokes their testimonial pact. "Well, you see, I was very fair. We didn't make any kind of interview. I didn't ask you any questions." Still hopeful, he laments a few instants later: "But we didn't talk about what I wanted to talk about. [...] The policy of the United States, of the State Department, of the Bermuda Conference. We didn't talk about this." Reams responds tit-for-tat: "We're not going to either."[102]

In these outtakes, a deafening silence haunts both the inaction of the State Department in the West and the destruction of European Jewry in the East. Evidencing neither remorse nor guilt, Reams only seemingly alludes to the Holocaust in the final moments of the interview. In what constitutes a rare reference to the Cold War in Lanzmann's archive of testimonies, he discloses his fear of an impending nuclear disaster. "And the only thing that scares everything out of me is the possibility or probability of an atomic war sometime in the future," he tells Lanzmann. As though reflecting on humanity's inability to learn from the recent past, he adds: "civilization as we know it will disappear and the human race may or may not be given another chance to see whether they have more sense than they did before."[103]

The landscape devoid of human presence described by Reams in the winter of 1978–1979 finds an echo in the décor of the contemporaneous interview with the Holocaust scholar Richard Rubenstein, which Lubtchansky recorded in the wetlands of the Florida Panhandle. In these one-hour-long outtakes, Lanzmann and Rubenstein sit on a boat going down the Wakulla River, in the eponymous state park, discussing the refugee question and, more specifically, the plight of stateless Jews during the years of persecution. This excluded material immediately calls to mind the opening sequence in *Shoah*, filmed only months before in Poland: Srebnik singing on a boat on the Ner River near the Chełmno death camp.

A reverse shot, captured in the West and left on the cutting room floor, of this non-site of memory in *Shoah*, the Floridian wetlands constitute for Rubenstein a perfect counter-representation of the machinery of destruction. "What we have here is an area in which nature has been completely unchanged," he explains, "and what the Holocaust represents is the most extreme form of man-made action and man-made project with a particular kind of destruction and with a peculiar kind of calculation, which [...] could never be present in nature."[104] In the finished film, the absence of traces or, even, of human life in present-day footage of extermination camps epitomizes the annihilation. Accordingly, the décor of the interview with Rubenstein also signifies by evocation. In this excluded material centered on the years of persecution, the landscape calls to mind the early—and ultimately aborted—Nisko Plan: the envisaged resettlement of Jews from Germany and occupied territories to the swampy area of Nisko in eastern Poland. The remote and untouched landscape found in these outtakes also approximates a space outside of the public sphere and, indeed, any social and political community: a space of exception, a zone of exclusion to which the stateless person and the refugee are relegated. Moreover, tracking shots of alligators—rather unexpected in Lanzmann's archive of the catastrophe—convey the vulnerability of the *apatride* and the *indésirable*. These individuals, writes Hannah Arendt in *The Origins of Totalitarianism*, are subjected to the "unrestricted and arbitrary domination," rather than protection, of the police, to whom totalitarian regimes allocate the task of handling those individuals situated "beyond the pale of the law."[105]

Although he never references the alligators that populate the wetlands of Florida, Rubenstein affirms that the "fundamental step that made possible the Holocaust was the denial of political rights to the Jews of Europe" who, in turn, were "left openly to the mercy of the government bureaucracy or police."[106] In this excluded interview, he begins by invoking the influence of Arendt's classic study on his own work, especially his 1975 essay *The Cunning of History*, which references *The Origins of Totalitarianism* and *Eichmann in Jerusalem*. Incidentally, in keeping with the setting of the filmed interview, Rubenstein observes in *The Cunning of History* that Auschwitz and its starved prisoners could be read as "a prophetic image of urban civilization at the end of its journey."[107]

FIGURES 4.14–15. Claude Lanzmann and Richard Rubenstein in the Floridian wetlands and the evocative image of an alligator (Created by Claude Lanzmann during the filming of *Shoah*. Used by permission of the United States Holocaust Memorial Museum and Yad Vashem, the Holocaust Martyrs and Heroes' Remembrance Authority, Jerusalem).

The intellectual presence of Arendt, whose name Lanzmann never utters, bears mentioning. Rather than a refutation of her 1961 accusations against the Jewish leaders, which underlies much of his filmic archive and returns, decades later, in *The Patagonian Hare* and *The Last of the Unjust*, her account of barbarism in the twentieth century permeates Rubenstein's major theses. One can only speculate as to whether Lanzmann's failure to acknowledge Arendt on camera is in fact deliberate.[108] This omission is nevertheless in keeping with his later decision to exclude from the finished film both the controversy surrounding *Eichmann in Jerusalem* and his investigation of the refugee question. Beyond Arendt, Lanzmann would also leave out the years of persecution (a period when "effective rescue," to quote Hilberg, could still be undertaken), along with any condemnation of Allied inaction during the Holocaust, including Rubenstein's criticism.[109] In the winter of 1978–1979, the author of *The Cunning of History* denounces in particular international indifference and apathy during the Évian Conference—an important episode in Lanzmann's investigation, as evidenced by the fact that the *Shoah* outtakes contain several rolls of location filming in Évian and at the Hôtel Royal where the 1938 conference was held.[110] Asked by Lanzmann if "the Holocaust would have been avoided" had England and America opened their doors to Jewish refugees in 1938, Rubenstein first asserts that the Germans would surely have acted quite differently. A few instants later, however, he blames the Allies, unequivocally invoking "a profound complicity of all the nations of Western Europe and America" in the catastrophe.[111]

The mise-en-scène recovered by the Reams and Rubenstein outtakes bears witness to an aesthetic dilemma raised during the making of *Shoah*: How to represent the Holocaust from the West? How to "incarnate" the distance, at once geographical and epistemological, separating the East from the West in the midst of an unprecedented tragedy? How to convey, even, what Treblinka could possibly have signified in 1943 for Allied leaders and officials living in Washington and New York? Despite their shared protagonists, what distinguishes *Who Shall Live and Who Shall Die?* from Lanzmann's unused investigation of the rescue and refugee question is, precisely, a certain demand of Holocaust representation.

Exemplified by the footage set in the Florida Panhandle, the mark of the docu-auteur further transpires in the excluded two-and-a-half-hour interview with John Pehle filmed weeks earlier in November 1978. The testimony of the former executive director of the WRB recorded at his home in Washington, DC, begins with a brief mise-en-scène striking for its banality. Perched in the woods that surround Pehle's house, the camera zooms in on a glass door behind which the protagonist and Lanzmann's assistant Irena Steinfeldt are preparing for the staged opening scene. Pehle steps outside alone: he extends his hand to see if it is raining and then proceeds to walk through his backyard and into the woods, picking up fallen branches along the way. The camera follows him intently during this three-minute-long take. Four more comparable takes follow, one of which introduces a slight variation: rather than merely walk through the woods, Pehle is raking leaves. "John, John, it's OK," Lanzmann calls out at the end of the first take, signaling him to return to the house.[112] While revealing his off-screen directing of these staged domestic scenes, the use of Pehle's first name evidences, in these opening moments of the interview, a familiarity reminiscent of certain male Jewish survivors' testimonies. Much like his generational identification with men such as Simha Rotem and Yehuda Lerner, who partook in armed resistance in ghettos and camps, Pehle's interview footage also unfolds a similar admiration on Lanzmann's part.

Akin to a non-site of memory, nothing remains in Pehle's banal gestures of his heroic wartime deeds: that of having chosen action over obstruction, resistance over complicity. During the Holocaust, Pehle worked to expose the State Department's "repression" (to borrow his terminology) of information on the extermination; to create the WRB, which "dramatically changed the policy of the US overnight"; and to attempt to save the remaining Jews of Europe in 1944, above all in Hungary.[113] If the bare trees and gray November day in Washington, DC, sharply contrast with the sunny winter afternoon in Panama City, Pehle and Reams embody the West's polar opposite reactions to the plight of the Jews. Through his mise-en-scène, Lanzmann possibly envisaged narrating the rescue and refugee question by means of two portraits of the State Department: Reams's silence both during the war and the making of *Shoah*, on the one hand; the testimony of the humble hero or ordinary man John Pehle, on the other hand, as conveyed by the walk in the woods and raking of leaves. This juxtaposition is further hinted at in the November 1978 interview when Lanzmann asks the former WRB director, in anticipation of the footage he would capture at the Bay Point resort community, if he could possibly film him golfing. "Oh no," Pehle replies, "you could show me raking leaves, but not playing golf."[114]

In Panama City, Lanzmann largely concealed his frustration—and surely his disdain—in the face of Reams's unceasing "repression" of an incriminating past (as he would, time and again, when interviewing perpetrators with the Paluche). Only once in these outtakes does the docu-auteur interrupt Reams's performance and subtly allude to his personal choices and actions in Vichy

France. Upon insisting in the final moments of the interview that he try to remember what he knew at the time of the Bermuda Conference in 1943 (Had he known of the annihilation? Had he heard of the Warsaw ghetto uprising?), Reams cuts him short and asks whether he would be able to recall the past. "I remember very well the year 1943—oh so well," Lanzmann retorts, quietly reminiscing about his activities in the French Resistance, which he detailed

FIGURE 4.16–17. A walk in the woods: the former WRB director John Pehle raking leaves and picking up branches (Created by Claude Lanzmann during the filming of *Shoah*. Used by permission of the United States Holocaust Memorial Museum and Yad Vashem, the Holocaust Martyrs and Heroes' Remembrance Authority, Jerusalem).

decades later in *The Patagonian Hare*. "But anyhow that was not my question," he quickly remarks, closing this short autobiographical parenthesis.[115] While Lanzmann never recounts his activities under the Occupation with Pehle, he does not conceal his admiration for the former WRB director. This admiration takes the form of a cinematographic homage by means of extreme close-ups of his face—a face, incidentally, evocative of an old western actor. "You stay on him *gros* [in close-up], I hope you were already," Lanzmann suddenly tells Lubtchansky during the filmed interview, before adding: "On his eyes—I find them absolutely astounding."[116]

A sense of urgency, too, permeates the end of the interview where Lanzmann sits next to Pehle, perusing wartime documents, including reports of the extermination. "Cut—I feel like I am forgetting something," Lanzmann suddenly exclaims in French. During these final moments, he often looks at his protagonist with fondness and emotion.[117] Beyond admiration for this ordinary man's courage and determination, the auteur insinuates Pehle's significance as receiver of the news of the annihilation, which messengers such as Karski transmitted to the Allied governments (while his face and blue eyes call to mind those of the Polish courier, Pehle stressed elsewhere the importance of Karski's mission during the summer of 1943 for the creation of the WRB).[118] His "absolutely astounding" eyes, then, take on another meaning: that of having been

FIGURE 4.18. The extreme close-up as homage in the excluded interview with John Pehle (Created by Claude Lanzmann during the filming of *Shoah*. Used by permission of the United States Holocaust Memorial Museum and Yad Vashem, the Holocaust Martyrs and Heroes' Remembrance Authority, Jerusalem).

able to see, to imagine, to believe—and to act accordingly—from the West the unprecedented horrors unfolding in the East.

During the final hour of the interview, the centrality of a paper memory—of reports, cables, and letters read by the protagonist and closely filmed by the camera—evidences Long and Reams's "repression" of information, as well as (to quote Lanzmann) "the complete discrepancy" between the urgent measures needed to rescue European Jewry and "the very slow and bureaucratic and red-tape" response of the State Department.[119] This paper memory also gestures toward a fundamental question underlying the making of *Shoah* as a whole: what Lanzmann calls, in his 1978 letter to Karski, "the problem of transmission of experience."[120]

In the finished film, this question subsists through the lens of a crisis of representation, epitomized in the omission of archival images as well as in the centrality of eyewitness testimony and non-sites of memory. In the excluded footage with "bystanders" of the West, it is repeatedly framed as an epistemological crisis. "One of the most difficult things to understand is really what does it mean to be ... informed," Lanzmann tells Pehle. He continues,

> When one lives here, in Washington or in New York, what is the meaning of Treblinka, what is the meaning of the extermination, what is the meaning of Auschwitz, what does it mean to know—I mean, does it penetrate the consciousness of the people? And I have the feeling that in many cases it didn't—at all. Even if they knew.[121]

Contrary to the accusatory premise of *Who Shall Live and Who Shall Die?* and, decades later, *The Messenger*, the controversial question of Allied inaction during the Holocaust is recast here as a more nuanced philosophical investigation into the crisis of imagination. The irremediable distance and confrontation between two worlds—the East and the West—put forward by Lanzmann also underlies the 2010 "Karski affair."[122] This is further evidenced in the *Shoah* archive by the recurring question, posed in many of the excluded interviews, "how to imagine Treblinka from Washington or New York?" More specifically, Justice Frankfurter's emblematic words after hearing the courier's eyewitness account of the annihilation ("I did not say that you are lying; I said that I don't believe you!") complicate Haenel's assertion in *The Messenger* that the Allies simply "knew."

This inquiry into "the problem of transmission of experience" in the West recovered by both the archive and *The Karski Report* approximates Deborah Lipstadt's important study on how the American press "repressed" news of the extermination. Aptly titled *Beyond Belief,* Lipstadt's study was published one year following the release of *Shoah*. "The magnitude of the horror was unfathomable. The tales of horror beggared the imagination," she writes in the epilogue before concluding on a more accusatory note characteristic of the book as a whole and of the historiographical current from which it emerged: "There were many failures in America's behavior during this period, and a failure of the imagination was one of them." If a crisis of imagination underlay the reception of reports about the first years of the extermination, Lipstadt observes that such an explanation becomes obsolete "by the time of the Bermuda Conference in 1943 and certainly by the time of the destruction of Hungarian Jewry in 1944" when numerous eyewitness accounts had reached the Allied governments.[123]

The individual actions of Pehle in 1943 and 1944, as well as those of Peter Bergson and Samuel Merlin during these same years, suggest exactly that. In keeping with Lipstadt's argument, Lanzmann himself attempted to reframe the question of Allied inaction in terms of a crisis of imagination, all the while collecting the testimonies of "bystanders" in the West who not only believed the news of the extermination but also acted on their own to alert the American public, particularly through the press. On camera, Pehle thus recounts how, in 1944 and despite governmental attempts to stop him, he put out a press release of the report on Auschwitz authored by the two escapees Alfred Wetzler and Rudolf Vrba. "Yes, we met him last week in New York," Lanzmann interjects, momentarily reframing Vrba's filmed testimony for *Shoah* through the lens—excluded in the finished film—of the reception of his report in the West.[124]

In November 1978, when he interviewed Pehle in Washington, Lanzmann also recorded Bergson and Merlin in New York, presumably in the vicinity of Orchard Street on the Lower East Side. Although devoid of any opening staged scenes, Lanzmann's decision to interview the two members of the "Bergson Group," outsiders in Washington and New York, together in a small, unassuming meeting room accentuates the collective nature of their wartime activities. These two followers of Vladimir Ze'ev Jabotinsky had come to the United States from Palestine in 1940. Three years later, led by Bergson, their group campaigned vigorously to alert the public of the impending catastrophe and of the need for drastic rescue measures. In the process, they sponsored hundreds of dramatic newspaper advertisements in the *New York Times* and *Washington Post*, among others (these are visible on the wall of the small meeting room where the camera films them carefully). Their other measures included a pageant titled *We Will Never Die*, which, two nights in a row, filled the twenty-two thousand seats of Madison Square Garden.

Neither of these two activists ever met with President Roosevelt during the war. In the decades following the Holocaust, Bergson repeatedly criticized

FIGURE 4.19. Peter Bergson (left) and Samuel Merlin (right) discussing the newspaper advertisements they sponsored in 1943 (Created by Claude Lanzmann during the filming of *Shoah*. Used by permission of the United States Holocaust Memorial Museum and Yad Vashem, the Holocaust Martyrs and Heroes' Remembrance Authority, Jerusalem).

American Jewish leaders and the president alike for failing to unite and save European Jewry. "There was no reaction while the murder went on," Bergson asserts bluntly in front of the camera in the *Shoah* outtakes. Merlin echoes the sentiment, observing, equally sarcastically, "But the truth of the matter is that the Jews were not divided, they were united in a certain indifference" (in the interview transcript used during the editing phase, both statements are underlined).[125] According to historians Richard Breitman and Allan J. Lichtman, the condemnations leveled at the president and, by extension, the Jewish leaders are themselves indicative of how "little understanding of American political culture" Bergson had as a foreigner during the Holocaust. "Roosevelt did not easily succumb to outside pressure," they observe in their more dispassionate assessment of FDR's wartime efforts on behalf of the Jews. "He would have shunned any actions that gave the impression that the United States was fighting a Jewish war regardless of views expressed by Jewish advocates either within or outside his circle of advisers" (upon being filmed for *Shoah*, Bergson affirms the exact contrary).[126]

Anticipating his critique of *The Messenger*, Lanzmann himself expresses skepticism several times during the interview at what he deems to be "very sharp" accusations of inaction voiced by the two "bystanders" in 1978. In keeping with his philosophical stance, he attempts to reframe their controversial historical interpretation in epistemological terms. "Yes, but the real point is the following, according to me: How do you explain this lack of reaction?" he asks the two men as he proceeds to reorient the discussion toward "the problem of transmission of experience." Lanzmann does not limit his inquiry to what Bergson and Merlin personally "imagine[d]" in 1943 when they spoke of the annihilation—a question left unanswered by the two activists who focus instead on their wartime "instinct" to rescue as many Jews as possible. He also probes, by way of these two outsiders' perspectives and wartime public campaigns, "what the average Jew in this country" or, even, "the Jews on Orchard Street" knew. For the unceasingly critical Bergson, the ordinary Jew, in contrast to the Jewish leaders, "reacted properly and would have reacted magnificently if he was given a chance."[127]

By excluding from *Shoah* the testimonies of the "bystanders" of the West, Lanzmann privileged, in the end, the perspective of ordinary Jews in the East. Among them, Ruth Elias, whose brief account of her deportation to Auschwitz in *Shoah* subsists as a trace of Lanzmann's broader investigation into the question of knowledge and transmission. "What is Auschwitz? I didn't know about Auschwitz anything," she exclaims in the finished film. "Men [...] told us that Auschwitz is a *Vernichtungslager*, an extermination camp, where they were gassing people, and we didn't believe." Her brief testimony ends with a repetition of these exact words, a repetition that posits the Holocaust as both unprecedented and unfathomable. "We didn't believe it," she declares once more on camera before affirming again, instants later in the outtakes, "Until you see anything... you don't believe."[128] A year before he filmed Elias in Tel Aviv, Lanzmann had intimated this crisis of representation during his interviews with Karski, Pehle, Bergson, and Merlin, all of whom he recorded only months after having visited for the first time the extermination camps in Poland. Reminiscent of these non-sites of memory that, in *Shoah*, stage a certain impenetrability of the catastrophe, Lanzmann later captured a dozen rolls of location shooting in New York, some of which he juxtaposed in the finished film with the testimonies of Karski and Vrba. Beyond the symbolic Statue of Liberty singled out by Haenel in *The Messenger*, the remaining rolls contain aerial shots of a hazy Manhattan, banal streets scenes, and low-angle shots of skyscrapers—excluded footage accentuating the city's own impenetrability and distance from the destruction.

Did Lanzmann anticipate a possible montage of shots of New York, a city located thousands of miles from Treblinka, and the joint testimony detailing the pressing actions of the Bergson group in 1943, a year that the filmmaker condemns in this interview as having been "entirely lost" by the State Department for the rescue of European Jewry?[129] The annotated transcript, which includes underlined and bracketed accusations made by the two activists, suggests so. Similar to Lanzmann's epistemological reframing, Bergson concedes in his closing statement that "the pressure of the constant horror, and the realization everyday of so many people killed, was just too much to comprehend."[130] The poignant despair that still haunts him in 1978 is itself reminiscent of the story of Zygielbojm.

"And the march of the Rabbis?" Lanzmann asks Bergson and Merlin toward the end of the interview.[131] After the pageant at Madison Square Garden in March 1943 and the various newspaper advertisements published that same year, the two activists describe the remarkable demonstration they organized in Washington, DC, on October 6, 1943, shortly before Yom Kippur. Several hundred rabbis walked from Union Station to the White House with a petition for the president requesting immediate measures to save the Jews of Europe (controversially, Roosevelt left his office on that day and did not meet with the rabbis).[132] "It must have been quite something, the arrival of this group of five hundred rabbis in the morning in Washington," Lanzmann observes, markedly moved by this unique scene of protest in the midst of the catastrophe. Even more affecting is the rabbis' arrival on the steps of Congress as the activists remember it: in the midst of a Senate session, Vice President Henry Wallace invited all the senators to join them outside. In their presence, the rabbis read the petition and recited a prayer. "Many of them cried very emotionally," Bergson tells Lanzmann in November 1978.[133]

Among the archival images recovered by the *Shoah* outtakes, but excluded from the finished film, are several close-ups of press photographs showing the delegation of rabbis, some weeping, on the steps of Congress. This homage in photographs approximates the poignant plea made by the two Jewish leaders in Warsaw for a hunger strike outside the government offices of the West. "Perhaps it will move humanity," they had told the Polish courier who, months later, relayed the message to the despairing Bund leader in London. If Lanzmann's archiving gesture captures his very own admiration for those who—to return to the words of Karski—did not abandon the Jews of Europe, the memory of the protesting rabbis in Washington also invokes the story of the Slovakian rabbi Michael Dov Weissmandl. Working alongside Gisi Fleischmann, the only woman in Lanzmann's narrative of rescue, Weissmandl established the underground organization known as the Bratislava Working Group, which attempted to halt deportations not only in Slovakia but throughout Europe. A messenger of the catastrophe whose despair calls to mind Czerniaków and Zygielbojm, Weissmandl foresaw Hitler's plan of annihilation as early as 1938. He later informed the West of the horrors unfolding in the East and frantically appealed for help to save the Jews.¹³⁴ In May 1944, Weissmandl relayed to the Jewish leaders in the free world Vrba's report of Auschwitz with a demand that the Allies bomb the train lines leading to the extermination camp.¹³⁵ After the war, he immigrated to the United States and founded the Nitra Yeshiva in Mount Kisco, New York, haunted until his death in 1957 by the world's inaction.

Over the course of filming *Shoah*, Lanzmann returns time and again to the story of Weissmandl, profoundly affected by the despair of this one man, even capturing footage of his yeshiva. "One of the main characters in this film," Lanzmann tells Shmuel Tamir in the outtakes, "one of the main protagonists in spite of the fact that I never met him and that he is dead—is Rabbi Weissmandel [sic]."¹³⁶ The archive bears witness for this witness by way of a series of excluded interviews, including one with the former member of the Bratislava Working Group Andre Steiner. "And you talked about the blue eyes of Weissmandel [sic]," Lanzmann tells Steiner in this excluded footage. "Can you [say] more about these eyes?" he adds, gesturing—in an echo to the Pehle footage—to the lucidity of this messenger of the catastrophe who foresaw, before attempting to stop, the destruction of European Jewry.¹³⁷

FIGURE 4.20. In search of Rabbi Weissmandl: Mr. Becher and Claude Lanzmann walking in November 1978 near the Nitra Yeshiva (Created by Claude Lanzmann during the filming of *Shoah*. Used by permission of the United States Holocaust Memorial Museum and Yad Vashem, the Holocaust Martyrs and Heroes' Remembrance Authority, Jerusalem).

AND THE WORLD REMAINED SILENT

"Dear Mr. Pehle: I have the honour to enclose four copies [...] of a report concerning a visit to the well-known Ghetto of Theresienstadt made by Dr. M. Rossel, Delegate of the International Committee of the Red Cross, on June 23, 1944. [...] The picture he presents of the Ghetto can unfortunately not be taken at face value."[138] With these words written in the fall of 1944, Roswell McClelland introduces his five-page "penetrating commentary of Rossel's report" (to borrow the words of Lucy Dawidowicz) in which he details what, precisely, the ICRC delegate did not see during the carefully orchestrated visit to Theresienstadt, which included a soccer match and a performance of a children's opera.[139]

The former WRB representative in Switzerland archived a copy of this letter in his correspondence with Dawidowicz, who had sent it to him in January 1975 after requesting permission to use it in an article about Rossel's inspection of the camp-ghetto. She published this piece that spring when Lanzmann attended the Holocaust conference in New York and met with her for several hours to discuss his film. In the weeks preceding his interview for *Shoah*, McClelland possibly received another copy from Irena Steinfeldt. In a letter dated September 14, 1978, the filmmaker's assistant offered to send him copies of the reports he had written for the WRB during the last two years of the war, in order to "refresh [his] memory for the filmed interview" (as Lanzmann had also suggested to Karski several months earlier).[140] During his interview with McClelland in November 1978, however, Lanzmann does not once question him about his strikingly perceptive assessment of Rossel as an unreliable witness. Instead, he interviewed Rossel at his home in the Swiss town of Tramelan, near Bern, over the course of three hours in the spring of 1979. Accordingly, the green label affixed on the tin canisters containing his testimony reads: "Theresienstadt."

In 1996, shortly before the outtakes were transferred to the USHMM, Lanzmann retrieved the unused footage featuring the former ICRC delegate, along with several tracking shots from the location filming in Terezín. The following year, he released *A Visitor from the Living*, the first of the five documentaries he would make using *Shoah* outtakes. This hour-long film edited by Sabine Mamou incorporates segments pertaining to Rossel's wartime visits, first to Auschwitz in 1943 and then to Theresienstadt in 1944. In the extermination camp, Rossel saw "nothing" of the annihilation—despite his knowledge that Jews deported there were "condemned," and despite crossing paths with several hundred "walking skeletons." He specifies: "Only their eyes were alive." In Theresienstadt, he also saw "nothing" of the farce staged by the Germans, all the while noting with anti-Semitic prejudice that this was a camp for "prominent" Jews whose "passivity" struck him profoundly.

More than the testimony of a "bystander" aged twenty-six at the time of the inspection and whose indifference and inaction approximate that of Reams in the State Department, *A Visitor from the Living* takes the form of an interrogation on Lanzmann's part, largely centered on the delegate's favorable report of Theresienstadt and failure as a witness or messenger of the catastrophe. For Brad Prager, "Lanzmann's intention to question aggressively and expose Rossel is unmistakable."[141] Indeed, in sharp contrast to his performance in the material with Reams where he never reveals his frustration or contempt, telling the former refugee specialist instead, "You are my master," Lanzmann intervenes at length over the course of this interview in French—half of which, in the original outtakes, centers on Theresienstadt alone. Positing himself as the "master," he quotes from and challenges the 1944 report in order to demonstrate to Rossel that the very scenes he "saw" in the camp-ghetto—as McClelland had already intimated in his letter to Pehle—"can unfortunately not be taken at face value." As Ophir Levy argues, Lanzmann assumes in *A Visitor from the Living* a radically different role than in *Shoah*, reinforced by the deployment of numerous reverse shots in the documentary. "He is no longer the one who records the witness (here devoid of all legitimacy as witness)," Levy writes, "but the one who lectures him, statistics and archival documents in hand."[142]

Despite this lecture, the former ICRC delegate and inspector of Theresienstadt admits neither error nor remorse in *A Visitor from the Living*. "Do you regret your report today?" Lanzmann asks him toward the end of the film, his voice-over juxtaposed with a tracking shot of an empty street in Terezín, a non-site of memory that insinuates a catastrophe unwitnessed. "I don't see how I could have written anything else. I'd sign it again," Rossel answers, unaffected by the ethical implication of the question posed. "Knowing everything that I told you?" the docu-auteur interjects. "Of course," he replies. In the face of Rossel's persistent indifference, and in a rare moment of desperation excluded from *A Visitor from the Living*, Lanzmann insists in the outtakes, "But don't you think if you had written another report, the world would have been alerted and that might have... helped to save [them]?" "Sir, I did not know anything," Rossel responds matter-of-factly.[143]

Silenced in *A Visitor from the Living*, this interrogation gestures toward an off-frame scene that haunts the making of *Shoah*. "The question of rescue of the Hungarian Jews will be one of the major topics of my film," Lanzmann had asserted in his first letter to McClelland in 1977. Two years later, the plight of this remaining Jewish community, whose mass deportation to Auschwitz coincides with the Theresienstadt visit, subsists silently as a striking reverse shot to what Lanzmann calls at the end of the documentary the "quite rosy" report penned by Rossel. Moreover, the very title, *A Visitor from the Living* or, in the original French, *Un vivant qui passe*, finds a tragic resonance in the unused testimony of Ehud Avriel, a former member of the Jewish Agency in Istanbul. Speaking in French, Avriel recounts how a despairing Joel Brand—already aware that the deportations in Hungary had begun—arrived in Istanbul and relayed to the agency in May 1944 the Germans' extraordinary offer to the Western Allies: the so-called "Blood for Goods" deal. "[Brand] was determined to return to hell," Avriel poignantly recalls in the *Shoah* outtakes, "and he spoke to us, you know, like a dead man on vacation [*un mort en vacances*]."[144]

Corresponding to the question of rescue voiced by the docu-auteur in the Rossel outtakes but omitted in the 1997 documentary, one might ask, why did Lanzmann choose as the first appendix to *Shoah* the story of a "bystander" of the West? Of a nonwitness, moreover, incarnating, according to Levy, "the symptom of a Europe who watched the Jews die while covering its eyes, opting later on to show contempt for the attitude of those who let themselves be 'led like sheep to the slaughter' instead of admitting its own complicit silence"?[145] What pressed Lanzmann to select, from his vast archive of testimonies, an interview with Karski's nemesis? After all, the Polish courier was just two years older than Rossel when he entered the Warsaw ghetto; he would continue to be, in sheer contrast to the former ICRC delegate, forever haunted by the abandonment of the Jews.

In the opening crawl text of *A Visitor from the Living*, Lanzmann situates the excluded material with the former ICRC delegate within the broader investigation of Theresienstadt he undertook over the course of making *Shoah*. This was a camp-ghetto, he explains, "both central and tangential to the origin and process of destruction of the Jews in Europe," to which Benjamin Murmelstein would later bear witness in *The Last of the Unjust* and Ruth Elias in *The Four Sisters*. Still, can we not read in the 1997 return of the footage with Rossel a refutation of the "quite rosy" depiction of rescue staged in *Schindler's List*? A refutation, that is, of this Holocaust fiction, which Lanzmann, retrospectively echoing the visit staged for the Red Cross, denounced three years earlier as having "distorted the truth"?[146]

A Visitor from the Living exceeds the accusations leveled at the former ICRC delegate to encompass a difficult confrontation between the filmmaker and the silence of a Europe that rendered possible the Final Solution; a silence that, much more than the inaction of the geographically distant State Department at the heart of Haenel's *The Messenger*, haunted Lanzmann during the twelve years he spent making *Shoah*. This confrontation is not only mediated but perhaps facilitated by the use of the French language in the Rossel interview, a language seldom spoken by eyewitnesses in either the outtakes or the finished film, which both exclude Vichy France and its complicity in the Holocaust. Of Lanzmann's nearly two hundred hours of interviews, the collaborationist regime of Pétain is referenced only in McClelland's unused testimony in English.

Between August 1941 and September 1942, McClelland and his wife Marjorie lived in Marseilles where they worked for the American Friends Service Committee, a Quaker organization that provided relief for both Jewish and Spanish Republican refugees in occupied France, including children in transit camps. Unvoiced in the outtakes is the story of Marjorie McClelland: she also played an active role in saving refugees during that period, particularly by organizing five convoys of children who made their way to the United States from France, via Lisbon.[147] In 1942, while working in Marseilles, Roswell McClelland wrote an unpublished account describing several French transit camps, the deportation of foreign Jews, and the treatment of Jewish children. That summer, during a trip to the town of Vichy, he met by chance with the French prime minister Pierre Laval (at the initiative of Laval and against German orders to deport only foreign Jews over the age of sixteen, children were sent to the East with their parents). Prompted by Lanzmann in November 1978, McClelland recounts this meeting on camera. He remembers in particular Laval's "tirade against Jews," during which he expressed the French government's desire "to be rid of them." At the same time, the French prime minister dismissed "as pure fiction" any report that the deported Jews were in fact not being resettled but exterminated.[148]

In Lanzmann's archive of the catastrophe, Europe's complicit silence is further encapsulated in the inaction and indifference of the Red Cross. During the making of *Shoah*, the filmmaker and his assistants turned to Saul Friedländer, once secretary to Nahum Goldmann between 1958 and 1960, for help in finding and contacting ICRC officials in Switzerland (as recounted in *When Memory Comes*, Friedländer's parents were turned away at the Swiss border before being murdered at Auschwitz).[149] The extensive investigation they conducted resulted, in the end, in only two filmed interviews: the Rossel footage and an equally confrontational meeting captured on April 19, 1979, with ICRC vice president Jean Pictet. Shot at the agency's headquarters in Geneva, this excluded material includes several mid-shots of the building and close-ups of the French acronym "CICR" on its facade, a mise-en-scène that, like the interview itself, functions to expose the Red Cross.

"You were in the center of things [*Vous avez été au cœur des choses*]": thus Lanzmann, in the opening moments, characterizes Pictet's position in the ICRC during the war.[150] A legal expert in the agency, he was also the close collaborator of its long-term president, Max Huber, whom he assisted as part of the Executive Committee's secretariat staff. Beyond the ICRC, he was also "in the center of things" in working in Geneva where the news of the Final

FIGURES 4.21–22. The ICRC headquarters in Geneva, where Jean Pictet is interviewed in the spring of 1979 (Created by Claude Lanzmann during the filming of *Shoah*. Used by permission of the United States Holocaust Memorial Museum and Yad Vashem, the Holocaust Martyrs and Heroes' Remembrance Authority, Jerusalem).

Solution first reached Gerhart Riegner in the summer of 1942. "I am trying to imagine how, how the rumor [of the annihilation] spread in Geneva," Lanzmann observes a few instants later (in keeping with this remark and in anticipation of a possible montage, the excluded location filming found in the archive includes tracking shots in the city of Geneva).[151] Accordingly, the contentious question of when exactly Pictet—and by extension the Executive Committee—learned of the extermination, constitutes the starting point, if not the very heart, of Lanzmann's investigation of the ICRC.

In these outtakes, the docu-auteur first poses what he terms "a question of the almost metaphysical sort." This question is evocative of the excluded footage with other "bystanders" in the West: namely, "What does Treblinka signify... in 1942?"[152] Rather than engage in a philosophical discussion, Lanzmann immediately reframes his question in order to elicit a factual answer. He does not simply ask when Pictet knew but, more importantly, when he believed the news of the destruction of European Jewry. "Oh, not before 1943," the ICRC official remarks before specifying that, while they were "extremely concerned already in 1942," they only became aware of the German plan of systematic annihilation the following year.[153]

Several times in these outtakes Lanzmann expresses skepticism at the date of 1943. Beyond alluding to Riegner's famous cable, he also mentions meetings in July 1942 between the WJC representative and Carl Burckhardt. Officially the vice president of the ICRC, Burckhardt served as the decision-maker in lieu of Huber, chronically ill throughout the war. "Burckhardt," writes the historian Gerald Steinacher, "was no great admirer of Hitler, but no particular friend of the Jews either."[154] While he would practice during the crucial years of 1942 and 1943 what Pictet terms "a policy of prudence" that, in the end, greatly restricted rescue efforts, he in fact had "early knowledge of the extermination," even confirming for the State Department in November 1942 the Germans' extermination plans.[155] Despite this knowledge, the ICRC failed to act until 1944. In the wake of the creation of the WRB and under significant pressure from the American government, the agency finally turned to the rescue of Hungarian Jewry. This "last chance operation" was not only supposed to save the remaining Jews still alive in Europe but also to provide the ICRC with the opportunity to redeem itself after years of inaction. As Pehle remarked in a letter to Goldmann in August 1944, "The ICRC [is] in general very proud of their success in [the] matter [of the] Hungarian Jews which they very much needed for their political position."[156]

Throughout the interview Pictet wavers between the year 1942 and the year 1943, remarking at one point that the need to go there and verify the rumors remained the crucial problem. Alluding to Rossel without ever revealing that he is also a protagonist of the film he is making, Lanzmann exposes a dilemma underlying this logic. "What is the point of describing what one sees if what one sees is false?" he asks, referring to the infamous report authored by the ICRC inspector of Theresienstadt.[157] Toward the end of the footage, Pictet is forced to admit that Lanzmann is possibly right regarding 1942. He also concedes that they had indeed known enough by the fall of that year to draft a declaration protesting Germany's violation of humanitarian law. At a meeting held on October 14, 1942, however, the Executive Committee voted to not release this document, thereby remaining silent and adopting the "policy of prudence" endorsed by Burckhardt.

"Me, what I don't understand, is what those risks were—that's what I am not able to see," a perplexed Lanzmann exclaims regarding this decision, which Steinacher casts as the "most shameful moment" in the noninterventionist stance of the ICRC.[158] For Pictet, these "risks" consisted first and foremost in potentially sabotaging the work of the Red Cross on behalf of prisoners of war in Germany. Yet insinuated in Lanzmann's remark and suppressed in Pictet's response is the agency's wartime violation of its principles of independence and neutrality engendered by what Steinacher qualifies as the "sometimes close and cozy relation between the ICRC and the Swiss government." If Pictet remembers acting as secretary during the October 14, 1942, meeting, he omits the presence of the Swiss federal president Philipp Etter, whose government felt the planned declaration of protest would surely "antagonize their [German] neighbour" and jeopardize national interests; during the meeting, he "made clear what kind of outcome the Swiss government wanted to see."[159] In 1979, the ICRC's consequential decision to remain silent despite its knowledge of the catastrophe returns symptomatically in Pictet's incapacity to pronounce the word "Jew" on camera. Instead, he resorts—as Lanzmann himself remarks—to a series of neutralizing euphemisms, including "political detainees" and "civilians."[160]

The final take of the footage recorded at the ICRC headquarters opens with a terse exchange indicative of the confrontational nature of these outtakes. "I was unable to provide a precise answer to the question of the date at which we began to realize there was an extermination...," Pictet begins. Lanzmann interrupts him. "You said that I caught you in a lie earlier [*je vous ai chopé*], but my intention was not at all to catch you lying," the exasperated filmmaker exclaims, alluding to a conversation between takes.[161] Rather than belonging to "the almost metaphysical sort," the contentious question of when the ICRC *knew* is of the profoundly moral and ethical kind. "What we know today is that they exterminated massively during all of 1942, during all of 1943 and ... during the first eight months of 1944," Lanzmann tells Pictet early on, implicitly delivering his verdict: during the years that the Jews were being murdered, the Red Cross remained indifferent. As though referring to his own difficult confrontation with the silence and inaction of the world that he excluded first in the editing room and then decades later in his critique of *The Messenger*, Lanzmann exclaims somewhat cryptically and in a rare personal tone: "And ... me ... but that's a question that will never be settled ... There will never be an answer."[162]

In 1993, at the dedication ceremony of the opening of the USHMM, Elie Wiesel would punctuate his remarks with a similar interjection upon evoking Allied inaction during the Holocaust. "Why weren't the railways leading to Birkenau bombed by Allied bombers?" asked the author of *Night*, a book originally titled in Yiddish Un di velt hot geshvign (*And the World Remained Silent*). He then added: "As long as I live I will not understand that."[163] A decade earlier inside the LTC film laboratory, Lanzmann had attempted to compose around the contentious topic of rescue and refugees before relegating it entirely to the margins of his Holocaust narrative. Recovered in the unused footage found at the USHMM, the world's resounding silence nevertheless haunts the representation of the catastrophe in the finished film. Beyond repeated shots of the railroad tracks leading to the entrance of Auschwitz and connoting "universal complicity" (to quote the French psychoanalyst Eric Didier), the docu-auteur ultimately chose to accentuate the sheer isolation *and* abandonment of the Jews of Europe upon confining his Holocaust opus to the East and to the Final Solution.[164] "I am the last Jew," Simha Rotem remembers saying to himself in the aftermath of the Warsaw ghetto revolt in May 1943, weeks after the Bermuda Conference and days after the suicide of Zygielbojm. Rotem's words are the final words we hear in Claude Lanzmann's *Shoah*.

Conclusion

THE DEEP TIME OF TESTIMONY

THE FOUR SISTERS opened at the New York Film Festival in October 2017, nearly half a century after the premiere of *Israel, Why* on the same occasion. Claude Lanzmann's final work using restored *Shoah* outtakes consists of four separate portraits of women survivors, each individually titled. "The Hippocratic Oath" (89 min.) and "Bałuty" (63 min.) center on the testimonies of Ruth Elias and Paula Biren, who both briefly appear in *Shoah*. "The Merry Flea" (51 min.) and "Noah's Ark" (68 min.) recover the excluded material with Ada Lichtman and Hanna Marton. The distinct names chosen for this four-part film, whose own title seemingly refers to Anton Chekhov's 1901 play *The Three Sisters*, each signify a defining event or place in the women's respective testimonies. "The Hippocratic Oath" refers to a pledge to save lives taken by the woman doctor in Auschwitz who gave Elias the morphine for her child; the Łódź ghetto, where Biren and her family were resettled in 1940, was situated in Bałuty, the city's poorest district; "The Merry Flea" was how SS officers in Sobibór named one of their villas, which Lichtman had to clean when she arrived in the extermination camp; Marton was aboard the special transport nicknamed "Noah's Ark" that carried 1,684 Jews from Hungary to Switzerland in 1944. A transnational narrative of the catastrophe, *The Four Sisters* offers a counterpoint to the perspectives and experiences of the male members—or "brothers"—of the *Sonderkommando* in *Shoah*.

What is striking about *The Four Sisters* is the relative absence of any montage. Rather than intertwine these four testimonies and connect them to footage of non-sites of memory—one of the "radical aesthetic transformation[s]" (to cite Gertrud Koch) *Shoah* had accomplished in 1985—Lanzmann utilizes in this final film what one might call a strategy of *negative editing*.[1] This strategy is typified by a sustained focus on the interviewees, reminiscent of "talking heads" and audiovisual testimonies. Absent from these four portraits of women survivors are present-day images of ghettos and camps. Instead, any evidence of montage takes the form of intermittent reverse or medium shots that include the filmmaker in the frame. In 2017, Lanzmann also resorts to documentary evidence to break the monotony of the "talking head" format. Specifically, he integrates several black-and-white images of the Łódź ghetto and its controversial leader Rumkowski in "Bałuty," as well as, in "Noah's Ark," a map of Transylvania and contemporary photographs of Marton's Romanian hometown of Cluj. In contrast to the centrality of the interpreters' voices in *Shoah*, Francine Kaufmann's translations from and to Hebrew are entirely excluded from "Noah's Ark," despite her presence in the unused Marton material. Finally, Lanzmann chose not to incorporate in *The Four Sisters* an opening text crawl used in all the other films made from excluded footage to provide historical background and shed light on his editorial choices between 1979 and 1985.

Undeniably, over the course of periodically producing new films from the outtakes, beginning with *A Visitor from the Living* in 1997, Lanzmann progressively moved away from his signature ethics of representation, which in *Shoah* included a largely off-screen authorial presence and the omission of archival images. Already in *A Visitor from the Living*, for instance, he deployed the shot reverse shot technique to convey the confrontational nature of his interview with Maurice Rossel. Similarly, in 2001, *Sobibór, October 14, 1943, 4 p.m.* opened with a black-and-white photograph showing a burial ceremony for German officers killed during the prisoner revolt. A more conspicuous and compelling contrast is found in the 2013 documentary *The Last of the Unjust*. Like flashbacks, segments of the outtakes with Benjamin Murmelstein poignantly intercut a present-day narrative centered on the aging director of *Shoah*, who returns to Theresienstadt and visits sites of memory in Prague and Vienna. Lanzmann also integrated in this three-and-a-half-hour documentary several scenes from the 1944 propaganda film made in the camp-ghetto—a strategy comparable to the use of archival images in "Bałuty."

More than anticipating *The Four Sisters*, however, the very structure of *The Last of the Unjust* evidences the negative editing of this final effort to recover *Shoah* outtakes. Unmistakably missing from *The Four Sisters* is the search for a form and the integration of the unused material into a broader narrative about the Holocaust. In the respective opening crawl texts of *A Visitor from the Living* and *The Last of the Unjust*, for example, Lanzmann situates the testimonies of Rossel and Murmelstein within his vast investigation of Theresienstadt. Devoid of either a crawl text or filmed footage of this non-site of memory, Elias's account of the camp-ghetto in "The Hippocratic Oath" subsists in the margins. Comparable is the absence in "Bałuty" and "Noah's Ark" of a crawl text that would have situated the testimonies of these two women as part of Lanzmann's extensive probing of the controversial topic of Jewish leadership during the Holocaust.

"This work in four parts provides several radically new elements in the way the extermination of the Jews is seen," writes David Frenkel, the producer of *The Four Sisters*, before underscoring the feminine perspectives offered by the film.[2]

In 2017, *The Four Sisters* was far from radical, either formally or conceptually. *Shoah* in fact would have been even more so in the eighties had it included the gendered narratives of these women survivors. The recovery in "The Hippocratic Oath" of the now-unedited opening line of Elias's testimony in *Shoah* and of her previously omitted pregnancy suggests as much. "This time it reached us, the transport to the East and *I knew I was pregnant*," she reveals in the 2017 film when she describes her deportation from Theresienstadt to Auschwitz. Actually, long before *The Four Sisters*, Elias had recounted the story of her pregnancy in the extermination camp several times, including at a packed auditorium at Yad Vashem in February 1985 and in her 1988 memoir *The Triumph of Hope*.[3] Similarly, Paula Biren and Ada Lichtman each told their story again in front of a camera after being interviewed for *Shoah*. Finally, privileged by the USHMM during the early years of preserving the outtakes, the testimonies of the women protagonists in Lanzmann's four-part work were among the first ones made available to the public in the 2000s. The museum even included Elias's unused gendered narrative in a compilation film titled *Shoah: The Unseen Interviews*, which premiered at the New York Jewish Film Festival in 2012.

"Women's histories of the Holocaust have proliferated since the first pathbreaking studies appeared in the 1980s. [...] Yet to a remarkable extent this work remains outside the mainstream of Holocaust studies," observes Doris Bergen in a recent assessment of the field. "Studies of gender and sexuality are accepted, but as 'different voices' [...], voices that speak from and for the most part to a 'separate sphere,' removed from what count as the big questions in the field."[4] By form alone, and in regrouping Elias, Biren, Lichtman, and Marton, *The Four Sisters* posits these women survivors not as protagonists but as "different voices," at once detached from a broader narrative of the Holocaust and from Lanzmann's oeuvre. Of all the films he has made from outtakes, these separate portraits resemble in their conventionality *The Karski Report* (2010). The first film to draw on the interview of a *Shoah* protagonist who, unlike the brief interventions of Elias and Biren, appears extensively in the nine-and-half-hour final version, it is also the only one to not have been planned by the filmmaker. A sense of urgency dictates the simple editing in *The Karski Report* (all the while including an opening text crawl), insofar as Lanzmann retrieved the excluded portions in the midst of the "affair" sparked by the 2009 publication of *The Messenger*.

A belated addendum to *Shoah*, *The Four Sisters* and its negative editing strategies gesture toward a similar sense of urgency, while problematizing the very nature of Lanzmann's final undertaking. If, by definition, the outtakes are composed of raw material, they also constitute, through their acquisition by the USHMM, archival footage. Is *The Four Sisters*, then, a documentary or a document? What distinguishes these minimally edited testimonies from the filmed interviews previously restored and digitized by the Steven Spielberg Film and Video Archive?

In *After the Fact: Holocaust Documentary in the Twenty-First Century* (2015), Brad Prager argues that a document, unlike a documentary, is "unframed" insofar as the footage is neither "placed in a context" nor "employed as part of a line of argumentation."[5] In *The Last of the Unjust*, the excluded testimony of Murmelstein is framed: it returns quite literally to illuminate the filmmaker's investigation of Theresienstadt, both in the past and in the present. In *The Four Sisters*, the unused material with Elias, Biren, Lichtman, and Marton subsists as an unframed document, which illuminates first and foremost the "anxiety of historical transmission" underlying the making of *Shoah*: the accelerated production of 230 hours of footage by the filmmaker who wanted to record witnesses of the catastrophe at all costs—regardless of whether they eventually would be included in his Holocaust opus and, even, regardless of whether this material would ever be seen.[6] "The most important thing for me was to have them on film," Lanzmann affirmed upon presenting *The Four Sisters* at the New York Film Festival in October 2017. Decades earlier, never could he have imagined that, in the twenty-first century, the USHMM would preserve these testimonies "in perpetuity" and render the Claude Lanzmann *Shoah* Collection part of a constellation of audiovisual archives that, in the digital age, have come to redefine Holocaust memory.[7]

A similar "anxiety of historical transmission" permeated, a decade after the release of *Shoah*, the extensive efforts of Michael Berenbaum and Raye Farr to acquire the outtakes and ensure the transmission of an unparalleled cinematic archive. "Lanzmann's deliberate attempt to pull each witness into a reliving of the event—as opposed to a retelling—has created a series of voyages into the place and the time and the pain and the paradox of Holocaust events, of Holocaust memories," Berenbaum and Farr wrote in their report of the interviews screened in Joinville-le-Pont in February 1996.[8] In moving from the unthinkable gendered trauma of Elias in "The Hippocratic Oath" to a reenactment of the past in "The Merry Flea," where Lichtman mends dolls in front of the camera as she had done in Sobibór, *The Four Sisters* captures such a transnational voyage. Yet what these outtakes evidence, and what this book has rendered visible and audible, is also a resistance to certain demands of Holocaust representation and a concomitant reshaping of testimonial performance. In the twenty-first century, the project of recovering the *Shoah* archive entails resisting a linear, progressive, universalizing approach to encountering horror. As this book has shown, it also means forging a model of reception premised not on deep memory but on *the deep time of testimony*: the recuperation of heterogeneous modalities of traumatic representation—both past and future.

NOTES

INTRODUCTION

6. "Letter from Raul Hilberg to Michael Berenbaum dated 18 March 1994," Film and Video Archive Administrative Files, USHMM, uncataloged.

7. Noah Shenker, *Reframing Holocaust Testimony* (Bloomington: Indiana University Press, 2015), 112–113.

8. Claude Lanzmann, "Letter to Roswell McClelland dated 16 February 1977," USHMM, 2014.500–Roswell and Marjorie McClelland Papers, Series 6, Folder 10, Files 3 and 4, 1.

9. Irena Steinfeldt (for Claude Lanzmann), "Letter to Roswell McClelland dated 14 September 1978," USHMM, 2014.500–Roswell and Marjorie McClelland Papers, Series 6, Folder 10, File 10. This rushed shooting schedule also intimates the financial difficulties encountered by Lanzmann that hindered the making of *Shoah* at various stages of the project. As his assistant Corinna Coulmas recalls, the filmmaker and his crew "almost stopped everything four or five times" due to lack of funds (Interview with Corinna Coulmas, 17 July 2016; my translation). Lanzmann never transferred to the USHMM the paper archive—such as invoices for film equipment, payroll reports, and fundraising letters—accumulated between 1973 and 1985, without which it is not possible to determine how *Shoah* was financed.

10. Thomas Trezise, *Witnessing Witnessing: On the Reception of Holocaust Testimony* (New York: Fordham University Press, 2013), 1. During the making of *Shoah*, Lanzmann filmed the New York City office of the American Jewish Committee (AJC), including their Wiener Oral History Library, which itself housed thousands of hours of audiotaped interviews with survivors. See "AJC Office—New York," USHMM, The Claude Lanzmann *Shoah* Collection, RG-60.5070.

11. Claude Lanzmann, "Letter to Roswell McClelland dated February 16, 1977," 1. I borrow the term "archival impulse" from Hal Foster. In his discussion of contemporary archival art, Foster suggests that this practice stems from a "sense of a failure in cultural memory, of a default in productive traditions." See Hal Foster, "An Archival Impulse," *October* 110 (Fall 2004): 21–22.

12. "Research Institute Establishes the Steven Spielberg Film and Video Archive," news release dated 28 October 1994, Film and Video Archive Administrative Files, USHMM, uncataloged.

13. For the filmmaker's critique of *Schindler's List*, see Claude Lanzmann, "Why Spielberg Has Distorted the Truth," *Guardian Weekly* (3 April 1994): 14. This article first appeared in *Le Monde* on 3 March 1994 under the title "Holocauste, la représentation impossible."

14. "A Proposal for the Acquisition and Educational Use of SHOAH Film Interviews" (1995), USHMM, Film and Video Archive Administrative Files, uncataloged.

15. "Letter from Raul Hilberg to Michael Berenbaum dated 17 August 1995," Film and Video Archive Administrative Files, USHMM, uncataloged.

16. Claude Lanzmann, "Material of 'Shoah'" (1994), Film and Video Archive Administrative Files, USHMM, uncataloged. *The Karski Report* was in fact not planned but prompted by the 2009 French publication of Yannick Haenel's novel *The Messenger* (see chapter 4). This film was the first Lanzmann made using outtakes restored by the USHMM, as would also be the case with *The Last of the Unjust* and *The Four Sisters*.

17. "*Shoah* Outtakes: Report on Paris Screening 20–29 February 1996" (4 March 1996), prepared by Raye Farr, Film and Video Archive Administrative Files, USHMM, uncataloged, 5–6.

18. Leslie Swift and Lindsay Zarwell, "Inside the Outtakes: A History of the Claude Lanzmann *Shoah* Collection at the USHMM," in *The Invention of Testimony: Claude Lanzmann in the Twenty-First Century*, ed. Erin McGlothlin, Brad Prager, and Markus Zisselsberger (forthcoming). Swift and Zarwell provide a detailed technical account of the acquisition, restoration, and digitization of the *Shoah* outtakes.

19. Swift and Zarwell, "Inside the Outtakes."

20. Swift and Zarwell, "Inside the Outtakes."

21. I borrow the term "docu-auteur" from Linda Williams who examined the intricate role played by postmodern docu-auteurs such as Lanzmann in "constructing and staging" narratives of trauma. See "Mirrors without Memories: Truth, History, and the New Documentary," *Film Quarterly* 46.3 (Spring 1993): 12.

22. "Letter from Raul Hilberg to Michael Berenbaum dated 17 August 1995."

23. Claude Lanzmann, "From Holocaust to 'Holocaust,'" in *Claude Lanzmann's "Shoah": Key Essays*, ed. Stuart Liebman (Oxford: Oxford University Press, 2007), 30, 34–35. On the identical terms deployed by Lanzmann in his critiques of *Holocaust* and *Schindler's List*, see Michael Rothberg, *Traumatic Realism: The*

Demands of Holocaust Representation (Minneapolis: University of Minnesota Press, 2000), 232–233.

24. Michel Ciment, "Décembre en cinéma," *Positif* 516 (February 2004): 45. My translation.

25. In 1987, Ziva Postec published an account of her work on *Shoah* emphasizing the collective nature of the editing phase (as denoted by her frequent use of the pronoun "we"). See "Le montage du film *Shoah*," accessed 22 November 2017, http://kefisrael.com/2011/01/26/le-montage-du-film-shoah-ziva-postec/. The Canadian director Catherine Hébert recently devoted a documentary to her work on *Shoah*. Titled *Ziva Postec: The Editor Behind the Film "Shoah,"* it premiered in November 2018 at the Montreal International Documentary Festival.

26. See Lawrence Langer, *Holocaust Testimonies: The Ruins of Memory* (New Haven: Yale University Press, 1991), 1–38. Recent scholarship that critically assesses the process of mediation underlying foundational oral history projects such as the Fortunoff Video Archive for Holocaust Testimonies also privileges the category of deep memory. See, for example, Amit Pinchevski, "The Audiovisual Unconscious: Media and Trauma in the Video Archive for Holocaust Testimonies," *Critical Inquiry* 39.1 (Autumn 2012): 154–158, as well as Shenker, *Reframing Holocaust Testimony*, 5.

27. Michael Renov, *The Subject of Documentary* (Minneapolis: University of Minnesota Press, 2004), 126.

28. Inversing the concept of "site of memory" popularized by the French historian Pierre Nora in 1984, Lanzmann describes the empty extermination camps filmed for *Shoah* as "non-sites of memory." See Marc Chevrie and Hervé Le Roux, "Site and Speech: An Interview with Claude Lanzmann about *Shoah*," in *Claude Lanzmann's "Shoah": Key Essays*, ed. Stuart Liebman (Oxford: Oxford University Press, 2007), 39.

29. See Sylvie Lindeperg, *"Night and Fog": A Film in History*, trans. Tom Mes (Minneapolis: University of Minnesota Press, 2014).

30. Stuart Liebman, "Introduction," in *Claude Lanzmann's "Shoah": Key Essays*, ed. Stuart Liebman (Oxford: Oxford University Press, 2007), 11.

31. On Ringelheim's interviews with women survivors in 1979, see "The Split Between Gender and the Holocaust," in *Women in the Holocaust*, ed. Ofer Dalia and Lenore J. Weitzman (New Haven: Yale University Press, 1998), 340–350. Subsequently head of the Department of Oral History at the USHMM, Ringelheim also partook in the acquisition of the *Shoah* outtakes. The paper trail of the negotiations includes a letter from Ringelheim to Hilberg dated 10 May 1994 in which she enquires about the physical characteristics and contents of Lanzmann's archive of testimonies (Film and Video Archive Administrative Files, USHMM, uncataloged).

32. Pinchevski, "The Audiovisual Unconscious," 147.

33. See Michael Rothberg, *Multidirectional Memory: Remembering the Holocaust in the Age of Decolonization* (Stanford: Stanford University Press, 2009).

34. Trezise, *Witnessing Witnessing*, 60.

35. Marianne Hirsch and Leo Spitzer, "Gendered Translations: Claude Lanzmann's *Shoah*" [1993], in *Claude Lanzmann's "Shoah": Key Essays*, ed. Stuart Liebman (Oxford: Oxford University Press, 2007), 187.

36. Lanzmann, "Why Spielberg Has Distorted the Truth," 14.

37. I wish to thank Samuel Weber for suggesting the phrase "to compose with the incompossible."

CHAPTER ONE

1. As Perlov explained in a 1981 interview, "the clear decision to make a diary and to call it *Diary* derived from a talk I had with Andre Schwartz-Bart [*sic*] who was here with his wife Simone, during the [Yom Kippur] war." Quoted in Irma Klein and Uri Klein, "An Interview with David Perlov," in *David Perlov's Diary*, ed. Mira Perlov and Pip Chodorov (Paris: Re:Voir Video, 2006), 14.

2. Raul Hilberg, "Letter to Michael Berenbaum dated 17 August 1995," Film and Video Archive Administrative Files, USHMM, uncataloged.

3. Claude Lanzmann, *The Patagonian Hare* [2009], trans. Frank Wynne (New York: Farrar, Straus and Giroux, 2012), 411.

4. Lanzmann, *The Patagonian Hare*, 411.

5. Sue Vice, *Shoah* (London: Palgrave Macmillan–British Film Institute, 2011), 17.

6. Lanzmann, "Letter to Roswell McClelland dated 16 February 1977," 1.

7. "It is not a documentary," he told *Cahiers du cinéma* shortly after the film's release. Quoted in Chevrie and Le Roux, "Site and Speech," 42.

8. Lanzmann, "Letter to Roswell McClelland dated 16 February 1977," 1–2.

9. Williams, "Mirrors without Memories," 15.

10. Pascal Bonitzer, *Le regard et la voix: Essais sur le cinéma* (Paris: 10/18, 1976), 11.

11. Libby Saxton, *Haunted Images: Film, Ethics, Testimony, and the Holocaust* (London: Wallflower Press, 2008), 45.

12. Noël Burch, *Theory of Film Practice* [1969], trans. Helen R. Lane (Princeton: Princeton University Press, 2014), 17.

13. Eyal Peretz, *The Off-Screen. An Investigation of the Cinematic Frame* (Stanford: Stanford University Press, 2017), 13.

14. Lanzmann, *The Patagonian Hare*, 422.

15. Interview with Corinna Coulmas, 17 July 2016. My translation.

16. Email correspondence with Irena Steinfeldt, 28 February 2009.
17. Email correspondence with Steinfeldt, 28 February 2009.
18. Lanzmann, *The Patagonian Hare*, 420.
19. Gitta Sereny, *Into That Darkness: An Examination of Conscience* (New York: Vintage Books, 1974), 112–113.
20. Sereny, *Into That Darkness*, 113.
21. Sereny, *Into That Darkness*, 257.
22. Sereny, *Into That Darkness*, 219.
23. Sereny, *Into That Darkness*, 119.
24. Sereny, *Into That Darkness*, 149; Chevrie and Le Roux, "Site and Speech," 42.
25. As Lanzmann explained in an interview, "Over the years, I thought of different titles. I had one that I liked a lot but it was a bit abstract: *Site and Speech*" (Chevrie and Le Roux, "Site and Speech," 39).
26. Raul Hilberg, *Perpetrators Victims Bystanders: The Jewish Catastrophe, 1933–1945* (New York: HarperCollins, 1992).
27. Sereny, *Into That Darkness*, 157.
28. Sereny, *Into That Darkness*, 205.
29. Translation of the Franz Suchomel Interview Transcript, trans. Uta Allers, USHMM, The Claude Lanzmann *Shoah* Collection, RG-60.5046, 4 and 51.
30. Sereny, *Into That Darkness*, 245.
31. Translation of the Richard Glazar Interview Transcript, trans. Uta Allers, USHMM, The Claude Lanzmann *Shoah* Collection, RG-60.5028, 144.
32. Jeffrey Shandler, *Holocaust Memory in the Digital Age* (Stanford: Stanford University Press, 2017), 154.
33. Lanzmann, *The Patagonian Hare*, 429.
34. Shenker, *Reframing Holocaust Testimony*, 12.
35. Williams, "Mirrors without Memories," 13.
36. As Libby Saxton notes, "most of the slave workers in Treblinka and other Reinhard camps were directly involved in one way or another in the extermination process, since this was the sole purpose of these camps, and in this respect their function bears comparison with that of the Auschwitz *Sonderkommandos*" (*Haunted Images*, 39).
37. Langer, *Holocaust Testimonies*, 6.
38. Rothberg, *Traumatic Realism*, 236.
39. Saxton, *Haunted Images*, 38.
40. Williams, "Mirrors without Memories," 12.
41. Janet Walker, *Trauma Cinema: Documenting Incest and the Holocaust* (Berkeley: University of California Press, 2005), 26.

42. Langer, *Holocaust Testimonies*, 1–38; Cathy Caruth, ed., "Introduction," in *Trauma. Explorations in Memory* (Baltimore: Johns Hopkins University Press, 1995), 153.

43. Trezise, *Witnessing Witnessing*, 60.

44. Sereny, *Into That Darkness*, 172.

45. Sereny, *Into That Darkness*, 212.

46. Translation of the Richard Glazar Interview Transcript, 84–85. The phrase "Please—*you must try*" is omitted from the transcript (emphasis mine).

47. Sereny, *Into That Darkness*, 246.

48. Simone de Beauvoir, "Preface," in Jean-François Steiner, *Treblinka* [1966], trans. Helen Weaver (New York: Meridian, 1994), xix.

49. Samuel Moyn, *A Holocaust Controversy: The Treblinka Affair in Postwar France* (Lebanon: Brandeis University Press, 2005), 1. On Glazar's "Open Letter," see 137–140.

50. Moyn, *A Holocaust Controversy*, 5.

51. Translation of the Richard Glazar Interview Transcript, 146, 149.

52. Moyn, *A Holocaust Controversy*, 9.

53. Simone de Beauvoir, Claude Lanzmann, and Richard Marienstras, "Entretien avec Simone de Beauvoir: 'Ils n'étaient pas des lâches,'" *Le Nouvel Observateur* 75 (27 April 1966): 15–16.

54. In the collection of essays titled *Shoah le film: Des psychanalystes écrivent* (Paris: Jacques Grancher, 1990), both Jean-Jacques Moscovitz and Anne-Marie Houdebine deploy the term "heroes" upon speaking of the *Sonderkommando* members. See Moscovitz, "Savoir et non-savoir en question" (41) and Houdebine, "L'écriture *Shoah*" (95).

55. Kaufmann defended her dissertation in 1976, three years prior to her work for *Shoah*. She subsequently published it as a book titled *Pour relire "Le dernier des Justes"* (Paris: Klincksieck, 1986).

56. De Beauvoir, Lanzmann, and Marienstras, "Entretien avec Simone de Beauvoir," 17.

57. Hannah Arendt, *Eichmann in Jerusalem: A Report on the Banality of Evil* [1963] (New York: Penguin Books, 2006), 125.

58. On the significance of Dawidowicz's book for the emergence of Holocaust memory in America, see Saul Friedländer, *Réflexions sur le nazisme: Entretiens avec Stéphane Bou* (Paris: Éditions du Seuil, 2016), 65.

59. Lucy Dawidowicz, "Letter to Roswell McClelland dated 4 March 1977," USHMM, 2014.500–Roswell and Marjorie McClelland Papers, Series 6, Folder 6, File 23.

60. Raul Hilberg, *The Politics of Memory: The Journey of a Holocaust Historian* (Chicago: Ivan R. Dee, 1996), 145.

61. Lanzmann, *The Patagonian Hare*, 426.

62. For a brief review of this conference, see Israel Shenker, "Holocaust Parley Has Few Answers," *New York Times*, 6 March 1975.

63. Yehuda Bauer and Malcolm Lowe, "Introduction," in *The Holocaust as Historical Experience: Essays and a Discussion*, ed. Yehuda Bauer and Nathan Rotenstreich (New York: Holmes & Meier, 1981), xi. Of the ten articles included in this volume, seven deal with the issue of Jewish leadership.

64. Quoted by Isaiah Trunk in Henry Feingold, Isaiah Trunk, et al., "Discussion: The *Judenrat* and the Jewish Response," in *The Holocaust as Historical Experience: Essays and a Discussion*, ed. Yehuda Bauer and Nathan Rotenstreich (New York: Holmes & Meier, 1981), 268; Lucy Dawidowicz, *The War Against the Jews: 1933–1945* [1975] (New York: Seth Press, 1986), 229.

65. Steiner, *Treblinka*, 81.

66. Lanzmann, "Letter to Roswell McClelland dated February 16, 1977," 1.

67. Joseph Rudavsky, *To Live with Hope, to Die with Dignity* (Lanham: University Press of America, 1987), 228.

68. See Leib Garfunkel, *The Destruction of Kovno's Jewry* [Hebrew] (Jerusalem: Yad Vashem, 1959).

69. Raul Hilberg and Stanislaw Staron, "Introduction," in *The Warsaw Diary of Adam Czerniakow: Prelude to Doom* [1979], ed. Raul Hilberg, Stanislaw Staron, and Josef Kermisz (Chicago: Ivan R. Dee, 1999), 67.

70. Original Leib Garfunkel Interview Transcript, USHMM, The Claude Lanzmann *Shoah* Collection, RG-60.5005, 1.

71. Lanzmann, *The Patagonian Hare*, 419.

72. Translation of the Motke Zaidel and Itzak Dugin Interview Transcript, trans. Anna Dhaliwal, USHMM, The Claude Lanzmann *Shoah* Collection, RG-60.5050, 11.

73. Translation of the Motke Zaidel and Itzak Dugin Interview Transcript, 7.

74. I borrow the phrase "the buried self" from Lawrence Langer, who adopts the terminology used by Charlotte Delbo in her posthumous first-person account of the camps, *Days and Memory* [1985], trans. Rosette Lamont (Evanston: Northwestern University Press, 2001). See *Holocaust Testimonies*, 3–4.

75. Original Leib Garfunkel Interview Transcript, 29–30; 31.

76. See Chevrie and Le Roux, "Site and Speech," 40–41.

77. I thank Corinna Coulmas for identifying Lanzmann's handwriting.

78. Lanzmann, *The Patagonian Hare*, 425.

79. Hannah Arendt and Gershom Scholem, *The Correspondence of Hannah Arendt and Gershom Scholem*, ed. Marie Louise Knott, trans. Anthony David (Chicago: University of Chicago Press, 2017), 203.

80. Saul Friedländer, *When Memory Comes* [1978], trans. Helen R. Lane (New York: Other Press, 2016), 111.

81. Needless to say, the Murmelstein interview is the longest of all the testimonies filmed for *Shoah*.

82. Lanzmann, "Material of 'Shoah,'" 7.

83. "Oral History Interview with Benjamin Murmelstein," Oral History Interviews of the Leonard and Edith Ehrlich Collection, USHMM, RG-50.862. I thank Anatol Steck at the USHMM for sharing and discussing the Ehrlich interviews with me. Their research on Murmelstein was published posthumously under the title *Choices under Duress of the Holocaust: Benjamin Murmelstein and the Fate of Viennese Jewry, Volume I: Vienna* (Lubbock: Texas Tech University Press, 2018).

84. Translation of the Benjamin Murmelstein Interview Transcript, trans. Lotti Eichorn, USHMM, The Claude Lanzmann *Shoah* Collection, RG-60.5009, Part II, 247.

85. Chevrie and Le Roux, "Site and Speech," 38.

86. Translation of the Benjamin Murmelstein Interview Transcript, Part II, 247.

87. Friedländer, *When Memory Comes*, 111.

88. Original Pery Broad Interview Transcript, USHMM, The Claude Lanzmann *Shoah* Collection, RG-60.5053, 1A–2A.

89. Lanzmann, *The Patagonian Hare*, 443–445.

90. Alain Bergala, Jean-Jacques Henry, and Serge Toubiana, "La sortie des usines Aäton (entretien avec Jean-Pierre Beauviala 2)," *Cahiers du cinéma* 286 (March 1978): 13. My translation.

91. See Clarice Fabre, "Jean-Pierre Beauviala: 'La caméra, comme un chat sur l'épaule,'" *Le Monde*, 11 October 2016, accessed 30 April 2018, http://www.lemonde.fr/cinema/article/2016/10/11/et-beauviala-reinventa-la-camera_5011573_3476.html.

92. Janet Bergstrom and Alain Bergala, "Genesis of a Camera (First Episode)," trans. Lynne Kirby, *Camera Obscura* 13–14 (Spring–Summer 1985): 165. In addition to two introductory texts by Bergstrom and Bergala, this article reproduces a conversation between Godard and Beauviala detailing their collaboration.

93. Email correspondence with Jean-Pierre Beauviala, 20 August 2016.

94. Anne-Marie Duguet, *Vidéo, la mémoire au poing* (Paris: Hachette, 1981), 186. My translation.

95. Antoine de Baecque, *Godard: biographie* (Paris: Bernard Grasset, 2010), 543. My translation.

96. Richard Brody, *Everything Is Cinema: The Working Life of Jean-Luc Godard* (New York: Metropolitan Book/Henry Holt and Company, 2008), 386; de Baecque, *Godard: biographie*, 540 (my translation).

97. Anthony Pierre, "*Le Père Nöel a les yeux bleus*: l'invasion du réel dans la fiction," in *Le court métrage français de 1945 à 1968: De l'âge d'or aux contrebandiers*, ed. Dominique Bluher and François Thomas (Rennes: Presses Universitaires de Rennes, 2005), 344.

98. Lanzmann, *The Patagonian Hare*, 409.

99. Michel Ciment and Yann Tobin, "William Lubtchansky: 'J'ai horreur du gris!'" *Positif* 475 (September 2000): 81. My translation.

100. On the Godard-Lanzmann dispute, see Saxton, *Haunted Images*, 46–67.

101. "Pery Broad," USHMM, The Claude Lanzmann *Shoah* Collection, RG-60.5053, FV3443, 08:29–08:32 (accessed 29 May 2018). My translation.

102. "Camionette [*sic*]," USHMM, The Claude Lanzmann *Shoah* Collection, RG-60.5058, FV3452 (accessed 29 May 2018).

103. Friedländer, *When Memory Comes*, 111. See also Lanzmann, *The Patagonian Hare*, 452.

104. Duguet, *Vidéo, la mémoire au poing*, 167–168. My translation.

105. Duguet, *Vidéo, la mémoire au poing*, 54. My translation.

106. See Original Franz Suchomel Interview Transcript, USHMM, The Claude Lanzmann *Shoah* Collection, RG-60.5046, 100. The exchanges in French between the filmmaker and the camera assistant are not included in the English translation of the interview. Lanzmann uses the code word *gros* in other *Shoah* outtakes as well. For instance, during the interview with the former War Refugee Board director John Pehle, he instructs his cameraman to sustain a close-up of Pehle's face. "*Tu restes gros sur lui* [you stay *gros* on him]," he exclaims in French. See Original John Pehle Interview Transcript, USHMM, The Claude Lanzmann *Shoah* Collection, RG-60.5021, 28.

107. Original Franz Suchomel Interview Transcript, 50.

108. Lanzmann, *The Patagonian Hare*, 453. As the outtakes confirm, Suchomel was accompanied by his wife. During the interview, she waits outside the room, knocking from time to time to check on her husband.

109. Translation of the Franz Suchomel Interview Transcript, 55.

110. "Franz Suchomel," USHMM, The Claude Lanzmann *Shoah* Collection, RG-60.5046, FV3759, 17:08–21:19 (accessed 29 May 2018). My translation.

111. Lanzmann, *The Patagonian Hare*, 453.

112. Translation of the Franz Suchomel Interview Transcript, 112–113.

113. Take 6 is described as a "general conversation." See Original Pery Broad Interview Transcript, 20.

114. Original Pery Broad Interview Transcript, 8A. Transcription modified.

115. Original Pery Broad Interview Transcript, 10A; Lanzmann, *The Patagonian Hare*, 527.

116. Original Pery Broad Interview Transcript, 4. In the outtakes, for instance, with Ada Lichtman and her husband, the two survivors of the Sobibór extermination camp estimate that "two, three kilometers" separated the railway station and the gas chamber. In fact, as Lanzmann tells them, it was only four hundred meters. See Translation of the Ada Lichtman Interview Transcript, USHMM, The Claude Lanzmann *Shoah* Collection, RG-60.5023, 29.

117. Walker, *Trauma Cinema*, 17, 19.

118. Original Pery Broad Interview Transcript, 10A.

119. Original Pery Broad Interview Transcript, 9A.

120. Original Pery Broad Interview Transcript, 132.

121. Quoted in Devin Pendas, *The Frankfurt Auschwitz Trials, 1963–1965: Genocide, History, and the Limits of the Law* (Cambridge: Cambridge University Press, 2006), 135.

122. Original Pery Broad Interview Transcript, 4A.

123. Original Pery Broad Interview Transcript, 6A.

124. Friedländer, *When Memory Comes*, 112.

125. This part of the outtakes is not included in the interview transcript. See "Pery Broad," FV3686, 01:31–02:27 (accessed 29 May 2018). My translation.

126. Lanzmann, *The Patagonian Hare*, 456. My emphasis.

127. James Naremore, "American Film Noir: The History of an Idea," *Film Quarterly* 49.2 (Winter 1995–1996): 24. For a more detailed exploration of this genre and its invention in postwar French cinephile circles, see Naremore's book-length study, *More than Night: Film Noir in Its Context* [1998] (Berkeley: University of California Press, 2008), 9–39.

128. In his presentation of the 1979 text republished in a volume of collected essays, Lanzmann explains that it was initially written as a "progress report" for the film's investors. See "De l'Holocauste à *Holocauste* ou comment s'en débarrasser," in *La Tombe du divin plongeur* (Paris: Gallimard, 2012), 369.

129. "Karl Kretschmer—Einsatzgruppen," USHMM, The Claude Lanzmann *Shoah* Collection, RG-60.5018, FV3246, 00:54–01:14 (accessed 29 May 2018). This conversation is not included in the transcript of the interview. For a detailed analysis of the Kretschmer footage, see Sue Vice, "Claude Lanzmann's Einsatzgruppen Interviews," in *Representing Perpetrators in Holocaust Literature and Film*, ed. Jenni Adams and Sue Vice (London: Valentine Mitchell, 2013), 47–68.

130. Lanzmann, *The Patagonian Hare*, 458–463. See also "Heinz Schubert—Einsatzgruppen," USHMM, The Claude Lanzmann *Shoah* Collection, RG-60.5013, FV3219, 19:03–21:07 (accessed 29 May 2018).

131. "Heinz Schubert—Einsatzgruppen," FV3216, 00:00–00:03 (accessed 29 May 2018). This conversation is not included in the transcript of the interview. My translation.
132. "Franz Schalling—Chelmno, Gas Van," USHMM, The Claude Lanzmann *Shoah* Collection, RG-60.5034, FV3355, 13:18–13:20 (accessed 29 May 2018). This conversation is not included in the transcript of the interview. My translation.
133. "Heinz Schubert—Einsatzgruppen," FV3217, 23:45–24:16 (accessed 29 May 2018). This conversation is not included in the transcript of the interview. My translation.
134. Translation of the Heinz Schubert Interview Transcript, trans. Lotti Eichorn, USHMM, The Claude Lanzmann *Shoah* Collection, RG-60.5013, 5.
135. Lanzmann, *The Patagonian Hare*, 458.
136. Interview with Corinna Coulmas, 17 July 2016; my translation. Steimle is listed in "Material of 'Shoah,'" the document Lanzmann drafted in 1994 for the USHMM. Rather than the "hidden camera" (as the Paluche is referred to in this document), a "hidden recorder" was used for this interview when Coulmas initially met with him. None of the interviews captured with a "hidden recorder" during the preliminary research phase were transferred to the USHMM.
137. Seibert, who received the same sentence at Nuremberg as Schubert and Steimle, passed away in March 1976, only weeks before Lanzmann would use the Paluche for the first time to film Suchomel.
138. The seven are Franz Suchomel, Franz Schalling, Walter Stier (all three appear in *Shoah*), Pery Broad, Heinz Schubert, Hans Geweke, and Eduard Kryshak. Willy Hilse, a German railroad worker at the Auschwitz train station, was possibly filmed with the Paluche: while only an audio-recording was transferred to the USHMM, Lanzmann asks Hilse in the middle of the interview if he can film him (the former railroad worker refuses).
139. Lanzmann, "Letter to Roswell McClelland dated 16 February 1977," 1.
140. "Gustav Laabs and Lettre Becker," USHMM, The Claude Lanzmann *Shoah* Collection, RG-60.5025, FV3293, 05:38–05:45 (accessed 29 May 2018). My translation. In the Broad outtakes, the camera also effects a close-up of an apartment window from the parked van.
141. "Gustav Laabs and Lettre Becker," FV3293, 07:50–07:52 (accessed 29 May 2018). My translation.
142. "Eduard Kryshak," USHMM, The Claude Lanzmann *Shoah* Collection, RG-60.5035, FV3360, 02:10–02:17 (accessed 29 May 2018). My translation.
143. "Eduard Kryshak," FV3357, 05:32–05:34 (accessed 29 May 2018). My translation.
144. Translation of the Eduard Kryshak Interview Transcript, trans. Uta Allers, USHMM, The Claude Lanzmann *Shoah* Collection, RG-60.5035, 6, 13.

145. Original Pery Broad Interview Transcript, 9A. My emphasis. Transcription modified.

146. "Rush, n.², adv., and adj.," in *OED Online*, accessed 3 January 2017, http://www.oed.com/view/Entry/169027?rskey=A0XRUM&result=2#eid24526541. I thank Samuel Weber for calling my attention to these older meanings.

147. Lanzmann, "Letter to Roswell McClelland dated 16 February 1977," 1.

148. "Abraham Bomba—Treblinka," USHMM, The Claude Lanzmann *Shoah* Collection, RG-60.5011, FV3205.2, 00:00–03:56 (accessed 29 May 2018).

149. Lanzmann, "Letter to Roswell McClelland dated 16 February 1977," 1.

150. Gottfried Wilhelm Leibniz, *Theodicy: Essays on the Goodness of God, the Freedom of Man, and the Origins of Evil* [1710], trans. E. M. Huggard (Chicago: Open Court, 1998), 242–243.

151. Michel Tournier, "Gilles Deleuze," trans. Walter Redfern, in *Deleuze and Religion*, ed. Mary Bryden (London: Routledge, 2001), 202. In *The Patagonian Hare*, where he describes these postwar years in Paris, Lanzmann recalls his strained friendship with Deleuze that culminated in a public rift in 1977. That year, the French minister of the interior censored Daniel Schmid's *The Shadow of Angels*, the film adaptation of Rainer Werner Fassbinder's controversial play *The Garbage, the City and Death* (1975), whose protagonist is a real estate developer solely referred to as "the Rich Jew." In a piece published in *Le Monde* on 18 February 1977, Deleuze praised and defended the film, going as far as asking: "Where is the anti-Semitism, where could it possibly be?" On February 23, 1977, in the midst of making *Shoah*, Lanzmann wrote a bitter rebuttal titled "Night and Fog," which decried the philosopher's supposed blindness to the film's blatant anti-Semitism. See Deleuze, "Le juif riche," reprinted in *Deux régimes de fous: Textes et entretiens 1975–1995* (Paris: Les Éditions de Minuit, 2003), 125 (my translation); Lanzmann, "Nuit et brouillard: réponse à Gilles Deleuze à propos de *L'Ombre des anges* de R. W. Fassbinder et D. Schmid," in *La Tombe du divin plongeur* (Paris: Gallimard, 2012), 348.

152. Gilles Deleuze, "Three Questions on *Six fois deux*" [1976], in *Negotiations 1972–1990*, trans. Martin Joughin (New York: Columbia University Press, 1995), 37–45.

153. Gilles Deleuze, "Cinéma cours 48 du 06/12/83," *La voix de Gilles Deleuze en ligne*, accessed 3 January 2017, http://www2.univ-paris8.fr/deleuze/article.php3?id_article=269.

154. Gilles Deleuze, *Cinema 2: The Time-Image* [1985], trans. Robert Galeta (Minneapolis: University of Minnesota Press, 1989), 131. See also Gilles Deleuze, *The Fold: Leibniz and the Baroque* [1988], trans. Tom Conley (Minneapolis: University of Minnesota Press, 1989), 62.

155. D. N. Rodowick, *Gilles Deleuze's Time Machine* (Durham: Duke University Press, 1997), 99.

156. Lanzmann, *The Patagonian Hare*, 184.
157. Lanzmann, *The Patagonian Hare*, 426, 439.
158. Lanzmann, *The Patagonian Hare*, 490.
159. Alison Landsberg, *Prosthetic Memory: The Transformation of American Remembrance in the Age of Mass Culture* (New York: Columbia University Press, 2004), 19.
160. Lanzmann, *The Patagonian Hare*, 70.
161. See Sylvie Lindeperg's account of the making of Resnais's documentary, *"Night and Fog": A Film in History*, 102–103.
162. Landsberg, *Prosthetic Memory*, 148.
163. Lanzmann, *The Patagonian Hare*, 75.
164. Julia Kristeva, *Powers of Horrors: An Essay on Abjection* [1980], trans. Leon S. Roudiez (New York: Columbia University Press, 1982), 4.
165. Dominique Villain, *Le montage au cinéma* (Paris: Cahiers du cinéma, 1991), 53. My translation.
166. Deleuze, *The Fold*, 81.
167. Chevrie and Le Roux, "Site and Speech," 46.
168. Chevrie and Le Roux, "Site and Speech," 46.
169. Lanzmann, *The Patagonian Hare*, 438.
170. Translation of the Simon Srebnik Interview Transcript, trans. Sarah Lippincott, USHMM, The Claude Lanzmann *Shoah* Collection, RG-60.5024, Part I, 9. Translation modified.
171. Lanzmann, *The Patagonian Hare*, 435.
172. Translation of the Simon Srebnik Interview Transcript, Part I, 14. Translation modified.
173. In a 2007 interview with Jean-Michel Frodon, Lanzmann provides an explanation for this shift from Hebrew to German: "I decided he should speak Hebrew, and we had to use an interpreter. And then it didn't work, it all seemed stiff, the shots seemed dead. So, we just spoke German." In *Cinema and the Shoah: An Art Confronts the Tragedy of the Twentieth Century* [2007], ed. Jean-Michel Frodon, trans. Anna Harrison and Tom Mes (Albany: State University of New York Press, 2010), 103.
174. Translation of the Simon Srebnik Interview Transcript, Part I, 16, 15.
175. Translation of the Simon Srebnik Interview Transcript, Part I, 5. Translation modified.
176. Claude Lanzmann, "Ce mot de 'Shoah'… Réponse à Henri Meschonnic" [2005], in *La Tombe du divin plongeur* (Paris: Gallimard, 2012), 363.
177. Interview with Corinna Coulmas, 17 July 2016.
178. De Beauvoir, "Preface," in *Treblinka*, xxiii.

179. Jean-Michel Frodon, "Intersecting Paths," in *Cinema and the Shoah: An Art Confronts the Tragedy of the Twentieth Century* [2007], ed. Jean-Michel Frodon, trans. Anna Harrison and Tom Mes (Albany: State University of New York Press, 2010), 12.

180. Francine Kaufmann, "Interview et interprétation consécutive dans le film *Shoah*, de Claude Lanzmann," *Meta: journal des traducteurs* 38.4 (December 1993): 665.

181. Lanzmann, *The Patagonian Hare*, 506.

CHAPTER TWO

1. Liat Benhabib, "*Memories of the Eichmann Trial*: Restoration of a 1979 film by David Perlov," *Yad Vashem Jerusalem* 61 (April 2011): 12.

2. Annette Wieviorka, *The Era of the Witness* [1998], trans. Jared Stark (Ithaca: Cornell University Press, 2006), 56.

3. Tom Segev, *The Seventh Million. The Israelis and the Holocaust* [1991], trans. Haim Watzman (New York: Owl Books, 2000), 211.

4. Captions identifying the interviewees were added to the restored version of *Memories of the Eichmann Trial*.

5. Arendt, *Eichmann in Jerusalem*, 6.

6. On the filming of the Eichmann trial, see Sylvie Lindeperg and Annette Wieviorka, "The Two Stages of the Eichmann Trial," in *Concentrationary Memories: Totalitarian Terror and Cultural Resistance*, ed. Griselda Pollock and Max Silverman (London: I. B. Tauris, 2014), 59–81.

7. Haim Gouri, *Facing the Glass Booth: The Jerusalem Trial of Adolf Eichmann* [1962], trans. Michael Swirsky (Detroit: Wayne State University Press, 2004), 40.

8. Uri Klein, "*Memories of the Eichmann Trial* / From Testimony to Proof," *Haaretz*, 1 May 2011, accessed 12 February 2017, http://www.haaretz.com/print-edition/features/memories-of-the-eichmann-trial-from-testimony-to-proof-1.359060. In his brief evocation of Perlov's film, *Cahiers du cinéma* critic Ariel Schweitzer also singles out Ross's performance, which he describes as the "most poignant testimony" in the film. See "Forgetting, Instrumentalization, and Transgression: The Shoah in Israeli Cinema," in *Cinema and the Shoah: An Art Confronts the Tragedy of the Twentieth Century* [2007], ed. Jean-Michel Frodon, trans. Anna Harrison and Tom Mes (Albany: State University of New York Press, 2010), 184.

9. Lawrence Douglas, *The Memory of Judgment* (New Haven: Yale University Press, 2001), 170.

10. Gouri, *Facing the Glass Booth*, 50.

11. Lanzmann, *The Patagonian Hare*, 424.
12. Quoted by Annette Wieviorka in *Le procès Eichmann* (Brussels: Éditions Complexe, 1989), 56. My translation.
13. Gouri, *Facing the Glass Booth*, 51.
14. Trezise, *Witnessing Witnessing*, 59.
15. Gouri, *Facing the Glass Booth*, 50.
16. Gouri, *Facing the Glass Booth*, 6, 8.
17. Hanna Yablonka, *The State of Israel vs. Adolf Eichmann* [2001], trans. Ora Cummings with David Herman (New York: Schocken Books, 2004), 60.
18. Amit Pinchevski and Tamar Liebes, "Severed Voices: Radio and the Mediation of Trauma in the Eichmann Trial," *Public Culture* 22.2 (Spring 2010): 278.
19. "The greatness of Claude Lanzmann's art," writes Simone de Beauvoir in her preface to the published testimonies of *Shoah*, "is [...] conveying the unspeakable through faces." See Claude Lanzmann, *Shoah: The Complete Text of the Acclaimed Film* (Boston: Da Capo Press, 1995), iii.
20. Shoshana Felman, "The Return of the Voice: Claude Lanzmann's *Shoah*," in Shoshana Felman and Dori Laub, *Testimony: Crises of Witnessing in Literature, Psychoanalysis and History* (New York: Routledge, 1992), 206.
21. For an analysis of Yoselewska's 1961 testimony, see Douglas, *The Memory of Judgment*, 170–173.
22. Yablonka, *The State of Israel vs. Adolf Eichmann*, 108. In this study published four decades after the Eichmann trial, Yablonka also posits Yoselewska as an exemplary witness. "It was with great excitement that I drove to the geriatric department of Tel Hashomer Hospital, one warm winter morning in 1994," she begins her introduction of *The State of Israel vs. Adolf Eichmann*. "I was going to meet recently widowed Rivka Yoselewska [...]. Rivka Yoselewska's had been the most horrific of all the testimonies at the trial of Adolf Eichmann thirty-three years before" (3).
23. Lanzmann, *The Patagonian Hare*, 425.
24. Lanzmann, *The Patagonian Hare*, 465–466.
25. Lanzmann, *The Patagonian Hare*, 425.
26. Gouri, *Facing the Glass Booth*, 31.
27. Trezise, *Witnessing Witnessing*, 224.
28. Gouri, *Facing the Glass Booth*, 31. In his foreword to *Facing the Glass Booth*, Alan Mintz also singles out Fleischmann's testimony as evidencing the beginning of "a marked shift in attitudes toward Holocaust survivors in Israeli society," especially regarding the question of passivity (xiii).
29. Gouri, *Facing the Glass Booth*, 51.
30. Douglas, *The Memory of Judgment*, 102.

31. *The Trial of Adolf Eichmann: Record of Proceedings in the District Court of Jerusalem* (Jerusalem: Trust for the Publication of the Proceedings of the Eichmann Trial, 1992), vol. 1, session 20, 324.
32. Translation of the Ada Lichtman Interview Transcript, 4.
33. *The Trial of Adolf Eichmann*, 325–326.
34. *The Trial of Adolf Eichmann*, 323. At the end of Lichtman's testimony, the prosecution suggested she testify again when the court would turn to "the chapter of the camps." However, the Sobibór survivor never came back to the witness stand.
35. Wieviorka, *The Era of the Witness*, 77. Most recently, the testimony of Ada Lichtman (whose first name is alternatively spelled Eda) was recalled by Deborah E. Lipstadt. In her account of the Eichmann trial, she in fact juxtaposes the testimonies of Lichtman and Yoselewska. See Deborah E. Lipstadt, *The Eichmann Trial* (New York: Nextbook and Schocken Books, 2011), 77.
36. Douglas, *The Memory of Judgment*, 103.
37. Gouri, *Facing the Glass Booth*, 26.
38. Douglas, *The Memory of Judgment*, 104. Filmed one last time in Israel in 1992, Lichtman replicated her courtroom demeanor by wearing sunglasses for the entirety of her testimony. See Oral History Interview with Eda Lichtman, USHMM, RG-50.120*0091.
39. *The Trial of Adolf Eichmann*, 324.
40. Tzvetan Todorov, *Facing the Extreme: Moral Life in the Concentration Camps* [1991], trans. Arthur Denner and Abigail Pollack (New York: Henry Holt, 1996), 16.
41. Original Abraham Bomba Interview Transcript, USHMM, The Claude Lanzmann *Shoah* Collection, RG-60.5011, 54. My translation.
42. Translation of the Ada Lichtman Interview Transcript, 21. Translation modified.
43. Translation of the Ada Lichtman Interview Transcript, 20.
44. Richard Rashke, *Escape from Sobibor* [1982] (New York: Delphinium Books, 2013), 326–327. When Rashke interviewed Lichtman in 1981, she had already retired.
45. Translation of the Ada Lichtman Interview Transcript, 28 and 32. Translation modified.
46. Lanzmann, *The Patagonian Hare*, 431–432.
47. See, for example, "Hier ist kein Warum," where Lanzmann denounces "an absolute obscenity in the project of understanding," in *Claude Lanzmann's "Shoah": Key Essays*, ed. Stuart Liebman (Oxford: Oxford University Press, 2007), 51. For a critique of Lanzmann's absolutism, see Dominick LaCapra, *History and Memory After Auschwitz* (Ithaca: Cornell University Press, 1998), 95–138.

48. Agnieszka Piotrowska, *Psychoanalysis and Ethics in Documentary Film* (London: Routledge, 2014), 163.
49. Translation of the Ada Lichtman Interview Transcript, 24. Translation modified.
50. Michel Chion, *The Voice in Cinema* [1982], trans. Claudia Gorbman (New York: Columbia University Press, 1999), 96–97.
51. Translation of the Ada Lichtman Interview Transcript, 30–31.
52. Jacques Mandelbaum, "Recovery," in *Cinema and the Shoah: An Art Confronts the Tragedy of the Twentieth Century* [2007], ed. Jean-Michel Frodon, trans. Anna Harrison and Tom Mes (Albany: State University of New York Press, 2010), 33.
53. Translation of the Motke Zaidel and Itzak Dugin Interview Transcript, 21. This interview took place on September 18, 1979, and is thus contemporaneous with the Lichtman footage.
54. Therese Lichtenstein, *Behind Closed Doors: The Art of Hans Bellmer* (Berkeley: University of California Press, 2001), 22.
55. Natalya Lusty, *Surrealism, Feminism, Psychoanalysis* (New York: Routledge, 2016), 132.
56. Moyn, *A Holocaust Controversy*, 102 and 196n6.
57. Sharon Geva, "'To Collect the Tears of the Jewish People': The Story of Miriam Novitch," *Holocaust Studies* 21.1–2 (2015): 80.
58. Miriam Novitch, *Sobibór: Martyrdom and Revolt* [1978] (New York: Holocaust Library, 1980), 55 and 61.
59. Piotrowska, *Psychoanalysis and Ethics in Documentary Film*, 141.
60. Thus Rothberg summarizes Lanzmann's dictum by calling attention to the filmmaker's flawed logic of representation: "Lanzmann paradoxically believes that his particular form of mise-en-scène of the genocide in artificial, but nonfiction, stagings (e.g., his renting of trains, the scene of the barbershop) bring the event back without the detour of mediation; the event cannot be explained or represented, but it can be reexperienced!" (*Traumatic Realism*, 127).
61. Lanzmann, *The Patagonian Hare*, 429. In his annotated list of the unused material for the USHMM, Lanzmann limits his description of the Bomba footage to a single word: "Magnificent." See "Material of 'Shoah,'" 3.
62. Piotrowska, *Psychoanalysis and Ethics in Documentary Film*, 162–163. For critical readings of this scene, see LaCapra, *History and Memory After Auschwitz*, 134–135, and Todorov, *Facing the Extreme*, 275–276.
63. Original Abraham Bomba Interview Transcript, 24.
64. As Bomba recalls on the terrace in Jaffa, "One day we had an order to get together a certain amount of barbers and go and cut the hair of the women. [...] That was another thing that was horrible. Unbelievable. They took the women in,

they undressed themselves and we were supposed to do a job. They didn't know they were going into the gas chamber. They didn't know they *were* in the gas chamber" (29–30).

65. Lanzmann, *The Patagonian Hare*, 435.

66. The testimony is itself shorter than two hours if we take into account the time of translation.

67. Translation of the Mordechai Podchlebnik Interview Transcript, trans. Margaret L. Roussel, USHMM, The Claude Lanzmann *Shoah* Collection, RG-60.5026, 18. Translation modified.

68. Francine Kaufmann provides these biographical details regarding the Yiddish interpreter in her essay devoted to translation in *Shoah*. See "The Ambiguous Task of the Interpreter in Lanzmann's Films *Shoah* and *Sobibor*: Between the Director and Survivors of the Camps and Ghettos," in *Interpreting in Nazi Concentration Camps*, ed. Michaela Wolf (New York: Bloomsbury, 2016), 169–170.

69. Lanzmann, *The Patagonian Hare*, 425.

70. In addition to the Eichmann trial, Podchlebnik took the witness stand two other times before being filmed for *Shoah*: in 1945, he was a key witness in the first Chełmno trial held in Kolo, where he recounted the traumatic memory of his wife and children; in 1963, he testified at the Bonn trial of the Chełmno personnel.

71. Gouri, *Facing the Glass Booth*, 116.

72. See Wieviorka, *The Era of the Witness*, 81–82, and Douglas, *The Memory of Judgment*, 169–170.

73. LaCapra, *History and Memory After Auschwitz*, 135.

74. Translation of the Ada Lichtman Interview Transcript, 36. Translation modified; my emphasis.

75. Lanzmann, *The Patagonian Hare*, 75.

76. Trezise, *Witnessing Witnessing*, 60.

77. Translation of the Ada Lichtman Interview Transcript, 33.

78. Eda Lichtman, "From Mielec to Sobibór: The Testimony of Eda Lichtman," accessed 9 July 2017, http://www.zchor.org/testimonies/lichtman.htm. On Lichtman's 1965 deposition collected for the Hagen trial, see Michael Bryant, *Eyewitness to Genocide: The Operation Reinhard Death Camp Trials, 1955–1966* (Knoxville: University of Tennessee Press, 2014), 182–184.

79. Trezise, *Witnessing Witnessing*, 53. Lichtman's account of the revolt is once again silenced in Richard Rashke's book *Escape from Sobibor*, which was later adapted for television by Jack Gold. In 1981, Rashke interviewed Lichtman and her husband at their home in Holon (Miriam Novitch served as the interpreter during their meeting; the disembodied voice of the interpreter in the Lichtman outtakes

captured for *Shoah* might in fact be hers). In his book, Rashke describes Lichtman as "a sweet little grandma" who, in contrast to her husband, has a poor memory (327–328). In a stark reversal to the filmed testimony recorded by Lanzmann only two years earlier, Rashke interviews Itzhak Lichtman almost exclusively.

80. Lanzmann, *The Patagonian Hare*, 435.
81. Original Abraham Bomba Interview Transcript, 30.
82. Translation of the Motke Zaidel and Itzak Dugin Interview Transcript, 30. My emphasis.
83. Translation of the Motke Zaidel and Itzak Dugin Interview Transcript, 33, 46.
84. Lanzmann, "Material of 'Shoah,'" 1.
85. On the discovery of the escape tunnel in 2016, see Merrit Kennedy, "Researchers Uncover Long-Lost Tunnel Used by Jews to Escape Extermination Pits," accessed 12 July 2017, http://www.npr.org/sections/thetwo-way/2016/06/29/484017541/researchers-uncover-long-lost-tunnel-used-by-jews-to-escape-extermination-pits. The article mentions the outtakes of the interview Lanzmann filmed with Dugin and Zaidel in 1979.
86. Todorov, *Facing the Extreme*, 20.
87. Lanzmann was born in 1925, the same year as Zaidel; Lerner was born in 1926, Vrba in 1924, Müller in 1922, and Glazar in 1920.
88. LaCapra, *History and Memory After Auschwitz*, 111.
89. Marianne Hirsch, *The Generation of Postmemory: Writing and Visual Culture after the Holocaust* (New York: Columbia University Press, 2012), 166.
90. For Lanzmann's account of his activities in the French Resistance, see *The Patagonian Hare*, 93–113. I refer here to Alison Landsberg's notion of "prosthetic memory" discussed in chapter 1.
91. Translation of the Simha Rotem and Itzhak Zuckerman Interview Transcript, trans. Jonathan Engler, USHMM, The Claude Lanzmann *Shoah* Collection, RG-60.5048, 34. Translation modified; my emphasis.
92. Todorov, *Facing the Extreme*, 47.
93. James Young, *The Texture of Memory: Holocaust Memorials and Meaning* (New Haven: Yale University Press, 1994), 173.
94. Segev, *The Seventh Million*, 179–180.
95. Translation of the Simha Rotem and Itzhak Zuckerman Interview Transcript, 15.
96. Gouri, *Facing the Glass Booth*, 42. In the seventies, Zuckerman approached Gouri to make a film about Jewish resistance during the Holocaust. Gouri then undertook *The 81st Blow*, in which he included images that had been collected by Miriam Novitch for the archive of the Ghetto Fighters' House.

97. Gouri, *Facing the Glass Booth*, 44–45.

98. Moyn, *A Holocaust Controversy*, 22–25. See also de Beauvoir, Lanzmann, and Marienstras, "Entretien avec Simone de Beauvoir," 15–16.

99. Kovner's account was included in the proceedings of the conference under the title "A First Attempt to Tell." See *The Holocaust as Historical Experience: Essays and a Discussion*, ed. Yehuda Bauer and Nathan Rotenstreich (New York: Holmes & Meier, 1981), 77–94.

100. Translation of the Abba Kovner Interview Transcript, trans. Charlotte Catz, USHMM, The Claude Lanzmann *Shoah* Collection, RG-60.5017, 1–2.

101. Translation of the Abba Kovner Interview Transcript, 8–9. The bracketed passages appear in the original interview transcript in French.

102. Translation of the Abba Kovner Interview Transcript, 18.

103. Translation of the Abba Kovner Interview Transcript, 22–23. My emphasis. During the interview with Rotem and Zuckerman, Lanzmann exclaims: "The leaders were themselves almost children" (14). Translation modified.

104. Segev, *The Seventh Million*, 140.

105. Translation of the Abba Kovner Interview Transcript, 22.

106. Translation of the Filip Müller Interview Transcript, trans. Uta Allers, USHMM, The Claude Lanzmann *Shoah* Collection, RG-60.5012, 27.

107. For a more detailed biography of Shilansky, see Segev, *The Seventh Million*, 236–239.

108. "Dov Schilanski [sic]," USHMM, The Claude Lanzmann *Shoah* Collection, RG-60.5071, FV3620, 05:30–07:59 (accessed 29 May 2018).

109. Translation of the Yad Vashem Transcript, trans. Lotti Eichorn, USHMM, The Claude Lanzmann *Shoah* Collection, RG-60.5073, 3, 6. Translation modified.

110. Translation of the Yad Vashem Transcript, 4, 8. Translation modified.

111. Yablonka, *The State of Israel vs. Adolf Eichmann*, 173, 176.

112. Translation of the Yad Vashem Transcript, 25. Translation modified. On the interpreter's biography, see Kaufmann, "The Ambiguous Task of the Interpreter in Lanzmann's Films *Shoah* and *Sobibor*," 171. On her identification with Hanna Zaidel, excluded from this English adaptation of her 1993 essay devoted to her work on *Shoah*, see "Interview et interprétation consécutive dans le film *Shoah*, de Claude Lanzmann," 671.

113. Translation of the Motke Zaidel and Itzak Dugin Interview Transcript, 50.

114. Quoted in Yablonka, *The State of Israel vs. Adolf Eichmann*, 81.

115. On *Eichmann and the Third Reich*, see Julie Maeck, "De l'écriture à l'histoire: le documentaire face au prétoire," in *Le moment Eichmann*, ed. Sylvie Lindeperg and Annette Wieviorka (Paris: Albin Michel, 2016), 128–129. On *Fighters of the Ghetto*, see Eran Neuman, who also provides in his book a detailed history of the

Ghetto Fighters' House, *Shoah Presence: Architectural Representations of the Holocaust* (London: Routledge, 2014), 15–17.

116. Zuckerman's seven-hundred-page memoir based on the sixty-hour recording was first published in Israel in 1991 before being translated into English under the title *A Surplus of Memory: Chronicle of the Warsaw Ghetto Uprising* [1990], trans. Barbara Harshav (Berkeley: University of California Press, 1993).

117. Jonathan Freedland, "The Day Israel Saw *Shoah*," 10 December 2015, accessed 20 July 2017, https://www.theguardian.com/world/2015/dec/10/the-day-israel-saw-shoah. For a detailed analysis of Lanzmann's reframing of the Warsaw ghetto revolt in the finished film, see Kekesi Zoltán, *Agents of Liberation: Holocaust Memory in Contemporary Art and Documentary Film* (New York: Central European University Press, 2015), 21–25. See, as well, LaCapra, *History and Memory After Auschwitz*, 116–118.

118. Lanzmann, *The Patagonian Hare*, 482.

119. Haim Gouri quoted in Segev, *The Seventh Million*, 182.

120. Translation of the Simha Rotem and Itzhak Zuckerman Interview Transcript, 8. Translation modified.

121. Translation of the Simha Rotem and Itzhak Zuckerman Interview Transcript, 16. For the English translation of her memoir, see Zivia Lubetkin, *In the Days of Destruction and Revolt* [1979], trans. Ishai Tubbin (Jerusalem: Hakibbutz Hameuchad, 1981).

122. Parts of this interview were used by Adam Benzine in his Oscar-nominated documentary short film, *Claude Lanzmann: Specters of "Shoah"* (HBO, 2015). The original PBS interview is available on YouTube: https://www.youtube.com/watch?v=7Ec_wxWy41U (accessed 21 July 2017).

123. Walter Benjamin, *Illuminations: Essays and Reflections*, ed. Hannah Arendt, trans. Harry Zohn (New York: Schocken Books, 1969), 257.

124. Lanzmann, "Letter to Roswell McClelland dated 16 February 1977," 1; Peter Novick, *The Holocaust in American Life* (Boston: Houghton Mifflin, 1999), 209.

125. Lanzmann, "From Holocaust to 'Holocaust,'" 31.

126. Omer Bartov, *The Jew in Cinema: From the "Golem" to "Don't Touch My Holocaust"* (Bloomington: Indiana University Press, 2005), 216.

127. Felman, "The Return of the Voice," 216.

128. Original Raul Hilberg Interview Transcript, Part II, USHMM, The Claude Lanzmann *Shoah* Collection, RG-60.5045, 111.

129. Lanzmann, "Material of 'Shoah,'" 4.

130. Original Yehuda Bauer Interview Transcript, USHMM, The Claude Lanzmann *Shoah* Collection, RG-60.5049, 2. Transcription modified.

131. Original Yehuda Bauer Interview Transcript, 19, 11.

132. Original Raul Hilberg Interview Transcript, Part II, 110.
133. Original Raul Hilberg Interview Transcript, Part II, 113, 115.
134. Hilberg, *The Politics of Memory*, 133.
135. Friedländer, *Réflexions sur le nazisme: Entretiens avec Stéphane Bou*, 130. My translation. In his comparative study of the influence of Zionism on Arendt and Hilberg, Nathaniel Popper remarks that, in their critique of the *Judenrat*, both had to "distance themselves from the weak Jews that they imagined they had left behind, and from whom they had hoped for so much more during the war." See "A Conscious Pariah," *The Nation*, 31 March 2011, accessed 28 July 2017, https://www.thenation.com/article/conscious-pariah/.
136. Christopher Browning, "Spanning a Career: Three Editions of Raul Hilberg's *Destruction of the European Jews*," in *Lessons and Legacies VIII: From Generation to Generation*, ed. Doris L. Bergen (Evanston: Northwestern University Press, 2008), 199.
137. On the absence of the word "collaboration" in the second edition of *The Destruction of the European Jews*, see Evgeny Finkel, *Ordinary Jews: Choice and Survival During the Holocaust* (Princeton: Princeton University Press, 2017), 72.
138. According to Browning, Hilberg's edition of the diary provided a "tragic rather than an accusatory framing of the issue" of Jewish leadership during the Holocaust ("Spanning a Career," 199).
139. Hilberg and Staron, "Introduction," 70.
140. Felman, "The Return of the Voice," 216.
141. Arendt, *Eichmann in Jerusalem*, 125.
142. Translation of the Abba Kovner Interview Transcript, 41, 48. Translation modified.
143. "Dov Schilanski [sic]," FV3620, 04:19–04:31 (accessed 29 May 2018).
144. This portion of the interview is not included in the transcript. See "Gustaw Alef-Bolkowiak—Warsaw," USHMM, The Claude Lanzmann *Shoah* Collection, RG-60.5037, FV3373, 05:37–06:13 (accessed 29 May 2018). My translation.
145. Todorov, *Facing the Extreme*, 16.
146. Leonard Tushnet, *The Pavement of Hell* (New York: St. Martin's Press, 1972), 164, 167.
147. Original Yehuda Bauer Interview Transcript, 28.
148. Barbara Epstein's important study, *The Minsk Ghetto 1941–1943: Jewish Resistance and Soviet Internationalism* (Berkeley: University of California Press, 2008), offers a detailed account of the unique and largely overlooked Jewish underground organization in Minsk. She notes that the literature on this ghetto is rather scant, with the exception of Smolar's memoirs (38).
149. Shandler, *Holocaust Memory in the Digital Age*, 122.

150. Original Translation of the Hersh Smolar Interview Transcript, USHMM, The Claude Lanzmann *Shoah* Collection, RG-60.5038, 26–27. On the cooperation of the underground movement and the *Judenrat* in the Minsk ghetto, see Epstein, *The Minsk Ghetto 1941–1943*, 17–18 and 92–93. In the *Shoah* outtakes, the camera also films the medals that adorn the winter coat of Israël Hertzl, a Polish Jew who served as a German interpreter in the Soviet Army. He intervenes during the interview filmed with Dr. Wiener in Krakow. See "Dr. Wiener—Cracow," USHMM, The Claude Lanzmann *Shoah* Collection, RG-60.5078, FV3880, 25:19–26:03 (accessed 29 May 2018).
151. Lanzmann, "Why Spielberg Has Distorted the Truth," 14.
152. On the history of the pharmacy, see Anna Pioro, "The Eagle Pharmacy: Regained Memory: The History of the Pharmacy as an Instance of Manipulating Collective Memory," in *The Eagle Pharmacy: History and Memory*, Jan Gryta et al. (Kraków: Muzeum Historyczne Miasta Krakow, 2013), 187–231.
153. Translation of the Tadeusz Pankiewicz Interview Transcript, trans. Uta Allers, USHMM, The Claude Lanzmann *Shoah* Collection, RG-60.5014, 26.

CHAPTER THREE

1. "Malka Goldberg—Warsaw," USHMM, The Claude Lanzmann *Shoah* Collection, RG-60.5068, FV3869, 00:17–00:20; 01:05–01:06. My translation.
2. In *Holocaust Memory in the Digital Age*, Jeffrey Shandler likens the use of Yiddish in audiovisual testimonies to "an act of defiance" (122).
3. "Malka Goldberg—Warsaw," FV3869, 03:22–03:23, 04:10–04:12.
4. Eyal Peretz, *The Off-Screen*, 30.
5. Pascal Bonitzer, "Deframings," in *Cahiers du cinéma, Volume Four, 1973–1978: History, Ideology, Cultural Struggle*, ed. David Wilson (London: Routledge, 2000), 198, 201.
6. In his analysis of Rembrandt's *The Sacrifice of Isaac* (1635), Eyal Peretz describes the angel, who enters the painting from an invisible outside, as "a messenger of the off-frame" (*The Off-Screen*, 10).
7. Bonitzer, "Deframings," 199, 201.
8. Hirsch and Spitzer, "Gendered Translations: Claude Lanzmann's *Shoah*," 178–180.
9. I thank Raye Farr, who spoke at length with Paula Biren in preparation for a 2006–2007 exhibit on the deportation of children from the Łódź ghetto at the USHMM, for the details pertaining to the interview filmed in Panama City. In the press kit of *The Four Sisters* (2017), Lanzmann provides a different version of the making of her interview: "I had planned to meet Paula in Cincinnati, but the

cost of the trip was beyond our means. She agreed to come to us, and we filmed for several days in the Florida sunshine" (*The Four Sisters* (Press Kit) [Paris: Arte Sales & Synecdoche], 11). The German eyewitness remembered by Biren appears in fact to be the former State Department refugee specialist Robert Borden Reams. While refusing to be interviewed about his wartime activities, he did allow Lanzmann to film him fishing and golfing in Panama City (see chapter 4).

10. I thank Raye Farr for this information regarding Biren's first encounter with Lanzmann in 1975, which he confirms in the press kit of *The Four Sisters* (11).

11. Original Paula Biren Interview Transcript, USHMM, The Claude Lanzmann *Shoah* Collection, RG-60.5001, 38.

12. Quoted in Chevrie and Le Roux, "Site and Speech," 42.

13. Original Paula Biren Interview Transcript, 35.

14. For the Murmelstein annotations, see 26 and 37. The document titled "Themes" is included in the folder containing the original paper version of the interview transcript archived at the USHMM. In this document, Lanzmann quotes her concise description of the ghetto as "the longest lasting, best organized, and most cut off from the world" (35).

15. For the Łódź footage captured during the winter of 1979, see "Location Filming in Poland—Retirages de *Shoah*," USHMM, The Claude Lanzmann *Shoah* Collection, RG-60.5080.

16. Original Paula Biren Interview Transcript, 24, 25. On this farm, see Filip Friedman, "Pseudo-Saviours in the Polish Ghettos: Mordechai Chaim Rumkowski of Lodz" (1954), in *Roads to Extinction: Essays on the Holocaust*, ed. Ada June Friedman (New York: The Jewish Publication Society of America, 1980), 342, and Tushnet, *The Pavement of Hell*, 19–20. These two texts inform Lanzmann's knowledge of the Łódź ghetto in the Biren outtakes.

17. Friedman, "Pseudo-Saviours in the Polish Ghettos," 343.

18. Primo Levi, *The Drowned and the Saved* [1986], trans. Raymond Rosenthal (New York: Simon & Schuster, 2017), 50, 54.

19. Richard L. Rubenstein, "Gray into Black: The Case of Mordecai Chaim Rumkowski," in *Gray Zones: Ambiguity and Compromise in the Holocaust and Its Aftermath*, ed. Jonathan Petropoulos and John K. Roth (New York: Berghahn Books, 2005), 308.

20. Original Paula Biren Interview Transcript, 13–14.

21. Original Paula Biren Interview Transcript, 14.

22. Original Paula Biren Interview Transcript, 17–18. Transcription modified.

23. Quoted in Tushnet, *The Pavement of Hell*, 73.

24. On the inability of the Jewish police to implement the September 1942 action, see: Tushnet, *The Pavement of Hell*, 75; Friedman, "Pseudo-Saviours in the Polish

Ghettos," 347; Isaiah Trunk, *Judenrat: The Jewish Councils in Eastern Europe under Nazi Occupation* (New York: Macmillan, 1972), 507.

25. Raul Hilberg, *The Destruction of the European Jews, Volume I* [1961], third edition (New Haven: Yale University Press, 2003), 235.

26. Trunk, *Judenrat*, 508. On the postwar trials of members of the Jewish police, see 548–569.

27. This photograph is available on the website of the USHMM: https://collections.ushmm.org/search/catalog/pa1418 (accessed 17 August 2017).

28. Trunk briefly describes the role of the women's squad in the Łódź ghetto in *Judenrat* (97, 496). He notes that a similar squad also existed in the Vilna ghetto.

29. Original Paula Biren Interview Transcript, 28–29. Transcription modified.

30. Original Paula Biren Interview Transcript, 32.

31. Finkel, *Ordinary Jews*, 73.

32. Calel Perechodnik, *Am I a Murderer? Testament of a Jewish Ghetto Policeman*, ed. and trans. Frank Fox (Boulder: Westview Press, 1996), 44–45.

33. Original Paula Biren Interview Transcript, 33.

34. Original Paula Biren Interview Transcript, 31.

35. Joan Ringelheim, "The Unethical and the Unspeakable: Women and the Holocaust," *Simon Wiesenthal Center Annual* 1 (1984): 69–87. In preparation for her interview with Biren, Ringelheim watched the outtakes of her testimony with Lanzmann. In 2005, Biren and Ringelheim briefly discuss *Shoah* and the way in which the interview with Lanzmann prompted her to break her silence and begin to tell her story. See Oral History Interview with Paula S. Biren, USHMM, RG-50.030*0500.

36. Zoë Waxman, *Women in the Holocaust: A Feminist History* (Oxford: Oxford University Press, 2017), 6. Waxman argues in her book that this assumption still permeates Holocaust studies.

37. Original Paula Biren Interview Transcript, 40. Transcription modified.

38. Original Society of the Survivors of the Riga Ghetto (New York)—Former Jewish Policemen and Baer Interview Transcript, USHMM, The Claude Lanzmann *Shoah* Collection, RG-60.5041, 1, 3.

39. A fourth policemen, who joins the group of survivors speaking to Lanzmann, later tells this story in the outtakes (12). Trunk also recounts this episode of the Riga ghetto police in *Judenrat* (522).

40. Original Society of the Survivors of the Riga Ghetto (New York)—Former Jewish Policemen and Baer Interview Transcript, 7–8.

41. Original Society of the Survivors of the Riga Ghetto (New York)—Former Jewish Policemen and Baer Interview Transcript, 14.

42. Trunk, *Judenrat*, 518.

43. Original Society of the Survivors of the Riga Ghetto (New York)—Former Jewish Policemen and Baer Interview Transcript, 12.

44. Following the testimony of these survivors, Lanzmann briefly interviews Fred Baer, a German Jewish veteran of World War I and survivor of the Oranienburg concentration camp. See Original Society of the Survivors of the Riga Ghetto (New York)—Former Jewish Policemen and Baer Interview Transcript, 16–21. Oppenheimer and Ziering most likely told Lanzmann in advance about the Jewish policemen and the veteran.

45. Francine Kaufmann, "The Ambiguous Task of the Interpreter in Lanzmann's Films *Shoah* and *Sobibor*," 173.

46. Original Society of the Survivors of the Riga Ghetto (New York)—Lore Oppenheimer and Hermann Ziering Interview Transcript, USHMM, The Claude Lanzmann *Shoah* Collection, RG-60.5051, 77.

47. Original Society of the Survivors of the Riga Ghetto (New York)—Lore Oppenheimer and Hermann Ziering Interview Transcript, 62.

48. Saul Friedländer, *Nazi Germany and the Jews, Volume 1: The Years of Persecution, 1933–1939* (New York: HarperCollins, 1997), 2.

49. Original Society of the Survivors of the Riga Ghetto (New York)—Lore Oppenheimer and Hermann Ziering Interview Transcript, 24.

50. Lanzmann, "Material of 'Shoah,'" 7.

51. Original Society of the Survivors of the Riga Ghetto (New York)—Lore Oppenheimer and Hermann Ziering Interview Transcript, 49–50.

52. Original Society of the Survivors of the Riga Ghetto (New York)—Lore Oppenheimer and Hermann Ziering Interview Transcript, 35–36. Rather than Hermann Kempinsky, the outtakes are labeled Hermann Ziering.

53. Original Gertrude Schneider Interview Transcript, USHMM, The Claude Lanzmann *Shoah* Collection, RG-60.5015, 40.

54. Neither woman is named in the outtakes. Instead, Schneider mentions her mother and sister in her book on the Riga ghetto. See *Journey into Terror: Story of the Riga Ghetto* (Westport: Praeger, 2001), ix and 120. According to the numbered reels, Lanzmann filmed the New York interviews in the following order:

New York, reels 3–10: Gertrude Schneider (October 1978)

New York, reels 48–57: Peter Bergson and Sam Merlin, who were part of a rescue committee (the interview is dated November 15, 1978)

New York, reels 58–77: annual meeting of the Society of Survivors of the Riga Ghetto

New York, reels 92–97: Gertrude Schneider and her family

55. Original Gertrude Schneider Interview Transcript, 1–2. On page 4, she mentions letters by Latvian Jewish survivors who blame the Jews from the Reich for the destruction of their community. Lanzmann immediately interjects: "I have one of those letters. [...] Fred Wildhauer [a Latvian Jewish survivor]?" "Yes, yes, I have this letter in my files," Schneider retorts.

56. In an essay titled "The Unfinished Road," Schneider details their deportation from Riga to the small camp of Gotentov in the eponymous Latvian village. Similarly, in a short text titled "How I Almost Did Not Make It," Rita Wasserman describes how the three women survived a death march from Gotentov in the final days of the war. See *The Unfinished Road: Jewish Survivors of Latvia Look Back*, ed. Gertrude Schneider (New York: Praeger, 1991), 1–25 and 167–173.

57. Marianne Hirsch, *Family Frames: Photography, Narrative, and Postmemory* (Cambridge: Harvard University Press, 1997).

58. Original Gertrude Schneider Interview Transcript, 52.

59. Original Gertrude Schneider Interview Transcript, 37.

60. Lanzmann, *The Patagonian Hare*, 438.

61. Schneider, *Journey into Terror*, 53–59.

62. Gertrude Schneider, ed., *Mordechai Gebirtig: His Poetic and Musical Legacy* (Westport: Praeger, 2000), 2.

63. Rothberg, *Multidirectional Memory*, 190. On the relationship between *Shoah* and cinema verité, see Joshua Hirsch, *Afterimage: Film, Trauma, and the Holocaust* (Philadelphia: Temple University Press, 2004), 63–84.

64. Original Gertrude Schneider Interview Transcript, 37–38. The phrase "your mother" is omitted in the transcript. Schneider also references this song and the modified lyrics in *Journey into Terror* (59). The original ending of the song is "*Dann ziehn die Moorsoldaten / Nie mehr mit den Spaten / Ins Moor* [Then will the peat bog soldiers march / No more with spades / To the bog]."

65. Original Gertrude Schneider Interview Transcript, 48. Transcription modified.

66. See "Theresienstadt," USHMM, The Claude Lanzmann *Shoah* Collection, RG-60.5081.

67. Saul Friedländer, *Nazi Germany and the Jews, Volume 2: The Years of Extermination, 1939–1945* (New York: HarperCollins, 2007), 352–353. Friedländer also explains that the "family camp" at Auschwitz was a "sham complement" to the Red Cross visit: in the event that the delegates asked to visit the place of resettlement of Jews from Theresienstadt, they could be shown the "family camp" (579–580).

68. Original Ruth Elias Interview Transcript, USHMM, The Claude Lanzmann *Shoah* Collection, RG-60.5003, 32.

69. Translation of the Benjamin Murmelstein Interview Transcript, Part II, 284–290.

70. Original Andre Steiner Interview Transcript, USHMM, The Claude Lanzmann *Shoah* Collection, RG-60.5010, 60. Lanzmann subsequently references Murmelstein's testimony.

71. Original Ruth Elias Interview Transcript, 7.

72. Friedländer, *When Memory Comes*, 112.

73. Kristeva, *Powers of Horror*, 4.

74. Hirsch and Spitzer, "Gendered Translations: Claude Lanzmann's *Shoah*," 177.

75. Original Ruth Elias Interview Transcript, 27. She continues: "One bucket for W.C., one bucket for water. The doors were closed and up there somewhere there was a window closed with barbed wire; the W.C. bucket was full so we all perched in one corner. Somebody tried to empty this bucket through the little window. With us were children, with us were elderly people. Children crying. This terrible odour. We could sleep inside only in one part, for sleeping, and the other part was for sitting in a corner. It went on for 2 days and one night." For the circled words "In Theresienstadt," see 6.

76. Langer, *Holocaust Testimonies*, 13.

77. Lawrence Langer, *Versions of Survival: The Holocaust and the Human Spirit* (Albany: State University of New York Press, 1982), 72–73. The story of Ruth Elias is also reminiscent of William Styron's 1978 novel and eponymous 1982 film adaptation by Alan J. Pakula *Sophie's Choice*.

78. Ruth Elias, *The Triumph of Hope: From Theresienstadt and Auschwitz to Israel* [1988], trans. Margot Bettauer Dembo (New York: John Wiley and Sons, 1998), 94.

79. Original Ruth Elias Interview Transcript, 12–13.

80. Original Ruth Elias Interview Transcript, 12–15.

81. Original Ruth Elias Interview Transcript, 21.

82. Original Ruth Elias Interview Transcript, 24.

83. Original Ruth Elias Interview Transcript, 34.

84. Original Gertrude Schneider Interview Transcript, 52–54. Steinfeldt's uttering of Biren's name is omitted from the transcript.

85. Elias, *The Triumph of Hope*, 118. Koni, in fact, did survive. However, immediately after the war, Elias filed for divorce. "I was happy to hear that he had survived," she writes in her memoir. "At the same time, I remembered the pain he had caused me and that had been deeply carved in my memory" (218).

86. Original Ruth Elias Interview Transcript, 20.

87. On the impact of the miniseries in 1979 on both West German public memory and the debate on the abolition of the statute of limitations for Nazi crimes, see

Jacob Eder, *Holocaust Angst: The Federal Republic of Germany and American Holocaust Memory since the 1970s* (Oxford: Oxford University Press, 2016), 30–46.

88. Original Mengele Factory Workers Interview Transcript, USHMM, The Claude Lanzmann *Shoah* Collection, RG-60.5074, 3, 6. My translation.

89. Original Ruth Elias Interview Transcript, 37–38.

90. Original Ruth Elias Interview Transcript, 47.

91. Trezise, *Witnessing Witnessing*, 59.

92. Original Ruth Elias Interview Transcript, 56. The phrase "you will kill my child" is omitted in the transcript. See "Ruth Elias—Theresienstadt, Auschwitz," USHMM, The Claude Lanzmann *Shoah* Collection, RG-60.5003, FV3118, 32:38–32:42 (accessed 29 May 2018).

93. Original Ruth Elias Interview Transcript, 57.

94. Original Inge Deutschkron Interview Transcript, USHMM, The Claude Lanzmann *Shoah* Collection, RG-60.5044, 55. My translation.

95. This unused material is reminiscent of Martin Gilbert's travelogue of Holocaust sites and memorials. Describing his visit to the Wannsee villa in 1996, he writes: "We walk down to the water's edge, a peaceful, almost idyllic scene. This is Heckshorn Point, a ferry stop, around which—to our left—are a number of popular restaurants. The statue of a lion looks out over the water, a memento of the German defense of this region in medieval times. From the lion, we can look into the Wannsee villa garden." See *Holocaust Journey: The Search of a Past* (New York: Columbia University Press, 1999), 43.

96. Original Place du Lion Interview Transcript, USHMM, The Claude Lanzmann *Shoah* Collection, RG-60.5044, 1. This four-page transcript in German corresponds to video FV3429 of the Deutschkron material.

97. Original Place du Lion Interview Transcript, 2. My translation.

98. Original Inge Deutschkron Interview Transcript, 59. In the archive, nothing remains of this audio recording. On the history of *Vergangenheitsbewältigung*, particularly in the eighties, see Wulf Kansteiner, "Losing the War, Winning the Memory Battle: The Legacy of Nazism, World War II, and the Holocaust in the Federal Republic of Germany," in *The Politics of Memory in Postwar Europe*, ed. Richard Ned Lebow, Wulf Kansteiner, and Claudio Fogu (Durham: Duke University Press, 2006), 102–146. In the Pery Broad footage captured shortly after the Deutschkron interview, the perpetrator skeptically mentions the concept of *Vergangenheitsbewältigung* upon discussing *Holocaust* with Coulmas and Lanzmann. See Original Pery Broad Interview Transcript, 2A–3A.

99. Original Inge Deutschkron Interview Transcript, 56. The portion of her testimony in the finished film from this final take continues for several lines, the first

of which was edited out: "And this is absolutely ridiculous, because they all saw it! They couldn't help seeing it. It wasn't a matter of one action, these were actions that were taking place for almost two years. Every fortnight people were thrown out of the houses. How could they escape it? How could they not see it?" (56).

100. Theodor W. Adorno, "The Meaning of Working through the Past" [1959], *Critical Models: Intervention and Catchwords*, trans. Henry W. Pickford (New York: Columbia University Press, 1998), 90.

101. Original Inge Deutschkron Interview Transcript, 57.

102. Original Inge Deutschkron Interview Transcript, 19–20.

103. Original Inge Deutschkron Interview Transcript, 10. In her important study of Jewish experience in Nazi Germany, Marion Kaplan asks: "Did the 'normality' of German daily life stand in opposition to the 'abnormality' of Jewish life, or did they actually coexist? Were they even deeply connected?" See *Between Dignity and Despair: Jewish Life in Nazi Germany* (Oxford: Oxford University Press, 1998), 9.

104. Original Inge Deutschkron Interview Transcript, 13–14.

105. Original Inge Deutschkron Interview Transcript, 38, 48.

106. Original Inge Deutschkron Interview Transcript, 45.

107. Original Inge Deutschkron Interview Transcript, 27.

108. For references to Ziering, see Original Inge Deutschkron Interview Transcript, 19–20.

109. Friedländer, *Nazi Germany and the Jews*, 2.

110. Lanzmann, *The Patagonian Hare*, 491, 439.

111. Translation of the Helena Pietyra Interview Transcript, trans. Bissie Bonner, USHMM, The Claude Lanzmann *Shoah* Collection, RG-60.5055, 5–6.

112. Translation of the Helena Pietyra Interview Transcript, 9.

113. Translation of the Helena Pietyra Interview Transcript, 1, 3–4.

114. Doris L. Bergen, "What Do Studies of Women, Gender, and Sexuality Contribute?," in *Different Horrors, Same Hell*, ed. Myrna Goldenberg and Amy H. Shapiro (Seattle: University of Washington Press, 2013), 21.

115. Translation of the Helena Pietyra Interview Transcript, 13.

116. Dominick LaCapra, "Lanzmann's *Shoah*: 'Here There Is No Why'" [1997], in *Claude Lanzmann's "Shoah": Key Essays*, ed. Stuart Liebman (Oxford: Oxford University Press, 2007), 214.

117. Excerpts of Erhard Michelsohn's postwar testimony are included in *Nazi Mass Murder: A Documentary History of the Use of Poison Gas* [1983], ed. Eugen Kogon, Hermann Langbein, and Adalbert Rückerl, trans. Mary Scott and Caroline Lloyd Morris (New Haven: Yale University Press, 1993), 75–76, 80.

118. Translation of the Franz Schalling Interview Transcript, trans. Uta Allers, USHMM, The Claude Lanzmann *Shoah* Collection, RG-60.5034, 27; Interview

with Corinna Coulmas, 17 July 2016. Reference to Erhard Michelsohn's postwar deposition is made in Christopher Browning, *The Origins of the Final Solution: The Evolution of Nazi Jewish Policy* (Lincoln: University of Nebraska Press, 2007), 542n145. See, as well, Translation of the Martha Michelsohn Interview Transcript, trans. Lotti Eichorn, USHMM, The Claude Lanzmann *Shoah* Collection, RG-60.5033, 18

119. In keeping with his interest in the theme of children, Lanzmann asks Michelsohn how the German children reacted to the horrors committed in Chełmno. "They were not affected [...]. They did not suffer moral damage by this," she affirms in front of the camera, as though referring to herself (36–37).

120. Marcel Ophüls, "Closely Watched Trains" [1985], in *Claude Lanzmann's "Shoah": Key Essays*, ed. Stuart Liebman (Oxford: Oxford University Press, 2007), 85.

121. Translation of the Martha Michelsohn Interview Transcript, 39.

122. Translation of the Martha Michelsohn Interview Transcript, 60.

123. Translation of the Martha Michelsohn Interview Transcript, 47.

124. Claudia Koonz, *Mothers in the Fatherland: Women, Family and Nazi Politics* [1987] (London: Routledge, 2013), 3.

125. Sarah Horowitz, "The Gender of Good and Evil: Women and Holocaust Memory," in *Gray Zones: Ambiguity and Compromise in the Holocaust and Its Aftermath*, ed. Jonathan Petropoulos and John K. Roth (New York: Berghahn Books, 2005), 172–173.

126. I borrow the genre, in Holocaust cinema, of "documentary of return" from Janet Walker. See "Moving Testimonies: 'Unhomed Geography' and the Holocaust Documentary of Return," in *After Testimony: The Ethics and Aesthetics of Holocaust Narratives for the Future*, ed. Jakob Lothe, Susan Rubin Suleiman, and James Phelan (Columbus: Ohio State University Press, 2012), 270.

127. Hirsch and Spitzer, "Gendered Translations: Claude Lanzmann's *Shoah*," 179; Kaplan, *Between Dignity and Despair*, 228.

128. Original Inge Deutschkron Interview Transcript, 1.

129. Original Inge Deutschkron Interview Transcript, 53–54.

130. Original Inge Deutschkron Interview Transcript, 53.

131. Hirsch and Spitzer, "Gendered Translations: Claude Lanzmann's *Shoah*," 183.

132. See "Inge Deutschkron," USHMM, The Claude Lanzmann *Shoah* Collection, RG-60.5044, FV3428, 26:41–27:05 (accessed 29 May 2018). Chapuis's response is barely audible, with the exception of the phrase "No, don't worry!" My translation.

133. This remark is omitted from the interview transcript. See "Karl Kretschmer—Einsatzgruppen," FV3247, 28:45–28:49 (accessed 29 May 2018). My translation.

134. Original Inge Deutschkron Interview Transcript, 26.

135. Kaplan, *Between Dignity and Despair*, 205.

136. Original Inge Deutschkron Interview Transcript, 11–12.
137. Translation of the Hanna Marton Interview Transcript, trans. Deborah S. Droller, USHMM, The Claude Lanzmann *Shoah* Collection, RG-60.5008, 35.
138. On the history of this album, see *The Auschwitz Album: The Story of a Transport* (Jerusalem: Yad Vashem and the Auschwitz-Birkenau State Museum, 2002), 74–86.
139. Segev, *The Seventh Million*, 255, 276.
140. Segev, *The Seventh Million*, 271.
141. Original Raul Hilberg Interview Transcript, Part II, 141.
142. Yehuda Bauer, *Jews for Sale? Nazi-Jewish Negotiations, 1933–1945* (New Haven: Yale University Press, 1994), 145.
143. Original Shmuel Tamir Interview Transcript, USHMM, The Claude Lanzmann *Shoah* Collection, RG-60.5040, 40.
144. Original Raul Hilberg Interview Transcript, Part II, 145–146.
145. Lanzmann, "Letter to Roswell McClelland dated February 16, 1977," 2.
146. Gouri, *Facing the Glass Booth*, 250.
147. Arendt, *Eichmann in Jerusalem*, 118.
148. Yablonka, *The State of Israel vs. Adolf Eichmann*, 96.
149. Translation of the Hansi Brand Interview Transcript, trans. Uta Allers, USHMM, The Claude Lanzmann *Shoah* Collection, RG-60.5002, 2.
150. Translation of the Hansi Brand Interview Transcript, Face A, 5.
151. Translation of the Hansi Brand Interview Transcript, 21.
152. Segev, *The Seventh Million*, 271.
153. Original Rudolf Vrba Interview Transcript, USHMM, The Claude Lanzmann *Shoah* Collection, RG-60.5016, 93.
154. Translation of the Hansi Brand Interview Transcript, 16.
155. Translation of the Hansi Brand Interview Transcript, 29.
156. Segev, *The Seventh Million*, 473, 471.
157. Original Raul Hilberg Interview Transcript, Part II, 143.
158. Translation of the Hanna Marton Interview Transcript, 19.
159. Translation of the Hanna Marton Interview Transcript, 31. In the original Hebrew, these remarks are followed by two rhetorical questions that remain untranslated. "But actually who is to blame? Are they to blame?" she asks, further refuting postwar claims of collaboration.
160. Debarati Sanyal, *Memory and Complicity: Migrations of Holocaust Remembrance* (New York: Fordham University Press, 2015), 24.
161. Translation of the Hanna Marton Interview Transcript, 35.
162. Original Raul Hilberg Interview Transcript, Part II, 143.
163. In his monograph devoted to wartime negotiations with the Germans, Yehuda Bauer summarizes the issues raised by the "Kasztner train": "Was it justifiable to

conduct negotiations with the Nazis to save Jews? And if it was, what were the limits to such contacts?" (*Jews for Sale?*, 145).

164. Original Andre Steiner Interview Transcript, 67.
165. Original Shmuel Tamir Interview Transcript, 25.
166. Original Raul Hilberg Interview Transcript, Part II, 148.
167. Lanzmann, *The Patagonian Hare*, 73.

CHAPTER FOUR

1. For an overview of the evolution of the term "bystander" in Holocaust scholarship, see David Cesarani and Paul A. Levine, ed., *'Bystanders' to the Holocaust: A Re-evaluation* (London: Routledge, 2002), 1–2.
2. Hilberg, *Perpetrators Victims Bystanders*, 217; on Karski specifically, see 221–223.
3. Elie Wiesel, *Night* [1958], trans. Marion Wiesel (New York: Hill and Wang, 2006), 3.
4. Wiesel, *Night*, 8.
5. Arthur D. Morse, *While Six Million Died: A Chronicle of American Apathy* (New York: Random House, 1968), 3.
6. For a detailed account of the reception of the "Riegner telegram" in the United States, see Richard Breitman and Allan J. Lichtman, *FDR and the Jews* (Cambridge: The Belknap Press of Harvard University Press, 2013), 199–210.
7. Popper, "A Conscious Pariah."
8. These figures are provided by Breitman and Lichtman, *FDR and the Jews*, 294.
9. Laurence Jarvik, "Letter to Roswell McClelland dated 12 October 1978," USHMM, 2014.500–Roswell and Marjorie McClelland Papers, Series 6, Folder 9, File 3.
10. Lanzmann, "Letter to Roswell McClelland dated 16 February 1977," 1.
11. Lanzmann, "Letter to Roswell McClelland dated 16 February 1977," 1. My emphasis.
12. For a history of publications on the topic of Allied rescue and refugee policy, see Deborah E. Lipstadt, "America and the Holocaust," *Modern Judaism* 10.3 (October 1990): 283–296.
13. Hilberg, *The Destruction of the European Jews, Volume III*, 1139, 1129.
14. Lanzmann, *The Patagonian Hare*, 411.
15. Lanzmann, "Letter to Roswell McClelland dated 16 February 1977," 1.
16. "Rescue was usually grey," concludes Timothy Snyder in his analysis of Karski's mission to inform the West. See *Black Earth: The Holocaust as History and Warning* (New York: Tim Duggan Books, 2015), 267.

17. Rothberg, *Traumatic Realism*, 241–242.
18. Lanzmann, "Why Spielberg Has Distorted the Truth."
19. "Nahum Goldmann," USHMM, The Claude Lanzmann *Shoah* Collection, RG-60.5082, FV3865, 05:17–05:22 (accessed 29 May 2018).
20. The labeled tin canisters in the editing room were not always preserved following the digitization of the *Shoah* outtakes. As such, it is impossible to determine which other interviews might have been assigned the red label "*La Solution.*"
21. Lanzmann, "Letter to Roswell McClelland dated February 16, 1977," 2.
22. Several hints suggest that the Goldmann outtakes were captured in late January 1975: the interview negatives were manufactured in France in 1975; Goldmann mentions the recently published book of Saul Friedman, *No Haven for the Oppressed: United States Policy Toward Jewish Refugees, 1938–1945* (Detroit: Wayne State University Press, 1973); in addition to Riegner, he evokes the imminent arrival of Stephen Roth, who also attended the Sixth Plenary Assembly of the World Jewish Congress.
23. Nahum Goldmann, *The Jewish Paradox*, trans. Steve Cox (New York: Grosset & Dunlap, 1978), 75. Lanzmann alludes to Goldmann in *The Patagonian Hare*. However, rather than describe the 1975 footage, he recalls how the Zionist leader arranged for him to meet with John McCloy, assistant secretary of war under Roosevelt, during the making of *Shoah* (452).
24. It is nevertheless possible that the Kodak original negative was in fact in color and simply misplaced or lost like the Riegner material. I thank Kevin Fallis, expert negative cutter for the USHMM, for the technical details pertaining to the Goldmann material.
25. Original Robert Reams Interview Transcript, USHMM, The Claude Lanzmann *Shoah* Collection, RG-60.5061, 24.
26. "Nahum Goldmann," FV3865, 00:07–01:04 (accessed 29 May 2018). See, as well, *The Autobiography of Nahum Goldmann: Sixty Years of Jewish Life* (New York: Holt, Rinehart and Winston, 1969), 146–148.
27. "Nahum Goldmann," FV3865, 05:50–05:53, and FV3866, 12:07 (accessed 29 May 2018).
28. "Nahum Goldmann," FV3866, 10:12–10:16 (accessed 29 May 2018).
29. Tushnet, *The Pavement of Hell*, 109.
30. The telegram is quoted in E. Thomas Wood and Stanisław M. Jankowski, *Karski: How One Man Tried to Stop the Holocaust* (New York: John Wiley & Sons, 1994), 150.
31. Original Jan Karski Interview Transcript, USHMM, The Claude Lanzmann *Shoah* Collection, RG-60.5006, 9. In their biography of Karski, Wood and Jankowski

suggest the Zionist leader was not Berman but Menachem Kirschenbaum (*Karski: How One Man Tried to Stop the Holocaust*, 117).

32. Original Jan Karski Interview Transcript, 48.

33. "Nahum Goldmann," FV3866, 16:02–16:21 (accessed 29 May 2018).

34. Original Henry Feingold Interview Transcript, USHMM, The Claude Lanzmann *Shoah* Collection, RG-60.5060, 39. Feingold is here alluding to the chapter he devoted to the Bermuda Conference in *The Politics of Rescue: The Roosevelt Administration and the Holocaust, 1938–1945* (New Brunswick: Rutgers University Press, 1970), 167–207.

35. Morse, *While Six Million Died*, 63–64.

36. Jan Karski, *Story of a Secret State: My Report to the World* [1944] (Washington, DC: Georgetown University Press, 2013), 315–319.

37. Quoted in Gay Block and Malka Drucker, *Rescuers: Portraits of Moral Courage in the Holocaust* (New York: Holmes & Meier, 1992), 174.

38. Jan Karski, "*Shoah*" [1986], in *Claude Lanzmann's "Shoah": Key Essays*, ed. Stuart Liebman (Oxford: Oxford University Press, 2007), 174. For Pola Nirenska's brief appearance in the outtakes, see "Jan Karski," USHMM, The Claude Lanzmann *Shoah* Collection, RG-60.5006, FV3135, 06:04–06:19 (accessed 29 May 2018). Her presence is also noted in the interview transcript (23).

39. Original Jan Karski Interview Transcript, 10.

40. Original Jan Karski Interview Transcript, 31–32.

41. "Letter from Claude Lanzmann to Jan Karski dated July 7, 1978," E. Thomas Wood Collection, Hoover Archives, Box 5, Folder 2, Epilogue (12).

42. Original Jan Karski Interview Transcript, 43, 38.

43. Yannick Haenel, *The Messenger* [2009], trans. Ian Monk (Berkeley: Counterpoint, 2011), 108.

44. Haenel, *The Messenger*, 105.

45. Haenel, *The Messenger*, 114–116.

46. Annette Wieviorka, "Faux témoignage," *L'Histoire* 349 (January 2010): 30–31.

47. Claude Lanzmann, "*Jan Karski* de Yannick Haenel: un faux roman," *Les Temps Modernes* 657 (January–March 2010): 4–5. This article was originally published under the same title in January 2010 in the French news magazine *Marianne*.

48. Richard J. Golsan, *The Vichy Past in France Today: Corruptions of Memory* (Lanham: Lexington Books, 2017), 91.

49. Lanzmann, "*Jan Karski* de Yannick Haenel: un faux roman," 9.

50. "You look at me [...] Not at this girl—*c'est la fille que vous regardez, c'est les filles* [it's the girl you are looking at, the girls]! [...] I don't know who is worse: if it is Hilberg or you." These remarks are excluded from the interview transcript.

See "Henry Feingold," USHMM, The Claude Lanzmann *Shoah* Collection, RG-60.5060, FV3571, 09:38–10:05 (accessed 29 May 2018).

51. Lanzmann, "*Jan Karski* de Yannick Haenel: un faux roman," 8–9 (my translation); Original Henry Feingold Interview Transcript, 49.

52. Haenel, *The Messenger*, 9.

53. Golsan, *The Vichy Past in France Today*, 95.

54. Remy Besson, "*The Karski Report*: A Voice with a Ring of Truth," trans. John Tittensor, *Études Photographiques* 21 (May 2011), accessed 26 October 2017, https://etudesphotographiques.revues.org/3467#bodyftn18.

55. Rothberg, *Traumatic Realism*, 237, 234.

56. Lucy Dawidowicz, "Indicting American Jews" [1983], in *What Is the Use of Jewish History?*, ed. Neal Kozodoy (New York: Schocken Books, 1992), 179–201.

57. "I hope you won't think it presumptuous of me," writes Dawidowicz to McClelland in July 1979, "but I have thought that perhaps you ought to consider writing your memoirs altogether about those war years and all your involvement in the rescue of Jews." See "Letter to Roswell McClelland dated July 9, 1979," USHMM, 2014.500–Roswell and Marjorie McClelland Papers, Series 6, Folder 6, File 31. McClelland had sent Dawidowicz his memoir in the hope that she might help him find a publisher.

58. Haenel, *The Messenger*, 122. Haenel also evokes Karski's meeting with Zygielbojm in the second part of the novel where he summarizes *Story of a Secret State* (88–89).

59. Karski, *Story of a Secret State*, 319.

60. "Letter from Claude Lanzmann to Jan Karski dated July 7, 1978."

61. The original verse is "No one / bears witness for the / witness." See "Aschenglorie/Ash-aureole," in *Selected Poems and Prose of Paul Celan*, trans. John Felstiner (New York: W. W. Norton, 2001), 260. Haenel appears to be quoting Antonio Tabucchi, who uses the same epigraph in *Tristano Dies: A Life*. Tabucchi integrates this line in the novel itself: "But who bears witness for the witness? Here's the point: no one bears witness for the witness..." See *Tristano Dies: A Life* [2004], trans. Elizabeth Harris (Brooklyn: Archipelago Books, 2015), 177.

62. See "Faivel Ziegelbaum," USHMM, The Claude Lanzmann *Shoah* Collection, RG-60.5072, FV3882, 38:20–39:51 (accessed 29 May 2018); see also Original Faivel Ziegelbaum Interview Transcript, USHMM, The Claude Lanzmann *Shoah* Collection, RG-60.5072, 15. Another archival image is found in the excluded portions of Filip Müller's interview. Here, the camera films Lanzmann and Müller leafing through a book containing one of the famous *Sonderkommando* photographs secretly captured at Auschwitz. See "Filip Müller—Auschwitz *Sonderkommando*,"

USHMM, The Claude Lanzmann *Shoah* Collection, RG-60.5012, FV3215, 14:10 (accessed 29 May 2018).

63. See Faivel Zygielbojm, *Der Koyeh tsu Shtarbn: Mishpohe Bukh* (Tel Aviv: Farlag Y. L. Perets, 1976).
64. Original Faivel Ziegelbaum Interview Transcript, 2.
65. Hilberg, Staron, and Kermisz, *The Warsaw Diary of Adam Czerniakow*, 70.
66. Original Faivel Ziegelbaum Interview Transcript, 4–5. My emphasis.
67. Original Faivel Ziegelbaum Interview Transcript, 10.
68. Original Faivel Ziegelbaum Interview Transcript, 8.
69. Original Faivel Ziegelbaum Interview Transcript, 9.
70. Karski, *Story of a Secret State*, 318; Original Jan Karski Interview Transcript, 51.
71. See Original Jan Karski Interview Transcript, 49–50.
72. Original Jan Karski Interview Transcript, 51.
73. Original Jan Karski Interview Transcript, 51. My emphasis.
74. Original Jan Karski Interview Transcript, 66. Spelling of names modified.
75. Original Jan Karski Interview Transcript, 45.
76. Original Jan Karski Interview Transcript, 47–49.
77. See "Jan Karski," FV3138, 02:01–02:29 (accessed 29 May 2018).
78. Original Jan Karski Interview Transcript, 72.
79. Lanzmann, "*Jan Karski* de Yannick Haenel: un faux roman," 2. My translation.
80. "Letter from Claude Lanzmann to Jan Karski dated July 7, 1978."
81. Lanzmann, *The Patagonian Hare*, 492–493.
82. "Contract from Les Films Aleph to Jan Karski dated May 28, 1982," E. Thomas Wood Collection, Hoover Archives, Box 5, Folder 2, Epilogue (12). According to this document, Karski was paid $1,500 in October 1978, $850 in December 1981, and $5,000 at the time he signed this contract.
83. The representation of these "bystanders" in the East in *Shoah* spurred particular controversy in Poland. See Jean-Charles Szurek, "*Shoah*: From the Jewish Question to the Polish Question," in *Claude Lanzmann's "Shoah": Key Essays*, ed. Stuart Liebman (Oxford: Oxford University Press, 2007), 149–169.
84. Quoted in Todorov, *Facing the Extreme*, 276.
85. "Letter from Claude Lanzmann to Jan Karski dated July 7, 1978." My emphasis.
86. Karski, "*Shoah*," 172.
87. Original Robert Reams Interview Transcript, 1. My translation and emphasis.
88. Lanzmann, "*Jan Karski* de Yannick Haenel: un faux roman," 8. My translation.
89. Morse, *While Six Million Died*, 32.
90. Original Henry Feingold Interview Transcript, 46.

91. Breitman and Lichtman, *FDR and the Jews*, 231–232.
92. Original John Pehle Interview Transcript, USHMM, The Claude Lanzmann *Shoah* Collection, RG-60.5021, 3–4.
93. Original Robert Reams Interview Transcript, 19, as well as Breitman and Lichtman, 309.
94. See "Robert Reams—Fish(ing Party)," USHMM, The Claude Lanzmann *Shoah* Collection, RG-60.5061, FV3878 (accessed 29 May 2018).
95. Morse, *While Six Million Died*, 32; Original Robert Reams Interview Transcript, 22.
96. I borrow the term "villain" from Breitman and Lichtman, who observe that Long was cast in Holocaust scholarship as "*the* villain responsible for an immoral American policy" (165).
97. See "Robert Reams—Fish(ing Party)," FV3875, 09:54–10:57 (accessed 29 May 2018).
98. Lanzmann, *The Patagonian Hare*, 422–423. Lanzmann writes that Paisikovic died shortly after of a heart attack and he never filmed him. He appears, however, to be confusing him with another *Sonderkommando* member. Paisikovic, who had previously testified (like Filip Müller) at the Frankfurt Auschwitz trials and told his story for the 1973 BBC documentary series *World at War*, passed away in 1988.
99. This phrase is omitted from the transcript. See "Robert Reams—Fish(ing Party)," FV3875, 19:56–19:59 (accessed 29 May 2018). My translation.
100. Original Robert Reams Interview Transcript, 6; Lanzmann, *The Patagonian Hare*, 453.
101. Original Robert Reams Interview Transcript, 7. For his despairing "*Oh la la la*," see 5, 7. My translation.
102. Original Robert Reams Interview Transcript, 11.
103. Original Robert Reams Interview Transcript, 28.
104. Original Richard Rubenstein Interview Transcript, USHMM, The Claude Lanzmann *Shoah* Collection, RG-60.5062, 1.
105. Hannah Arendt, *The Origins of Totalitarianism* [1951] (New York: Schocken Books, 2004), 366, 365.
106. Original Richard Rubenstein Interview Transcript, 3.
107. Richard Rubenstein, *The Cunning of History: The Holocaust and the American Future* (New York: Harper & Row, 1975), 95.
108. The influence of Arendt can be seen, for instance, in Rubenstein's remark, with which Lanzmann concurs, that "when a stateless committed a crime, committed an offense, he was more protected" (6). This approximates Arendt's observation in *The Origins of Totalitarianism* that stateless people "benefit legally from committing a

crime," above all because "it seems to be easier to deprive a completely innocent person of legality than someone who has committed an offense" (374).

109. "The most effective rescue," writes Hilberg in the third volume of *The Destruction of the European Jews*, "is that which is undertaken before the danger point had been reached. In the Jewish case this meant emigration before the outbreak of the war" (1194).

110. In his 1979 critique of the miniseries *Holocaust*, Lanzmann also mentions the Évian Conference and suggests it will be an episode in the film he is making. "In my film," he writes, "the Final Solution could not be the culmination of the story, it would be its point of departure. The full impact of the Évian scandal will not be felt unless the gas trucks are already in action and the spectator has been gripped by the mind-boggling acceleration of history, between Évian and the first gassing of the Jews of the Wartheland *only three years* passed" ("From Holocaust to *Holocaust*," 34).

111. Original Richard Rubenstein Interview Transcript, 13, 14.

112. This remark is omitted from the interview transcript. See "John Pehle—Allies," USHMM, The Claude Lanzmann *Shoah* Collection, RG-60.5021, FV3259, 03:01–03:03 (accessed 29 May 2018).

113. Original John Pehle Interview Transcript, 16, 2.

114. Original John Pehle Interview Transcript, 29.

115. Original Robert Reams Interview Transcript, 28.

116. Lanzmann's comments are excluded from the interview transcript. See "John Pehle—Allies," FV3262, 29:16–29:24 (accessed 29 May 2018). My translation.

117. "John Pehle—Allies," FV3264, 05:49–05:54 (accessed 29 May 2018). My translation.

118. Wood and Jankowski, *Karski: How One Man Tried to Stop the Holocaust*, 201.

119. Original John Pehle Interview Transcript, 6.

120. "Letter from Claude Lanzmann to Jan Karski dated July 7, 1978."

121. Original John Pehle Interview Transcript, 26–27.

122. See, for instance, Original Robert Reams Interview Transcript, 28; Original Peter Bergson and Samuel Merlin Interview Transcript, USHMM, The Claude Lanzmann *Shoah* Collection, RG-60.5020, 13–14; and Original Siegmunt Forst Interview Transcript, USHMM, The Claude Lanzmann *Shoah* Collection, RG-60.5004, 42.

123. Deborah E. Lipstadt, *Beyond Belief: The American Press and the Coming of the Holocaust, 1933–1945* (New York: The Free Press, 1986), 274.

124. Original John Pehle Interview Transcript, 27–28. See, as well, Lipstadt, *Beyond Belief*, 265–267.

125. Original Peter Bergson and Samuel Merlin Interview Transcript, 6, 9.

126. Breitman and Lichtman, *FDR and the Jews*, 218. The Jewish leaders, Bergson explains to Lanzmann, would simply have "had to pressure the American government, which would have yielded, in my opinion, I don't think there is any question about it. If the proper pressure had come up [...] I think Roosevelt would have taken the necessary steps" (17).

127. Original Peter Bergson and Samuel Merlin Interview Transcript, 12–14.

128. Original Ruth Elias Interview Transcript, 31.

129. Original Peter Bergson and Samuel Merlin Interview Transcript, 29.

130. Original Peter Bergson and Samuel Merlin Interview Transcript, 46–47.

131. Original Peter Bergson and Samuel Merlin Interview Transcript, 42.

132. On the march of the rabbis, see Breitman and Lichtman, *FDR and the Jews*, 229–230.

133. Original Peter Bergson and Samuel Merlin Interview Transcript, 45–46.

134. In his filmed interview for *Shoah*, Siegmunt Forst tells Lanzmann that, following the Anschluss in 1938, Weissmandl "foresaw that Hitler would not stop there." See Original Siegmunt Forst Interview Transcript, 5.

135. In the *Shoah* outtakes, Lanzmann discusses the various proposals made in 1944 to bomb the railways, as well as Auschwitz, with Bergson and Merlin, Feingold, McClelland, Pehle, and Rubenstein. In the Pehle interview, the camera films several archival documents pertaining to this contentious topic, including a letter dated July 4, 1944, from the War Department and signed by John McCloy informing Pehle that the WRB's request to bomb the railways in order to halt the deportations of the Hungarian Jews had been denied. See "John Pehle—Allies," FV3264, 21:36–22:10 (accessed 29 May 2018).

136. Original Shmuel Tamir Interview Transcript, 1.

137. Original Andre Steiner Interview Transcript, 24. Steiner also provides the most detailed portrait of Gisi Fleischmann in Lanzmann's archive of testimonies. In addition to Forst, Steiner, and Tamir, Mr. Becher and Hermann Landau also bear witness to the life of Weissmandl in the *Shoah* outtakes. See "Becher—Mount Kisco/Weissmandel [sic]"(USHMM, The Claude Lanzmann *Shoah* Collection, RG-60.5052) and "Hermann Landau" (USHMM, The Claude Lanzmann *Shoah* Collection, RG-60.5007).

138. "Letter from Roswell McClelland to John Pehle dated 26 October 1944," USHMM, 2014.500–Roswell and Marjorie McClelland Papers, Series 6, Folder 6, File 9.

139. Lucy Dawidowicz, "Bleaching the Black Lie: The Case of Theresienstadt," *Salmagundi* 29 (Spring 1975): 138n19.

140. Irena Steinfeldt (for Claude Lanzmann), "Letter to Roswell McClelland dated September 14, 1978."

141. Brad Prager, "Interpreting the Visible Traces of Theresienstadt," *Journal of Modern Jewish Studies* 7.2 (2008): 188.
142. Ophir Levy, "La forteresse et l'aveu: A propos d'*Un vivant qui passe* de Claude Lanzmann," *Témoigner: Entre histoire et mémoire* 107 (2010): 55. My translation.
143. Translation of the Maurice Rossel Interview Transcript, trans. Lotti Eichorn, USHMM, The Claude Lanzmann *Shoah* Collection, RG-60.5019, 54.
144. Translation of the Ehud Avriel Interview Transcript, trans. Hazel Keimowitz, USHMM, The Claude Lanzmann *Shoah* Collection, RG-60.5000, 31. Translation modified.
145. Levy, "La forteresse et l'aveu," 59. My translation.
146. Lanzmann, "Why Spielberg Has Distorted the Truth."
147. The story of Marjorie McClelland was recently recovered, along with that of other women who rescued Jews, by Deborah Dwork. See Judy Maltz, "The American Women Who Risked It All to Save Jews During the Holocaust," *Haaretz*, 27 January 2014, accessed 15 November 2017, https://www.haaretz.com/jewish/features/.premium-1.570700.
148. Original Roswell McClelland Interview Transcript, USHMM, The Claude Lanzmann *Shoah* Collection, RG-60.5047, 6–7.
149. Saul Friedländer, *Where Memory Leads: My Life* (New York: Other Press, 2016), 56–64; *When Memory Comes*, 88.
150. Translation of the Jean Pictet Interview Transcript, trans. Lotti Eichorn, USHMM, The Claude Lanzmann *Shoah* Collection, RG-60.5054, 1.
151. Translation of the Jean Pictet Interview Transcript, 4.
152. Translation of the Jean Pictet Interview Transcript, 1–2. Translation modified.
153. Translation of the Jean Pictet Interview Transcript, 10.
154. Gerald Steinacher, *Humanitarians at War: The Red Cross in the Shadow of the Holocaust* (Oxford: Oxford University Press, 2017), 29.
155. Translation of the Jean Pictet Interview Transcript, 34; Steinacher, *Humanitarians at War*, 42–43.
156. Steinacher, *Humanitarians at War*, 68.
157. Translation of the Jean Pictet Interview Transcript, 33. Translation modified.
158. Translation of the Jean Pictet Interview Transcript, 34. Translation modified. Steinacher borrows the term from *The Economist*. See *Humanitarians at War*, 42, 48, and 243.
159. Translation of the Jean Pictet Interview Transcript, 15; Steinacher, *Humanitarians at War*, 44–45,
160. Translation of the Jean Pictet Interview Transcript, 11, 13.
161. This exchange is only partially included in the transcript; see Translation of the Jean Pictet Interview Transcript, 53–54. Translation modified.

162. Translation of the Jean Pictet Interview Transcript, 19–20. Translation modified.
163. "Elie Wiesel's Remarks at the Dedication Ceremonies for the United States Holocaust Memorial Museum, April 22, 1993," accessed 15 May 2018, https://www.ushmm.org/information/about-the-museum/mission-and-history/wiesel; *Un di velt hot geshvign* (Buenos Aires: Tsentral-Farband fun Poylishe Yidn, 1956).
164. Eric Didier, "De l'impensable à l'irréparable," in *Shoah le film: Des psychanalystes écrivent* (Paris: Jacques Grancher, 1990), 21. My translation.

CONCLUSION

1. Gertrud Koch, "The Aesthetic Transformation of the Image of the Unimaginable: Notes on Claude Lanzmann's *Shoah*," in *Claude Lanzmann's "Shoah": Key Essays*, ed. Stuart Liebman, trans. Jamie Owen Daniel and Miriam Hansen (Oxford: Oxford University Press, 2007), 129.
2. *The Four Sisters* [Press Kit], 6.
3. On Elias's 1985 testimony at Yad Vashem, see Jonathan Broder, "Auschwitz Survivors Recall Horror of Nazi Experiments," *Chicago Tribune*, 7 February 1985, accessed 26 November 2017, http://articles.chicagotribune.com/1985-02-07/news/8501080137_1_josef-mengele-israel-and-west-germany-auschwitz.
4. Bergen, "What Do Studies of Women, Gender, and Sexuality Contribute?," 17. Bergen references here the anthology edited by Carole Rittner and John K. Roth, *Different Voices: Women and the Holocaust* (St. Paul: Paragon House, 1993).
5. Brad Prager, *After the Fact: Holocaust Documentary in the Twenty-First Century* (New York: Bloomsbury, 2015), 13–14.
6. Trezise, *Witnessing Witnessing*, 1.
7. In *Holocaust Memory in the Digital Age*, Jeffrey Shandler observes that the digital age permits archives such as the Shoah Foundation to preserve survivor testimonies "in perpetuity" (40).
8. "*Shoah* Outtakes: Report on Paris Screening 20–29 February 1996," 5; emphasis in original.

BIBLIOGRAPHY

ARCHIVAL COLLECTIONS

Film and Video Archive Administrative Files, United States Holocaust Memorial Museum, uncataloged.
Oral History Interview with Eda Lichtman, United States Holocaust Memorial Museum, RG-50.120*0091.
Oral History Interview with Benjamin Murmelstein, Oral History Interviews of the Leonard and Edith Ehrlich Collection, United States Holocaust Memorial Museum, RG-50.862.
Oral History Interview with Paula S. Biren, United States Holocaust Memorial Museum, RG-50.030*0500.
Roswell and Marjorie McClelland Papers, United States Holocaust Memorial Museum, 2014.500.1.
The Claude Lanzmann *Shoah* Collection, United States Holocaust Memorial Museum, 1996.166.
The Eichmann Trial Channel, Yad Vashem and the Israel State Archives.
The E. Thomas Wood Collection, Hoover Institution Archives, 2000C114.

INDIVIDUAL INTERVIEW BY AUTHOR

Corinna Coulmas, 17 July 2016.

EMAIL CORRESPONDENCE WITH AUTHOR

Jean-Pierre Beauviala, 20–21 August 2016.
Irena Steinfeldt, 28 February 2009.

PUBLISHED SOURCES

Adorno, Theodor W. "The Meaning of Working through the Past" [1959]. *Critical Models: Intervention and Catchwords*, 89–104. Translated by Henry W. Pickford. New York: Columbia University Press, 1998.

Arendt, Hannah. *The Origins of Totalitarianism* [1951]. New York: Schocken Books, 2004.

———. *Eichmann in Jerusalem: A Report on the Banality of Evil* [1963]. New York: Penguin Books, 2006.

Arendt, Hannah, and Gershom Scholem. *The Correspondence of Hannah Arendt and Gershom Scholem*. Edited by Marie Luise Knott. Translated by Anthony David. Chicago: University of Chicago Press, 2017.

Baecque, Antoine de. *Godard: biographie*. Paris: Bernard Grasset, 2010.

Bartov, Omer. *The Jew in Cinema: From the "Golem" to "Don't Touch My Holocaust."* Bloomington: Indiana University Press, 2005.

Bauer, Yehuda. *Jews for Sale? Nazi-Jewish Negotiations, 1933–1945*. New Haven: Yale University Press, 1994.

Bauer, Yehuda, and Malcolm Lowe. "Introduction." In *The Holocaust as Historical Experience: Essays and a Discussion*, edited by Yehuda Bauer and Nathan Rotenstreich, vii–xiv. New York: Holmes & Meier, 1981.

Beauvoir, Simone de. "Preface." In Jean-François Steiner, *Treblinka* [1966], xix–xxiv. Translated by Helen Weaver. New York: Meridian, 1994.

———. "Preface." In Claude Lanzmann, *Shoah: The Complete Text of the Acclaimed Film* [1985], vii–x. Boston: Da Capo Press, 1995.

Beauvoir, Simone de, Claude Lanzmann, and Richard Marienstras. "Entretien avec Simone de Beauvoir: 'Ils n'étaient pas des lâches.'" *Le Nouvel Observateur* 75 (27 April 1966): 14–17.

Benhabib, Liat. "*Memories of the Eichmann Trial*: Restoration of a 1979 Film by David Perlov." *Yad Vashem Jerusalem Quarterly Magazine* 61 (April 2011): 12. https://www.yadvashem.org/sites/default/files/yv_magazine61.pdf.

Benjamin, Walter. *Illuminations: Essays and Reflections*. Edited by Hannah Arendt. Translated by Harry Zohn. New York: Schocken Books, 1969.

Bergala, Alain, Jean-Jacques Henry, and Serge Toubiana. "La sortie des usines Aäton (entretien avec Jean-Pierre Beauviala 2)." *Cahiers du cinéma* 286 (March 1978): 5–14.

Bergen, Doris L. "What Do Studies of Women, Gender, and Sexuality Contribute?" In *Different Horrors, Same Hell*, edited by Myrna Goldenberg and Amy H. Shapiro, 16–37. Seattle: University of Washington Press, 2013.

Bergstrom, Janet, and Alain Bergala. "Genesis of a Camera (First Episode)." Translated by Lynne Kirby. *Camera Obscura* 13–14 (Spring–Summer 1985): 162–194.

Besson, Remy. "*The Karski Report*: A Voice with a Ring of Truth." Translated by John Tittensor. *Études Photographiques* 21 (May 2011). Accessed 26

October 2017, https://journals.openedition.org/etudesphotographiques/3467.

Bonitzer, Pascal. *Le regard et la voix. Essais sur le cinéma*. Paris: 10/18, 1976.

———. "Deframings." In *Cahiers du cinéma, Volume Four, 1973–1978: History, Ideology, Cultural Struggle*, edited by David Wilson, translated by Chris Darke, 197–204. London: Routledge, 2000.

Block, Gay, and Malka Drucker. *Rescuers: Portraits of Moral Courage in the Holocaust*. New York: Holmes & Meier, 1992.

Breitman, Richard, and Allan J. Lichtman. *FDR and the Jews*. Cambridge: The Belknap Press of Harvard University Press, 2013.

Broder, Jonathan. "Auschwitz Survivors Recall Horror of Nazi Experiments." *Chicago Tribune*, 7 February 1985. Accessed 26 November 2017. http://articles.chicagotribune.com/1985-02-07/news/8501080137_1_josef-mengele-israel-and-west-germany-auschwitz.

Brody, Richard. *Everything Is Cinema: The Working Life of Jean-Luc Godard*. New York: Metropolitan Book/Henry Holt and Company, 2008.

Browning, Christopher. *The Origins of the Final Solution: The Evolution of Nazi Jewish Policy*. Lincoln: University of Nebraska Press, 2007.

———. "Spanning a Career: Three Editions of Raul Hilberg's *Destruction of the European Jews*." In *Lessons and Legacies VIII: From Generation to Generation*, edited by Doris L. Bergen, 191–202. Evanston: Northwestern University Press, 2008.

Bryant, Michael. *Eyewitness to Genocide: The Operation Reinhard Death Camp Trials, 1955–1966*. Knoxville: University of Tennessee Press, 2014.

Burch, Noël. *Theory of Film Practice* [1969]. Translated by Helen R. Lane. Princeton: Princeton University Press, 2014.

Caruth, Cathy, ed. *Trauma: Explorations in Memory*. Baltimore: Johns Hopkins University Press, 1995.

Celan, Paul. *Selected Poems and Prose of Paul Celan*. Translated by John Felstiner. New York: W. W. Norton, 2001.

Cesarani, David, and Paul A. Levine, ed. *'Bystanders' to the Holocaust: A Re-evaluation*. London: Routledge, 2002.

Chevrie, Marc, and Hervé Le Roux. "Site and Speech: An Interview with Claude Lanzmann about *Shoah*." In *Claude Lanzmann's "Shoah": Key Essays*, edited by Stuart Liebman, 37–49. Translated by Stuart Liebman. Oxford: Oxford University Press, 2007.

Chion, Michel. *The Voice in Cinema* [1982]. Translated by Claudia Gorbman. New York: Columbia University Press, 1999.

Ciment, Michel. "Décembre en cinéma." *Positif* 516 (February 2004): 44–47.
Ciment, Michel, and Yann Tobin. "William Lubtchansky: 'J'ai horreur du gris!'" *Positif* 475 (September 2000): 76–80.
Dawidowicz, Lucy. "Bleaching the Black Lie: The Case of Theresienstadt." *Salmagundi* 29 (Spring 1975): 125–140.
———. *The War Against the Jews: 1933–1945* [1975]. New York: Seth Press, 1986.
———. "Indicting American Jews" [1983]. In *What Is the Use of Jewish History?*, edited by Neal Kozodoy, 179–201. New York: Schocken Books, 1992.
Delbo, Charlotte. *Days and Memory* [1985]. Translated by Rosette Lamont. Evanston: Northwestern University Press, 2001.
Deleuze, Gilles. "Cinéma cours 48 du 06/12/1983." *La voix de Gilles Deleuze en ligne*. Accessed 3 January 2017. http://www2.univ-paris8.fr/deleuze/article.php3?id_article=269.
———. *Cinema 2: The Time-Image* [1985]. Translated by Robert Galeta. Minneapolis: University of Minnesota Press, 1989.
———. *The Fold: Leibniz and the Baroque* [1988]. Translated by Tom Conley. Minneapolis: University of Minnesota Press, 1989.
———. "Three Questions on *Six fois deux*" [1976]. In *Negotiations 1972–1990*, 37–45. Translated by Martin Joughin. New York: Columbia University Press, 1995.
———. "Le juif riche" [1977]. In *Deux régimes de fous: Textes et entretiens 1975–1995*, 123–126. Paris: Les Éditions de Minuit, 2003.
Didier, Eric. "De l'impensable à l'irréparable." In *Shoah le film: Des psychanalystes écrivent*, 21–25. Paris: Jacques Grancher, 1990.
Douglas, Lawrence. *The Memory of Judgment*. New Haven: Yale University Press, 2001.
Duguet, Anne-Marie. *Vidéo, la mémoire au poing*. Paris: Hachette, 1981.
Eder, Jacob. *Holocaust Angst: The Federal Republic of Germany and American Holocaust Memory since the 1970s*. Oxford: Oxford University Press, 2016.
Ehrlich, Edith, and Leonard H. Ehrlich. *Choices under Duress of the Holocaust: Benjamin Murmelstein and the Fate of Viennese Jewry, Volume I: Vienna*. Lubbock: Texas Tech University Press, 2018.
Elias, Ruth. *The Triumph of Hope: From Theresienstadt and Auschwitz to Israel* [1988]. Translated by Margot Bettauer Dembo. New York: John Wiley and Sons, 1998.
Epstein, Barbara. *The Minsk Ghetto 1941–1943: Jewish Resistance and Soviet Internationalism*. Berkeley: University of California Press, 2008.
Fabre, Clarice. "Jean-Pierre Beauviala: 'La caméra, comme un chat sur l'épaule.'" *Le Monde*, 11 October 2016. Accessed 30 April 2018. http://www.lemonde.

fr/cinema/article/2016/10/11/et-beauviala-reinventa-la-camera_5011573_3476.html.

Feingold, Henry. *The Politics of Rescue. The Roosevelt Administration and the Holocaust, 1938–1945*. New Brunswick: Rutgers University Press, 1970.

Feingold, Henry, Isaiah Trunk, et al. "Discussion: The *Judenrat* and the Jewish Response." In *The Holocaust as Historical Experience: Essays and a Discussion*, edited by Yehuda Bauer and Nathan Rotenstreich, 223–271. New York: Holmes & Meier, 1981.

Felman, Shoshana, and Dori Laub. *Testimony: Crises of Witnessing in Literature, Psychoanalysis and History*. New York: Routledge, 1992.

Finkel, Evgeny. *Ordinary Jews: Choice and Survival During the Holocaust*. Princeton: Princeton University Press, 2017.

Foster, Hal. "An Archival Impulse." *October* 110 (Fall 2004): 3–22.

Freedland, Jonathan. "The Day Israel Saw *Shoah*." *The Guardian*, 10 December 2015. Accessed 20 July 2017. https://www.theguardian.com/world/2015/dec/10/the-day-israel-saw-shoah.

Friedländer, Saul. *Nazi Germany and the Jews, Volume 1: The Years of Persecution, 1933–1939*. New York: Harper Collins, 1997.

———. *Nazi Germany and the Jews, Volume 2: The Years of Extermination, 1939–1945*. New York: Harper Collins, 2007.

———. *Réflexions sur le nazisme: Entretiens avec Stéphane Bou*. Paris: Éditions du Seuil, 2016.

———. *When Memory Comes* [1978]. Translated by Helen R. Lane. New York: Other Press, 2016.

———. *Where Memory Leads: My Life*. New York: Other Press, 2016.

Friedman, Filip. "Pseudo-Saviours in the Polish Ghettos: Mordechai Chaim Rumkowski of Lodz" [1954]. In *Roads to Extinction: Essays on the Holocaust*, edited by Ada June Friedman, 333–352. New York: Jewish Publication Society of America, 1980.

Frodon, Jean-Michel. "Intersecting Paths." In *Cinema and the Shoah: An Art Confronts the Tragedy of the Twentieth Century* [2007], edited by Jean-Michel Frodon, 1–14. Translated by Anna Harrison and Tom Mes. Albany: State University of New York Press, 2010.

———. "The Work of the Filmmaker: An Interview with Claude Lanzmann." In *Cinema and the Shoah: An Art Confronts the Tragedy of the Twentieth Century* [2007], edited by Jean-Michel Frodon, 93–106. Translated by Anna Harrison and Tom Mes. Albany: State University of New York Press, 2010.

Garfunkel, Leib. *The Destruction of Kovno's Jewry* [Hebrew]. Jerusalem: Yad Vashem, 1959.

Geva, Sharon. "'To Collect the Tears of the Jewish People': The Story of Miriam Novitch." *Holocaust Studies* 21.1–2 (2015): 73–92.

Gilbert, Martin. *Holocaust Journey: The Search of a Past*. New York: Columbia University Press, 1999.

Glazar, Richard. *Trap with a Green Fence: Survival in Treblinka* [1992]. Translated by Roslyn Theobald. Evanston: Northwestern University Press, 1995.

Goldmann, Nahum. *The Autobiography of Nahum Goldmann. Sixty Years of Jewish Life*. New York: Holt, Rinehart and Winston, 1969.

———. *The Jewish Paradox*. Translated by Steve Cox. New York: Grosset & Dunlap, 1978.

Golsan, Richard J. *The Vichy Past in France Today: Corruptions of Memory*. Lanham: Lexington Books, 2017.

Gouri, Haim. *Facing the Glass Booth. The Jerusalem Trial of Adolf Eichmann* [1962]. Translated by Michael Swirsky. Detroit: Wayne State University Press, 2004.

Gutman, Israel, and Bella Gutterman. *The Auschwitz Album: The Story of a Transport*. Jerusalem: Yad Vashem and the Auschwitz-Birkenau State Museum, 2002.

Haenel, Yannick. *The Messenger* [2009]. Translated by Ian Monk. Berkeley: Counterpoint, 2011.

Hilberg, Raul. *Perpetrators Victims Bystanders: The Jewish Catastrophe, 1933–1945*. New York: HarperCollins, 1992.

———. *The Politics of Memory: The Journey of a Holocaust Historian*. Chicago: Ivan R. Dee, 1994.

———. *The Destruction of the European Jews* [1961], third edition. New Haven: Yale University Press, 2003.

Hilberg, Raul, Stanislaw Staron, and Josef Kermisz, ed. *The Warsaw Diary of Adam Czerniakow: Prelude to Doom* [1979]. Chicago: Ivan R. Dee, 1999.

Hirsch, Joshua. *Afterimage: Film, Trauma, and the Holocaust*. Philadelphia: Temple University Press, 2004.

Hirsch, Marianne. *Family Frames: Photography, Narrative, and Postmemory*. Cambridge: Harvard University Press, 1997.

———. *The Generation of Postmemory: Writing and Visual Culture after the Holocaust*. New York: Columbia University Press, 2012.

Hirsch, Marianne, and Leo Spitzer. "Gendered Translations: Claude Lanzmann's *Shoah*" [1993]. In *Claude Lanzmann's "Shoah": Key Essays*, edited by Stuart Liebman, 175–190. Oxford: Oxford University Press, 2007.

Horowitz, Sara. "The Gender of Good and Evil: Women and Holocaust Memory." In *Gray Zones: Ambiguity and Compromise in the Holocaust and Its Aftermath*, edited by Jonathan Petropoulos and John K. Roth, 165–178. New York: Berghahn Books, 2005.

Houdebine, Anne-Marie. "L'écriture *Shoah*." In *Shoah le film: Des psychanalystes écrivent*, 83–150. Paris: Jacques Grancher, 1990.
Kaplan, Marion. *Between Dignity and Despair: Jewish Life in Nazi Germany*. Oxford: Oxford University Press, 1998.
Kansteiner, Wulf. "Losing the War, Winning the Memory Battle: The Legacy of Nazism, World War II, and the Holocaust in the Federal Republic of Germany." In *The Politics of Memory in Postwar Europe*, edited by Richard Ned Lebow, Wulf Kansteiner, and Claudio Fogu, 102–146. Durham: Duke University Press, 2006.
Karski, Jan. "*Shoah*" [1986]. In *Claude Lanzmann's Shoah: Key Essays*, edited by Stuart Liebman, 171–174. Oxford: Oxford University Press, 2007.
———. *Story of a Secret State: My Report to the World* [1944]. Washington, DC: Georgetown University Press, 2013.
Kaufmann, Francine. *Pour relire "Le dernier des Justes."* Paris: Klincksieck, 1986.
———. "Interview et interprétation consécutive dans le film *Shoah*, de Claude Lanzmann." *Meta: journal des traducteurs* 38.4 (December 1993): 664–673.
———. "The Ambiguous Task of the Interpreter in Lanzmann's Films *Shoah* and *Sobibor*: Between the Director and Survivors of the Camps and Ghettos." In *Interpreting in Nazi Concentration Camps*, edited by Michaela Wolf, 161–180. New York: Bloomsbury, 2016.
Kennedy, Merrit. "Researchers Uncover Long-Lost Tunnel Used by Jews to Escape Extermination Pits." *NPR*, 26 June 2016. Accessed 12 July 2017. https://www.npr.org/sections/thetwo-way/2016/06/29/484017541/researchers-uncover-long-lost-tunnel-used-by-jews-to-escape-extermination-pits.
Klein, Irma, and Uri Klein. "An Interview with David Perlov" [1981]. In *David Perlov's Diary*, edited by Mira Perlov and Pip Chodorov, 13–19. Paris: Re:Voir Video, 2006.
Klein, Uri. "*Memories of the Eichmann Trial* / From Testimony to Proof." *Haaretz*, 1 May 2011. Accessed 12 February 2017. http://www.haaretz.com/print-edition/features/memories-of-the-eichmann-trial-from-testimony-to-proof-1.359060.
Koch, Gertrud. "The Aesthetic Transformation of the Image of the Unimaginable: Notes on Claude Lanzmann's *Shoah*." In *Claude Lanzmann's "Shoah": Key Essays*, edited by Stuart Liebman, 125–132. Translated by Jamie Owen Daniel and Miriam Hansen. Oxford: Oxford University Press, 2007.
Kogon, Eugen, Hermann Langbein, and Adalbert Rückerl, ed. *Nazi Mass Murder: A Documentary History of the Use of Poison Gas* [1983]. Translated by Mary Scott and Caroline Lloyd Morris. New Haven: Yale University Press, 1993.

Koonz, Claudia. *Mothers in the Fatherland. Women, Family and Nazi Politics* [1987]. London: Routledge, 2013.

Kovner, Abba. "A First Attempt to Tell." In *The Holocaust as Historical Experience: Essays and a Discussion*, edited by Yehuda Bauer and Nathan Rotenstreich, 77–94. New York: Holmes & Meier, 1981.

Kristeva, Julia. *Powers of Horrors: An Essay on Abjection* [1980]. Translated by Leon S. Roudiez. New York: Columbia University Press, 1982.

LaCapra, Dominick. *History and Memory After Auschwitz*. Ithaca: Cornell University Press, 1998.

———. "'Here There Is No Why'" [1997]. In *Claude Lanzmann's "Shoah": Key Essays*, edited by Stuart Liebman, 191–229. Oxford: Oxford University Press, 2007.

Landsberg, Alison. *Prosthetic Memory: The Transformation of American Remembrance in the Age of Mass Culture*. New York: Columbia University Press, 2004.

Langer, Lawrence. *Versions of Survival: The Holocaust and the Human Spirit*. Albany: State University of New York Press, 1982.

———. *Holocaust Testimonies: The Ruins of Memory*. New Haven: Yale University Press, 1991.

Lanzmann, Claude. "Why Spielberg Has Distorted the Truth." *Guardian Weekly*, 3 April 1994, 14.

———. "Hier ist kein Warum" [1988]. In *Claude Lanzmann's "Shoah": Key Essays*, edited by Stuart Liebman, 51–52. Translated by Claude Lanzmann. Oxford: Oxford University Press, 2007.

———. "From Holocaust to *Holocaust*" [1979]. In *Claude Lanzmann's "Shoah": Key Essays*, edited by Stuart Liebman, 27–36. Oxford: Oxford University Press, 2007.

———. "*Jan Karski* de Yannick Haenel: un faux roman." *Les Temps Modernes* 657 (January–March 2010): 1–10.

———. "Nuit et brouillard: réponse à Gilles Deleuze à propos de *L'Ombre des anges* de R.W. Fassbinder et D. Schmid" [1977]. In *La Tombe du divin plongeur*, 346–350. Paris: Gallimard, 2012.

———. "De l'Holocauste à *Holocauste* ou comment s'en débarrasser" [1979]. In *La Tombe du divin plongeur*, 369–381. Paris: Gallimard, 2012.

———. "Ce mot de 'Shoah'... Réponse à Henri Meschonnic" [2005]. In *La Tombe du divin plongeur*, 363–368. Paris: Gallimard, 2012.

———. *The Patagonian Hare* [2009]. Translated by Frank Wynne. New York: Farrar, Straus and Giroux, 2012.

Lanzmann, Claude, David Frenkel, and Fabrice Puchault. *The Four Sisters* (Press Kit). Paris: Arte Sales & Synecdoche, 2017.

Leibniz, Gottfried Wilhelm. *Theodicy: Essays on the Goodness of God, the Freedom of Man, and the Origins of Evil* [1710]. Translated by E. M. Huggard. Chicago: Open Court, 1998.

Levi, Primo. *The Drowned and the Saved* [1986]. Translated by Raymond Rosenthal. New York: Simon & Schuster, 2017.

Levy, Ophir. "La forteresse et l'aveu: A propos d'*Un vivant qui passe* de Claude Lanzmann." *Témoigner: Entre histoire et mémoire* 107 (2010): 53–64.

Lichtenstein, Therese. *Behind Closed Doors: The Art of Hans Bellmer*. Berkeley: University of California Press, 2001.

Lichtman, Eda. "From Mielec to Sobibór: The Testimony of Eda Lichtman" [1965]. Accessed 9 July 2017. http://www.zchor.org/testimonies/lichtman.htm.

Liebman, Stuart. "Introduction." In *Claude Lanzmann's Shoah: Key Essays*, edited by Stuart Liebman, 3–24. Oxford: Oxford University Press, 2007.

Lindeperg, Sylvie. *"Night and Fog": A Film in History*. Translated by Tom Mes. Minneapolis: University of Minnesota Press, 2014.

Lindeperg Sylvie, and Annette Wieviorka. "The Two Stages of the Eichmann Trial." In *Concentrationary Memories: Totalitarian Terror and Cultural Resistance*, edited by Griselda Pollock and Max Silverman, 59–81. London: I. B. Tauris, 2014.

Lipstadt, Deborah E. *Beyond Belief: The American Press and the Coming of the Holocaust, 1933–1945*. New York: The Free Press, 1986.

———. "America and the Holocaust." *Modern Judaism* 10.3 (October 1990): 283–296.

———. *The Eichmann Trial*. New York: Nextbook and Schocken Books, 2011.

Lubetkin, Zivia. *In the Days of Destruction and Revolt* [1979]. Translated by Ishai Tubbin. Jerusalem: Hakibbutz Hameuchad, 1981.

Lusty, Natalya. *Surrealism, Feminism, Psychoanalysis*. New York: Routledge, 2016.

Maeck, Julie. "De l'écriture à l'histoire: le documentaire face au prétoire." In *Le moment Eichmann*, edited by Sylvie Lindeperg and Annette Wieviorka, 119–138. Paris: Albin Michel, 2016.

Maltz, Judy. "The American Women Who Risked It All to Save Jews During the Holocaust." *Haaretz*, 27 January 2014. Accessed 15 November 2017. https://www.haaretz.com/jewish/features/.premium-1.570700.

Mandelbaum, Jacques. "Recovery." In *Cinema and the Shoah: An Art Confronts the Tragedy of the Twentieth Century* [2007], edited by Jean-Michel Frodon, 25–41. Translated by Anna Harrison and Tom Mes. Albany: State University of New York Press, 2010.

Morse, Arthur D. *While Six Million Died: A Chronicle of American Apathy*. New York: Random House, 1968.

Moscovitz, Jean-Jacques. "Savoir et non savoir en question." In *Shoah le film: Des psychanalystes écrivent*, 35–63. Paris: Jacques Grancher, 1990.

Moyn, Samuel. *A Holocaust Controversy: The Treblinka Affair in Postwar France*. Lebanon: Brandeis University Press, 2005.

Naremore, James. "American Film Noir: The History of an Idea." *Film Quarterly* 49.2 (Winter 1995–1996): 12–28.

———. *More than Night: Film Noir in Its Context* [1998]. Berkeley: University of California Press, 2008.

Neuman, Eran. *Shoah Presence: Architectural Representations of the Holocaust*. London: Routledge, 2014.

Novick, Peter. *The Holocaust in American Life*. Boston: Houghton Mifflin, 1999.

Novitch, Miriam. *Sobibór: Martyrdom and Revolt* [1978]. New York: Holocaust Library, 1980.

OED Online, s.v. "Rush, n.^{2}, adv., and adj." Accessed 3 January 2017. http://www.oed.com/view/Entry/169027?rskey=A0XRUM&result=2#eid24526541.

Ophüls, Marcel. "Closely Watched Trains" [1985]. In *Claude Lanzmann's "Shoah": Key Essays*, edited by Stuart Liebman, 77–87. Oxford: Oxford University Press, 2007.

Pendas, Devin. *The Frankfurt Auschwitz Trials, 1963–1965. Genocide, History, and the Limits of the Law*. Cambridge: Cambridge University Press, 2006.

Perechodnik, Calel. *Am I a Murderer? Testament of a Jewish Ghetto Policeman*. Edited and translated by Frank Fox. Boulder: Westview Press, 1996.

Peretz, Eyal. *The Off-Screen. An Investigation of the Cinematic Frame*. Stanford: Stanford University Press, 2017.

Pierre, Anthony. "*Le Père Nöel a les yeux bleus*: l'invasion du réel dans la fiction." In *Le court métrage français de 1945 à 1968: De l'âge d'or aux contrebandiers*, edited by Dominique Bluher and François Thomas, 341–347. Rennes: Presses Universitaires de Rennes, 2005.

Pinchevski, Amit. "The Audiovisual Unconscious: Media and Trauma in the Video Archive for Holocaust Testimonies." *Critical Inquiry* 39.1 (Autumn 2012): 142–166.

Pinchevski, Amit, and Tamar Liebes. "Severed Voices: Radio and the Mediation of Trauma in the Eichmann Trial." *Public Culture* 22.2 (Spring 2010): 265–291.

Pioro, Anna. "The Eagle Pharmacy: Regained Memory: The History of the Pharmacy as an Instance of Manipulating Collective Memory." In Jan Gryta et al., *The Eagle Pharmacy. History and Memory*, 187–231. Kraków: Muzeum Historyczne Miasta Krakow, 2013.

Piotrowska, Agnieszka. *Psychoanalysis and Ethics in Documentary Film.* London: Routledge, 2014.
Popper, Nathaniel. "A Conscious Pariah." *The Nation*, 31 March 2011. Accessed 28 July 2017. https://www.thenation.com/article/conscious-pariah/.
Postec, Ziva. "Le montage du film *Shoah*" [1987]. Accessed 22 November 2017. http://kefisrael.com/2011/01/26/le-montage-du-film-shoah-ziva-postec/.
Prager, Brad. "Interpreting the Visible Traces of Theresienstadt." *Journal of Modern Jewish Studies* 7.2 (2008): 175–194.
———. *After the Fact: Holocaust Documentary in the Twenty-First Century.* New York: Bloomsbury, 2015.
Rashke, Richard. *Escape from Sobibor* [1982]. New York: Delphinium Books, 2013.
Renov, Michael. *The Subject of Documentary.* Minneapolis: University of Minnesota Press, 2004.
Ringelheim, Joan. "The Unethical and the Unspeakable: Women and the Holocaust." *Simon Wiesenthal Center Annual* 1 (1984): 69–87.
———. "The Split Between Gender and the Holocaust." In *Women in the Holocaust*, edited by Ofer Dalia and Lenore J. Weitzman, 340–350. New Haven: Yale University Press, 1998.
Rittner, Carole, and John K. Roth, eds. *Different Voices: Women and the Holocaust.* St. Paul: Paragon House, 1993.
Rodowick, D. N. *Gilles Deleuze's Time Machine.* Durham: Duke University Press, 1997.
Rothberg, Michael. *Traumatic Realism: The Demands of Holocaust Representation.* Minneapolis: University of Minnesota Press, 2000.
———. *Multidirectional Memory: Remembering the Holocaust in the Age of Decolonization.* Stanford: Stanford University Press, 2009.
Rubenstein, Richard L. *The Cunning of History: The Holocaust and the American Future.* New York: Harper & Row, 1975.
———. "Gray into Black: The Case of Mordecai Chaim Rumkowski." In *Gray Zones: Ambiguity and Compromise in the Holocaust and Its Aftermath*, edited by Jonathan Petropoulos and John K. Roth, 299–310. New York: Berghahn Books, 2005.
Rudavsky, Joseph. *To Live with Hope, to Die with Dignity.* Lanham: University Press of America, 1987.
Sanyal, Debarati. *Memory and Complicity: Migrations of Holocaust Remembrance.* New York: Fordham University Press, 2015.
Saxton, Libby. *Haunted Images: Film, Ethics, Testimony, and the Holocaust.* London: Wallflower Press, 2008.

Schneider, Gertrude, ed. *The Unfinished Road: Jewish Survivors of Latvia Look Back.* New York: Praeger, 1991.

———, ed. *Mordechai Gebirtig: His Poetic and Musical Legacy.* Westport: Praeger, 2000.

———. *Journey into Terror: Story of the Riga Ghetto* [1979]. Westport: Praeger, 2001.

Schweitzer, Ariel. "Forgetting, Instrumentalization, and Transgression: The Shoah in Israeli Cinema." In *Cinema and the Shoah: An Art Confronts the Tragedy of the Twentieth Century* [2007], edited by Jean-Michel Frodon, 181–188. Translated by Anna Harrison and Tom Mes. Albany: State University of New York Press, 2010.

Schwiefert, Peter. *L'Oiseau n'a plus d'ailes.* Translated by Claude Lanzmann. Paris: Gallimard, 1974.

Segev, Tom. *The Seventh Million: The Israelis and the Holocaust* [1991]. Translated by Haim Watzman. New York: Owl Books, 2000.

Sereny, Gitta. *Into That Darkness: An Examination of Conscience.* New York: Vintage Books, 1974.

Shandler, Jeffrey. *Holocaust Memory in the Digital Age.* Stanford: Stanford University Press, 2017.

Shenker, Israel. "Holocaust Parley Has Few Answers." *New York Times*, 6 March 1975.

Shenker, Noah. *Reframing Holocaust Testimony.* Bloomington: Indiana University Press, 2015.

Snyder, Timothy. *Black Earth: The Holocaust as History and Warning.* New York: Tim Duggan Books, 2015.

Steinacher, Gerald. *Humanitarians at War: The Red Cross in the Shadow of the Holocaust.* Oxford: Oxford University Press, 2017.

Styron, William. *Sophie's Choice* [1979]. London: Vintage, 2004.

Swift, Leslie, and Lindsay Zarwell. "Inside the Outtakes: A History of the Claude Lanzmann *Shoah* Collection at the USHMM." In *The Invention of Testimony: Claude Lanzmann in the Twenty-First Century*, edited by Erin McGlothlin, Brad Prager, and Markus Zisselsberger. Forthcoming.

Szurek, Jean-Charles. "*Shoah*: From the Jewish Question to the Polish Question." In *Claude Lanzmann's "Shoah": Key Essays*, edited by Stuart Liebman, 149–169. Oxford: Oxford University Press, 2007.

Tabucchi, Antonio. *Tristano Dies: A Life* [2004]. Translated by Elizabeth Harris. Brooklyn: Archipelago Books, 2015.

Todorov, Tzvetan. *Facing the Extreme: Moral Life in the Concentration Camps* [1991]. Translated by Arthur Denner and Abigail Pollack. New York: Henry Holt and Company, 1996.

Tournier, Michel. "Gilles Deleuze." In *Deleuze and Religion*, edited by Mary Bryden, 201–204. Translated by Walter Redfern. London and New York: Routledge, 2001.

Trezise, Thomas. *Witnessing Witnessing: On the Reception of Holocaust Testimony*. New York: Fordham University Press, 2013.

Trunk, Isaiah. *Judenrat: The Jewish Councils in Eastern Europe under Nazi Occupation*. New York: Macmillan, 1972.

Tushnet, Leonard. *The Pavement of Hell*. New York: St. Martin's Press, 1972.

Vice, Sue. *Shoah*. London: Palgrave Macmillan–British Film Institute, 2011.

———. "Claude Lanzmann's Einsatzgruppen Interviews." In *Representing Perpetrators in Holocaust Literature and Film*, edited by Jenni Adams and Sue Vice, 47–68. London: Valentine Mitchell, 2013.

Villain, Dominique. *Le montage au cinéma*. Paris: Cahiers du cinéma, 1991.

Walker, Janet. *Trauma Cinema: Documenting Incest and the Holocaust*. Berkeley: University of California Press, 2005.

———. "Moving Testimonies: 'Unhomed Geography' and the Holocaust Documentary of Return." In *After Testimony: The Ethics and Aesthetics of Holocaust Narratives for the Future*, edited by Jakob Lothe, Susan Rubin Suleiman, and James Phelan, 269–288. Columbus: Ohio State University Press, 2012.

Waxman, Zoë. *Women in the Holocaust: A Feminist History*. Oxford: Oxford University Press, 2017.

Wiesel, Elie. *Un di velt hot geshvign*. Buenos Aires: Tsentral-Farband fun Poylishe Yidn, 1956.

———. "Elie Wiesel's Remarks at the Dedication Ceremonies for the United States Holocaust Memorial Museum, April 22, 1993." Accessed 22 November 2017. https://www.ushmm.org/information/about-the-museum/mission-and-history/wiesel.

———. *Night* [1958]. Translated by Marion Wiesel. New York: Hill and Wang, 2006.

Wieviorka, Annette. *Le procès Eichmann*. Brussels: Éditions Complexe, 1989.

———. *The Era of the Witness* [1998]. Translated by Jared Stark. Ithaca and London: Cornell University Press, 2006.

———. "Faux témoignage." *L'Histoire* 349 (January 2010): 30–31.

Williams, Linda. "Mirrors without Memories: Truth, History, and the New Documentary." *Film Quarterly* 46.3 (Spring 1993): 9–21.

Wood, E. Thomas, and Stanisław M. Jankowski. *Karski: How One Man Tried to Stop the Holocaust*. New York: John Wiley & Sons, 1994.

Yablonka, Hanna. *The State of Israel vs. Adolf Eichmann* [2001]. Translated by Ora Cummings with David Herman. New York: Schocken Books, 2004.

Young, James. *The Texture of Memory: Holocaust Memorials and Meaning.* New Haven: Yale University Press, 1994.

Zoltán, Kekesi. *Agents of Liberation: Holocaust Memory in Contemporary Art and Documentary Film.* New York: Central European University Press, 2015.

Zuckerman, Yitzhak "Antek." *A Surplus of Memory: Chronicle of the Warsaw Ghetto Uprising* [1990]. Translated by Barbara Harshav. Berkeley: University of California Press, 1993.

Zygielbojm, Faivel. *Der Koyeh tsu Shtarbn: Mishpohe Bukh.* Tel Aviv: Farlag Y. L. Perets, 1976.

INDEX

"abjection of the Nazi crime" (Kristeva), 49, 143, 145–46
Adorno, Theodor, 153
affiliative identification, 86
affiliative memory, 86. *See also* Hirsch, Marianne
affiliative postmemory, 94
Aid and Rescue Committee. *See* Vaada
Alef-Bolkowiak, Gustaw, 106–7
"anxiety of historical transmission," xxiv, xxxi, 230
Apfelbaum, Fanny, 76–77
Apteka Pod Orłem (Under the Eagle pharmacy), 109–12
"archival impulse," xxiv, 231n6
Arendt, Hannah, 18, 268n108
  on collaboration, 14, 16, 106
  criticism of *Judenrat* (Jewish council), xxx, xxxii, 16, 62, 102, 106, 107, 252n135
  Eichmann in Jerusalem: A Report on the Banality of Evil, xxxiv, 14, 16, 25, 64, 106, 168, 170, 207, 208
  Gershom Scholem and, 25
  interviews, 107
  Lanzmann and, 25, 62, 170, 173, 206–8
  The Origins of Totalitarianism, 207, 268n108
  Rudolf Kasztner and, 168
Arnon, Ya'akov, 106

Aron, Raymond, 52
artisans, 21, 23
Aubouy, Bernard, xxx, 33, 39, 51, 113
"Auschwitz Album," 166–67, 174
Auschwitz-Birkenau Memorial and Museum, 49
Auschwitz concentration camp, 37, 166, 207, 225
  deportations to, 62, 126, 128, 141, 144, 166, 171, 172, 175–77, 215, 220, 229
  escapes from, 213. *See also* Vrba, Rudolf
  extermination process at, 38–39, 170
  Filip Müller on, 92
  Hungarian Jews at, 166–67, 170
  John Pehle and, 213, 270n135
  Julia Kristeva on, 49
  Lanzmann on, 180, 212
  map of, 36, 37
  Maurice Rossel's visit to and report on, 218–20
  Paula Biren and, 120, 121, 128. *See also* Biren, Paula
  people's (un)awareness of, 167, 170–72, 181, 213, 215, 218–19. *See also* Kasztner, Rudolf: Auschwitz and
  Pery Broad and, 25, 29, 36–39
  prisoner uprising in fall 1944, 37, 83, 141

287

Auschwitz concentration camp *(continued)*
  proposals to bomb, 217, 270n135
  the question of rescue from, 180
  Rudolf Kasztner and, 62, 166–68, 170. *See also* Kasztner, Rudolf: negotiations with Eichmann
  Rudolf Vrba's report on, 37, 166, 170, 171, 213, 217
  Ruth Elias and choice and survival in, 140–50. *See also* Elias, Ruth
  Ruth Elias on, 215, 229
  Shoah and, 92, 120, 149
  Theresienstadt family camp at, 141, 144, 146–48, 150, 257n67
Avriel, Ehud, 220
"Azoy muss sein" ("That's the Way It Has to Be"), 133–35, 136f, 138

Barmore, Shalmi, 93–94
Baron, Salo, 102
Bartoszewski, Władysław, 200
Bartov, Omer, 102
Bauer, Yehuda, 6, 26, 103, 107
  background and overview, 103
  Hungarian Jews and, 6
  interviews and testimony, 17, 103, 106, 107
  on *Judenrat*, 103–4
  Lanzmann and, 6, 52, 103–4, 106
  outtakes, 103, 107
  "The Holocaust—A Generation After" (conference) and, 17–18
Beauviala, Jean-Pierre, xxxiv, 30, 34, 41
Becher, Mr., 217f
Becker, August, 42
Beit Ha'am theater (and auditorium), 56, 57, 60, 63–66, 88

Bellmer, Hans, 72
Benjamin, Walter, 101
Berenbaum, Michael, xxii–xxv, xxvii, 230
Bergen, Doris, 157, 229
Bergson, Henri, 47, 50
Bergson, Peter (Hillel Kook), 177–79, 213–16
  on American Jewish leaders, 177, 213–15, 270n126
  background and overview, 177
  photograph, 214f
  Roosevelt and, 214–15, 270n126
Bergson Group, 213
Berlin, choice and survival in, 151–65
Berman, Adolf, 186
Bermuda Conference, xxxvi–xxxvii, 186, 205, 210, 213
Besson, Remy, 191
Biren, Paula S., 253nn9–10
  Chaim Rumkowski and, xxxv, 121–26
  choice and survival in Łódź ghetto, 117–28
  Joan Ringelheim and, 127, 255n35
  testimony, xxviii, 227, 229, 255n35
  in *The Four Sisters*, 229, 230
"Blood for Goods" deal, 166, 168, 177, 220
Bomba, Abraham, 74, 145
  background, 67
  as "barber of Treblinka," 67, 69, 74, 247n64
  characterizations of, 82–83
  escape from Treblinka, 10, 11, 74, 83
  Lanzmann and, 10, 69, 73–75, 75f, 80, 82–84

The Patagonian Hare (Lanzmann)
and, 10, 47, 74, 82
photographs, 46f, 75f
silencing performances, xxxiv, xxxv, 45, 81
staged reenactment in the barbershop with, 11, 12, 21, 45, 57, 67, 69, 71, 74, 80, 82, 83, 188, 205
tears, xxx, 82
bombing railways and camps, proposals for, 270n135
Bonitzer, Pascal, 5, 116
Borges, Jorge Luis, 47
Brand, Hansi, 172
Kasztner and, 168–69, 172
languages spoken by, 170
Lanzmann and, 169, 171, 172
negotiations with Eichmann, 168–70
outtakes, 172, 174
on people's awareness of the extermination, 171
photograph, 169f
role in Vaada, 168–69
Rudolf Vrba and, 170, 171
testimony, 169, 169f, 170
Brand, Joel, 168, 169, 220
Bratislava Working Group, 142, 175, 216, 217
Breitman, Richard, 214
Broad, Pery, 259n98
Auschwitz and, 25, 29, 36–39
interviews and testimony, 25, 29, 36–38, 44
Lanzmann and, 29, 36–38, 44
outtakes, 32–33, 36
silence and testimonial resistance, 36, 37, 39, 43, 205
"Broad Report," 29, 37

Browning, Christopher, 105
Budapest. *See also* Kasztner, Rudolf: negotiations with Eichmann
choice and survival in, 165–74
Budapest committee. *See* Vaada
Burckhardt, Carl, 223–24
"buried self," 21, 237n74
"bystanders," xx, xxxvii, 175, 178, 179, 186, 191–192, 197, 199, 205, 212–215, 219–220, 223. *See also* "messengers of the catastrophe"

Cahiers du cinéma, 4, 119, 133
"camera car," 31–33
camera, hidden. *See* Paluche
Caruth, Cathy, 12
Champetier, Caroline, xxx, 30
Chapuis, Dominique, xxix–xxx, 31, 33, 42, 161, 164–165, 188,
Chełmno extermination camp, 123–24. *See also* Podchlebnik, Mordechai; Srebnik, Simon
children's reactions to the horrors committed in, 261n119
Mordechai Podchlebnik's escape from, 83
Mordechai Podchlebnik's testimony regarding, 79, 83
Simon Srebnik's experiences in, 51
Simon Srebnik's staged return to, 11, 21, 50–52, 137, 140
Simon Srebnik's testimony in, 50–52
"singing child" of. *See* Srebnik, Simon
Chełmno trials, 41–42, 248n70
childbirth and labor, 73, 149. *See also* pregnant women

Chion, Michael, 70
choice, tragedy of, 49, 128, 167, 168, 173
  editing *Shoah* and, 53
  Gertrude Schneider and, 134
  and the incompossible, xxxv, 53, 117, 125, 144, 173
  Judenrat and, 21, 125, 127
  Lanzmann on, 173
  Rudolf Kasztner and, 167, 173. See also Kasztner, Rudolf: negotiations with Eichmann
  Ruth Elias and, 144
  women survivors and, 117, 168, 173
"choiceless choice," 145. See also Langer, Lawrence
Chomsky, Marvin, xxix, 17, 53, 101, 152
"collaboration," 104. See also complicity
complicity. See also "collaboration"
  claims of, 16, 103
  "like sheep to the slaughter," xxxiv, 14–15, 18, 62, 64, 88, 90–94, 220
composing with incompossibles. See incompossible(s): composing with
Coulmas, Corinna, 6, 40–42, 51, 113, 158
  camera concealed in the handbag of, 29, 36, 38, 39, 43f. See also Paluche
  Eduard Kryshak and, 42, 43, 43f
  Heinz Schubert and, 39
  Irena Steinfeldt and, 6, 40
  Pery Broad and, 29, 36, 38, 39
  photographs, 13f, 43f

in *Shoah*, 6
  tasks as Lanzmann's assistant, 6–7, 29
critical trend in Holocaust studies, 178
Czerniaków, Adam, 102, 104
  diary, 8, 18, 19, 21, 23, 102–5, 193, 195, 195f
  Faivel Zygielbojm and, 195
  Judenrat (Jewish council) and, 8, 18–19, 21, 23, 101, 102, 104, 105, 107
  Lanzmann and, 49, 102–6, 193
  Raul Hilberg and, 8, 18–19, 21, 23, 49, 101, 103, 105–6, 173, 193, 195, 198–99
  resistance and, 8, 18, 104, 107
  Shoah and, 18–19, 21, 49, 102, 103, 105–6, 187, 193, 198–99
  suicide, 8, 49, 187, 192
  Szmul Zygielbojm and, 185
  Warsaw ghetto and, 8, 18, 49, 101, 102, 105–7, 185, 187, 192, 195, 195f
Częstochowa, women from, 74

Dawidowicz, Lucy
  correspondence with Roswell McClelland, 17, 191, 218, 266n57
  Judenrat (Jewish council) and, 17, 18
  Lanzmann and, 17
  Raul Hilberg and, 17, 18
  on rescue efforts, 191
  Shoah and, 17
  The War Against the Jews: 1933–1945, 17, 18
de Beauvoir, Simone, 14–16, 52

deep memory, xxxii, 11, 12, 80
  Ada Lichtman and, xxxv, 80
  Lanzmann and, xxxv, 21, 76, 77, 80
  Shoah and, xxx, xxxi, 11, 12, 21, 100
deep time of testimony, 230
Deleuze, Gilles, 242n151
  and the incompossible, 45–47
  Lanzmann and, 45–47, 242n151
  Leibniz and, 46, 47, 50
  writings, 47, 242n151
Destruction of Kovno's Jewry, The (Garfunkel), 19–23, 171
Destruction of the European Jews, The (Hilberg), 8, 14, 17, 20, 101–5, 123, 125, 178
Deutschkron, Inge, 161, 165
  choice and survival in Berlin, 151–65
  interviews and testimony, xxxvi, 151–58, 156f, 160–62, 162f, 163f, 165
  languages spoken by, 161
  Lanzmann and, 151, 155, 161, 164, 165
  Outcast (memoir), 154
  outtakes, 151, 155, 161
  photographs, 162f–64f
Diary (Perlov's film), 1–3, 5, 6, 55, 62, 234n1
Douglas, Lawrence, 57, 64–65, 80
Dugin, Itzhak, 7, 20–21, 72, 83–84, 88, 130, 150
Duguet, Ann-Marie, 34

Eagle pharmacy. *See* Apteka Pod Orłem
Ehrlich, Edith, 26, 238n83
Ehrlich, Leonard H., 26, 238n83

Eichmann, Adolf. *See also* Eichmann trial
  negotiations with Jewish leaders, xxxvi, 62, 166–73. *See also* "Blood for Goods" deal
Eichmann in Jerusalem: A Report on the Banality of Evil (Arendt), xxxiv, 14, 16, 25, 64, 168, 170, 207, 208. *See also* Arendt, Hannah
  "collaboration" of *Judenrat* and, 106
Eichmann trial, 56, 167. See also *Eichmann in Jerusalem*; *Facing the Glass Booth*; specific topics
  audio and video recordings, 60
  David Perlov and, 56, 60, 61. See also *Memories of the Eichmann Trial*
  effect on Israeli youth, 94
  Gideon Hausner and, 59–61, 64, 78f, 79, 80, 88, 97
  Hanna Yablonka on, 60, 94, 245n22
  Hannah Arendt and, 102. See also *Eichmann in Jerusalem*
  in *In Thy Blood Live*, 55
  Judenrat and, 102, 106
  Lanzmann and, 55, 66, 78–80
  Lanzmann's dismissal of, xxxiv, 25, 62
  Lanzmann's recasting of memorable testimonies of, 80
  in the media, 55, 60–62, 64, 65
  omission from *Shoah*, xxx
  radio, 60–61
  resistance, complicity, and, 94
  Rivka Yoselewska and, 57–64, 90, 245n22, 246n35. See also *Memories of the Eichmann Trial*
  Shoah and, 62, 80

Eichmann trial witnesses, 62, 63, 76, 78, 102. *See also* Lichtman, Ada; Podchlebnik, Mordechai; Yoselewska, Rivka
in *Shoah*, 62
81st Blow, The (Gouri's film), 59, 95, 249n96
Eitan, Rafael, 56
elderly Jews, persecution of, 104, 124, 125, 141
Elias, Ruth, 230
Holocaust experiences, 45, 48, 215, 227–29, 258n75
choice and survival in Auschwitz, 140–50
interviews and testimony, xxviii, 48, 144–50, 145f, 151f, 227, 229
Koni (husband) and, 147–48, 258n85
outtakes, 144, 147–50
in *Shoah*, xxxvi, 215, 227
in *The Four Sisters*, 151f, 220, 227–30
Éluard, Paul, 72
Emergency Committee to Save the Jewish People of Europe, 177
Epstein, Barbara, 252n148
"Es brent." *See* "Undzer shtetl brent!"
Escoffier, Jean-Yves, 33–35
ethics and aesthetics, 3–5
ethics of care, 74, 80
ethics of editing, xxxv, 5–6, 106
ethics of listening to survivors, 81–82
ethics of representation, xxxiii, 1, 2, 5, 23, 69, 101, 105, 150, 184, 193
Etter, Philipp, 224
"Europa Plan," 142, 173

Évian Conference, xx, 177, 208, 269n110
exemplary performances, 11, 12, 20, 21, 35, 111, 116
exemplary witness(es), 158. *See also specific individuals*
Ada Lichtman as, 65
Inge Deutschkron as, 154
Martha Michelsohn as, 160
Noah Shenker on, 11
Paula Biren as, 122
Rivka Yoselewska as, 57, 63, 245n22
extermination process, 235n36

Facing the Glass Booth: The Jerusalem Trial of Adolf Eichmann (Gouri), 56, 58, 60, 61, 63–64, 80, 88, 90, 168
familial memory, 135
familial postmemory, 94
"family camp." *See also* Auschwitz concentration camp
Farr, Raye, xxiii–xxv, xxvii, 230
Feiner, Leon, 186
Feingold, Henry
on Bermuda Conference, 186
on Breckinridge Long, 201
interviews, 17, 179, 190
Lanzmann and, 17, 178, 190
Lucy Dawidowicz and, 17
outtakes, 186, 190, 201
writings, 178, 179, 190, 201
Felman, Shoshana, 61, 102, 105–6
Finkel, Evgeny, 126
Fleischmann, Gisi, 142, 175, 176, 216
Fleischmann, Morris, 63–64

Fortunoff Video Archive for Holocaust Testimonies, xxxi, 12, 45, 145
Four Sisters, The (Lanzmann's film), xxvii, 220, 227–30
press kit, 253nn9–10
France. *See also* Paris; *Six fois deux*
postwar, 14–16, 39, 52. *See also* "Treblinka affair"
refugees in, 221
Shoah and, xxxi, 87–88, 221
Vel d'Hiv roundup, 48
Vichy, 88, 209–10, 221
Frankfurt Auschwitz trials, 29, 37
Frankfurter, Felix, 190, 196–97, 212
Frauenlager (women's camp), 148, 149
French cinematographers, xxix–xxx. *See also specific individuals*
French government and the deportation and extermination of Jews, 221
French language, 29, 36, 107, 122, 135, 139f, 142, 220, 239n106
Lanzmann's use of, 23, 34–36, 38, 40, 107, 142, 164, 205, 211, 219–21, 239n106
testimony in, 72, 138, 221
French New Wave, xxix, xxx, 30, 99
French publications, 14–16, 72, 114. *See also* Kovner, Abba: 1942 manifesto/proclamation; *Messenger*
French Resistance, Lanzmann's activities in, xxxiv, 86, 210–11
French television, 101, 106, 149, 190
French translations, 14, 72, 91–93, 110, 179

French witnesses, exclusion of, 44
Frenkel, David, 228
Friedländer, Saul
Benjamin Murmelstein and, 25, 28, 29
on the "family camp" at Auschwitz, 257n67
Franz Suchomel and, 29, 33, 36, 38
on Hilberg and the Jewish council, 105
Holocaust experiences, 25
ICRC and, 221
on an "integrated" history of the Holocaust, 132
interviews, 25
Lanzmann and, 25, 29, 38
Shoah and, 25, 36
on voices of survivors, 155
When Memory Comes (autobiography/memoir), 25, 29, 33, 52, 143, 221
Friedman, Filip
on Chaim Rumkowski, 123
Lanzmann and, 123, 178
writings, 123, 178, 201

Garfunkel, Leib
death, xxvii, 90
The Destruction of Kovno's Jewry, 19–23, 171
Holocaust experiences, 19
interviews and testimony, xxvii, xxviii, 16, 19–23, 22f, 24f, 25–27, 50, 90, 106, 171, 181, 184
Judenrat (Jewish council) and, 21, 23, 171, 181
Kovno ghetto and, xxvii, 21, 106

Garfunkel, Leib *(continued)*
  outtakes, xxx, 20, 21, 172
  photograph, 22f
  wartime diary, 19
Gebirtig, Mordechai, 114, 137
genetic criticism, xxxii
Gens, Jacob, 104, 106
Gerard Behar Center. *See* Beit Ha'am theater
Geva, Sharon, 73
Gewecke, Hans, 40
Ghetto Fighters' House, 55, 72, 86, 87, 96–98, 100f
ghetto uprisings, 14–15, 83, 93. *See also* Jewish resistance
ghettos, 20. *See also specific ghettos*
Gilbert, Martin, 259n95
Give Me Your Children (Rumkowski's speech), 124
Glasberg, Jimmy, 31, 51
Glazar, Richard
  background and Holocaust experiences, 10
  escape and survival, 11, 14, 16, 83
  Franz Suchomel and, xxxiii, 7–9, 13–14
  Gitta Sereny and, xxxiii, 8–10, 12–14
  interviews and testimony, xxxiii, 7, 9, 10, 12–15, 83, 108
  Jean-François Steiner and, 14, 15
  on Jews as incapable of violence, 15
  Lanzmann and, 13f, 13–15
  outtakes, 10, 12, 83
  photograph, 13f
  on resistance, 15
  in *Shoah*, xxxiii, 7, 9, 13, 14, 67
  Treblinka extermination camp and, 10, 11, 13–15
  on Treblinka revolt, 10, 14, 83
  at Treblinka trial, xxxiii
Godard, Jean-Luc, xxix, xxx, 30–32, 35, 47, 238n92
Gol, Shlomo, 7
Goldberg, Jacob, 113, 114, 114f
Goldberg, Malka, 116
  Holocaust experiences, 113
  interviews and testimony, 113–15
  Lanzmann, 113–15
  outtakes, 113–17, 128
  photograph, 114f
  singing, 114–15, 138
Goldmann, Nahum, 186, 190–92
  accusations against, 185
  background and life history, 180–81
  characterizations of, 181, 185, 185f
  criticism of Jewish leadership, 184
  Évian Conference and, 177
  as first messenger of the catastrophe, 180–81, 184–85
  interviews and testimony, 178–86, 183f
  Jan Karski and, 186
  Lanzmann and, 178–86, 264n23
  outtakes, 181, 193, 264n22
  photographs, 183f, 185f
  the question of the unseen expressed by, 184–85
  Shoah and, 180, 181
  Szmul Zygielbojm and, 185, 193
Golsan, Richard, 190, 191
Gouri, Haim, 64, 65, 88, 98, 126
  The 81st Blow (film), 59, 95, 249n96

Facing the Glass Booth: The Jerusalem Trial of Adolf Eichmann, 56, 58, 60, 61, 63–64, 80, 88, 90, 168
  Hausner and, 60, 64, 79
  Lanzmann and, 79–80
  Morris Fleischmann and, 63–64
  report of May 8, 1961, 58
  Rivka Yoselewska and, 57–61, 64, 79
  Yitzhak "Antek" Zuckerman and, 98
gray zone, 123, 150, 172
Gruenwald, Malchiel, 167, 168
Grynszpan, Shmuel, 65

Haenel, Yannick, xxxvii, 189–93. See also *Messenger*
  Roosevelt and, 189, 190, 197
Halevy, Benjamin, 167, 168, 170
Hareven, Alouph, 4, 179
Hausner, Gideon, 88
  at Ghetto Fighters' House, 97
  Mordechai Podchlebnik and, 79, 80
  opening statement in Eichmann trial, 59–60
  photograph, 78f
  on resistance, 64
  Rivka Yoselewska and, 59–61
Hilberg, Raul, xxiii, xxix, 119, 178, 182f
  at 1975 Holocaust conference, 119
  Adam Czerniaków and, 18–19, 49, 101, 103, 105–6, 125, 168, 173, 193, 195, 198–99
  Adam Czerniaków's diary and, 8, 18, 19, 21, 23, 102, 103, 107, 125, 172, 193
  on collaboration, 14, 103
  The Destruction of the European Jews, 8, 14, 17, 20, 101–5, 123, 125, 178
  ghettos and, 18–19, 195
  heroism and, 105
  interviews and testimony, xxviii, 21, 101–4, 107, 112, 125, 181, 190, 193
  Isaiah Trunk and, 18
  Judenrat (Jewish council) and, 18, 101, 103–7, 123, 125, 252n135
  Lanzmann and, xxiii, 2–3, 17, 38, 52, 101–7, 173, 178
  Lanzmann on, 181, 190, 265n50
  Łódź ghetto and, 125
  Lucy Dawidowicz and, 17
  outtakes, 103, 104, 167, 168
  on rescue, 208, 269n109
  Rudolf Kasztner and, 167, 168
  Shoah and, xxiii, xxv, xxix, 2–3, 8, 16, 18, 21, 38, 49, 52, 106, 107, 112, 125, 181, 193
  United States Holocaust Memorial Museum (USHMM) and, xxiii, xxiv, xxix
  Wise and, 177
  on World War II, 178
  writings
    Perpetrators Victims Bystanders: The Jewish Catastrophe, 1933–1945, 175
    The Destruction of the European Jews, 14, 17, 20, 101–5, 123, 125, 178
    The Politics of Memory, 17, 105
  Yehuda Bauer and, 103
Hirsch, Fredy, 141, 144

Hirsch, Marianne
 on (absence of) feminine perspectives and women in *Shoah*, xxxv, 116, 144, 161, 164
 on affiliative memory, 86
 on photographs, 86
 on postmemory, 86, 94, 135
 writings, xxxv, 116, 135
Hirschhorn, Charlotte (mother of Gertrude Schneider), 133, 134, 164, 256n54
 Holocaust experiences, xxxvi
 interviews and testimony, 134, 136
 Lanzmann and, 137, 138
 photograph, 136f
 Shoah and, xxxvi, 81, 116, 135
 singing, xxxvi, 81, 133, 136f, 136–38
Holocaust
 warnings about, 180–81, 184–85
Holocaust (Chomsky's miniseries), 17, 148
 Lanzmann on, xxix, 29, 101, 269n110
 plot, 101–2
 resistance vs. passivity in, 101–2
 Shoah and, xxx, 39, 53, 101
"Holocaust"
 omission of the word from the title of *Shoah*, xxx, 53
Holocaust and Heroism Memorial Day (Israel), 87
Holocaust as Historical Experience, The (Bauer and Rotenstreich), 18
Holocaust conference (1975), 119, 178
Holocaust controversy of 1966, 16
Holocaust museums, 87, 111. *See also* Ghetto Fighters' House; United States Holocaust Memorial Museum; Yad Vashem
Holocaust survivors, ethics of listening to, 81–82
"Holocaust—A Generation After, The" (conference), 17–18, 88, 178
Horowitz, Sara, 160
Huber, Max, 222
Hungarian Jews, xxxvi. *See also* Kasztner train
 at Auschwitz, 166–67, 170
 deported to Auschwitz, 62, 166, 167
 in Lanzmann's memoir, 174
 moral dilemmas faced by Jewish leaders, 169
 rescue of, 5, 6, 101, 168, 219–20, 223
 Rudolf Kasztner and, 169, 170. *See also* Kasztner, Rudolf: negotiations with Eichmann
 and the question of knowledge of extermination, 170–72, 174
Hungary, 168, 171
hymn(s)
 of resistance, 114
 Treblinka, 13, 29, 35

In Thy Blood Live (Perlov's film), 55
incompossible(s), 79, 125, 150, 167, 168, 171, 173. *See also Patagonian Hare*
 "Any choice in murder," 48–49, 53
 coexistence (vs. exclusion) of, 47, 82
 composing with, xxxvii, 50, 180, 234n32
 defined, xxxiv, 45, 48, 49
 Deleuze and, 45–47. *See also* Deleuze, Gilles

Lanzmann on, 48–49, 53, 180
Lanzmann's task of composing with incomposibles, 45
Leibniz and, 45–48, 81, 167. See also Leibniz, Gottfried Wilhelm
nature of, 48–49
and negotiations between Eichmann and Jewish leaders, xxxvi
notion of, 167, 173–74
"the possible and incompossible." See *Shoah*: editing
Shoah and, xxxiv, xxxv, 49, 50, 53, 81, 82
and the tragedy of choice, xxxv, 53, 117, 125, 144, 173
writings on, 47, 48
infanticide, 45, 69, 73, 145, 149, 227
Into That Darkness: An Examination of Conscience (Sereny), 8–10, 13, 14, 20, 35. See also Sereny, Gitta
Israel, 14, 58, 63, 64, 87. See also Eichmann trial; Kasztner, Rudolf; *specific topics*
and commission of *Shoah*, 4
founding of the state of, 87, 93, 95–96
Holocaust and Heroism Memorial Day, 87
hostile attitudes toward the Jewish councils in, 106
media in, 55–57, 60–62, 64, 65
memory politics in, 93, 168
Israel, Why (Lanzmann's film), 3, 4, 96, 182, 227
"Israel" (imposed name), 132, 133
Israelis, 64
attitudes toward Holocaust survivors, 60–61, 95, 245n28

Eichmann trial and, 60, 61

Jacob, Lili, 167
Jaffa, footage captured on terrace in, 67, 74, 80, 83, 247n64
Jakubowska, Wanda, 48
Jan Karski (Haenel). See *Messenger*
Jarvik, Laurence, 175, 177–78, 191
Jewish Aid and Rescue Committee. See Vaada
Jewish army (to fight alongside the Allies), 177
Jewish council. See *Judenrat*
Jewish leaders. See also *Last of the Unjust*; Murmelstein, Benjamin
Jewish resistance, xxxiv, 62, 83, 86, 104–105, 109, 113, 249n96. See also ghetto uprisings; Sobibór revolt of 1943; underground activities
goals of, 109
Jewish Underground in Warsaw, 186, 195
Jews
"passing" of guilt from the Nazis to the, 172–73
Joinville-le-Pont, screening in, xxv–xxviii, 230
Journey into Terror: Story of the Riga Ghetto (Schneider), 134–35
Judenrat (Jewish council), 16, 25. See also Czerniaków, Adam; Garfunkel, Leib; Murmelstein, Benjamin
absence of revolt on the part of, 18
"collaboration," 106
critiques of, 252n135
Hannah Arendt on, 102, 106
in Minsk ghetto, 109

Kaplan, Marion, 154
Karski, Jan, 8, 11, 175–77
  interviews and testimony, xxxvii, 197–99, 215
  Lanzmann and, 197, 199, 218
  Lanzmann's letters to, 199, 200, 212
  meeting with Roosevelt, 190, 192, 196–98
  Pehle and, 211
  photograph, 198f
  reenactment, 186, 188, 189, 197–98
  Shoah and, 199
  Szmul Zygielbojm and, 8, 185–87, 191–92, 195–98, 198f
  Warsaw ghetto and, 197–99
  writings, 198, 200
"Karski Affair," xxxvii, 189–92, 212. See also *Messenger*
Karski Report, The (Lanzmann's film), xxvi, 190, 191, 197, 212, 229, 232n11
Kasztner, Rudolf (Rezső), 173
  accusations against, 167–71
  assassination of, 168
  Auschwitz and, 62, 166–68, 170
  Hanna Marton and, 171–74
  in Israel, 167
  Lanzmann and, 170, 173
  Malchiel Gruenwald and, 167
  negotiations with Eichmann, 62, 166–73. See also "Blood for Goods" deal; Eichmann, Adolf: negotiations with Jewish leaders; Kasztner train
Kasztner train ("Noah's Ark"), 167–74, 227, 262n163

Kasztner trial (*Attorney-General of the Government of Israel v. Malchiel Gruenwald*), 167–68, 170, 172
Katz, Esther, 127
Katzenelson, Itzhak, 107
Kaufmann, Francine, 16, 19, 94, 248n68
  Antek Zuckerman and, 98, 99, 100f, 101
  dissertation, 16, 236n55
  Hanna Marton and, 171, 228
  interpreting/translations, 92–94, 98, 99, 171, 228
  Lanzmann and, 20, 53, 86, 89, 93–95
  photograph, 100f
Kazik. See Rotem, Simha "Kazik"
Klarsfeld, Serge, 167
Klein, Uri, 56–57
Koch, Gertrud, 227
Kook, Hillel. See Bergson, Peter
Koonz, Claudia, 160
Kovner, Abba, 14, 16, 88, 90
  1942 manifesto/proclamation, 88–93, 95
  at 1975 Holocaust conference, 119
  characterizations of, 14, 108
  death, 88
  at Eichmann trial, 88
  Holocaust experiences, 88, 90
  interviews and testimony, 16, 18, 88–92, 89f, 94, 106
  on *Judenrat*, 106
  at Kibbutz Ein HaHoresh, 88, 89f
  Lanzmann and, 89, 92
  "like sheep to the slaughter," 14, 18, 62, 88, 91–93, 95, 104
  outtakes, 62, 88, 92, 94, 95

photograph, 89f
resistance and, xxxiv, 14, 88, 91, 108
Steiner's *Treblinka* and, 92
Vilna ghetto and, 14, 62, 90, 91, 93, 108
Kovno, Jews of, 21
The Destruction of Kovno's Jewry (Garfunkel), 19–23, 171
Kovno ghetto, 23
Leib Garfunkel and, xxvii, 21, 106. See also *Destruction of Kovno's Jewry*
Kovno *Judenrat*, 19, 21
Kraków ghetto pharmacy. See Apteka Pod Orłem
Kretschmer, Karl, xxviii, 39, 165
Kristeva, Julia, 49, 143
Kryshak, Eduard, 42–43

Laabs, Gustav, 41–42, 158
LaCapra, Dominick, 80, 85–86, 157, 159
Landsberg, Alison, 48
Langer, Lawrence, xxxi, 12, 145, 233n21
Lanzmann, Claude. See also *specific topics*
 demands of Holocaust representation, 20
 dissertation, 48
 lifestyle and daily life, xxiv
 physical interactions with interviewees, 74, 75f, 76, 77, 77f
 "position of an attentive listener" adopted by, 20
 research assistants, 6–7, 184. See also *specific individuals*
 turning the camera on himself, 142
 use of pseudonym "Dr. Sorel," 29, 39–42, 151
Last of the Unjust, The (Lanzmann's film), xxvi, xxvii, 16, 25, 26, 142, 208, 228
 Benjamin Murmelstein and, 16, 25, 26, 141, 220, 228, 230
 prologue, 141
 "last of the unjust," 27
Laval, Pierre, 221
Leibniz, Gottfried Wilhelm, 47, 50
 Gilles Deleuze and, 46, 47, 50
 and the incompossible, 45–48, 81, 167
 Lanzmann and, 45, 48, 49, 81
Lerner, Yehuda
 Holocaust experiences, 84
 interviews and testimony, 84–85, 92
 Lanzmann and, 84, 209
 photograph, 85f
 Sobibór, October 14, 1943, 4 p.m. and, 16, 84
 Sobibór revolt and, 16, 84
Les Quatre Soeurs. See *Four Sisters*
Les Temps Modernes, 39, 41, 52, 101, 190
Levi, Primo, 7, 123, 150, 172
Levy, Ophir, 219–20
Lichtman, Ada, xxxi
 deep memory and, xxxv, 80
 interviews, 63–73, 68f, 80–82, 84, 229, 248n79
 personality, 249n79
 photographs, 66f, 68f, 71f
 physical appearance, 246n38
 reenactment, 67, 69, 73, 80, 82, 230

Lichtman, Ada *(continued)*
  Richard Rashke on, 248n79
  on Sobibór revolt, 82, 84, 248n79
  speaking Yiddish, 65, 81
  testimony of
    at Eichmann trial, xxxi, 64, 65, 66f, 72, 246nn34–35, 246n38
    gender reversal in the, 69–71
    in *The Four Sisters*, 71f, 227, 229, 230
Lichtman, Allan J., 214
Lichtman, Eda. *See* Lichtman, Ada
Lichtman, Itzhak, 70–71, 71f
Liebes, Tamar, 60
Liebman, Stuart, xxxii
Lindeperg, Sylvie, xxxii
Lipstadt, Deborah, 175, 212–13
Łódź ghetto, 56, 128, 227–28
  Chaim Rumkowski and, 121–26, 227
  characterizations of, 121
  choice and survival in, 117–28
  Henryk Ross and, 56, 125–26
  Lanzmann and, 121, 122, 127, 135
  Paula Biren and, 117–28, 144, 227
  "resettlement" of children, 124
Łódź ghetto police, 125–30
  women's squad, 126, 127
Łódź photographer. *See* Ross, Henryk
Long, Breckinridge, 202, 212
LTC film laboratory, xxv, 6, 43, 45, 50, 62, 180, 225
  David Perlov at, 3, 62
  editing work and editorial decisions at, xxx, xxxvii, 5, 47–49, 179, 197
  segment of *Diary* shot at, 3
  Yael Perlov at, 2, 2f

Lubetkin, Zivia, 55, 88, 96, 99
Lubtchansky, William "Bob," 35, 206
  background, 34
  Caroline Champetier and, xxx, 30
  cinematography, xxx, xxxiv, 15, 16, 30–31, 35, 52, 74, 76, 88, 99–100, 113, 117, 119, 128, 130, 137, 140–42, 144, 158, 160, 161, 165, 171, 184, 193, 203
  clapboard, 32
  Jean-Luc Godard and, 30–32
  Lanzmann and, xxix, 3, 15, 16, 31, 32f, 33–35, 83, 113, 117, 188, 205, 211
  photograph, 118f
  Shoah and, xxix, xxx, 31–34, 76, 83, 113, 117, 130

Mamou, Sabine, xxi, xxiii, xxv, xxx, 218
Mandelbaum, Jacques, 71
march of the Rabbis. *See* Rabbis' march
Marienstras, Richard, 52
Marrus, Michael, 175
Marton, Ernst, 165–66, 172
  diary, 165–66, 172
  photograph, 166f
Marton, Hanna, 171
  Arendt and, 173
  Auschwitz and, 172
  interviews and testimony, 165, 171, 172, 262n159
  on Kasztner train ("Noah's Ark"), 171, 227
  on Kasztner trial, 172
  Lanzmann and, 165, 166f, 173
  outtakes, 173, 174

and "passing" of guilt from the
Nazis to the Jews, 172–73
photograph, 166f
Rudolf Kasztner and, 171–74
Shoah and, 173
story of choice and survival,
171–73
The Four Sisters and, 227–30
"Material of 'Shoah'" (Lanzmann),
xxiv, xxvi, xxviii, 26, 241n136
McClelland, Marjorie, 221
McClelland, Roswell, 177–78, 221
"Blood for Goods" deal and,
168, 177
correspondence with Lucy
Dawidowicz, 17, 191, 218,
266n57
interviews and testimony, 17, 45,
101, 178, 179, 218, 221
Irena Steinfeldt and, xxiv, 218
John Pehle and, 218, 219
Lanzmann and, xxiv, 4–6, 8, 17,
19, 21, 30, 41, 44, 101, 168, 178,
181, 190, 218, 220
letters from, 17, 218, 219
letters to, xxiv, 4–6, 8, 17, 19, 21,
30, 41, 44, 101, 168, 178, 181,
191, 220, 266n57
Maurice Rossel and, 218, 219
rescue and, xxiv, 4, 17, 168, 177,
178, 191
Shoah and, xxiv, 4, 17, 19, 30, 41,
44, 101, 177–79, 218
War Refugee Board (WRB) and,
xxiv, 4, 17, 168, 177, 178
Memories of the Eichmann Trial
(Perlov's film), 55–57, 57f,
61–62, 81

Rivka Yoselewska and, 57, 59f,
59–63, 81
Mengele, Josef, 45, 148–49, 197
Mengele factory, 148, 149, 152, 161
Merlin, Samuel, 213–15
interviews and testimony, 215, 216
on Jewish leadership, 177, 214
Lanzmann and, 213, 215
outtakes, 178, 179, 214
photograph, 214f
on rescue, 177, 215
Messenger, The (Haenel), 189,
191–93, 215
on Allies' inaction and indifference
to the plight of the Jews, xxxvii,
212, 221
"Karski Affair" and, xxxvii, 189–92,
198, 199, 232n11
Lanzmann's criticism of, xxxvii,
190, 191, 198, 201, 214, 225
publication, xxxvii, 189, 229,
232n11
"messengers of the catastrophe,"
xxxvii, 175–76, 180–200. *See also
specific individuals*
Meyer, Saly, 177–78
Michelsohn, Erhard, 158–60
Michelsohn, Martha, 156–60
minivan, xxxiv, 30–34, 38–42, 151,
165. *See also* Paluche
as "camera car," 31
filming and footage of, 30, 32, 33,
43, 53, 152, 203
footage inside, 32, 33
Paluche and, xxxiv, 34, 38
Minsk ghetto, 108–10, 252n148
Mitlaufer (fellow traveler), 158, 160
Moishe the Beadle, 176, 185

Morse, Arthur D., 176, 178–79, 187
Moyn, Samuel, 14–15, 72
Müller, Filip, 29, 83
　Holocaust experiences, 11, 141
　Lanzmann and, 6, 37, 92
　in *Shoah*, 3, 11, 37, 83, 141
　testimony, xxv, xxviii, xxx, 37, 83, 92
　Yehuda Bauer and, 6
Murmelstein, Benjamin, 25, 28, 122, 146, 167, 220
　background, 16
　Gershom Scholem's condemnation of, 25, 106
　interviews and testimony, xxvii, 16, 25–28, 28f, 106, 119, 141, 143, 170, 181, 183, 228
　Judenrat (Jewish council) and, 16, 25, 26, 28, 106, 119, 170, 181
　Lanzmann and, 16, 25–28, 28f, 119, 120f, 141–43, 228
　The Last of the Unjust (Lanzmann's film) and, 16, 25, 26, 141, 220, 228, 230
　outtakes, 16, 26–27, 119, 142, 228, 230
　photograph, 28f
　Saul Friedländer and, 25, 28, 29
Mushkin, Ilya, 109

negative editing, 227–29
　overview and nature of, 227
Nirenska, Pola, 187–88
"Noah's Ark." *See* Kasztner train
Novitch, Miriam, 72–73, 248n79

Operation Reinhardt, 8

Oppenheimer, Lore, 130, 133
　interviews and testimony, xxxvi, 130, 132–35, 143, 179
　Lanzmann and, 128, 133–35
　outtakes and, 130, 179
　photograph, 131f
　Society of Survivors of the Riga Ghetto and, 128, 130
Ostthema ("theme of the East"), 133, 143–144, 154, 160, 179

Paisikovic, Dov, 203, 268n98
Paluche ("hidden camera"), xxxiv, 29–31, 34, 241nn136–38
　as "a very fine investigation instrument," 30
　caught fire and abandoned by Lanzmann, 38–39
　description, 34
　discovered (by interviewee), 39
　handbag containing, 29, 36, 38, 39, 43f
　filming Franz Suchomel, 30, 31, 33–36, 41, 181
　and the secret recording of perpetrators (1976–1979), 29–43
　in *Shoah*, 29–30
　William Lubtchansky and, xxxiv, 31. *See also* Lubtchansky, William
Pankiewicz, Tadeusz, 109–12
　Holocaust experiences, 109, 110
　Lanzmann and, 110–12
　outtakes, 109–12
　photographs, 110f, 111f
　reenactment in pharmacy, 111, 111f
　in *Schindler's List*, 109

Paris, xxiii
  David Perlov in, 1, 55
  Lanzmann in, xxiii, xxv, 4, 6,
    48–49, 53, 242n151
Pártos, Ödön, 55
Patagonian Hare, The (Lanzmann),
    xxvii, 4, 7, 10, 29, 31, 34, 35,
    38–40, 47–50, 53, 66, 69, 86,
    98, 99, 137, 173–74, 199, 205,
    208, 211
  Bomba and, 74, 82
  Eichmann trial and, 62, 78
  incompossible discussed in, 48–49
  Jewish councils discussed in, 23, 62
  Lanzmann's selection process
    discussed in, xxxiv
  Shoah discussed in, xxxiii
  subjects absent from, 15, 17, 203
  use of the first-person plural
    pronoun in, 74
Pehle, John, 209
  characterization of, 209
  close-ups of, 211, 211f
  and the extermination, 209
  heroic wartime deeds, 209
  on ICRC, 223
  interviews and testimony, 177–79,
    202, 208–9, 211, 211f, 213, 215,
    217, 239n106, 270n135
  Jan Karski and, 211
  Lanzmann and, xxvii, 209,
    211, 212
  photographs, 210f, 211f
  press release of the report on
    Auschwitz, 213
  and proposal to bomb railways and
    Auschwitz, 270n135
  refugees and, 202, 209

Roswell McClelland and, 218, 219
  U.S. government attempts to
    censor, 213
  War Refugee Board (WRB) and,
    177, 209, 211, 239n106,
    270n135
Perechodnik, Calel, 126–27
Peretz, Eyal, 6, 47, 116
Perlov, David, 1–3
  André Schwarz-Bart and, 1, 16
  Diary (autobiographical opus), 1–3,
    5, 6, 55, 62, 234n1
  Eichmann trial and, 56, 60,
    61. See also *Memories of the
    Eichmann Trial*
  interview with Rivka Yoselewska,
    57, 60–63
  Lanzmann and, 2, 3, 50, 62
  life history, 1
  at LTC film laboratory, 3, 62
  reenactment and, 56, 57, 60–63
  Shoah and, 1–4
  Thy Blood Live (documentary
    short), 55
Perlov, Mira, 1
Perlov, Yael, 1–2, 2f, 50
pharmacy. *See* Apteka Pod Orłem
Pictet, Jean, 221–25
Pietyra, Helena, 156–57
Pinchevski, Amit, 60
Piotrowska, Agnieszka, 69, 73, 74
Piwonski, Jan, 67
Podchlebnik, Mordechai (Michael),
    78, 79
  crying, 76–77
  Haim Gouri and, 79
  heroism, 51, 83, 84
  Holocaust experiences, 79, 83

Podchlebnik, Mordechai (Michael) *(continued)*
    interviews and testimony, 62, 70, 76, 78f, 78–80, 84, 100, 248
    Lanzmann and, 76, 77, 77f, 79–80, 83, 84
    outtakes, 76, 79, 98
    photographs, 77f, 78f
    in *Shoah*, 62, 76–77, 100, 113, 150
police, Jewish. *See also* Łódź ghetto police
    of Riga ghetto, 128–30, 129f
POLIN Museum of the History of Polish Jews, 87
Popper, Nathaniel, 252n135
Postec, Ziva, xxi, xxx, 2–3, 50, 223n20
postmemory, 94–96. *See also* Hirsch, Marianne
Pottecher, Frédéric, 58
Prager, Brad, 219, 230
pregnant women, 45, 73, 144, 146–49, 229. *See also* childbirth and labor

Quatre Soeurs, Les. See *Four Sisters*

Rabbis' march (1943), 216
railways to extermination camps, proposals to bomb, 270n135
rape, 73. *See also* sexual violence
Rapoport, Nathan, 87, 96, 99
Rashke, Richard, 248n79
Reams, Robert Borden, 184, 200–201, 203, 205–6
    anti-Semitism, 201
    Breckinridge Long and, 201, 212
    characterization of, 201–3
    on Cold War, 205
    indifference, silence, and inaction, 205, 209, 212, 219
    interviews and testimony, 184, 200, 203, 205, 206, 210, 219, 254n9
    Lanzmann and, 117, 184, 200–201, 203, 204f, 209–10, 219, 254n9
    photograph, 202f, 204f
    State Department and, 184, 200–203, 219, 254n9
    William Lubtchansky and, 203
reenactment, 5, 12, 29, 33, 34, 83, 137, 164. *See also* Bomba, Abraham; songs, melodies, and singing
    of Ada Lichtman, 67, 69, 73, 80, 82, 230
    David Perlov and, 56, 57, 60–63
    of Jan Karski, 186, 188, 189, 197–98
    Lanzmann and, 42–43, 69, 82
    Łódź photographer (Henryk Ross) and, 56, 57, 81
    nature of and characterizations of, 12, 57, 85
    reframing, 63–82
    Rivka Yoselewska and, 61, 62, 81
    silencing, xxxv, xxxvi, 12, 81–82
    by singing, 29, 116, 133, 146. *See also* "Azoy muss sein"
    of Tadeusz Pankiewicz in pharmacy, 111, 111f
Reinhardt, Operation, 8
reliving of past events, 11. *See also* deep memory
Renov, Michael, xxxi
representational ethics. *See* ethics of representation
rescue, xxxvi, 178–80, 190, 212, 215–16
    from Auschwitz, 180

Bergson Group and, 213
of Hungarian Jews, 5, 6, 101, 168, 219–20, 223
Lanzmann and, xxx, xxxvii, 168, 170, 179–80, 200, 202, 208, 209, 216, 219–20, 225
Lucy Dawidowicz and, 191
Nahum Goldmann and, 186
pleading with Allies for, 175
of Polish Jewry, 185
politics of, xxx
Raul Hilberg on, 208, 269n109
Roswell McClelland and, 45, 101, 177, 266n57
Samuel Merlin on, 177, 215
Shoah and, xxx, 178, 179, 220
U.S. State Department and, 209
Zionist leadership and, 177
rescue efforts, 223. *See also* Bermuda Conference
of War Refugee Board (WRB), 7, 177
rescue operations, 62. *See also* "Europa Plan"; Kasztner, Rudolf: negotiations with Eichmann; Kasztner train; Vaada
Andre Steiner's, 142
Schindler's List and, xxxvii, 110, 179–80, 220. See also *Schindler's List*
Rescue Resolution, 177, 202. *See also* War Refugee Board: creation of
rescue strategy of Chaim Rumkowski, 123. *See also* Rumkowski, Mordechai Chaim
rescuers, Polish, 202
Resnais, Alain, 48
revenants, 57, 63, 83, 95
defined, 57–58

revisionist Zionists, 93, 105, 177
Riegner, Gerhart, 176, 178, 179, 181, 223
Riga ghetto, 134, 135. *See also* Society of Survivors of the Riga Ghetto
choice and survival in, 128–40
Jewish police of, 128–30, 129f
singing in, 133, 137, 138, 146. *See also* Schneider, Gertrude: singing
Ringelheim, Joan, xxxii, 127, 233n26, 255n35
Rodowick, D. N., 47
Roosevelt, Franklin Delano, xxxvi, 177, 192, 213–14, 216
Jan Karski's meeting with, 190, 192, 196–98
Peter Bergson and, 214–15, 270n126
War Refugee Board (WRB) and, 177, 190
Yannick Haenel and, 189, 190, 197
Roosevelt administration, 178–79
Rosenblatt, Roger, 100
Ross, Henryk (Łódź photographer), 56
in *Memories of the Eichmann Trial* (Perlov's film), 56–57, 244n8
photograph of, 57f
recorded scenes of Łódź ghetto, 56, 125–26
reenactment and, 56, 57, 81
Ross, Stefania, 57f
Rossel, Maurice, 141, 218–20
interviews and testimony, 218, 219, 221, 228
Lanzmann and, 218–21, 224, 228
Lucy Dawidowicz and, 218
outtakes, 219, 220

Rossel, Maurice *(continued)*
  Rossel's visit to and report on Theresienstadt ghetto, 218–20, 224, 228
  Roswell McClelland and, 218, 219
  Shoah and, 141, 218
  visit to and report on Auschwitz, 218–20
  A Visitor from the Living and, xxvi, 141, 218–20, 228
Rotem, Simha "Kazik," 225
  heroism, 87, 93, 97
  "I am the last Jew," 97, 164, 225
  interviews and testimony, 86, 87, 91, 96–100, 164, 187, 225
  Lanzmann and, 86, 87, 93, 97, 99
  reflections, 86, 164, 225
  resistance and, 86, 87, 96, 97, 99, 100, 187, 209, 225
  in *Shoah*, 97, 164, 255
  Warsaw Ghetto Uprising and, 86, 93, 96, 97, 100, 187, 225
  Yitzhak "Antek" Zuckerman and, 86, 91, 96–99
Rotenstreich, Nathan, 18
Rothberg, Michael, 73, 138, 247n60
  on *Schindler's List*, 180, 191
  on *Shoah*, 73, 138, 180, 247n60
Rubenstein, Richard, 206–8
Rumkowski, Mordechai Chaim
  background, 123
  characterizations of, 123, 125
  compliance/complicity/cooperation, 121, 123–25
  Give Me Your Children speech, 124, 125
  as *Judenrat* leader, 121, 123, 126
  Lanzmann and, 123–24, 128, 227–28
  Łódź ghetto and, 121–26, 227
  Paula Biren and, xxxv, 121–26
  women's squad and, 126

Sanyal, Debarati, 172–73
Saxton, Libby, 5, 235n36
Schindler, Oskar, 180
Schindler's List (film), xxv, 179, 220
  Holocaust and, xxv, xxix, xxx, xxxvii
  Lanzmann on, xxv, xxix, xxx, xxxvii, 180
  rescue and, xxxvii, 110, 220
  Shoah and, xxxvii, 180, 191
  Steven Spielberg and, xxiv, xxix, xxx, xxxvii, 110, 180
Schneider, Gertrude, 256–57nn54–56
  choice and survival in Riga ghetto, 134–40
  Holocaust experiences, 147
  Lanzmann and, 134, 135, 137, 147
  outtakes, 133–35, 136f, 146, 147
  photograph, 136f
  in *Shoah*, xxviii, xxxvi, 81, 116–17, 135
  singing, 81, 133–34, 137–38, 140, 146
  testimony, xxviii, xxxvi, 81, 133–35, 137–38, 139f, 140, 144, 165, 256n54
  writings, 134–35, 257n56
Scholem, Gershom, 25, 106
Schrobsdorff, Angelika, 26
Schubert, Heinz, 39–41, 63
Schwarz-Bart, André, 1, 1–2, 16, 16
Schweifert, Peter, 26
second generation, 86, 94, 95, 101
Segev, Tom, 167, 171

Sereny, Gitta. See also *Into That Darkness*
   Franz Suchomel and, xxxiii, 8, 9, 35
   Lanzmann and, 7–10
   Richard Glazar and, xxxiii, 8–10, 12–14
   on Stanislaw Szmajzner, 8–9
   visit to Treblinka, 9
sexual violence, 72, 73
Shandler, Jeffrey, 10, 108
Shenker, Noah, 11
Shilansky, Dov, 92–95, 106
Shoah (Lanzmann's film). See also *specific topics*
   characterizations of, 4
   collaborators in the making of, xxix–xxx
   commissioned by Israel, 4. See also Hareven, Alouph
   criticisms of, 44, 74
   editing (1979–1985), 44–53
   final words in, 164, 225
   first filmed interviews (1975–1976), 17–28
   first interview shot for, 16, 19
   gender bias, 44, 75, 144. See also women survivors
   initial conception of, 4
   Lanzmann's choosing the title for, 53. See also "Holocaust"
   Lanzmann's vision for, 179
   "most poignant testimony" in, 244n8. See also Ross, Henryk: in *Shoah*
   narrative lacunae in, 84
   opening sequence and opening interviews, 50, 143, 184, 206, 222
   preliminary research and interviews (1973–1974), 3–16
   purposes, 4
Shoah: Four Sisters (*Les Quatre Soeurs*). See *Four Sisters*
Shoah: The Unseen Interviews (compilation film), 229
"Shoah," Lanzmann on the word, 53
Shoah outtakes. See also *specific topics*
   cardboard boxes containing, xxvi
   recovering the, xxxi–xxxvii
Šiauliai ghetto, 93
"silencing reenactment," xxxv, xxxvi, 12, 81–82
Silvart, Andrés, 33
Six fois deux (Godard's television series), 31–32, 35, 47
Smolar, Hersh, 107–9, 112
Sobibór: Martyrdom and Revolt (Novitch), 72
Sobibór, October 14, 1943, 4 p.m. (Lanzmann's film), 16, 84
Sobibór revolt of 1943, xxiv–xxv, 16, 65, 70, 72, 73, 82, 84, 228
   Ada Lichtman on, 82, 84, 248n79
   aftermath, 96
   role of women in, 82
   Yehuda Lerner and, 16, 84
Society of Survivors of the Riga Ghetto, 128, 130, 132, 134
Sonderkommando at Auschwitz, 173
   revolt of 1944, 37, 83, 141
songs, melodies, and singing, 138, 139f. See also hymn(s); Yiddish melodies, songs, and chants
   "Azoy muss sein," 133–35, 136f, 138
   Lanzmann and, 50, 81, 138, 140

songs, melodies, and singing *(continued)*
"Mały biały domek," xi, 137, 139–140
reenactment through, 116, 133, 146. See also "Azoy muss sein" in *Shoah*, 81, 140
"Undzer shtetl brent!," 114–16, 115f
Sorel, Dr. (pseudonym of Lanzmann), 29, 39–42, 151
Sperber, Manès, 52
Spielberg, Steven, xxiv, xxix, xxx, xxxvii, 180. See also *Schindler's List*
   Lanzmann and, 110, 180
   Lanzmann's criticism of, xxix, xxx, xxxvii, 110, 180
   Schindler's List and, xxiv, xxix, xxx, xxxvii, 110, 180
   Survivors of the Shoah Visual History Foundation and, xxiv
Spitzer, Leo, xxxv, 116, 144, 161, 164
Srebnik, Simon
   Chelmno survivor, xxv
   compared with Stanislaw Szmajzner, 8
   at Eichmann trial, 62
   German language and, 51
   Holocaust experiences and life history, 9, 51, 52, 62, 133
   Lanzmann and, 9, 11, 21, 47, 50–52, 133, 137, 140, 162
   outtakes, 50–52
   personality and demeanor, 51, 52
   in *Shoah*, xxv, 8, 9, 11, 50, 52, 62, 143, 184, 206
   silence, 51, 52
   singing, 11, 47, 50, 133, 137, 140, 143, 206

   testimonial performance, 11, 50, 140, 143, 184
   testimony and interviews, 11, 50–52, 162
Staron, Stanislaw, 103, 195
Steimle, Eugen, 40–41
Stein, Irene. *See* Steinfeldt, Irena
Steinacher, Gerald, 223–24
Steiner, Andre, 142–43, 143f, 146, 173, 217
Steiner, Jean-François. See also *Treblinka*
   Abba Kovner and, 92
   interviews conducted by, 14
   Jewish passivity and, 16
   Lanzmann and, xxvii, 15, 16, 93
   Richard Glazar and, 14, 15
Steinfeldt, Irena, 19, 21, 209
   background, 6
   Lanzmann and, xxiv, 6, 19, 23, 147, 209
   photograph, 22f
   Roswell McClelland and, xxiv, 218
   and the search for witnesses, 7, 40
   Shoah and, 6, 7, 23, 40
   translations, 21, 23, 171
Steven Spielberg Film and Video Archive, 230
   Claude Lanzmann *Shoah* Collection acquired by, xxvii
   establishment of, xxv
   women's testimonies and, xxviii
Suchomel, Franz, 241n137–138
   filmed with Paluche ("hidden camera"), 30, 31, 33–36, 41, 181
   Gitta Sereny and, xxxiii, 8, 9, 35, 38

interviews and testimony, 2, 7, 9, 13–14, 29–31, 32f, 33–36, 38, 41, 47, 67, 181, 205
  Lanzmann and, 7, 13, 14, 31, 34–36, 47, 205
  outtakes, 9, 13, 14, 31, 34, 35
  Richard Glazar and, xxxiii, 8, 9, 35, 38
  Saul Friedländer and, 29, 33, 36, 38
  on Treblinka extermination camp, 9, 13–14, 35, 38
  Treblinka hymn sung by, 13, 35
Survivors of the Shoah Visual History Foundation, xxiv, xxv. *See also* USC Shoah Foundation
Switzerland. *See* Kasztner train
Szmajzner, Stanislaw, 8–9

Tamir, Shmuel, 167, 168, 171, 173, 217
testimonial performance, 11, 12, 38, 140
  of Abraham Bomba, 11, 67, 73, 76, 188
  of Ada Lichtman, xxxv, 66, 80, 81
  excluded, 107–8
  of Franz Suchomel, xxxiii, 9, 35
  of Gertrude Schneider, 137, 140
  of Hermann Ziering, 130
  of Jan Karski, 188, 197, 199
  Lanzmann and, xxix, xxx, 11, 35, 52
  of Łodź photographer (Henryk Ross), 57. *See also* Ross, Henryk: in *Memories of the Eichmann Trial*
  of Pery Broad, 38

  reshaping, 230
  of Simon Srebnik, 11, 50, 140, 143, 184
  of Tadeusz Pankiewicz, 111
Theresienstadt family camp, 141, 144, 146–48, 150, 257n67
Theresienstadt ghetto, 140, 146, 230
  Benjamin Murmelstein and, 25, 228
  deportations to, 10, 128, 142–44, 143f, 229
  deportees from, 141, 144
  Fredy Hirsch and, 141
  Lanzmann at, 142, 228
  Lanzmann on, 141
  Maurice Rossel's visit to and report on, 218–20, 224, 228
  Paula Biren and, 128
  photograph, 140f
  Ruth Elias and, 141, 144, 146, 229
  visits to, 218–20
Todorov, Tzvetan, 84, 87, 107
Tournier, Michel, 46
tragedy of choice. *See* choice, tragedy of
traumatic memory, Caruth's theory of, 12
Treblinka: The Revolt of an Extermination Camp (Steiner), 14, 15, 18, 52. *See also* Steiner; "Treblinka affair"
  Abba Kovner's manifesto and, 88, 92
  accusations of collaboration sparked by, 84
  criticism of, 14
  Lanzmann and, 92
  Simone de Beauvoir on, 14, 15, 52

"Treblinka affair" (controversy over Steiner's *Treblinka* in postwar France), 14, 15, 52, 72, 84, 92, 93
Treblinka extermination camp, 15, 84, 235n36. See also *Into That Darkness*
  "barber of Treblinka." *See* Bomba, Abraham
  escapes from, 10, 11, 83
  Franz Suchomel on, 9, 13–14, 35, 38. See also Suchomel, Franz
  Lanzmann and, 15, 35, 180
  meaning of, and what it signifies, xxxvii, 208, 212, 223
  memorial, 9
  the question of rescue from, 180
  readings/accounts of, 7–8
  Richard Glazar and, 10, 11, 13–15
  Saul Friedländer on, 29
  trains to, 42, 43
Treblinka hymn, 13, 29, 35
Treblinka revolt, 10, 14–15, 83. See also *Treblinka*
Trezise, Thomas, 12, 58, 81
  on "anxiety of historical transmission," xxiv
  on listening to survivors, 81–82
  on "possibility of a survival beyond revictimization," 82
  on "silencing reenactment," xxxiv
Trunk, Isaiah, 18, 125, 130
Tushnet, Leonard, 107

Under the Eagle pharmacy. *See* Apteka Pod Orłem
underground activities, 88. *See also* French Resistance; Jewish resistance
underground movement in Minsk ghetto, 108–10
underground organizations. *See* Bratislava Working Group
"Undzer shtetl brent!" ("Our Town Is Burning!"), 114–16, 115f
United States Holocaust Memorial Museum (USHMM), xxv, xxviii, 28, 84, 103, 127, 132, 225
  Claude Lanzmann *Shoah* Collection and, xxxi, 230
  The Four Sisters and, 229, 230
  Lanzmann's first visit to, xxiv, xxv, 26, 103, 241n136
  Raul Hilberg and, xxiii, xxiv, xxix
  Shoah archive in, xxiii, xxix, xxxii, 3, 50
  Shoah outtakes at, xxv, xxvii–xxix, 190, 218, 229
  Shoah to be screened in, xxiv
  Steven Spielberg Film and Video Archive, xxv
United States State Department, "repression" of information on extermination by, 209
University of Southern California Shoah Foundation. *See* USC Shoah Foundation
USC Shoah Foundation, xxiv, 10. *See also* Survivors of the Shoah Visual History Foundation

Vaada (Aid and Rescue Committee), 166–70
Vatican, 7
Villain, Dominique, 49
Visitor from the Living, A (Lanzmann's film), xxiii, xxvi, 141, 218–20, 228

Volkswagen minivan. *See* minivan
Vrba, Rudolf, 217
   escape from Auschwitz, 83,
     166, 170
   Hansi Brand and, 170, 171
   Lanzmann and, 6, 37, 170
   on Rudolf Kasztner, 170
   in *Shoah*, 83, 141, 166, 213
   testimony, 37, 83, 141, 170,
     213, 215
   as witness in Frankfurt Auschwitz
     trials, 29

Walker, Janet, 12, 37
Wallace, Henry, 216
War Refugee Board (WRB)
   creation of, 177, 190, 209, 211, 223
   John Pehle and, 177, 209, 211,
     239n106, 270n135
   Lanzmann and, 7, 190
   rescue efforts, 7, 200, 223
   Roosevelt and, 177, 190
   Roswell McClelland and, xxiv, 4,
     17, 168, 177, 178, 191
Warsaw ghetto, underground in,
   186, 195
Warsaw Ghetto Diary, The
   (Czerniaków), 102–3, 195. *See
   also* Czerniaków, Adam: diary
Warsaw Ghetto Uprising (1943), 55,
   87, 88, 102, 113, 186
   Adolf Berman and, 186
   in *Holocaust* (Chomsky's
     miniseries), 142
   Lanzmann on, 87, 97, 99, 107
   Malka Goldberg and, 113
   Shoah and, xxxvi, 107, 187
   Simha Rotem and, 86, 93, 96, 97,
     100, 187, 225
   suppression of, 187
   Yitzhak "Antek" Zuckerman and,
     55, 86, 87, 97, 99
Wasserman, Rita (sister of Gertrude
   Schneider), 136–38
   interviews and testimony, 134, 135,
     137, 140, 147
   Lanzmann and, 138, 147
   photograph, 136f
   in *Shoah*, 134, 136f
   singing, 134, 136f, 137
Weissmandl, Michael Dov, 142, 175,
   176, 178, 216–17, 217f
Wetzler, Alfred, 213
Wiesel, Elie, 176, 225
Wieviorka, Annette, 80, 189–90
Williams, Linda, 5, 11, 232n16
Wise, Stephen, 176–77, 181, 196
*Witnessing Witnessing: On the
   Reception of Holocaust Testimony*
   (Trezise). *See* Trezise, Thomas
"witnessing witnessing," 58–59, 61,
   90, 100
women (and the Holocaust), 127,
   134, 146–47, 160, 169
   in death camps, 67, 73, 147–49.
     See also Bomba, Abraham: as
     "barber of Treblinka"
   extermination of, 38
   in gas chambers, 67, 69, 247n64
   pregnant, 45, 73, 144, 146–49,
     229. *See also* childbirth and
     labor
   role in Sobibór revolt, 82
   roles in Holocaust, 157, 160
   survival strategies in ghettos and
     camps, xxxii
   violence against, 72, 73
women interpreters, 34

women survivors, testimonies of, xxviii, 127, 173, 227–29. See also *Four Sisters*; women; *specific individuals*
   and the juxtaposition of feminine and masculine perspectives, xxxvi
   Lanzmann and, xxxii, xxxv, xxxvii, 63, 75–76, 160
   omitted from *Shoah*, xxviii, xxx, xxxii, xxxv, xxxvii, 12, 44, 53, 75–76, 112, 117, 130, 137, 168, 173. See also Hirsch, Marianne and Spitzer, Leo
   in 1970s, xxxii
   in *Shoah*, xxxi, xxxv, xxxvi, 116–17, 119, 130, 133, 144, 149, 150, 156, 160, 161, 216, 227
   in Warsaw ghetto, 112
women's squad (Łódź ghetto police), 126, 127
Wyman, David, 190

Yablonka, Hanna, 60, 94, 245n22
Yad Vashem, 87, 95, 96, 112, 167
   debate at, 93, 94, 96
   education at, 93, 95f
   Israel, Why and, 3
   Lanzmann and, 3, 6
   library and archives, xxvii, 3, 6, 96
   military students at, 93, 96f
Yad Vashem outtakes, 96
Yad Vashem Visual Center, 55
Yiddish
   Ada Lichtman's testimony in, 64–67, 70, 81
   Eichmann trial testimony in, 58, 59, 61, 64–66, 79
   Franz Suchomel's testimony in, 35
   Gertrude Schneider's testimony in, xxxvi, 133, 137–138
   Hersh Smolar's testimony in, 108
   Leib Garfunkel's diary, 19
   letters of Szmul Zygielbojm, 193
   Malka Goldberg's testimony in, 113–114
   Mordechai Podchlebnik's testimony in, 76
Yiddish melodies, songs, and chants, 35, 114, 133, 137, 138
Yiddish spoken in outtakes, 107–8
   functions of, 108
Yoselewska, Rivka
   Ada Lichtman contrasted with, 65
   characterizations of, 57–58, 63
   daughter (Marta), 58
   David Perlov's interview with, 57, 60–63
   description, overview, and characterizations of, 57, 63
   Haim Gouri and, 57–61, 64, 79
   heart attack, 57, 61, 62
   Holocaust experiences, 57, 58
   Lanzmann and, 62–63, 66
   Memories of the Eichmann Trial (Perlov's film) and, 57, 59f, 59–63, 81
   reenactment and, 61, 62, 81
   as a revenant, 57, 63
Young, James, 87

Zabotinsky, Vladimir Ze'ev, 105
Zaidel, Hanna, 94–95
Zaidel, Motke, 7, 20, 83–84
Ziering, Hermann, 130, 132, 133
   Holocaust experiences, 130, 132, 133, 135

interviews and (excluded) testimony, xxxvi, 130–35, 143, 155, 179
   Lanzmann and, 130–31, 134, 135
   photograph, 131f
   Society of Survivors of the Riga Ghetto and, 130
Zionist leadership, 177. *See also specific leaders*
Zionists, revisionist, 93, 105, 177
Zuckerman, Yitzhak "Antek," 96, 249n96
   characterizations of, 55, 97, 108
   Eichmann trial and, 55, 88
   interviews and testimony, 62, 86, 88, 91, 97–101
   Jewish Resistance and, xxxiv, 55
   Lanzmann and, 87, 98, 99, 101
   photograph, 100f
   Ponar forest and, 88
   resistance and, 55, 108, 249n96
   Simha "Kazik" Rotem and, 86, 91, 96–99
   Warsaw ghetto and, 62, 108
   Warsaw ghetto uprising and, 55, 86, 87, 97, 99

Zygielbojm, Faivel, 8, 193–96, 194f
Zygielbojm, Rivka (Rivkele), 193, 195
Zygielbojm, Szmul "Artur," 8, 187, 192, 195, 196, 200, 216
   Adam Czerniaków and, 185, 195
   as Bund leader, 8, 185, 187, 192, 193
   characterizations of, 192
   Faivel Zygielbojm and, 8, 193–96, 194f
   Judenrat (Jewish council) and, 185, 192
   Lanzmann and, 185, 192, 196–98
   The Messenger (Haenel) and, 191–92
   Nahum Goldmann and, 185, 193
   outtakes, 186, 187, 194f, 196
   photograph, 194f
   suicide, xxxvii, 8, 187, 192, 195–97
   testimony, 193–94, 197
   Warsaw ghetto and, 185, 192–95, 197–98
   Warsaw ghetto revolt and, xxxvii, 187

www.ingramcontent.com/pod-product-compliance
Ingram Content Group UK Ltd.
Pitfield, Milton Keynes, MK11 3LW, UK
UKHW041915140426
5217IPUK00013B/167